I0303279

Michael Ferrebee Sadler

The Epistles of St. Paul to the Colossians, Thessalonians and Timothy

Michael Ferrebee Sadler

The Epistles of St. Paul to the Colossians, Thessalonians and Timothy

ISBN/EAN: 9783337381332

Printed in Europe, USA, Canada, Australia, Japan

Cover: Foto ©Lupo / pixelio.de

More available books at **www.hansebooks.com**

THE EPISTLES OF ST. PAUL

TO THE

COLOSSIANS, THESSALONIANS

AND

TIMOTHY

WITH NOTES CRITICAL AND PRACTICAL

BY THE REV. M. F. SADLER

LATE RECTOR OF HONITON AND PREBENDARY OF WELLS

LONDON

GEORGE BELL AND SONS

1898

THE EPISTLE TO THE COLOSSIANS.

INTRODUCTION.

THE authenticity of the Epistle to the Colossians as being the writing of St. Paul, and received from the first as Canonical, has never been doubted in the Christian Church till the present century. It has latterly been pronounced by some German critics to contain references to Gnostical heresies which were not developed till a later period. We shall show, however, that the germs of Gnosticism were abroad in the world long before this.

There are apparent allusions to some of its statements in Clement of Rome and the longer recension of Ignatius, but the first undeniable reference is in—

Justin Martyr, ch. lxxxv.: "For every demon, when exorcised in the name of this very Son of God—Who is the firstborn of every creature." (Dial. lxxxv.) "We have been taught that Christ is the firstborn of God." (Apol. xlvi.)

In the Muratorian Fragment of the Canon it is reckoned as fourth among the Pauline Epistles. "Ad Corinthios (prima), ad Ephesios (secunda) ad Philippenses (tertia) ad Colossienses (quarta)," &c.

Irenæus quotes the Epistle to the Colossians nearly twenty times. Thus Book iii. 14: "And again he says in the Epistle to the Colossians, Luke the beloved Physician greets you."

Clement of Alexandria quotes this Epistle about twenty-five times. In the Stromata, i. 1, he mentions it by name: "Also in the Epistle to the Colossians he writes, admonishing every man, and teaching every man in all wisdom" (i. 28).

Tertullian quotes the Epistle frequently; sometimes by name, thus:—"He testifieth of philosophy by name that it ought to be shunned: writing to the Colossians, 'Beware lest any one beguile you through philosophy and vain deceit after the tradition of men,'" &c.

CITY OF COLOSSE.

Colossæ (or Colosse) was formerly a large city of Phrygia, within a short distance (twelve miles) of two others, Laodicea and Hierapolis, and situated in the valley of the Lycus, a tributary of the Meander, which it joins a few miles further down to the west. In the time of St. Paul it was a declining city, and the ruins which remain are of no architectural importance. Xenophon describes Colossæ in his time as a great city, populous and flourishing; and Pliny classes it amongst the *oppida celeberrima* of Phrygia; and so it continued for some centuries after the Christian era, decaying, however, gradually, and Chonas, three miles to the south, at the foot of the mountain, grew up in its place. It is now absolutely uninhabited.

A most interesting account of the cities of the Lycus is given by Bishop Lightfoot in the preface to his volume on the Epistle to the Colossians, but it seems to throw no light whatsoever on the contents of the Epistle. A remarkable circumstance, however, mentioned by Theodoret, seems to show that the cultus of angels reached far into Christian times. "Those who upheld the law also induced them to worship angels, saying that the law had been given through their intervention. This evil custom remained long in Phrygia and Pisidia. Hence a synod, which met in Laodicea of Phrygia, prohibited by law the worship of angels, and to this very day an oratory, dedicated to St. Michael, is to be seen in these parts."

The Byzantine writer, Nicetas Choniates, who was a native of Chonas, also makes mention of it. The neighbourhood (visited by Pococke) was explored by Mr. Arundell ("Seven Churches," p. 158; "Asia Minor," ii., p. 160), but Mr. Hamilton was the first to determine the actual site of the ancient city, which appears to be at some little distance from the modern village of Chonas. ("Researches in Asia Minor," i., p. 508, abridged from Smith's "Bible Dictionary.")

BY WHOM WAS COLOSSE FIRST EVANGELIZED?

We should gather from i. 7, "As ye have ("also" to be omitted) learned of Epaphras," &c., that Epaphras was the first preacher of the Gospel to them.

Alford and Bishop Lightfoot, and most expositors, consider that St. Paul includes the Colossians, to whom he was writing, when he speaks of "as many as have not seen my face in the flesh." The remarks of the latter are, "this is a purely grammatical question; therefore it is uncertain whether St. Paul's language here implies his personal acquaintance with his correspondents, or the contrary. But in all such cases the sense of the context must be our guide. In the present instance, *καὶ ὅσοι* is quite out of place, unless the Colossians and Laodiceans also were personally unknown to the Apostle. There would be no meaning in singling out *individuals* who were unknown to him, and then mentioning comprehensively *all* who were unknown to him. Hence we may infer from the expression here that St. Paul had never visited Colosse."

On the other hand, Theodoret amongst the ancients, and Dr. Lardner amongst the moderns, have contended that St. Paul first evangelized this and the two neighbouring cities. Alford, in his Prolegomena to this Epistle, gives sixteen reasons from Lardner why St. Paul should have been their Evangelist. The great point which seems to turn the scale in favour of Epaphras having been the founder of the Church, is that the Apostle never claims to be their spiritual father as he does in the cases of the Thessalonian, Corinthian, Galatian, and Philippian Churches (1 Thess. i. 5; ii. i-4; Gal. i. 6; 1 Cor. iii. 6-10; Phil. ii. 16). If he had been their father in Christ, much referred to in the Epistle would have led him to claim their obedience on that score.

FOR WHAT PURPOSE WAS THIS EPISTLE WRITTEN?

A large portion of this Epistle is directly controversial or polemic. The whole of the second chapter is written to warn his converts against (apparently) two forms of false teaching, the one Judaizing, the other Gnosticism. He sometimes has the one principally before him, as when he writes: "Let no man judge you in meat or in drink, or in respect of an holyday, or of the new moon, or of the Sabbath days" (ii. 16). And he looks apparently to the other as a distinct form of evil teaching when he writes: "Let no man beguile you of your reward in a voluntary humility and worshipping of angels, intruding into those things which he hath not seen, vainly puffed up by his fleshly mind" (ii. 18). This latter certainly, at first sight, does not seem to present any features of a perverted Judaism, and yet there is an almost general consensus of authorities that St. Paul contended against *one* heresy—the Colossian heresy—so called because it seems at that time to be peculiar to this and perhaps the two neighbouring cities; and not to have been so rife at Ephesus, inasmuch as in the Epistle to the Ephesians the Apostle seems to take no notice of it.

The following account of it is given by Dollinger: "The wonted Judaism in its Pharasaic form, to which nothing was so dear as the universal force of the law, and the perpetual prerogatives of the Jewish Nationality—the Judaism St. Paul attacked so sharply—never succeeded in forming separate congregations, at least for any time, and in the later Apostolic period this danger seems to have been no longer important. On the other hand, a doctrine of far more seductive tendency crept increasingly into the communities—a Gnostic Judaism—producing serious disorders, and entailing on the Apostles and their first successors a difficult contest. It is uncertain when, and under what influences, this Gnostic tendency and admixture of Jewish and Gentile teaching found entrance among the Jews of the dispersion. In Palestine it only appeared among the Essenes, and there is no trace of their spreading or having influence out of Palestine. We can only say that the old Orphic Pythagorean ideas, and the notion long before brought into the West by the Babylonian Magicians of various classes of Demons, both higher and ministering spirits, and the conditions of their action, had gained admission also amongst the Jews of Asia Minor."

"The false teachers against whom Paul warned the believers of Colossæ were Jewish converts, who held to the law and circumcision, and required an observance of the Old Testament rules about meats, and the Jewish feasts and moons, and Sabbaths. To this they added, against the body as the defiling prison of the soul, a violent and unmeasured Asceticism, and an angel worship founded, as the Apostle says, on a false humility. They make the angels, according to the heathen idea, mediators whom men must apply to because the Supreme God was incomprehensible and out of reach. Without doubt they thus degraded the dignity of Christ as being a Prophet to whom only one of these cosmic angels, and an angel of a lower order, had revealed himself, whence Paul here insists so emphatically on the majesty of the Only born. The Apostle's warning, 'Beware that none rob you of your reward through philosophy and vain deceit after the tradition of men' proves that the doctrine was drawn from an heathen philosophy as it was with the Essenes."

The consideration of this early form of Gnosticism is important as bearing upon the genuineness of this Epistle. It (or at least parts of it) have been pronounced by German rationalizing critics to be of later date than the times of St. Paul, because the Gnosticism is in their view more developed than it could have been at the time of the writing of this Epistle. But this is said without due consideration of the fact that the Gnosticism alluded to in the Epistle is as undeveloped as it can well be. It is all contained in the sentence "worshipping of angels": "Let no man beguile you of your reward, in a voluntary humility and *worshipping of angels.*" This is the only direct reference to that feature common to all Gnosticism, of the interposition of a series of supernatural existences between God and man. There is no reference whatsoever to the Dual idea, by which the origin of evil is attempted to be accounted for: and the rigorous asceticism reprobated, is quite as much Essene as Gnostic.

Now it is allowed on all hands that the fountain-head of Gnosticism is in the ancient Persian or Zoroastrian religious speculation, and this undoubtedly contains the invocation of intermediate beings. Mr. Ll. Davies, at the end of his commentary on the Colossians, gives the beginning of the first of the Yaćnas or Liturgical Invocations. Thus: "I invoke Ahura Mazda . . . . who created us, who formed us, who keeps us, the noblest among the heavenly," and then the worshipper is directed to call upon six intermediate beings, whose names are Vohumano, Asha-vahista, Kshathra-vairya, Spenta armaiti, Hauwut, and Ameretat, and a seventh, Seroch, appears to have not yet been revealed, and is said to answer to the Messiah, so that Gnosticism would be no Gnosticism at all, unless it recognized these intermediate beings.

Besides this, we find in the two most ancient accounts of Simon Magus (considered by all ancient writers to be the founder of the Gnosticism which affected Christianity), that his doctrine is described as being, in its leading features, Angelology. Thus Irenæus, Book i. ch. 23, "Declaring that this woman, Ennæa, leaping forth from him, and comprehending the will of her father, descended to the lower regions of space, and generated angels and powers by whom also he declares this world was formed." Again, "He conferred salvation upon men by making himself (Simon Magus) known to them. For since the angels ruled the world ill, because each one of them coveted the principal power for himself, he had come to amend matters, and had descended, transfigured and assimilated to powers, and principalities, and angels, so that he might appear among men to be a man, while he was yet not a man, and that thus he was thought to have suffered in Judæa when he had not suffered," &c.

Again, we gather from Hippolytus, that Simon's creed, if such it can be called, was largely tinctured with angelology, even ascribing the creation of the world to angels. "For the angels who created the world," he said, "made whatever enactments they pleased, thinking by such words to enslave those who listened to them," &c. Hippolytus, "Refutation of all Heresies," book vi. ch. xiv.

These angels, or successions of angelic intermediate beings developed into the æons of the gnostical systems of the conclusion of the first century and the beginning of the next, but St. Paul's allusion to them is the simplest possible, and it seems to me equally applicable to a rudimentary, or to a more fully developed Gnosticism. He avoided saying a syllable about them, except that the recognition of them was incompatible with loyalty to the eternal Son.

TIME AND PLACE OF WRITING.

The Epistle to the Colossians was written about the same time as those to the Ephesians and Philemon during the last part of St. Paul's first imprisonment at Rome, and was sent from Rome to Asia Minor by Tychicus, with whom was associated Onesimus (Coloss. iv. 7, 8, 9; Ephes. vi. 21, 22).

The verbal coincidences between it and the Epistle to the Ephesians are such, that that they must have been written when the great truths, and the expression of those truths, which are common to both, were fresh in the Apostle's mind, and yet each has its separate dominant truth—that in the Epistle to the Ephesians being the unity of the Church as one Body under Christ as its Head, and that to the Colossians being the unity of Christian truth in the same Christ, the Eternal Son of God Incarnate.

So that in the Ephesian letter the Apostle dwells upon the election of Jew and Gentile in Christ, and both being raised up in Christ, and made to sit together at God's right hand in Christ, and being built up as one holy temple in Christ, and being united and increasing under one Apostolic ministry in Christ, whilst in the Colossian Epistle the Godhead and Divine Sonship of the Lord and His creation of all things visible and invisible, is the root of all Christian truth, from which men fall if they are captivated by either Judaistic or Gnostic teaching, or by both combined.

In considering the distinctive teaching of the Epistle to the Colossians, we must remember that though written by the Apostle with the view of combating certain errors of the times, it was designed by the inspiring Spirit to be for the instruction of the Church in all ages and generations, and the dogmatic truths asserted in it are just as much lost sight of in England in the nineteenth century, as in Colosse in the first. We have in our popular theology nothing like the position which is ascribed in the first chapter to the Eternal Son, as the Creator of all things visible and invisible, and the Head of His mystical Body, or in the second chapter to the fulness of the Godhead dwelling bodily in Him. I do not deny for a moment that these truths are confessed by us in our creeds, but in this Epistle the loftiest truths are made the foundation for the performance of the lowliest every-day duties. One instance will abundantly suffice. The most mysterious truth that we are risen with Christ—that we are dead in Him, and that our life is hid with Christ in God, is assigned as the reason that we should mortify such sins as fornication, uncleanness, inordinate affection, and evil concupiscence—that we should put off anger, wrath, malice, and blasphemy, and that as the elec of God we should put on bowels of mercies, kindness, humbleness of mind, meekness, long-suffering, and forbearance. So that dogma and duty are in this Epistle inseparably connected. There cannot be deeper truths than that Christ is the image of the invisible God—that He is the author of Creation visible and invisible, that in Him dwelleth the fulness of Godhead bodily, and yet these deepest of truths are to be the root of a daily life of purity. truthfulness, mutual forgiveness, and charity.

A COMMENTARY.

THE EPISTLE TO THE COLOSSIANS.

CHAP. I.

PAUL, [a] an apostle of Jesus Christ by the will of God, and Timotheus *our* brother, [a] Eph. i. 1.

2 To the saints [b] and faithful brethren in Christ [b] 1 Cor. iv. 17. Eph. vi. 21.

---

1. "Paul, an apostle of Jesus Christ by the will of God, and Timotheus our brother." "An apostle of Jesus Christ by the will of God." If there was a strong Jewish element in the city, and probably in the Church, it was well for St. Paul to assert that his apostleship was as much as that of the first-called apostles "by the will of God."

"By the will of God." Christ says of the twelve, "thine they were and thou gavest them me," and the calling of St. Paul indubitably set forth that he was a vessel of election, "separated from his mother's womb and called by God's grace."

"And Timotheus our brother." In seven epistles, those to the Corinthians, the Philippians, this and the Epistle to Philemon, and in those to the Thessalonians, St. Paul joins Timothy with himself as joint senders of the letters, and yet each letter is wholly St. Paul's, written in the first person singular, and evidently every word of it the production of one mind and will. This could only be for one purpose, viz., that others should be associated with the Apostle in his peculiar apostolical authority, so that when God should remove him from the scene, the apostolic ministry should not cease to be continued in the Church.

2. "To the saints and faithful brethren in Christ which are at

which are at Colosse: [c] Grace *be* unto you, and peace, from God our Father and the Lord Jesus Christ.

c Gal. i. 3.

2. "From God our Father, and the Lord Jesus Christ." So א, A., C., F., G., most Cursives, f, g, Copt., Arm., Æth.; but B., D., E., K., L., 17, 39, 46, 109, 115, 177, 178, 219, 238, d, e, Vulg. (Cod. Amiat.), Syriac, omit "and the Lord Jesus Christ."

Colosse." The "saints" marks out Christians as persons dedicated to God and set apart for His service; the "faithful brethren" seems to indicate their joint belief in the Son of God, and brotherly love amongst themselves. Wesley says, "'Saints'—this word expresses their union with God, 'and brethren,' this their union with their fellow Christians."

"From God our Father, and from the Lord Jesus Christ." The reader, by referring to the critical note, will see that the words "from the Lord Jesus Christ" are not contained in five of the principal Uncials, B, D, E, K, L, but are contained in א, A, C, F, G. Origen notices the omission. "To the Colossians indeed, (he says) 'Grace to you and peace from God our Father,' and does not add, 'and from our Lord Jesus Christ.'" And Chrysostom also, "Whence cometh grace to you? Whence peace? *From God*, he says, *our Father*, although he useth not in this place the Name of Christ."

Seeing that in every other epistle grace is invoked conjointly from Christ and God, this omission gives a singularly unfinished character to the prayer here. Theological reasons have been assigned for this omission, one being expressed as follows: "Could it have been suggested to St. Paul's mind in connection with his special desire to emphasize the true Godhead of Christ, so obvious in this epistle, by an instinctive reluctance to use in this case any phrase, however customary with him, which might even seem to distinguish His nature from the Godhead?" (Bishop Barry.) But may not a simpler reason be assigned? We are told by almost every commentator on this Epistle, that compared with others it presents decided marks of roughness and want of finish in the style, as if it had been written in greater haste. May not this most unique omission be a case in point?

3. "We give thanks to God and the Father of our Lord Jesus Christ, praying," &c. St. Paul in this, and at the beginning of every epistle, puts thanksgiving before prayer, and the reason is obvious. In every epistle he writes to churches which had been

3 [d] We give thanks to God and the Father of
our Lord Jesus Christ, praying always for you,
4 [e] Since we heard of your faith in Christ Jesus,
and of [f] the love *which ye have* to all the saints,

d 1 Cor. i. 4. Eph. i. 16. Phil. i. 3. & iv. 6.
e ver. 9. Eph. i. 15. Philem. 5.
f Heb. vi. 10.

---

3. "To God and the Father of," *i.e.* "To the God and Father of." So ℵ, A., E., K., L., P., all Cursives, f, Vulg., Arm.; but B., C., D., F., G., d, e, g, Syriac, Copt., Æth., read, "To God the Father of our Lord Jesus Christ."

4. "Which ye have." So ℵ, A., C., D., E., F., G., P., most Cursives, d, e, f, g, Vulg., Copt.; but B. omits.

gathered out from among the heathen by astonishing acts of grace, and had, to the time of his writing, more or less steadfastly held fast their profession, and exhibited the reality of that profession by good works. He must consequently first give thanks for these tokens of grace in the past, as being pledges of help for the future.

"Praying always for you." Not merely mentioning hurriedly the names of each Church, but entering into particulars respecting the distinct spiritual requirements of each. Thus we have in each Epistle different prayers, and if we knew their spiritual state as God knew it, we should find that in the case of each particular Church its spiritual state was known to the Apostle, and he was led to plead with God accordingly.

4. "Since we heard of your faith in Christ Jesus, and of the love which," &c. "Your faith in Christ Jesus." We are told that the preposition here denotes the sphere in which their faith moves, rather than the object to which it is directed; but surely the working of faith in the Person of Christ as the Eternal Son of the Ruler of the Universe, is an astonishing miracle when we consider what the state of mind of any Colossian or any other heathen was before the Gospel came to him. He embraced the belief that the world was redeemed by the Blood of a crucified Jew, and the Resurrection from the dead of the same Jew was the pledge that not only was the Redemption complete, but that instead of at the best a dreamy surmise respecting the immortality of his soul, he was assured that he should live for ever in a spirit united to a glorified body, raised up in the likeness of the Body of the Son of God.

It seems a miracle of power and grace that an ordinary heathen mind should have been able to entertain such an idea, much more to embrace it, and conform his outer and inner life to its spirit.

5 For the hope [g] which is laid up for you in heaven, whereof ye heard before in the word of the truth of the gospel;

[g] 2 Tim. iv. 8. 1 Pet. i. 4.

And so St. Paul may well give thanks that the Colossian Christians should have laid aside heathenism, and acknowledged Jesus Christ crucified, risen, and ascended, to be the Son of God, the Saviour of the world.

"And of the love which ye have to all the saints." Next to the astonishing miracle of the implantation in heathen minds of such a faith was the appearance in the world of the new brotherhood, knitted together in the bonds of a love never before known or even imagined in this world of hate and lust. This love was first of all love to the Crucified—without this it could not have existed—and then love to those who loved Him ; so that discipleship was manifested by love. "By this shall all men know that ye are my disciples, if ye have love one towards another" (John xiii. 35).

5. "For the hope which is laid up for you in heaven." Some interpret this as if the faith and the love were the products of the hope : but surely this is inverting the order of things : there must first come the faith of the Gospel, or the hope which rises directly out of the facts of the Gospel (especially the Resurrection) could have no root. Christians hope for that future blessedness which the Gospel assures to them, because the Gospel is the Revelation of that Risen Lord Who said, "Because I live, ye shall live also." We think then, notwithstanding great names, that the hope must follow upon "We give thanks ; " it is as if he said, "Hearing of your faith and love, we thank God that these graces will not be ineffectual, but that you have the assured hope that you will be rewarded for what ye do and endure."

But what is "the hope laid up for you in heaven"? It is the hope of the resurrection of your bodies, changed after the likeness of Christ's glorious Body. This hope is laid up in heaven because Christ is there, and "our life is hid with Christ in God," so that "when He shall appear, then shall ye also appear with Him in glory" (iii. 3, 4). The hope can be no other than this, for this is, in its very nature, the highest hope that any human being can have.

"Whereof ye heard before in the word of the truth of the gospel."

6 Which is come unto you, [h] as *it is* in all the world; and [i] bringeth forth fruit, as *it doth* also in you, since the day ye heard *of it*, and knew [k] the grace of God in truth:

h Matt. xxiv. 14. Mark xvi. 15. Rom. x. 18. ver. 23.
i Mark iv. 8. John xv. 16. Phil. i. 11.
k 2 Cor. vi. 1. Eph. iii. 2. Tit. ii. 11. 1 Pet. v. 12.

---

6. "Unto you, as it is in all the world, and bringeth forth fruit." So E**, F., G., K., L., most Cursives, d, e, f, g, Vulg., Syriac; but ℵ, A., B., C., D., E*, P., a few Cursives (10), Copt., Arm., Æth. (omitting καὶ), read, "Coming unto you as it is in all the world, bringing forth fruit." After "bringing forth fruit," ℵ, A., B., C., D., E., F., G., L., P., and eighty Cursives, d, e, f, g, Vulg., &c., read, "and increasing."

"Ye heard of this hope when the Gospel was first preached to you, for the Gospel which Epaphras preached was the same as mine, that Christ died, and was buried, and rose again, and if Christ be risen from the dead, He is risen as the first-fruits, and so 'as in Adam all die, even in Christ shall all be made alive.'"

This was the first form in which the Gospel was preached, as we learn from 1 Corinth. xv. 1-10.

6. "Which is come unto you, as it is in all the world; and bringeth forth fruit." The more probable reading is followed by the Revisers, "which is come unto you, even as it is also in all the world bearing fruit and increasing, as it doth in you also, since the day ye heard and knew the grace of God in truth." If so rendered, the hyperbole is avoided, or at least softened, for what the Apostle seems to assert is not the absolute presence of the Gospel everywhere, but that wherever it is present it bears fruit and increases.

We are to remember that the Apostle never speaks of all the world as meaning the whole habitable globe as known to us; but if the Gospel was preached as far south as Ethiopia by the eunuch, the treasurer of Candace, and north by himself at the shores of the Black Sea and Illyricum, and also at Rome and Gaul, and in Mesopotamia, he would look upon it as no exaggeration to say that it was preached to the whole world.

And wherever it is preached it bears fruit and increases. It bears the fruits of righteousness and holiness amongst those who have received it, and it adds to its number by making converts of the surrounding heathen.

"Since the day ye heard of it and knew the grace of God in truth." It would seem from this, that as soon as they heard the preaching of the Gospel they received it in sincere belief.

7 As ye also learned of [l] Epaphras our dear fellowservant,
who is for you [m] a faithful minister of Christ;
8 Who also declared unto us your [n] love in the
Spirit.
9 [o] For this cause we also, since the day we
heard *it*, do not cease to pray for you, and to de-
sire [p] that ye might be filled with [q] the knowledge

l ch. iv. 12. Philem. 23.
m 2 Cor. xi. 23. 1 Tim. iv. 6.
n Rom. xv. 30.
o Eph. i. 15, 16. ver. 3, 4.
p 1 Cor. i. 5.
q Rom. xii. 2. Eph. v. 10, 17.

---

7. "Also" (καὶ) omitted by ℵ, A., B., C., D., F., G., P., d, e, f, g, Vulg., Goth., Syriac; retained by E., K., L., and most Cursives.

"For you." So C., E., K., L., P., most Cursives, d, e, f, Vulg., Goth., Syriac, Copt., Arm., Æth.; but ℵ, A., B., D., F., G., 3, 13, 33, 43, 52, 80, 91, 109, read "for us."

7. "As ye also learned of Epaphras." Epaphras appears, from this notice of him, to have been the first Evangelist of Colosse. St. Paul here calls him his fellow-servant; the only instance in which he uses the word. He is mentioned elsewhere in Col. iv. 12, and in Philemon 23, as St. Paul's fellow-prisoner in Jesus Christ. Antiquity represents him as Bishop of Colosse. This is denied, or at least doubted, by modern writers; but after the Apostle's death he would, if he had continued connected with the Church, have undoubtedly been its chief governor, for how could another have been put over the head of this fellow-servant and fellow-prisoner of the Apostle, his intimate friend, who knew all his mind? Such an one could be trusted to carry on the Apostolic government.

8. "Who also declared unto us your love in the Spirit." He declared the Gospel to you, and brought me back the welcome news of its success, in that it bore within you the fruit of love, the first grace of the Holy Spirit.

9. "For this cause we also, since the day we heard it, do not cease to pray," &c. He now begins to tell them what his prayer was on their behalf, but first he lets them know that it was no new thing that he should pray for them. He had done this from his first hearing of their faith and love. "Since the day we heard it" —he had prayed for them during many years, and that without ceasing.

"And to desire." Rather to ask, to entreat. His desire expressed itself in the words which follow.

"That ye might be filled with the knowledge of his will in all wisdom," &c. "With the knowledge," rather, with the thorough, or

of his will [r] in all wisdom and spiritual understanding;

10 [s] That ye might walk worthy of the Lord [t] unto all pleasing, [u] being fruitful in every good work, and increasing in the knowledge of God:

[r] Eph. i. 8.
[s] Eph. iv. 1. Phil. i. 27. 1 Thess. ii. 12.
[t] 1 Thess. iv. 1.
[u] John xv. 16. 2 Cor. ix. 8. Phil. i. 11. Tit. iii. 1. Heb. xiii. 21.

---

10. "In the knowledge of God." So E**, K., L., most Cursives; but ℵ, A., B., C., D., E*, F., G., P., 17, 71, 73, Vulg. (Amiat.) read, "by the knowledge."

perfect knowledge, ἐπίγνωσις, something far beyond the γνῶσις, to which the Gnostic falsely pretended.

"The knowledge of his will." Not merely of the speculative knowledge of the beings betwixt Himself and us, but of the knowledge of His will concerning us, how it is to regulate our hearts and lives.

"In all wisdom and spiritual understanding." Wisdom in the Bible is always of the highest moral nature, and regulates the heart and life; spiritual understanding is the faculty by which we enter into the exceeding depth and length of the meaning of what God reveals. Wisdom is mentioned first because the heavenly wisdom which makes us truly apprehend God and His will makes us also understand its perfection. Chrysostom makes this wisdom to be divine wisdom in contrast to human wisdom. His comment is a very good introduction to what follows: "'That ye might be filled with the knowledge of his will.' That is, ye must be brought unto Him by the Son, and no more by angels. Now that ye must be brought unto Him ye have learnt, but it remains for you yet to learn further why He sent the Son. For had it been that we were to have been saved by angels, He would not have sent the Son, He would not have given Him up. 'In all wisdom,' he saith, 'and spiritual understanding.' For since the philosophers deceived them, 'I wish you,' he saith, 'to be in spiritual wisdom, not after the wisdom of men.'"

10. "That ye might walk worthy of the Lord unto all pleasing." The Lord is here the Lord Jesus. Walking worthy of Him is walking in His footsteps, after His example. In some places it is "walking worthy of God, who hath called us unto his kingdom and glory." In other places it is "being imitators of God, as dear children."

x Eph. iii. 16. & vi. 10. y Eph. iv. 2. z Acts v. 41. Rom. v. 3. a Eph. v. 20. ch. iii. 15.

11 [x] Strengthened with all might, according to his glorious power, [y] unto all patience and long-suffering [z] with joyfulness;

12 [a] Giving thanks unto the Father, which hath

"Unto all pleasing." Walking worthy of the Lord is so to walk as to please Him in all things. And how, as Chrysostom asks, "unto all pleasing"? The answer is—

"Being fruitful in every good work, and increasing," &c., *i.e.*, doing and progressing. If we are fruitful in good works we shall increase in the knowledge of God—that is, thorough knowledge—the same word (ἐπίγνωσις) as before. Some, however, render it, "increasing *by* the knowledge of God."

11. "Strengthened with all might, according to his glorious power." Literally, "strength with all strength, according to the might of His glory." What is the might of His glory? The most probable way of understanding it is as the Authorized, "according to his glorious power." The glory, however, may here mean the Holy Spirit, the finger of God, by Whom even the Lord, in the days of His humiliation, did His miracles. Thus Chrysostom, in explaining Rom. viii. 30, "Whom he justified, them he also glorified," says, "by His Spirit."

"Unto all patience and longsuffering with joyfulness." From this it would seem that they were then under persecution. The difference between patience and long-suffering is explained by Archbishop Trench as being, that patience is bearing the ill-will of persons; long-suffering is bearing the evil things, such as pain or distress, with which God may chastise us.

"With joyfulness." What the Apostle inculcated he practised himself. Thus he says in this chapter (verse 24), "Who now rejoice in my sufferings for you." Again, 2 Cor. vii. 4, "I am exceeding joyful in all our tribulation." On this verse Wesley says, "This is the highest point. Not only to know, to do, to suffer the whole will of God; but to suffer it to the end, not barely with patience, but with thankfulness." It is difficult to believe that every evil thing which we suffer for Christ's sake will be recompensed, but it assuredly will be so.

12. "Giving thanks unto the Father, which hath made us meet." The Father, as that person in the Godhead Who is the ultimate

made us meet to be partakers of [b] the inheritance of the saints in light:

13 Who hath delivered us from [c] the power of darkness, [d] and hath translated *us* into the kingdom of † his dear Son:

b Acts xxvi. 18. Eph. i. 11.
c Eph. vi. 12. Heb. ii. 14. 1 Pet. ii. 9.
d 1 Thess. ii. 12. 2 Pet. i. 11.
† Gr. *the Son of his love*, Matt. iii. 17. Eph. i. 6.

---

12. "Made us meet." So A., C., D., E., F., G., K., L., P., most Cursives, d, e, f, g, Syriac; but ℵ, B., 4, 23, 80, 15, Vulg. (Amiat.), &c., read, "made you meet."

fountain of all blessings; even those which we receive through the Son and Spirit come from Him, because the Son is "of" the Father, and the Spirit "of" the Father and "of" the Son.

"Who hath made us meet." Who hath made us fit, or competent. Here the Apostle speaks of an action of God in past time, so that he does not mean that all to whom he writes are absolutely now fit in all respects for their heavenly inheritance, but that God has on His part done all that is needful. He hath provided an atonement for all sin. He hath shed abroad abundantly His Spirit. He hath baptized men into His Son's Body. He hath given His Word and His Sacraments, and He has begun a good work in all those who now believe.

"To be partakers of the inheritance,"—rather, "for the part of the lot of the Saints," seemingly having reference to the division by lot of the promised land amongst the Israelites. Chrysostom makes use of this allusion to show that the inheritance is not by works. "Why doth he call it inheritance (or lot?) To show that by his own good works no one obtains the Kingdom, but as a lot is rather the result of good fortune, so, in truth, it is here also. For a life so good as to be counted worthy of the Kingdom doth no one shew forth, but the whole is of His free gift."[1]

"In light." See Revel. xxi. 23: "And the city had no need of the sun, neither of the moon, to shine in it, for the glory of God did lighten it, and the lamb is the light thereof."

13. "Who hath delivered us from the power of darkness." The power of darkness was at its height when it was on the eve of being destroyed. Our Lord said, "this is your hour and the power of

---

1 The translator of Chrysostom (C. Marriot) here appends a note: "The whole passage shows that he uses this word merely to imply man's insufficiency, and not at all to introduce the notion of chance as opposed to Divine Agency."

14 [e] In whom we have redemption through his blood, *even* the forgiveness of sins:

15 Who is [f] the image of the invisible God, [g] the firstborn of every creature:

[e] Eph. i. 7.
[f] 2 Cor. iv. 4. Heb. i. 3.
[g] Rev. iii. 14.

---

14. "Through his blood" omitted by ℵ, A., B., C., D., E., F., G., K., L., P., most Cursives, Vulg. (Amiat.), Syriac, Copt.; retained by only a few Cursives.

darkness" (the same words as here), Thus "through death He destroyed him that had the power of death" (Heb. ii. 14). Thus, having utterly broken the power of evil, He introduced a contrary state of things in the shape of a kingdom, and this no other than the Kingdom of His dear Son, the kingdom of grace into which we have been transferred, so completely transferred, that to us belongs the promise, "Sin shall not have dominion over you, for ye are not under the law, but under grace" (Rom. vi. 14).

14. "In whom we have redemption through his blood, even the forgiveness of sins." The words "through his blood," are not in the oldest authorities, and are probably an interpolation from Ephes. i. 7.

"Redemption through his blood, even the forgiveness of sins." Here Redemption seems limited to forgiveness, and the first benefit in point of time which the sinner receives is forgiveness; but Redemption, in its fulness, is our being brought into Christ, and being made members of Himself, and in Him we have not only forgiveness, but a new life; and a new life, not only to enable us to live the life of Christ in the world, but which will survive death, and will raise up our bodies in the likeness of His glorious Body: and so this Apostle speaks in Rom. viii. 23, of "looking for the adoption, to wit, the redemption of our bodies."

15. "Who is the image of the invisible God, the firstborn of every creature." "Image" signifies such perfection in the likeness as is opposed to shadow (Heb. x. 1), which is mere outline. More especially is this true as respects the Son of God, if we compare the places in which it is said that the Father reveals Himself through Him. Thus "No man hath seen God at any time; the only begotten Son, who is in the bosom of the Father, he hath declared Him" (John i. 18). This implies such a setting forth of the hidden nature of the Father as no mere creature is capable of. Again, "He that seeth me seeth him that sent me," and, "He that hath seen me

16 For [h] by him were all things created, that

[h] John i. 1 Cor. viii. 6. Eph. iii. 9. Heb. i. 2.

---

hath seen the Father" (John xii. 45; xiv. 9), seem to carry out the idea of perfect Divine likeness, as far as it is possible to be apprehended by us creatures. Again, this leads up to "the brightness of His glory and the express image of His person" of Heb. i. 3, which should more properly be rendered, "shining forth of His Glory," and express image of His person should be rather, "express image of His substance," not of His exterior manifestations, but of His substance—of what He really is in Himself.

Putting these together as the words of the Spirit of God, it is clear that we must give the Highest Divine Significance to this expression, "Image of the Invisible God." But is He the image of the Invisible God with respect to His Divine or His Human Nature? Now His title of Logos implies that He represents, or shows forth, what is in God to all intelligences; but that He did not cease to be the perfect image of God when He was made in the likeness of men, is evident from the fact that, in the days of His flesh He said of Himself, "He that hath seen me hath seen the Father."

"The first-born of every creature." Does St. Paul mean by this that the Eternal Son is included in God's creation as a creature—the first of creatures; or does it mean that the Son is as regards His divine and eternal existence prior to all creation? Unquestionably the latter. For he proceeds to say, "by him were all things created that are in heaven and that are in earth." He could not give as a reason for His being the first of creatures that He was the author of creation. Creation is the work of the supreme Uncreated Being, and, as far as we can see, cannot belong to any creature. It is the sole prerogative of God to create.

Perhaps, if it be lawful to coin a word, first-born ought to be rendered pre-begotten, and instead of "of" (of every creature), we ought to substitute fore-begotten before all creatures; in fact, anticipating the words of the creed, "begotten of His Father before all worlds."

For further elucidation of this phrase ("first begotten of all creatures"), I would refer the reader to a note of Bishop Lightfoot on this verse, which seems for all practical purposes to exhaust this subject.

16. "For by him were all things created." "For," that is be-

are in heaven, and that are in earth, visible and invisible, whether *they be* thrones, or [i] dominions, or principalities, or powers: all things were created [k] by him, and for him:

[i] Rom. viii. 38. Eph. i. 21. ch. ii. 10, 15. 1 Pet. iii. 22.
[k] Rom. xi. 36. Heb. ii. 10.

---

cause He is the fore-begotten before all things, "by him were all things created." Thrice is this asserted: once here, once in John i. 3 ("All things were made by him, and without him was not anything made that was made"), once in Heb. i. 2 ("By whom also he made the worlds"). And to this we may add, Prov. viii. 22, "The Lord possessed me in the beginning of his way, before his works of old. . . . . When he prepared the heavens I was there: when he set a compass upon the face of the depth: then I was by him as one brought up with him, and I was daily his delight, rejoicing always before him." Every word of this most sublime passage implies that the uncreated, the God-begotten Wisdom was infinitely above the sphere of the creature, and was in the sphere of the Creator.

"By him," literally, "in Him." In Him as compassing all things, penetrating all space, nay the author of space itself as a condition of the creature, were all things created.

"In the heavens and upon the earth, visible and invisible, whether they be thrones or dominions, or principalities, or powers." Does the Apostle mention these orders of spirits because he desired to show that the angelic beings or æons which formed so prominent a part of the gnostical speculations were, if they had any existence at all, subordinate to the Son, or Logos, and created by Him? I do not think so. He mentioned them because it was a part of his idea of the unseen world that it was not one vast solitude, but that it was peopled by spiritual existences absolutely innumerable. Thus Heb. xii. 22, and also Matth. xviii. 10. And in the next place he assuredly believed that this mighty host of intelligences was under government; it had gradations and ranks, so that there were "principalities and powers in heavenly places."

Now putting aside all reference to gnostical speculations, which he might or he might not have entertained, it seems clear that it would from his point of view immeasurably enhance the glory of the Eternal Son if He was the Creator of this unseen spiritual

17 [l] And he is before all things, and by him all things consist. [l] John i. 1, 3. & xvii. 5. 1 Cor. viii. 6.

18 And [m] he is the head of the body, the church: [m] 1 Cor. xi. 3. Eph. i. 10, 22. & iv. 15. & v. 23.

---

universe, and so believing in its existence, and believing in its order and subordination, he writes this sublime act of faith and praise. "By Him were all things created that are in heaven and that are in earth, visible and invisible, whether they be thrones or dominions, or principalities, or powers, all things were created by Him and for Him, and He is before all things, and by Him all things consist."[1]

"All things were created by him and for him." By Him as the instrument or agent of the Father, &c. "By whom he (the Father) made the world," "for Him," *i.e.* for His glory as well as for the glory of the Father.

17. "And he is before all things." Not He was, but He is. Thus He says of Himself, "Before Abraham was I am."

"And by him all things consist," *i.e.* cohere, hold together, not merely physically, but as part of a system or plan which was in His Mind and Will when He created them, and which He continues to carry out.

18. "And he is the head of the body, the church: who is the beginning," &c. Having glorified the Lord Jesus as the author and upholder of all creation, visible and invisible, he now goes on to speak of Him as the author or originator of the Church: "He is the head of the body, the church: Who is the beginning." This title of beginning, or arché, is one which He takes to Himself in His message to the churches. He is the beginning (*ἀρχή*) of the creation of God: and He is the Alpha and Omega, the beginning and the end. And so being the *ἀρχή*, He is, if one may so say, naturally the Head of the Church, for the head being the seat of intelligence and direction is beyond comparison the principal part

---

1 The reader may be glad to be reminded that several of the most ancient Liturgies mention these orders of spiritual existences in those parts which correspond to our Tersanctus. Thus the Clementine, "Thee, the innumerable hosts of angels, archangels, thrones, dominions, principalities, authorities, powers, thine everlasting armies, adore. The Cherubim and Seraphim with six wings . . . let all the people say with them, Holy, Holy, Holy is the Lord of Sabaoth." So also the Liturgies of St. James, St. Mark, and the Roman.

who is the beginning, [n] the firstborn from the dead; that ‖ in all *things* he might have the pre-eminence.

19 For it pleased *the Father* that [o] in him should all fulness dwell;

[n] Acts xxvi. 23. 1 Cor. xv. 20, 23. Rev. i. 5.
‖ Or, *among all.*
[o] John i. 16. & iii. 34. ch. ii. 9. & iii. 11.

---

of the body: so that the beginning of creation and the beginning of redemption, as it exists in one Redeemed and glorified Body, is one and the same.

It has been said, even by some of the fathers, that as God He is the ἀρχή of the old creation, and as man the ἀρχή of the new; but are we justified altogether in making this distinction? For the relations of Christ to the Church as its Head in heaven, whilst the Church is militant on earth, require a substratum of Divine all-sufficiency to sustain them. He is Head over all things to the Church, which is His Body, which seems to require an omnipotence, omniscience, and omnipresence absolutely divine and infinite.

"The first born from the dead." As He is the first-begotten of all creations, so He is first-begotten of the dead. This means far more than that He is the first-fruits of them that slept. Just as He is the fore-begotten of creation, because in Him all things were created, so He is fore-begotten of the dead, because in Him the dead rise again: "As in Adam all die, even so in Christ shall all be made alive" (1 Cor. xv.).

"That in all things he might have the pre-eminence." That is, in both worlds, in the natural and in the spiritual. The state of things which followed upon, and had its roots in the Death and Resurrection of the Son of God was the New Creation, a new spiritual and eternal world of which He was the Beginning, and of which He is the Head and Completion. It was fitting that He should be the ἀρχή of the seen and the unseen, the old and the new, because the physical and the spiritual are reconciled and made one in Him.

19. "For it pleased the Father that in him should all fulness dwell." "In him," that is in His human nature; for in the next chapter (verse 9), we have, "in him dwelleth all the fulness of the Godhead bodily.".

The word Father is in italics, and is not in the original, but it must be supplied, for the Son by taking human nature became a

20 And, ‖ [p] having made peace through the blood of his
cross, [q] by him to reconcile [r] all things unto him-
self; by him, *I say*, whether *they be* things in earth,
or things in heaven.

‖ Or, *making peace.*
p Eph. ii. 14, 15, 16.
q 2 Cor. v. 18.
r Eph. i. 10.

---

creature of God, so that He could say, "I ascend unto my Father and your Father, and to my God and your God." He consequently received from His Father in His human nature what it became a creature to receive from God. Thus He prayed, "Now, O Father, glorify me with thine own self, with the glory which I had with thee before the world was" (John xvii.), and He said, "All power is *given* unto me in heaven and in earth."

The pleroma or fulness here is, I think, not to be considered to refer to any Gnostical pleroma, but simply to this, that in His human nature His Father had accorded that there should dwell the fulness of Deity with all its divine attributes: in Him dwell all power, all wisdom, all knowledge, all grace: "all things that the Father hath are his" (John xvi. 15).

20. "And having made peace through the blood of his cross, by him to reconcile," &c. This place seems to teach that the effects of the Atonement wrought upon the Cross are not confined to this world, but are as wide as the universe. We must have a double care respecting this verse, that we do not unduly narrow it, as well as that we do not unduly extend it. Many places in Scripture forbid us to build upon it any hope respecting the restoration of evil spirits, and yet it is clear that "things in heaven" are included in the reconciliation, and things in heaven can only be angelic existences.

It is impossible to suppose that the "things in heaven" are souls in paradise, for respecting one of the greatest of these it is said, "David is not ascended into the heavens" (Acts ii. 34); but is it not possible to suppose that the power and virtue of the Blood of Christ extends to them so as to bring them nearer to God, so as to purchase for them perseverance in the love and service of God? Created natures which have not sinned may yet require further union with God, and this may be called reconciliation.

But upon this it is useless, perhaps wrong, to speculate, because it is unrevealed, but what is revealed is that the Sacrifice of Christ affects all intelligence, and this we must hold as an article of faith.

21 And you, [s] that were sometime alienated and enemies ‖ in *your* mind [t] by wicked works, yet now hath he reconciled

22 [u] In the body of his flesh through death, [x] to present you holy and unblameable and unreproveable in his sight:

[s] Eph. ii. 1, 2, 12, 19. & iv. 18.
‖ Or, *by your mind in wicked works.*
[t] Tit. i. 15, 16.
[u] Eph. ii. 15, 16.
[x] Luke i. 75. Eph. i. 4. & v. 27. 1 Thess. iv. 7. Tit. ii. 14. Jude 24.

---

21. "Hath he reconciled." So all authorities except B., 17, which read, "ye were reconciled."

It is set forth to us as reconciliation in the sense that we are citizens of one city. (Hebr. xii. 22, 23), "Ye are come unto Mount Sion, and unto the city of the living God, the heavenly Jerusalem, and to an innumerable company of angels, to the general assembly and church of the first-born which are written in heaven, and to God the Judge of all, and to the spirits of just men made perfect."

21. "And you that were some time alienated and enemies in your mind by wicked works." There is first alienation or estrangement in heart through original sin, and then this alienation is increased and strengthened by actual deeds of wickedness in our lives. We have injured God so far as such a Being can be injured by disobedience, and so we hate, and turn away from Him Whom we have injured. The scene in the garden of Eden is reproduced in each soul. "And Adam and his wife hid themselves from the presence of the Lord God among the trees of the garden." (Gen. iii. 8.)

21, 22. "Now hath he reconciled in the body of his flesh through death, to present you holy," &c. How is it that the Apostle here so specifically mentions that the sphere of reconciliation was "in the body of his flesh, through death"? We have to connect together three passages to arrive at some approach to a conclusion; first, "It pleased the Father that in Him should all fulness dwell;" secondly, this place, "you hath he reconciled, in the body of his flesh through death," and again, ii. 9, "In him dwelleth all the fulness of the Godhead bodily." We are not then to look upon His Reconciliation as a mere mental or even spiritual matter, but as a life through death, and that the death of His Body. There is first of all the Son taking our flesh and assuming a human body; then there is God granting to this Body that in it

23 If ye continue in the faith [y] grounded and settled, and *be* [z] not moved away from the hope of

[y] Eph. iii. 17. ch. ii. 7.
[z] John xv. 6.

---

should dwell the fulness of the Godhead: then, following on this, this Body was given for the life of the world; then it resumed the Life it had surrendered, and became the source of Life to the New Creation—the Church.

So that we are not merely to look upon this place as an implied protest against certain docetic errors, which it may be, for the idea of regarding the flesh, the body, the material substance, as intrinsically evil, was very early in the Gnostical forms of error, but we are to look upon it as God bringing Life and Immortality through Death—through the death of the Body of the God-man.

This is one of those passages in which the extraordinary power and virtue of the crucified and risen Flesh of the Lord is brought into exceeding prominence, so that not only His Mental or Spiritual Sufferings, but His Bodily Sufferings terminating in death are to be regarded as inseparable from the Atonement.

"To present you holy and unblameable and unreproveable in his sight." All sacrificial Atonement is to the end that our bodies, souls and spirits may be made at one—at-one-d to God. Through His Sacrifice of His Body, we have to present our bodies living sacrifices, holy, acceptable to God, our reasonable service. (Rom. xii. 1.)

23. "If ye continue in the faith grounded and settled." This faith is beyond doubt the faith of Ephes. iv., "One Lord, one faith, one Baptism." It is the word respecting the Son of God Incarnate, Crucified, Risen and Ascended. It is that *faith* into the unity of which we pray all may come (Ephes. iv. 13). If the Colossians entertained the Gnostical errors by which they were then seduced by false teachers this faith was made void, for there was a series of angelic existences or æons betwixt the Supreme Being and Christ which destroyed the truth of His Godhead, Incarnation, and Atoning Sacrifice—in fact, would deprive Him of that Body, that Flesh by which He was one of us.

"And be not moved away from the hope of the gospel." The hope of the gospel is more particularly the hope of the Lord's Second Advent, and the Resurrection of the Body. This is the one hope of our calling. We know that a few years later than the writing of this Epistle false teachers moved away disciples from

[a] Rom. x. 18.
[b] ver. 6.
[c] Acts i. 17. 2 Cor. iii. 6. & iv. 1. & v. 18. Eph. iii. 7. ver. 25. 1 Tim. ii. 7.
[d] Rom. v. 3. 2 Cor. vii. 4.
[e] Eph. iii. 1, 13.
[f] 2 Cor. i. 5, 6. Phil. iii. 10. 2 Tim. i. 8. & ii. 10.
[g] Ephes. i. 23.

the gospel, which ye have heard, [a] *and* which was preached [b] to every creature which is under heaven; [c] whereof I Paul am made a minister;

24 [d] Who now rejoice in my sufferings [e] for you, and fill up [f] that which is behind of afflictions of Christ in my flesh for [g] his body's sake, which is the church;

---

this hope by saying that the Resurrection is past already, "and overthrew the faith of some." (2 Tim. ii. 18.)

"Which ye have heard, and which was preached to every creature which is under heaven." This of course is an hyperbole. St. Paul meant nothing more by it than to assert a preaching of the Gospel throughout the then known world, but he probably means to assert rather the sameness of the Gospel which was everywhere preached, as contrasted with the errors and false gospels which, being the production of human minds, were everywhere manifold, and differed from the true Gospel, and from one another.

24, 25. "Whereof I Paul am made a minister; who now rejoice in my sufferings for you, and fill up that which is behind." The Sufferings of Christ are always set forth in the Scriptures as all-sufficient in atoning virtue, but they were not so ordered by God as to relieve the Church from taking part with Him in suffering, and so taking part with Him in reigning, according to the well-known words, "If we suffer with him, we shall also reign with him" (2 Tim. ii. 12). These words have been pronounced to be startling, but we are only startled by them because we do not realize, as the Apostle did, the oneness betwixt Christ and His Church, so in Him that it should be as it were one being—one organization. In the great conflict between good and evil, there is in the counsels of God a certain amount of suffering required to fulfil His all-wise purposes. Christ drank most fully of the cup, and yet He said to two faithful disciples, and if to two, to all, "Ye shall drink indeed of my cup."

But why does the Apostle proceed to say, "For his body's sake"? Because all the sufferings, both of Christ and of His saints, are

25 Whereof I am made a minister, according to [h] the dispensation of God which is given to me for you, ‖ to fulfil the word of God;

26 *Even* [i] the mystery which hath been hid from ages and from generations, [k] but now is made manifest to his saints:

27 [l] To whom God would make known what *is* [m] the riches of the glory of this mystery among the Gentiles; which is Christ ‖ in you, [n] the hope of glory:

[h] 1 Cor. ix. 17. Gal. ii. 7. Eph. iii. 2. ver. 23.
‖ Or, *fully to preach the word of God,* Rom. xv. 19.
[i] Rom. xvi. 25. 1 Cor. ii. 7. Eph. iii. 9.
[k] Matt. xiii. 11. 2 Tim. i. 10.
[l] 2 Cor. ii. 14.
[m] Rom. ix. 23. Eph. i. 7. & iii. 8.
‖ Or, *among you.*
[n] 1 Tim. i. 1.

---

for the sake of the Church, not by way of atoning sacrifice, but still by way of sacrificial devotion. The free-will offerings on the part of St. Paul and other saints, are like the "offerings to God of a sweet-smelling savour" which call down blessings on the whole mystical Body. The oft-repeated saying, "The blood of the martyrs is the seed of the Church," gives us the key of the whole matter.

25. "Whereof I am made a minister, according to the dispensation," &c. This place is strictly parallel to Ephes. iii. 1-10, and both should be studied together. The place in the Epistle to the Ephesians is much fuller. It speaks of the mystery as being that the Gentiles should be "fellow heirs, and of the same body, and partakers of God's promise in Christ." It speaks of the mystery as being "hid in God." It speaks of the working out of the mystery being so ordered that "to the principalities and powers in heavenly places might be known by the Church the manifold wisdom of God."

"To fulfil the word of God." This may be taken in one of two ways, either that the dispensation or stewardship was given to St. Paul as the chief instrument by which the call of the Gentiles, and their incorporation into the Church of Christ was fulfilled; or that the word or Gospel of God, including those features of it which were so contrary to the wishes of the Jews, should be fulfilled. The former seems much more in accordance with the context.

26, 27. "Even the mystery which hath been hid from ages and from generations . . . which is Christ in you, the hope of glory."

o Acts xx. 20, 27, 31.
p 2 Cor. xi. 2. Eph. v. 27. ver. 22.

28 Whom we preach, [o] warning every man, and teaching every man in all wisdom; [p] that we may present every man perfect in Christ Jesus:

What is this mystery? It is Christ in us. Christ so in us, that it can be said of us sinful creatures, "We are members of His Body, of His flesh, and of His bones." It is the mystery set forth in John vi. and in John xv. "I am the vine," &c.

I do not think that this mystery, once hidden, now revealed, is merely the free admission of the Gentiles on equal terms to the privileges of the Covenant. It is rather the mode of that admission, that God has sent His Son into the world as the Second Adam, the Second Head of the race, so that men, without distinction of race or condition, should be engrafted into Him and become members of His Body, "He in them, and they in Him, that they all should be made perfect in one." The fact that the Gospel should be preached to the Gentiles and that they should receive it, is many times asserted or implied in the Old Testament, as for instance, where God says to Abraham, "In thee shall all the nations of the earth be blessed," and in Psalm ii. 8, and in all the latter part of Psalm xxii., and in Isaiah xlix. 6; but the mode of admission, that all should be alike grafted into one organized Body, and *that* the Body of the Son of God, is, even now that it is revealed, the deepest of all mysteries, and the one which even now very many excellent Christians have the greatest difficulty in realizing.

28. "Whom we preach, warning every man, and teaching every man in all wisdom." This seems to tell us that the Apostle's ministry was not a ministry to bodies of men, but to individuals. Thus he says to the elders of Ephesus, "I have taught you publicly and from house to house . . . and by the space of three years, I ceased not to warn every man night and day with tears." (Acts xx. 20, 31.)

"That we may present every man perfect in Christ Jesus." So that the aim of the Apostle in his teaching was not to save souls only, but to present each soul perfect at the last, at the day of Christ. So in the office for the ordering of priests, "Wherefore consider with yourselves the end of your ministry towards the children of God, towards the Spouse and Body of Christ; and see

29 [q] Whereunto I also labour, [r] striving [s] according to his working, which worketh in me mightily.

q 1 Cor. xv. 10.
r ch. ii. 1.
s Eph. i. 19. & iii. 7, 20.

---

that you never cease your labour, your care and diligence, until you have done all that lieth in you, according to your bounden duty, to bring all such as are or shall be committed to your charge, unto that agreement in the faith and knowledge of God, and to that ripeness and perfectness of age in Christ, that there be no place left among you either for error in religion, or for viciousness in life."

29. "Whereunto I also labour, striving according to his working," &c. Here he reverts again to the first person singular. In the last verse he joins with himself all his fellow labourers in an emphatic "we;" now he reverts to himself as one with many, "I *also* labour."

"Striving according to his working, which worketh in me mightily." As he says of the individual Christian, "It is God that worketh in you both to will and to do of his good pleasure," so he now says the same of himself as a minister, "I labour according to his working, which worketh in me mightily." Did God contend mightily in him, he with all his might seconded this Divine Energy.

CHAP. II.

FOR I would that ye knew what great ‖ [a] conflict I have for you, and *for* them at Laodicea, and *for* as many as have not seen my face in the flesh;

‖ Or, *fear*, or, *care*.
a Phil. i. 30. ch. i. 29. 1 Thess. ii. 2.

---

1. "For I would that ye knew what great conflict I have for you." "Great conflict," *i.e.* conflict in prayer, wrestling with God as did Jacob. If they knew the deep anxiety he had respecting them they might have more anxiety about themselves.

"For you, and for them at Laodicea, and for as many as have not seen," &c. Does this imply that the Apostle had never preached the Gospel at Colosse or Laodicea? Modern commentators, as par-

2 [b] That their hearts might be comforted, [c] being knit together in love, and unto all riches of the full assurance of understanding, [d] to the acknow-

b 2 Cor. i. 6.
c ch. iii. 14.
d Phil. iii. 8. ch. i. 9.

---

ticularly Bishop Lightfoot, contends that it does. Chrysostom seems not to speak certainly. His comment is, "He shews here after a divine manner that they saw him constantly in the spirit." Theodoret writes: "Some argue from these words that the divine Apostle had never been at Colosse. But they ought to have examined the general tenour of the words. His meaning is, 'I have much anxiety not only for you, but also for those who have never seen me.' For he cannot be supposed to imply that he has no solicitude for those who have seen him. Accordingly the blessed Luke has informed us that the Apostle went through the region of Galatia and Phrygia, in which Colosse is situated."

2. "That their hearts might be comforted, being knit together in love." "Comforted"—strengthened, perhaps, or encouraged as well as comforted. "Knit together in love"—if they were all united in love the enemy would have the less power against them.

"Unto all riches of the full assurance of understanding," &c. God has so made the various Christian graces to depend upon one another, that if one is wanting the others are incomplete, or even wanting also. Here the "understanding," which we should suppose was in the domain of the intellect, is brought under the influence of the heart; thus St. John: "He that loveth his brother abideth in the light, and there is none occasion of stumbling in him. But he that hateth his brother is in darkness," &c. (1 John ii. 10, 11).

"Assurance" in this and many other places seems to mean "certainty"; the "full assurance of understanding" seems to mean that we surely and certainly understand what is revealed, *i.e.* so far as regards ourselves.

"To the acknowledgment of the mystery of God, and of the Father," &c. The true reading of the latter part of this verse must, in our present state of critical knowledge, be a matter of conjecture.[1] We must, first of all, endeavour to ascertain from the context what is the mystery to which the Apostle alludes. Beginning

---

1 At the end of this chapter I give an extract from Scrivener's "Introduction" examining the various readings.

ledgment of the mystery of God, and of the Father, and of Christ;

---

2. "Mystery of God, and of the Father, and of Christ" (τοῦ Θεοῦ καὶ πάτρος καὶ τοῦ χριστοῦ). So E., K., L., most Cursives; but ℵ, A., C., 4, "Of God, father of Christ," and B. reads (with Hilary), τοῦ Θεοῦ χριστοῦ, which Bishop Lightfoot seems to prefer, putting, however, a comma after Θεοῦ, and paraphrasing, "Of God's mystery, which is nothing else than Christ." D^b, P., 37, 67, 71**, 80, 116, "of God" simply.

with verse 26 of the last chapter, where it is first mentioned, and going on till we come to verse 19 of this chapter, the mystery is evidently the fact that human beings are capable of being "in Christ," so that, being in Him, they should partake, so far as creatures are able, of all the treasures of wisdom and knowledge, and so should be above the reach of Gnosticism; then that they should be rooted and built up in Him, and be complete in Him and have been circumcised, so as to need no circumcision made with hands, having been buried with Him in baptism, and be quickened together with Him, and so account all Judaizing rites and ceremonies as shadows, utterly out of place in such a system of realities as the Christian; and be no longer in danger of being beguiled by Gnostic angelologies, which never can have place in the minds of those who hold the Head.

Such is the mystery, and if it exists at all, it is the mystery of the universe—nothing in regard of mystery can come near to it.

Now this is the mystery of God. It was first determined by God the Father. He committed it to the Son, Who, in order to receive it and act it out, must have been the full partaker of the Divine Nature, and must have the fulness of the Divine Nature in His very Body; for the mystery is a Mystery of Body as well as of Spirit, insomuch as His Risen and ascended Body is the root of all—His Body, raised from the dead, is endowed with Divine Life to be communicated to those whom He chooses to be His members, so that they should be baptized into Him, feed eucharistically upon Him, live in Him, be holy and without blame in Him, and at last be raised up in Him. Now the contemplation of all this minimizes the importance of the difference of readings. It is the mystery of God because hid in Him from eternity. It is the mystery of God (even) Christ, for Christ must have dwelling in Him the fulness of God to be its recipient and divine agent in carrying it out. It is the mystery of God the Father and of Christ, because it equally

3 ‖ [e]In whom are hid all the treasures of wisdom and knowledge.

4 And this I say, [f]lest any man should beguile you with enticing words.

5 For [g]though I be absent in the flesh, yet am I with you in the spirit, joying and beholding [h]your order, and the [i]stedfastness of your faith in Christ.

‖ Or, *Wherein.*
e 1 Cor. i. 24. & ii. 6, 7. Eph. i. 8. ch. i. 9.
f Rom. xvi. 18. 2 Cor. xi. 13. Eph. iv. 14. & v. 6. ver. 8, 18.
g 1 Cor. v. 3. 1 Thess. ii. 17.
h 1 Cor. xiv. 40.
i 1 Pet. v. 9.

---

pertains to the Father and the Son. It cannot be without the Father, and it cannot be without the Son.

3. "In whom are hid all the treasures of wisdom and knowledge." They must be if He is the Wisdom as well as the Power of God; they must be if He is the Truth; they must be if He is the Word by Whom all things were created.

"Hid," not that they should continue to be hid, but that they should be sought for from Him, and from Him alone: for He alone can dispense them. If we seek them from Him, He will be to us wisdom (1 Cor. i. 30). This wisdom and knowledge reaches even to the Father, for "no man knoweth the Father save the Son and he to whomsoever the Son shall reveal him" (Matt. xi. 27, &c.).

4. "And this I say, lest any man should beguile you with enticing words." What are these enticing words, except those which would entice men to seek Gnosis from anyone except Christ?

5. "For though I be absent in the flesh, yet am I with you in the spirit." "In the spirit." This may mean that his spirit was present with them, joying, and beholding their order, because he had learnt it from Epaphras, and so beheld it in his imagination, which he knew did not exceed the reality; or it may be that the Spirit of God for his consolation revealed it to him supernaturally; but the former sense is more probable.

And he said not "faith," but "steadfastness," as to soldiers standing in good order but firmly. Now that which is steadfast, neither deceit nor trial shall shake asunder. "Not only, he saith, have ye not fallen, but no one hath so much as thrown you into disorder. He hath set himself over them, that they may fear him as though present, for thus is order preserved." (Chrysostom.)

6 [k] As ye have therefore received Christ Jesus the Lord, *so* walk ye in him:

7 [l] Rooted and built up in him, and stablished in the faith, as ye have been taught, abounding therein with thanks.

k 1 Thess. iv. 1. Jude 3.
l Eph. ii. 21, 22. & iii. 17. ch. i. 23.

Some (as Blunt) have noticed that "this is the language of one who was personally known to those whom he was addressing, and who himself had sometimes witnessed conduct on which his words were grounded."

6. "As ye have therefore received Christ Jesus the Lord, so walk ye," &c. This does not mean the true doctrine of Christ Jesus, though that of course is comprehended in it; but as ye have received Himself as the God-man, the Head of the mystical Body, the Second Man, the true Adam, "as ye have been grafted into him, so walk ye in him."

7. "Rooted," that is, as a tree rooted in the best soil, or rather, perhaps, as a branch rooted in the stem (compare John xv. 1-10, and Romans xi. 17).

"Built up," as a building is erected on its foundation (compare Ephes. ii. 19). Here are apparently, from a critic's point of view, three incompatible figures: Walking as in a way, rooted as in ground, built up as a temple on its foundations; and yet the true Christian has to realize all three. He has to walk in Christ as the way, he has to be rooted in Christ as in the true Vine, he has to be built up upon or in Him as a lively or living stone (1 Peter ii. 4, 5).

"Stablished in the faith, as ye have been taught," *i.e.* as ye have been taught at the first, perhaps by Epaphras, perhaps by the Apostle himself. They were taught the one true Gospel when they were first converted. Any other Gospel which they were in some danger of receiving would be not another *Gospel.*

"Abounding therein with thanks." The blessings comprehended under the words "being in Christ" are such, that if realized they must make the recipient abound in thanksgiving.

8. "Beware lest any man spoil you through philosophy and vain deceit." "Spoil you," *i.e.* "lead you captive." By having been brought into the kingdom of God's dear Son, ye are translated into

m Jer. xxix. 6. Rom. xvi. 7. Eph. v. 6. ver. 18. Heb. xiii. 9.
n Matt. xv. 2. Gal. i. 4. ver. 22.
‖ Or, *elements.*
o Gal. iv. 3-9. ver. 20.
p John i. 14. ch. i. 19.

8 [m] Beware lest any man spoil you through philosophy and vain deceit, after the [n] tradition of men, after ‖ the [o] rudiments of the world, and not after Christ.

9 For [p] in him dwelleth all the fulness of the Godhead bodily.

---

a kingdom of liberty: ye partake of the liberty wherewith Christ makes free. Beware lest you be taken captive again.

"Through philosophy and vain deceit." "Through his philosophy and vain deceit," so Alford and Revisers. The absence of both preposition and article in the second clause shows that vain deceit describes and qualifies philosophy (Lightfoot), so that St. Paul does not here denounce all philosophy, but that philosophy, falsely so called, which neutralized the Gospel.

"After the tradition of men." These traditions may not have been Jewish traditions, for we must remember that in Apostolic language traditions simply meant knowledge delivered from the teacher to the taught. Thus St. Paul praises the Corinthian Christians that they kept the traditions as he delivered them unto them (1 Cor. xi. 2); and he bids the Thessalonians hold the traditions which they have been taught, whether by word or by his Epistle (2 Thess. ii. 15). If, then, any Gnostical teachers delivered to those who listened to them a system of æons, this would then be called "tradition" as much as any doctrine handed down by the Jewish elders could be called tradition.

"After the rudiments of the world." These are the same words as in Gal. iv. 3: "Even so when we were children, we were in bondage under the elements of the world," in which the Apostle evidently refers to Judaism. The immediate context, especially the following two verses of this place, seem to refer to Gnostical speculations respecting the Pleroma. But is it not most probable that the words immediately following, "not after Christ," teach us that the Apostle here refers to all worldly rudimentary knowledge, Jewish, or Gnostical, or heathen, apart from Christ?

9. "For in him dwelleth all the fulness of the Godhead bodily." This is one of the most mysterious as well as one of the most suggestive passages in the New Testament. It is the counterpart of

10 [q] And ye are complete in him, [r] which is the head of all [s] principality and power: [q] John i. 16. [r] Eph. i. 20, 21. 1 Pet. iii. 22. [s] ch. i. 16.

John i. 14: "And the Word was made flesh, and dwelt amongst us, and we beheld his glory, the glory as of the only begotten of the Father, full of grace and truth."[1] Parallel places are, "He that hath seen me hath seen the Father." "I and the Father are one." "The Father that dwelleth in me He doeth the works." If the reader will consider a moment, he will see that the wondrous discourse in John vi. respecting Christ's flesh being for the life of the world, postulates the doctrine here revealed to Christ's Apostle by the Holy Ghost. It puts out of court, as it were, all that mere human reasoning which insists upon limiting the attributes or powers of the Flesh of Christ by the qualities of our flesh. His Flesh is human Flesh, His Body is a human Body, but in it dwells the fulness of the Godhead. How can we profess to measure the properties, to lay down the limitations of such a body?[2] We hope ourselves, when we are raised again, to possess bodies which will have qualities far above those of our present natural bodies: what must, then, be the attributes of the glorified Body of the Lord, of Him in Whom dwells corporeally the fulness of Godhead?

10. "And ye are complete in him, which is the head of all principality and power." Ye have no need of any pleroma, any fulness in angelic powers, for ye are complete in Him. Ye have all fulness in Him Who, if there be angelic power, no matter how exalted, is its Creator. Ye have in Him the supply of all need, both for the life of holiness here, and the life of glory hereafter.

11. "In whom also ye are circumcised with the circumcision

---

1 If the Word was made flesh and became incarnate, so that Jesus Christ was Very God and Very Man, then the fulness of the Godhead dwelt in Jesus Christ; for the Persons of the Adorable Godhead have not the Godhead parted amongst Them, but each One has the whole Godhead. In Christ the Son of God, then, there dwells the fulness of the Godhead bodily.

2 Thus Cyril of Alexandria: "If the nature of flesh be looked at in itself, it is not life-giving. It will give life to nothing, but rather needs a power to give life to itself. But if you take the mystery of the Incarnation into account, and learn Who it is Who dwells in this flesh, you will by all means be disposed to allow, unless you speak against the Divine Spirit Itself, that It is able to give life, even though the flesh by itself profit nothing. For when it is united to the Life-producing Word, It becomes of Itself wholly Life-producing. Mounting up to the level of that which is better than Itself, and not bringing down to Itself that which cannot be debased." On John vi. 64.

t Deut. x. 16. & xxx. 6. Jer. iv. 4. Rom. ii. 2 Phil. iii. 3.
u Rom. vi. 6. Eph. iv. 22. ch. iii. 8, 9.
x Rom. vi. 4.

11 In whom also ye are [t] circumcised with the circumcision made without hands, in [u] putting off the body of the sins of the flesh by the circumcision of Christ:

12 [x] Buried with him in baptism, wherein also

---

11. "Ye are circumcised." "Were circumcised."
"The body of the sins of the flesh." ℵ, A., B., C., E., F., G., P., 17, 71, 73, 116, 118, 120, 178, Vulg., Ital., Copt., omit "of the sins;" but K., L., most Cursives, and Syr.ac retain the words.

12. Revisers translate more correctly, "Having been buried with him in baptism, wherein ye were also raised with him, through faith in the working of God."

made without hands." The words "made without hands," are frequently used in the New Testament to signify what is heavenly and spiritual in contradiction to what is earthly and carnal. Thus (2 Cor. v. i.), "We have a building of God, an house not made with hands, eternal in the heavens." And again, the sphere of redemption by Christ's Blood is called "a greater and more perfect tabernacle, not made with hands." (Heb. ix. 11), "Ye are circumcised with the circumcision made without hands," signifies the spiritual circumcision; and this, in the next verse, is explained as being buried with Christ in Baptism, which is the circumcision of Christ.

But what is the signification of "putting off the body (of the sins) of the flesh by the circumcision of Christ"? The allusion is probably to the fact that in the Jewish circumcision only a part pertaining to one member of the body, the foreskin, was cut off, whereas in Christian Baptism the whole body is (or is assumed to be), submerged; so that not one form of carnal lust, but the whole body of the old man, in which sin resides, is mystically destroyed, and this is clear from what follows.

12. "Buried with him in baptism, wherein also ye are risen with him." The whole body is assumed to die and to be buried; and the whole body is assumed to emerge out of the water in a renewed state. The connection with the past is severed, for the body, the man, is buried, and the future which opens out is a state of being "in Christ," partaking of His fulness or completeness in all that is against sin, and on the side of righteousness, or rather newness of life.

"Wherein also ye are risen with him through the faith of the operation of God, who," &c. Perhaps this would be clearer if it was

[y] ye are risen with *him* through [z] the faith of the

[y] ch. iii. 1.
[z] Eph. i. 19. & iii. 7.

---

translated as the Revisers render it, "Wherein ye were also raised with him through faith in the working of God." The parallel passage in Rom. vi. will assist us materially to realize the idea of the Apostle. "Knowing this (Rom. vi. 6), that our old man is crucified with him, that the body of sin might be destroyed, that henceforth we should not serve sin." This is parallel to "putting off the body of the sins of the flesh by the circumcision of Christ. Buried with him in Baptism." But though buried in the Holy Rite, we are not to continue buried, but are to be raised again out of the water as He was raised out of the tomb, or state of death, and this being raised again is a Resurrection to a new state, a state of grace, a state in which the virtue of Christ's Resurrection is ours, if we will believe it and plead it. Baptism has a double significance. It represents a Death and a Resurrection, both of Christ—a death to sin by mystical union with His Death in our being put under the water, and a Resurrection to newness of life by mystical union with His Resurrection to a life to God ("in that he liveth, he liveth unto God"). Unless the Christian Church held fast to the Resurrection of Christ it could not observe Baptism, and so all who are baptized by and into the Christian Church, are so baptized because they believe in the working of God in having raised Him from the dead.

So that, according to the Apostle's reasoning, there is an extraordinary supernatural working of God in the spiritual world taking place at the ministration of every Baptism. The man (or the child), baptized, is united to Christ in His Death and Resurrection—in His Death, so that he may partake of the virtue of that Death in receiving forgiveness for the sins for which Christ died; and in His Resurrection, so that he may partake of that new life against the power of sin, and for the service of God, which Christ received when He rose by the power of God.

This extraordinary work of God in Baptism the Apostle himself firmly believed, or he could not possibly have written this passage in this Epistle, and the parallel one in Rom. vi., for they are precisely the same in meaning. And their meaning is that every baptized person at his baptism receives what we now should call an interest in the Death and also in the Resurrection of Christ; an interest in the Death of Christ so that he may have the forgiveness

[a] Acts ii. 24. operation of God, [a] who hath raised him from the dead.

---

which is the result of that Death, and an interest in the Resurrection so that he may have a part in that Life which Christ received at His Resurrection.

Only the Apostle uses a much stronger term than "receiving an interest" in these things of Christ. He speaks as if the tomb of Christ was always open, so that we might descend into it and leave our sinful flesh there, and emerge out of it with a renewed nature.

The question for us is not, how can this be? for, if we believe in God at all, we must believe that He can bring about anything; but how can we believe it in our own case? If we can believe it, it will be a most blessed thing for us, giving us a power against sin, and a confident reliance on the ever present grace of the New Covenant, which grace is being "in Christ."

Now the first step to believing it is belief in the Divine Nature of the Lord—that the Head of the Church and the Ordainer of Sacraments is the God-Man, Who is ever present in the Church and in all parts of it, to make each administration of the Sacrament one and the same, so that in every case, no matter how unfavourable, or mean, or commonplace the surroundings are, He is present to make it a Death, Burial, and Resurrection with Himself.

If the effect of Baptism is described in extraordinary terms, we have to remember that the whole dispensation is extraordinary. Its beginning in the Incarnation of the Lord, its continuance by the power of His Resurrection, and its conclusion by the resurrection of our own bodies are alike extraordinary.

But here we are met by the objection that this Death, Burial, and Resurrection in the Sacrament is only ascribed to the Baptism of believers, called so for the purpose of excluding children from the operation of the Lord's mercy in this respect. But looking at my own experience as a parish priest, I feel obliged to say that the Baptism of those of riper years has been one of the most difficult parts of it. For those who have demanded this ministration at my hands have been always either spiritual or unspiritual. If spiritual, then all that men commonly account regeneration had taken place before, perhaps long before, and there seemed to be no place for such a thing as a Death and Resurrection with Christ. If, how-

13 [b] And you, being dead in your sins and the [b Eph. ii. 1, 5, 6, 11.]

13. "In your sins." So A., C., D., E., F., G., K., P., most Cursives; but ℵ, B., L., some Cursives, read, "through" or "on account of."

ever, they came in an unspiritual, not to say sinful state, then they certainly were not converted, or rendered spiritual by the administration. Whereas in the case of the Baptism of Infants there seems to be no difficulty. They receive Incorporation into the New or Second Adam (*i.e.*, a Burial and Resurrection in Him), in the same state of helpless unconsciousness as they received Union with the Old at their fleshly conception, or birth: and those who have the charge of their yet pliant minds have to see to it that they are reminded that they have received a blessing from Christ, and that this has to be believed by them, and they have to make it good and to retain it, and to yield their wills to it.

Now nothing can be a better guide in this respect than the use which is made in our own Baptismal Service of the conduct of Christ towards infants. "Doubt ye not therefore, but earnestly believe that He will likewise favourably receive this present Infant," &c. Here we appeal to the unchangeableness of the God-man—that He will act towards all infants now as He did in the days of His Flesh—that, in spite of their tender years, He will give them all that they can then receive, and assuredly, if they have received evil from Adam they can equally receive good from Him, which good thing is the being buried and raised again in Him.

I have dwelt upon this before, in my notes on Rom. vi., but have now considered it fully a second time, as it is the key to enable us to apprehend somewhat St. Paul's view of Union with Christ. It is also necessary to be understood if we would rightly apprehend the definition of the grace of Baptism in our Catechism—"a death unto sin and a new birth unto righteousness." A death unto sin by Sacramental Union with Christ's Death, and a New Birth, or, to use the words of the Apostle, a Resurrection in Christ unto Righteousness. The reader will also find the comparison of the two Adams very fully treated in Bishop Jeremy Taylor's "Liberty of Prophesying," vol. v. pp. 540-590, Edon's edition.

13. "And you, being dead in your sins and the uncircumcision of your flesh." "Dead," *i.e.*, dead to God, and to all hopes of a glorious immortality.

uncircumcision of your flesh, hath he quickened together with him, having forgiven you all trespasses:

[c] Eph. ii. 15, 16.

14 [c] Blotting out the handwriting of ordinances that was against us, which was contrary to us, and took it out of the way, nailing it to his cross;

"Having forgiven you." L., P., and a few Cursives; but ℵ, A., B., C., D., E., F., G., K., most Cursives, Goth., Syriac, read, "us."

"And the uncircumcision of your flesh." The uncircumcision here denotes that they were without that type of a purity hereafter to be bestowed, which was given to the chosen people; they had not even the figure of something better than their then degraded state. There was not even that mark in the flesh which was the token of God's regard.

"Hath he quickened together with him," *i.e.*, with Christ. A repetition of the same idea of Resurrection in Christ to a new and better life, which was in the previous verse.

"Having forgiven you," rather "us." So all the older MSS. The change in the person from you to us emphasizes the sharing alike of both Jews and Gentiles in the Redemption.

14. "Blotting out the handwriting of ordinances that was against us, which was contrary to us." This apparently can only mean the Jewish ordinances of exclusion which before the Death and Resurrection of Christ were "against us," this "us" being rather the Gentile Body with which St. Paul, for the time, identifies himself here; or it may mean that the law, or handwriting, or ordinance was against the Jews themselves to whom it was given, as it clearly taught that the way to God was not yet made manifest till a new and better state of things was introduced. The figure of a handwriting against us seems to be the same as "the law of commandments contained in ordinances" of Ephes. ii. 15, and which was the same in its separating effect as the middle wall of partition of the previous verse.

May not the Apostle have meant that any ordinances of exclusion in a religion ordained by the Father of all, must betoken very imperfect reconciliation, so that the very existence of the handwriting of ordinances was against—was contrary to—the chosen people themselves, as well as against the Gentiles, who were more formally and pointedly excluded?

15 *And* [d]having spoiled [e]principalities and powers, he made a shew of them openly, triumphing over them || in it.

[d] Gen. iii. 15. Ps. lxviii. 18. Is. liii. 12. Matt. xii. 29. Luke x. 18. & xi. 22. John xii. 31. & xvi. 11. Eph. iv. 8. Heb. ii. 14.
[e] Eph. vi. 12.
|| Or, *in himself.*

"And took it out of the way, nailing it to his cross." I confess that I do not understand the allusion here. It seems to refer to some ancient custom which was connected with release from debt, the memory of which is forgotten. It seems as if, when Christ was on the Cross, He satisfied the claims against us on account of our sins, and so, in a figure, He took the bill or bond which was against us, and nailed it to His Cross with our sign-manual erased, so that all might see, if they looked to the Cross, that the debt was cancelled. Blunt interprets it thus: "The idea here is that of Christ Himself bearing away the bond, and making it part of Himself, when being made sin for us, Who knew no sin, He was nailed to the Cross." This appears to be mainly the interpretation of Theodoret.

15. "And having spoiled principalities and powers, he made a shew of them openly," &c. The meaning of this extremely difficult verse seems to be this: Christ put off from Himself principalities and powers, *i.e.*, the powers of evil, when He divested Himself of His Body, for it was only through His Body that the spirits of evil had power over Him. [This is your hour and the power of darkness.] By submitting to the Death of the body He put off (not spoiled) the powers of evil, and apparently He did more than this, for when His disembodied Spirit descended into the unseen world He enjoyed a triumph (the circumstances of which are not revealed) over the powers of darkness, of which all the dwellers in Hades were witnesses.

Such seems to be the idea which Chrysostom had of the meaning of the passage, "'Having stripped off principalities and powers.' He means the diabolical powers, either because human nature had arrayed itself in these, or because they had, as it were, a hold (on it); when He became man He put away from Himself that hold. This is the meaning of 'He made a shew of them.' And well said He so, for never yet was the devil in so shameful a plight. For whilst expecting to have Him, he lost even those he had, and when that Body was nailed to the Cross, the dead arose. Then

16 Let no man therefore [f] judge you || [g] in meat,
or in drink, or || in respect [h] of an holyday, or of
the new moon, or of the sabbath *days*:
17 [i] Which are a shadow of things to come; but
the body *is* of Christ.

f Rom. xiv. 3, 10, 13.
|| Or, *for eating and drinking.*
g Rom. xiv. 2, 17. 1 Cor. viii. 8.
|| Or, *in part.*
h Rom. xiv. 5. Gal. iv. 10.
i Heb. viii. 5. & ix. 9. & x. 1.

---

16. "Or in drink." B. alone of authorities reads "and" in drink.

the devil received his wound having met his death-stroke from a dead body."

"Triumphing over them in it," *i.e.*, "by the Cross." So He triumphed over them by the symbol of that extremity of shame and death which they brought upon Him.

16. "Let no man therefore judge you." Suffer no man to blame you, or to call you to account.

"Therefore." Here in what he is about to say he seems to revert to verses 8-10, and the intervening verses seem to be somewhat parenthetical.

"In meat or in drink." That is in the matter of eating and drinking unclean meats or abstinence from wine. Ye are complete in Him and are emancipated from the bondage; see that ye are not again ensnared by it.

"Or in respect of an holyday, or of the new moon, or of the sabbath days." This is said with respect to the Jewish side of the errors or heresies into which the Colossian Christians were tempted to fall, just as verse 18 looks to the Gnostical side of such errors.

"Of the sabbath days." This of course refers to the keeping of the seventh day of the week rather than of the first. The first day of the week, the Lord's day, had not at that time been enforced by Church authority as a day of rest, though it was recognized as the day for the celebration of the Eucharist. See notes on Gal. iv. 10. It is now enforced, and if professing Christians habitually disregard it they deprive their fellow Christians of that day of rest and refreshment, and opportunity to attend the service of God, which Christ has emphatically declared to be theirs when He said, "The Sabbath was made for man."

17. "Which are a shadow of things to come; but the body is of Christ." The very sabbath itself was a shadow. It shadowed forth "the rest which remaineth to the people of God," as we are

18 [k] Let no man || beguile you of your reward † in a voluntary humility and worshipping of angels, intruding into those things [l] which he hath not seen, vainly puffed up by his fleshly mind,

k ver. 4.
|| Or, *judge against you.*
† Gk. *being a voluntary in humility*, ver. 23.
l Ezek. xiii. 3. 1 Tim. i. 7.

---

18. "Which he hath not seen." So K., L., P., most Cursives, f, g, Vulg., Goth., Syriac, &c.; but ℵ, A., B., D., and several references in Fathers read, "Which he hath seen."

taught by the remarkable reasoning of Hebrews iv. For the principle which underlies the rejection by the Church of Jewish festivals, and the religious keeping of Christian ones, I must refer the reader to my notes on the Epistle to the Galatians, especially on Chap. iv. 10. Suffice it to say here that the keeping of a Jewish festival as such was in a converted Gentile a sign of deep-seated unbelief—unbelief in the all-sufficiency of Christ as the Head of the Christian system—whereas the keeping of a Christian festival was a sign of faith, that Christ as Incarnate, Born, Crucified, Risen and Ascended, should be glorified to the uttermost not only in the recesses of the Christian soul, but in the very lapse of time itself—so that there should not be only earthly but Christian seasons, the very course of the year proclaiming the Gospel of the grace of God.

18. "Let no man beguile you of your reward in a voluntary humility and worshipping of angels, intruding," &c. The Revisers translate this "Let no man rob you of your prize," &c.

The meaning seems to be somewhat of this sort: You are in danger of losing your eternal reward by these teachers imbuing you with a false humility, making you think that you are not worthy to be joined directly to the supreme God through Christ, but that there must be a series of æons or angels whom you must invoke who are the links between God and Christ, and between Christ and you. He who thus teaches you intrudes into those things which he hath not seen,[1] and upon the truth of which neither

---

1 "Which he hath not seen." Some ancient authorities read, "which he hath seen," and this being the more unlikely reading is preferred by some. But what sense can be made of the words, "intruding into those things which he *hath* seen"? It is explained by importing the words "in vision." The persons alluded to profess to have seen the unseen world of æons or angels in visions or revelations; but still it seems a strange sense, "intruding into those things which he hath seen in his visions and trances," but may

19 And not holding [m] the Head, from which all the body by joints and bands having nourishment ministered, and knit together, increaseth with the increase of God.

[m] Eph. iv. 15, 16.

---

he nor any other human being can pronounce. Such an one is vainly puffed up by his fleshly mind—it is not the spiritual but the fleshly mind which dwells upon speculations of this sort. The truly spiritual mind, that is the mind informed and enlightened by the Spirit of God, will rather dwell upon the things of Christ, especially the great truth that He is the Head and Saviour of the body.

19. "And not holding the Head;" *i.e.*, not holding fast or firmly to the Head. If a man firmly holds to the Head, he firmly holds to the truth that Christ is the Son of God, and the Head of the Church ("Head over all things to the Church which is His Body," Ephes. i. 22, 23). Now if his faith has anything like a firm grasp of this truth, there is no room for any system of æons or angels mediating anywhere in the spiritual universe. There can be no system of æons between the Father and the Son, for the Son and the Father are one; neither is there room for any angelic system, or system of Gnostical æons betwixt Christ and the Christian, for the Christian is a member of the mystical body of which Christ is the Head. In this Body Christ is the Head, and the ministers of the word and sacraments, and not angelic natures, are the joints and bands.

"From which all the body by joints and bands having nourishment ministered, and knit together." Ephes. iv. 16 is a strictly parallel passage, "The head, even Christ: from whom all the body fitly framed and knit together through that which every joint supplieth (or through every joint of the supply), according to the working in due measure of each several part," &c.

I have shown by a comparison of this passage in the Ephesians, with the context which leads up to it, that "every joint of supply"

---

much as it cannot be allowed that he has really seen these things in visions, another word still has to be interpolated, which he *professes* to have seen. So that in order not to violate the Canon which enjoins us to choose the most unlikely and difficult reading, we have to render "which he hath seen," by, "which he professes or supposes himself to have seen in his visions."

20 Wherefore if ye be [n] dead with Christ from [o] the || rudiments of the world, [p] why, as though living in the world, are ye subject to ordinances,

n Rom. vi. 3, 5. & vii. 4, 6. Gal. ii. 19. Eph. ii. 15.
o ver. 8.
|| Or, *elements.*
p Gal. iv. 3, 9.

---

20. "Wherefore" omitted by A., B., C., D., E., F., G., K., L., P., twenty-five Cursives, d, e, f, g, Vulg. (Amiat.), Goth., Copt., Arm., Æth.; but retained by א and most Cursives, &c.

means the ministerial system, and so it must be here. The body is not a piece of formless or inorganic flesh, but a number of members related to one another, joined together and made one living organization by the nerves running from the guiding and intelligent head, and conveying life and powers of fitting action to all the limbs of the body. This system of "joints and bands" which knits the body unto one organization and at the same time contributes to its power of growth, is the apostolic ministry of bishops, priests, and deacons, existing throughout the Catholic Church, unifying it, not by teaching merely, but by the administration of Sacraments, as it is said respecting Baptism. "By one Spirit are we all baptized into one body"; and there is "one Lord, one faith, one Baptism." And it is said respecting the Holy Eucharist, "We being many are one bread and one body, for we are all partakers of that one Bread" (1 Cor. x. 16, 17).

20. "Wherefore if ye be dead with Christ from the rudiments of the world," &c. They who were baptized into Christ, and so partook of His Death, not only died to sin, but to the old state of things (whatever that might have been) in which they had been brought up. They died to the whole Jewish system, legal and ceremonial. The ordinances to which they were once under subjection were shadows; the substance had now come in Christ, and so it was apostasy from Him to revert to the shadows (Gal. v. 2-5). The same equally applied to any heathen, or philosophical, or Gnostical, or Essene elements in which they had once lived. To whatever might be called elements or rudiments of this present state of things they had died, and they had entered into a new kingdom in which Christ was all in all.

"Why, as though living in the world?" Why, as though the old world, the old state of things, had not passed away, and ye were yet living in *it?*

"Are ye subject to ordinances?" Do ye subject yourselves to

q 1 Tim. iv. 3. 21 ([q] Touch not; taste not; handle not;
22 Which all are to perish with the using;)
r Isa. xxix. 13. Matt. xv. 9. Tit. i. 14. [r] after the commandments and doctrines of men?
s 1 Tim. iv. 8. 23 [s] Which things have indeed a shew of wis-

---

ordinances? (Revisers.) "Are ye having prescribed to you?" (Alford.) Ye are not in the world, he saith, and how is it that ye are subject to its elements? how to its observances?

21, 22. "(Touch not; taste not; handle not; which all are to perish with the using)." The "touch not; taste not; handle not," I need scarcely tell the well-informed reader, are not the words of the Apostle, but of the Judaizing or Gnostical teacher. Thus we have in 1 Tim. iv. 3, "commanding to abstain from meats"—pronouncing things unclean which the Lord hath cleansed (Mark vii. 19, notes; Acts x. 15).

"Which all are to perish with the using." These are evidently the words of the Apostle, and have the same signification as the words of the Lord: "Are ye so without understanding also? Do ye not perceive that whatsoever thing from without entereth into the man cannot defile him, because it entereth not into his heart, but into the belly, and goeth out into the draught?" (Mark vii. 18-19).

Augustine, however, supposes that he refers to Gnostical teaching, rather than to Jewish; and so Tertullian, quoted in Cornelius à Lapide: "Taxat, inquit, eos qui ex visionibus angelicis, quasi de angelicâ superstitione docebant certis cibis abstinendum esse." Et Clemens III. Stromata "solentibus, inquit angelos et demones, curæ est vino, esu carnis, et venere abstinere."

"After the commandments and doctrines of men." The Gnostical prohibitions, of course, were purely human, but so also were, in truth, the Judaizing ones, for after the Lord had freed men from their yoke, the re-imposing of them was through the self-will and perversity of man, and had no Divine authority whatsoever.

23. "Which things have indeed a shew of wisdom in will-worship, and humility, and neglecting of the body," &c. The very different interpretations of this verse show that it is one of very great difficulty.

"Which things have a shew" (λόγος) lit., a word or reason, a talk; the expression, being a contemptuous one signifies that it is in word only—that is, in shew or appearance—that there is wisdom.

dom in [t]will worship, and humility, and || neglecting of the body; not in any honour to the satisfying of the flesh.

[t] ver. 18.
|| Or, *punishing, or, not sparing.*

"In will-worship"—religious service, not according to the revelation of God, but according to the mere will, or wilfulness of man.

"And humility," *i.e.*, of course, false or feigned humility, used, as in verse 18, in a bad sense. According to Bishop Lightfoot, the word ἐθελο should be understood before it, signifying voluntary humility—humility, the appearance of which is put on at will.

[And] "neglecting of the body." Neglecting of the body, not sparing of the body, hard treatment of the body through ascetic practices.

"Not in any honour to the satisfying of the flesh." The greatest possible difference prevails in the interpretation of this clause. Bishop Lightfoot takes honour (τιμὴ) to mean pay and then value, and interprets the clause, "yet not really of any value to remedy indulgence of the flesh." This yields an excellent sense, and one strictly in accordance with the whole context; but still to give to the words "satisfying or indulgence of the flesh" an exactly opposite meaning by violently importing into them the idea of remedying indulgence of the flesh, seems unwarrantable.

Others, as Bishop Wordsworth, take "not in any honour" with the preceding words, and paraphrase "which things have a shew of wisdom in will-worship . . . . and in mortification of the body, not held in any honour, and tending to the pampering of the flesh." But how can mortification of the body tend to the pampering of the flesh?

A tolerable meaning *may* be given to this by keeping to the word in the Authorized "satisfying," and by having regard to the undoubted fact that there is a satisfaction in the most rigid and cruel ascetic practices (witness the fakeers of India), which satisfaction is not of the Spirit, but of the flesh—feeding pride, self-sufficiency, and self-satisfaction, all which are works of the flesh.

Then there is another turn of meaning which is not unworthy of notice, which is that God intends the flesh to be honoured by being not harshly treated, but by being kept under due restraint; and that if we dishonour the flesh by neglecting it, and taking no notice of it, our contempt of it turns shortly into the indulgence of it, as was the case with some of the Gnostic sects. The best way of honouring the flesh is by such subjugation of it to the spirit that we may obey the Spirit's godly motions in righteousness and true holiness.

I cannot say that I can give any satisfactory meaning. The real meaning of the Apostle, whatever may be the translation of his words, must be that self-imposed, self-willed asceticism is of no value, either in preventing the indulgence of the flesh, or in mortifying that pride which is in reality as much a work of the flesh as self-indulgence.

CRITICAL NOTE ON THE READINGS OF II. 2.

τοῦ μυστηρίου τοῦ Θεοῦ καὶ πατρὸς καὶ τοῦ χριστοῦ, "Of the mystery of God the Father, and of Christ." The reading of B. (approved by Lachmann, by Tischendorf in his eighth edition, by Tregelles, Westcott and Hort, Bp. Chr. Wordsworth, and Bp. Ellicott), τοῦ μυστηρίου τοῦ Θεοῦ χριστοῦ ("ita cod. nihil interponens inter Θεοῦ et χριστοῦ," Mai, 2nd ed.). [Tischendorf, however, boldly interposes a comma between the words (see p. 605, note) and is followed by Westcott and Hort and by Bp. Lightfoot, whose note on this passage is very elaborate. This mode of punctuation would set χριστοῦ in apposition to μυστηρίου, in support of which construction ch. i. 27, 1 Tim. iii. 16 are alleged. This is not, however, the sense favoured by Hilary ("in agnitionem sacramenti Dei Christi," and again, "Deus Christus Sacramentum est"), and would almost call for the article before χριστοῦ. In meaning it would be equivalent to D*, &c. (ὅ ἐστιν χς')], has every appearance of being the original reading, and that from which the many perplexing variations have arisen. At present it stands in great need of confirmation, since Hilary (de Trin. ix.) alone supports it (but καὶ χριστοῦ, Cyril), though the Scriptural character of the expression is upheld by the language of ch. i. 27, just preceding, and by the Received Text in 1 Tim iii. 16. Some who feel a difficulty in understanding how χριστοῦ was removed from the text, if it ever had a place there, conceive that the verse should end with Θεοῦ, all additions, including χριστοῦ, the simplest, being *accretions* to the genuine passage. These alleged accretions are, τοῦ Θεοῦ ὅ ἐστι χριστός, manifestly an expansion of χριστοῦ, and derived from ch. i. 27; του Θεοῦ πατρὸς τοῦ χριστοῦ; τοῦ Θεοῦ καὶ πατρὸς καὶ τοῦ χριστοῦ, the final form of the Received Text. Now of these four readings, τοῦ Θεοῦ, the shortest, and according to Griesbach, Scholz, Tischendorf in his seventh edition, Alford, and Dr. Green, the true one, is found only in the late Uncial P, and in a few, though professedly good Cursives—37, 71, 80, 116 (καὶ Θεοῦ, 23), and the important Second-hand of 67, witnesses too few and feeble. . . . Of the longer readings, ὅ ἐστιν χριστός is favoured by D. (though obelized by the Second-hand, which thus would read only τοῦ Θεοῦ), d, e, whose parallel Greek speaks differently, by Augustine and Vigilius of Thapsus, but apparently by no Cursives. The form best vouched for appears to be that of א, A., C., 4, of the Thebaic according to Griesbach. . . . and of an Arabic Codex of Tischendorf, τοῦ Θεοῦ πατρὸς τοῦ (א* omits τοῦ) χριστοῦ. To these words "ihu" is simply added by f (F, G, g are unfortunately lost here), and by other MSS. of the Vulgate (Amiat. fuld., &c.), though the Clementine edition has "Dei patris et Christi Jesu," the Complutensian "Dei et Patris et C. I." With the Clementine Vulgate agree the Memphitic and (omitting Ἰησοῦ) the Peshito Syriac, Arabic, 47, 73, Chrysostom; while 41, 115, 213, 221, 253* (τοῦ Θεοῦ καί π. τοῦ χρ) so far strengthen the case of א, A., C. The Received Text is found in (apparently) the great mass of Cursives, in D. (tertiâ manu), E., K., L., the Philoxenian Syriac (but the καὶ after πατρὸς marked with the asterisk), Theodoret, John Damascene, and others. . . . On reviewing the whole mass of conflicting evidence, we may unhesitatingly reject the shortest form, τοῦ Θεοῦ, some of whose maintainers do not usually found their text on Cursive MSS. almost exclusively. We would gladly adopt τοῦ Θεοῦ χριστοῦ, so powerfully do internal considerations plead in its favour, were it but a little better supported; the important doctrine which it declares, Scriptural and Catholic as that is, will naturally make us only the more cautious in receiving it unreservedly. Yet the more we think over this reading, the more it grows upon us as the source from which all the rest are derived. At present, perhaps, τοῦ Θεοῦ πατρὸς τοῦ χριστοῦ may be looked upon as the most strongly attested, but in the presence of so many opposing probabilities, a very small weight might suffice to turn the critical scale. (From Scrivener's "Introduction to Criticism of the New Testament," third edition, p. 634.)

CHAP. III.

IF ye then [a]be risen with Christ, seek those things which are above, where [b] Christ sitteth on the right hand of God.

[a] Rom. vi. 5. Eph. ii. 6. ch. ii. 12.
[b] Rom. viii. 34. Eph. i. 20.

---

1. "If ye then be risen with Christ." Rather, as Revisers, "If ye were raised together with Christ," &c.

1. "If ye then be risen with Christ, seek those things which are above." This is the fourth time he recurs to the idea of a supernatural life received from above, by reason of union with a Crucified and Risen Lord in the matter of His Death and Resurrection.

(1) In ii. 6: "As ye have received Christ Jesus the Lord, so walk ye in him, rooted and built up in him." (2) In ii. 10: "Ye are complete in him." (3) In ii. 12: "Buried with him in Baptism, wherein also ye are risen with him." (4) In ii. 13: "You being dead in your sins hath he quickened together with him." (5) In ii. 20: "Wherefore if ye be dead with Christ," &c.

The words in the original point more distinctly to the particular time of the first reception of this supernatural life. They are not, "if ye then be risen," but rather "if ye then were raised." "If ye be risen" gives a wrong meaning—in this respect, that it implies that they were then in a risen state, which they might not be if they had wilfully returned to their former sinful state; whereas "if ye were raised" implies that the fact of their being raised had taken place, and that they were responsible for it, and must live to it.

2 Set your ‖ affection on things above, not on things on the earth.

‖ Or, mind.

"If ye then be risen with Christ," implies much more than if ye were converted from idolatry, and began to serve God. It means that after ye were converted, so as to see the vanity of idols, ye embraced or put yourselves under a supernatural system, at the very commencement of which ye partook of the Death and of the Resurrection of One Who is now at the right hand of God, at the head of the universe. And this participation in His Death and Resurrection took place in order that you might have your trespasses forgiven you, by virtue of Union with His Death, and have a new life wherewith to live before God in righteousness and holiness by virtue of Union with Him in His Resurrection.

"If ye then be risen with Christ, seek those things which are above, where Christ sitteth," &c. Christ, when He rose again, rose not to live in this world, but to ascend up to heaven, and to live at the right hand of God. And so must ye, in heart and mind, thither ascend, and with Him continually dwell.

But what are the things which we are continually to seek? Evidently the life, the power, the goodness, and grace which are in Him, and are treasured up in Him, in order that they may be given to us. Thus he prays for the Ephesians, when he wrote: "I make mention of you in my prayers that the God of our Lord Jesus Christ may give you . . . that ye may know what is the exceeding greatness of his power . . . according to the working of his mighty power which he wrought in Christ when . . . he set him on his own right hand in heavenly places" (Ephes. i. 16-20).

2. "Set your affection on things above, not on things on the earth." Set your affection—rather "think of," "mind," by constantly meditating or dwelling upon them.

"On things above"—that is, on Christ and the things belonging to Him, not on things on the earth, *i.e.*, its riches, pleasures, honours, rewards: but has not the world become Christian, and have not Christians, professing ones at least, to rule the world, to manage it, to conduct its business, to administer justice in its courts, to command its soldiery, to guide, if possible, its opinions so that they may flow in right channels? Yes, this is that outer life which all must live; but all this is to be done with the distinct consciousness that there is an inner life, which is not yet fully revealed, but which waits to

3 [c] For ye are dead, [d] and your life is hid with Christ in God.

4 [e] When Christ, *who is* [f] our life, shall appear, then shall ye also appear with him [g] in glory.

c Rom. vi. 2. Gal. ii 20. ch. ii. 20.
d 2 Cor. v. 7. ch. i. 5.
e 1 John iii. 2.
f John xi. 25. & xiv. 6.
g 1 Cor. xv. 43. Phil. iii. 21.

---

4. ℵ, C., D., F., G., P., 17, 47, 52, 73, 109, 116, d. e, f, g, Vulg., Goth., Arm., Æth., read, "your life"; but "our life" in B., K., L., most Cursives, Syriac, Copt.

be revealed. The world is not only to be benefited but to be served, but in serving the world we must see to it that we serve not ourselves, but God; and to do this most effectually, we must see to it that we realize the apostolic words, "All that is in the world, the lust of the flesh, and the lust of the eyes, and the pride of life, is not of the Father, but of the world, and the world passeth away and the lust thereof" (1 John ii. 16). If we are to benefit the world we must live above it with the hidden life.

3. "For ye are dead, and your life is hid with Christ in God." Not "ye are dead," but "ye died when ye were buried and raised in Him." The Apostle's argument is this, "when ye sank under the Baptismal water, ye disappeared for ever to the world. You rose again, it is true, but you rose only to God. The world henceforth knows nothing of your new life, and as a consequence your new life must know nothing of the world."—(Bp. Lightfoot.)

There is no special mystery about this assertion beyond this, that Christ is our veritable Head, and we the members of His Body; for, on this hypothesis, the life dwells in the head, and as the Head is in heaven so is our life. We have it not as a gift to ourselves, so that it should be permanently in us apart from our connection with the Head. From moment to moment we depend upon the life residing in the Head, which flows down into us through "the joints and bands" before mentioned by the Apostle.

4. "When Christ, who is our life, shall appear, then shall ye also appear," &c. Christ and His people will be glorified together. When He appears He will appear in glory, and we shall then be glorified, for as St. John writes, "It doth not yet appear what we shall be, but we know that when He shall appear we shall be like Him for we shall see Him as He is." (1 John iii. 2.)

h Rom. viii. 13. Gal. v. 24.
i Rom. vi. 13.
k Ephes. v. 3.

5 [h] Mortify therefore [i] your members which are upon the earth; [k] fornication, uncleanness, inor-

---

5. "Mortify therefore your members which are upon the earth; fornication, uncleanness," &c. The sins which he enumerates are not the actual members of our bodies and yet he says "mortify your members." This has been explained as if sin itself was a body, and the particular sins members of this body: but he means, I think, something plainer, we are to mortify our members which are upon the earth, *i.e.*, the members of our unrenewed bodies in which sin resides, by denying—indeed, if possible, by extirpating the evil motions of those sins which dwell in them. As he says elsewhere, "They that are Christ's have crucified the flesh with its affections and lusts." (Gal. v. 24.)

"Fornication, uncleanness, inordinate affection, evil concupiscence," &c. It is to be noted how that in every case where St. Paul mentions the sins which Christians must avoid on peril of incurring the wrath of God and forfeiting their right to their eternal inheritance, fornication and other breaches of the Seventh Commandment are mentioned first. Thus in the first of all his Epistles, that to the Thessalonians, he commences the practical part with "This is the will of God even your sanctification, that ye should abstain from fornication." Again he commences his list of the works of the flesh in Gal. v. 19, with "Adultery, fornication, uncleanness, lasciviousness." Again, in the Epistle to the Ephesians, "Fornication and all uncleanness . . . . let it not be once named among you," &c., v. 3. And in the Epistles to the Corinthians, he evidently has more anxiety about this sin than about any other. (1 Cor. v. vi. 15, 20.)

Now what inference are we to draw from this? Are we to infer that fornication and kindred vices were the especial sins of that age, because that his converts having been converted to Christ from a state in which these evil things were not accounted sins, they were not delivered from the habits contracted in their heathen state; or are these sins of the flesh the besetments of human nature itself, constantly reappearing in times when the Gospel is preached with all possible plainness and fervour, so that this nineteenth century, with all its education and refinement, seems as much a prey to these sins as any before it? Certainly, in answer, we must

dinate affection, [l] evil concupiscence, and covetousness, [m] which is idolatry: l Thess. iv. 5. m Ephes. v. 5.

---

say that these Apostolic warnings are written for all time, and for every age. The statistics of prostitution, so far as they can be got at—the statistics of illigitimacy in all the great cities of Europe—Protestant as well as Romanist—in Amsterdam, Berlin, Berne, Brussels, seem to teach that the population of these cities have as little sense of the sinfulness of such sins as the great cities of old, Ephesus, Colosse, and the country towns of Galatia seem to have had.

It is then the plain duty of ministers of Christ, when speaking of sin, to put these sins as St. Paul did, in the first place. Prudence and common sense, of course, must rule our conduct in this, as in all other respects, but not false delicacy, nor the fear of certain respectables who may be listeners.

But says one to me. " What you have to do is to preach conversion. If people are converted they will naturally avoid such sins." No, I rejoin, this is not apostolic procedure. If any one was successful in converting to Christ men of all ranks and classes and characters it was St. Paul, and yet he puts these sins in the foreground, always in the foreground, and you had better do so, if you would be free from men's blood. The preaching of conversion is not sufficient unless there be joined with it the preaching of the holiness of the body.

And again, if you preach conversion ever so strongly, you are not likely to convert more than a part of your hearers, and how about the remainder? They are certainly baptized, and in that baptism they were certainly dedicated to God. St. Paul would have said that they had been made therein members of Christ. Well, dare you say that their baptism was so empty a form that they will be little or none the worse if they are overcome by such sins? You scarcely dare say this. You would shrink with horror if such teaching was to be applied to the members of your own family, would you not?

Again, you must remember that you are the pastor of the poor as well as of the rich, and if you know anything about the poor, you well know that they have nothing like the feeling against the commission of these sins that the so called respectable classes have: very, very few, as far as my experience goes, shun those of their neighbours who lead immoral lives.

n Rom. i. 18. Ephes. v. 6. Rev. xxii. 15.
o Ephes. ii. 2.

6 [n] For which things' sake the wrath of God cometh on [o] the children of disobedience:

---

6. "Cometh on the children of disobedience." So ℵ, A., C., D., E., F., G., H., K., L., P., all Cursives, d, e, f, g, Vulg., Syriac; but "on the children of disobedience" omitted in B. and Sahidic.

So that the apostolic reprobation of these sins is to be very diligently and prayerfully laid to heart by the members of Christ's body, the Church.

"Fornication." Adultery is not mentioned because it was an acknowledged crime.

"Uncleanness." That is, every sort or form of impurity.

"Inordinate affection." One word, "pathos." By the Revisers it is translated "passion," by Alford, "hurtful passion."

"Evil concupiscence," that is, lust and dwelling complacently on evil and impure objects of desire. Both these, "passion" and "evil concupiscence," are the sinful dispositions in the heart which have their gratification, in the two first forms of evil, fornication and uncleanness.

"And covetousness which is idolatry." The use of the article "and *the* covetousness which is idolatry" seems to stamp what the Apostle now mentions as a separate sort of sin, not to be identified with lust in its usual signification, but as meaning greed or greediness of any worldly advantage, whether riches, money, lands, glory, honours, power; for all these things become masters of the spirit, and so really occupy the throne in each man's heart which is by right reserved for God only. In the parallel place in the Epistle to the Ephesians it is "covetous man who is an idolater."

It seems a severe thing to say that covetousness is idolatry, but the Apostle must be believed as saying this in the Spirit. He seems to imply that the inordinate desire of any earthly thing may as effectually interpose between God and the soul as the worship of a false god.

6. "For which things' sake the wrath of God cometh on the children of disobedience." In the Epistle to the Ephesians the Apostle adds, "Let no man deceive you with vain words." Such vain words as that your passions are strong, the flesh is weak, such temptations are natural, almost all are more or less involved in them, and so forth. All such words are vain, for we are

7 [p] In the which ye also walked some time,
when ye lived in them.
8 [q] But now ye also put off all these; anger,
wrath, malice, blasphemy, [r] filthy communication
out of your mouth.

p Rom. vi. 19, 20. & vii. 5. 1 Cor. vi. 11. Ephes. ii. 2. Tit. iii. 3.
q Eph. iv. 22. Hebr. xii. 1. James i. 21. 1 Pet. ii. 1.
r Ephes. iv. 29. & v. 4.

---

assumed to be partakers of a new life against sin, even the life of Christ's Resurrection.

"The wrath of God upon the children (or sons) of disobedience." One MS., B., and some versions omit "upon the children of disobedience;" but the vast majority of authorities, are in favour of retaining it. And, indeed, it seems necessary, for the wrath of God cometh not upon any single transgression, yielded to through stress of severe temptation, and immediately confessed and repented of, but on those who go on sinning wilfully and deliberately—for such only are the children or sons of disobedience.

7. "In the which ye also walked some time, when ye lived in them." They lived in religions and states of society which were impure to the very core, and to this state of things they freely conformed, and walked in the commission of these abominations. (Compare Gal. v. 25.)

8. "But now ye also put off all these; anger, wrath, malice, blasphemy," &c. Having spoken against sins of uncleanness and avarice, he now proceeds to speak of sins of temper—breaches of the spirit of the sixth commandment.

"Anger, wrath." The one seems to be the sudden outbreak; the other, the settled continuance of the passion.

"Malice." Malicious, envious, revengeful disposition. Blasphemy means violent, abusive language against our fellow-creatures, as well as against God. The parallel place is Ephes. iv. 31: "Let all bitterness and wrath and anger and clamour and evil-speaking be put away from you, with all malice," which suggests that the filthy communication should be rather understood as base slander and detraction, or, as some interpret, coarse railing; but the arrows of polished wit are often dipped in far more deadly venom than the coarse abuse.

9. "Lie not one to another, seeing that ye have put off the old man," &c. In the words of the Catechism, "Seeing that ye have renounced the devil, and all his works;" and of the devil the Lord

s Lev. xix. 11. Ephes. iv. 25.
t Ephes. iv. 22, 24.
u Rom. xii. 2.
x Ephes. iv. 23, 24.
y Eph. ii. 10.

9 [s] Lie not one to another, [t] seeing that ye have
put off the old man with his deeds;
10 And have put on the new *man*, which [u] is
renewed in knowledge [x] after the image of him that
[y] created him:

---

says, "He was a murderer from the beginning, and abode not in the truth. When he speaketh a lie, he speaketh of his own, for he is a liar, and the father of it" (John viii. 44).

The old man is, of course, the old nature, which we have not only undertaken to renounce, but which we have sacramentally put off in Holy Baptism.

10. "And have put on the new man, which is renewed in knowledge." I have interpreted (in Ephes. iv.) this New Man of Christ Himself, in Whom we were buried, and raised again, thereby putting off the Old Man and putting on the New. And the Apostle speaks, in Rom. xiii. 14, of a continuous putting on of the Lord Jesus. The meaning is, that we have put Him on by having been united to Him, and made His members; and we must constantly, by acts of faith, renew and cement our union.

But the reader will observe that the Apostle changes the words, "which after God is created in righteousness and true holiness," which appear in Ephes. iv. 24, into "which is renewed in knowledge after the image of him that created him." This seemingly refers to ii. 3, "In whom are hid all the treasures of wisdom and knowledge." The mind of the Apostle is now full of the false gnosis, and that those for whose benefit he writes, have, if they will realize it, the true gnosis: and so he speaks of the Lord Whom we are to put on, the Second Adam, as being renewed in knowledge after the image of Him Who, with regard to His human nature, created Him.[1]

---

1 It has been denied by some (as by Bishop Lightfoot) that this "new man" is Christ, but that it is rather the regenerate man formed after Christ. The matter is exceedingly mysterious, but the interpretation that the "new man" is Christ is borne out by such decisive places in the writings of this Apostle, that I cannot see how we can have two opinions about the matter. First we have the Apostle saying, "As many of you as have been baptized into Christ have put on Christ" (Gal. iii. 27). This is at the very commencement, every Christian's new life being supposed to begin at his baptism. Now at his baptism he is supposed to put on Christ, not by the putting on of the profession of the faith of Christ, nor, as we might have supposed, by the putting before him the example of

11 Where there is neither [z] Greek nor Jew, cir-

[z] Rom. x. 12. 1 Cor. xii. 13. Gal. iii. 28. & v. 6. Ephes. vi. 8.

---

11. "Where there is neither Greek nor Jew, circumcision nor uncircumcision, Barbarian," &c. "Where"—that is, in Christ the New Man. This following close upon the clause, "put on the New Man," is an additional proof that that New Man is Christ: for after the Apostle, in his Epistle to the Galatians, had written, "as many of you as have been baptized into Christ have put on Christ," he proceeds, "There is neither Jew nor Greek, there is neither bond nor free, there is neither male nor female"—an exactly parallel assertion.

We have wonderful proofs of this in the journals of our present missionaries. In the accounts which I have heard from the lips of Bishop Horden, of Moosonee, it seems that, so far as the fulness of the reception of Christ is concerned, it makes no difference whether a man be an inheritor of centuries of the most cruel and degraded barbarism, or whether he be an inheritor of centuries of Christianity and civilization. When the power of the grace of God overcomes and converts a Red Indian, he exhibits the same power of the same regenerating and enlightening grace as the inhabitant of an English town or village who is turned from a life of sin to God and Christ; so that it is an absolute fact that in Christ Jesus there is neither Englishman nor Hindoo, Red Indian, or Japanese, or Malay. The lineaments of the same Divine Character are patent in each. If it is pointed out to us that sin is not extirpated in the

---

Christ, but by being united with Christ as one Who died to sin, was buried, and rose again to newness of life. This is mentioned twice in the Pauline Epistles—once in Rom vi., once in this Epistle (ch. ii. 12). This is the root or origin of that expression, "in Christ," with which some of the Pauline Epistles abound. If we are in Christ we must have been received into Him, which I take it is equivalent to our having put Him on—at least it belongs to a class of analogous expressions. But can it be said that there can be a continuous putting on of Christ? Now we have this in Rom. xiii. 14, "Put ye on the Lord Jesus Christ;" and the same idea is expressed in another form in the Epistle to the Galatians (iv. 19), "My little children, of whom I travail in birth again, till Christ be formed in you." And again to the Corinthians, "Know ye not how that Christ is in you" (2 Cor. xiii. 5). Again, Adam and Christ are opposites—Adam as the Old Man, Christ as the New. If we put off the old, with its sins and infirmities, we put away the Old Adam within us, but we put him off that we may put on that which is his opposite—the New Man, even Christ.

There is a very deep reason for the use of this mysterious language—which is that our new, our better self, is not a creation in ourselves apart from Christ, but in Him. We can but feel after this truth, but it is assuredly what the Apostle teaches.

cumcision nor uncircumcision, Barbarian, Scythian, bond *nor*
free: [a] but Christ *is* all, and in all.
12 [b] Put on therefore, [c] as the elect of God, holy

[a] Eph. i. 23.
[b] Eph. iv. 24.
[c] 1 Thess. i. 4. 1 Pet. i. 2. 2 Pet. i. 10.

---

heathen convert, but that much of the Old Adam remains, we rejoin that it is precisely the same with the Englishman. He, too, has daily to put off the Old Man, and daily to put on the New.

"Barbarian" is the word which the Greeks apply to all who have not inherited their civilization. A Scythian was the lowest type of Barbarian.

"Bond nor free." Of this there were continual proofs before their eyes in the transformation wrought by the Gospel among slaves—so much so that the slave was frequently a pattern to the household.

"But Christ is all, and in all." This is a further proof that the New Man which they have put on is not a regenerate nature, merely after the pattern of Christ's, but Christ Himself.

"Christ is all." He is all to the true believer—His wisdom, righteousness, sanctification—the way, the truth, and the life—the Mediator, Redeemer, and Judge.

"And in all." It was then one of the first truths of Christianity (certainly with St. Paul), that Christ was in all Christians, and yet it was a matter of self-examination for each one to ascertain that Christ was in him. "Examine yourselves whether ye be in the faith; prove your own selves. Know ye not your own selves, how that Jesus Christ is in you, except ye be reprobates?" (2 Cor. xiii.5). "But Christ, saith he, is all, and in all—that is, Christ will be all things to you, both rank and descent, and Himself in you all. Or he says another thing—to wit, that ye all are become one Christ, being His Body" (Chrysostom).

12. "Put on therefore, as the elect of God, holy and beloved, bowels of mercies, kindness," &c. How are ye to put on Christ? It is not a matter of imagination, of mysticism, of spiritual exaltation—not a matter of mere faith, even. It is a matter of charity rather than of anything else. If ye seek to be imbued with mercy, kindness, humility, meekness, long-suffering, through the grace of the Spirit, then ye put on Christ, for these graces are His, and He accompanies them; and so He is formed within you.

"As the elect of God." It is a very singular fact that this is the

and beloved, [d] bowels of mercies, kindness, humbleness of mind, meekness, longsuffering;

13 [e] Forbearing one another, and forgiving one another, if any man have a || quarrel against any: even as Christ forgave you, so also *do* ye.

[d] Gal. v. 22. Ephes. iv. 2, 32. Phil. ii. 1.

[e] Mark xi. 25. Ephes. iv. 2, 32.

|| Or, *complaint*.

---

13. "As Christ forgave you." So C., E., K., L., P., most Cursives, Syriac, Sah., Copt., Æth., Goth.; but ℵ, A., B., D., F., G., d, e, f, g, Vulg., read, "the Lord," and ℵ* reads, "God."

only allusion to God's election or choice in this Epistle, whereas in that Epistle which is, one might say, its twin sister, that to the Ephesians, the election of God occupies the most prominent place. Did the Spirit reveal to St. Paul that the Ephesian Christians needed the truth respecting God's choice of men, and the Colossian Christians did not? There must be a reason, one would think, why the Apostle should dwell on this mysterious truth in the one case, and not in the other.

"Holy and beloved." Holy, because consecrated to God; beloved, because they must have been first loved of God if He made them partakers of His grace.

"Bowels of mercies." An Old Testament expression. Thus it is said of Joseph that his bowels yearned over his brethren; and, in Isaiah, Israel is supposed to remonstrate with the Lord in such words as, "Where is the sounding of thy bowels, and of thy mercies toward me?" (lxiii. 15). And our Apostle, "I long after you all in the bowels of Jesus Christ" (Phil. i. 8).

"Kindness, humbleness of mind, meekness, longsuffering." These are all closely connected. Nothing hinders kindness so much as pride, because pride is self-contemplating, and, therefore, in its very essence, selfish; and so meekness cannot but be longsuffering. The true Christian never forgets that he deserves discipline, and that what others inflict upon him may be a chastening of his Father's hand.

13. "Forbearing one another, and forgiving one another . . . if any have," &c. Some MSS. read "the Lord," but the Son of God is meant.

"Even as Christ forgave you." When Christ prayed for the soldiers who crucified Him, it is not to be supposed that His prayer reached only to them. They were in one sense the most

f 1 Pet. iv. 8.
g John xiii. 34. Rom. xiii. 8. 1 Cor. xiii. Eph. v. 2. ch. ii. 2. 1 Thess. iv. 9. 1 Tim. i. 5. 1 John iii. 23. & iv. 21.
h Eph. iv. 3.
i Rom. xiv. 17. Phil. iv. 7.

14 [f] And above all these things [g] *put on* charity, which is the [h] bond of perfectness.

15 And let [i] the peace of God rule in your hearts,

---

15. "The peace of God." So E., K., L., 17, most Cursives, Goth.; but ℵ, A., B., C., D., F., G., P., six Cursives, d, e, f, g, Vulg., Syriac, Sah., Copt., read, "Peace of Christ."

innocent, because they were mere tools. He must have prayed for Pilate, for the chief priests, for the multitude; and all these were but the instruments of sinful man. Our sins drove the nails through His hands and feet, and pierced His side.

This place also proves the Lord's Godhead. "All power is given to me," includes all power of forgiveness. But there is that within us which may limit Christ's power of forgiveness, and that is our implacability. "Forgive us our trespasses as we forgive them that trespass against us." If ye forgive not men their trespasses, neither will your heavenly Father forgive you your trespasses.

14. "And above all these things put on charity, which is the bond of perfectness." "For since it is possible for one who forgives, not to love: yea, he saith, thou must love him too, and he points out a way whereby it becomes possible to forgive. For it is possible for one to be kind, and meek, and humble-minded, and long-suffering, and yet not affectionate, and therefore he said at the first, bowels of mercies, both love and pity. And above all these things charity, which is the bond of perfectness. Now what he wishes to say is this, that there is no profit in these things, for all these things fall asunder except they be done with love; this is it which clenches them all together: whatsoever good thing it be thou mentionest, if charity be away it is nothing, it melts away" Chrysostom. The idea of St. Paul is expressed in 1 Cor. xiii. 3, "Though I bestow all my goods to feed the poor . . . . and have not charity, it profiteth me nothing."

15. "And let the peace of God rule in your hearts, to the which also ye are called in one body." The oldest MSS. and versions read "the peace of Christ," and the Christian peace is emphatically the peace of Him Who said, "Peace I leave with you, my peace I give unto you: not as the world giveth, give I unto you" (John xiv. 27). But the peace of God and of Christ is the same,

[k] to the which also ye are called [l] in one body; [m] and be ye thankful.
16 Let the word of Christ dwell in you richly

k 1 Cor. vii. 15.
l Eph. ii. 16, 17, & iv. 4.
m ch. ii. 7. ver. 17.

---

and so he says in the Epistle to the Philippians, "The peace of God which passeth all understanding" (iv. 7).

"Rule in your hearts." This is the best translation for English readers, being the most intelligible; but the Greek verb signifies to act as umpire, and is so explained by Chrysostom. "Let the peace of God act as umpire in your hearts. If two thoughts are fighting together, set not anger, set not spitefulness to hold the prize, but peace: for instance, suppose one to have been insulted unjustly, of the insult are born two thoughts, the one bidding him to revenge, the other to endure; and these wrestle with one another; if the Peace of God stands as umpire, it bestows the prize on that which bids endure, and puts the other to shame. How? By persuading him that God is peace, in that He hath made peace with us."

"To the which also ye are called in one body." We are called to peace—to the peace of God, because we are called not as separate stones in a heap, but as members of one body, which must act together and no member have separate interests, if the body is to be in a healthy state and act as one body.

"Be ye thankful." This is the second time this precept "to be thankful" occurs in this letter. We had it in ii. 7, "Abounding therein with thanksgiving," and we shall have it again in verse 17.

16. "Let the word of Christ dwell in you richly in all wisdom," &c. This is explained as meaning Christ Himself in the heart, and not any definite truths respecting Him, but why then does the Apostle not say the presence of Christ instead of the word of Christ? A reference to a very important part of the written word, the Psalms, follows immediately upon this.

The Apostle began to preach the word in Asia seven years before this, and the Gospel of St. Matthew, particularly rich in the words of Christ, had been published many years before, and it is probable that St. Luke's Gospel had also been finished and begun to be copied and put in the hands of the disciples. Either of these Gospels would furnish the Church with a rich store of the very words of Christ. Surely if our missionaries take care that their

in all wisdom; teaching and admonishing one another

---

converts should be furnished with New Testaments in their own languages, St. Paul would not have been behindhand in so obvious a duty. And if it be objected that books then required to be copied out, the reader must remember that either of the Gospels I have mentioned could have been fairly written out in less than a month by a person of ordinary industry. If St. Paul had not furnished his churches with some written Gospel he would have, in a great measure, left them at the mercy of the Judaizers, whose great strength was the letter of the Old Testament.

About the present application of the Apostle's language to Christians there can be no doubt. Brahminical teachers are, I have heard, required to spend many years in committing to memory their Vedas in the Sanscrit, now a dead language, and some effort should be made by Christian students not to be put to shame by the adherents of false religions. Bishop Ridley speaks of having committed to memory the whole of the Epistles during the time he was an undergraduate at Cambridge, and it is no impossible task. It only requires perseverance for three or four years in learning, say, three verses a day.

"Hearken ye, as many as are in the world and have charge of wife and children; how to you too he commits especially the reading of Scripture, and that not to be done lightly, or in any sort of way, but with much earnestness."

"And tarry not for another to teach thee, for thou hast the oracles of God. No man teacheth thee as they, for he indeed (the preacher) oft concealeth much for vain glory's sake and envy. Hearken, I entreat you, all ye that are careful for this life, procure books that will be medicines for the soul. If ye will not any other, yet get you at least the New Testament . . . . if grief befal thee, dive into them as into a chest of medicines; take thence comfort for thy trouble, be it loss, or death, or bereavement of relations; or rather dive not into them merely, but take them wholly to thee, keep them in thy mind. This is the cause of all evils, the not knowing the Scriptures. We go into battle without arms, and how should we come off safe?" (Chrysostom.)

"Teaching and admonishing one another in psalms and hymns." Psalms are most probably the psalms of the Old Testament, which

[n] in psalms and hymns and spiritual songs, [n] 1 Cor. xiv. 26. Eph. v. 19.
singing [o] with grace in your hearts to the Lord. [o] ch. iv. 6.
17 And [p] whatsoever ye do in word or deed, *do* [p] 1 Cor. x. 31.

---

16. "To the Lord." So E., K., L., most Cursives, Goth., Copt.; but ℵ, A., B., C., D., F., G., 17, 47, 67**, 73, 179, d, e, f, g, Vulg., Sah., Syriac, read, "to God."

formed a large portion of the synagogue worship, and naturally passed from the Jews to the Christians. Hymns would be forms of adoration and praise to God and Christ. Pliny speaks of the worship of the Christians in his time, that "They sang among themselves alternately a hymn to Christ as God."

"Spiritual songs," as distinguished from psalms and hymns may be odes of a didactic character; but all distinctions between these three acts of praise are purely conjectural. Chrysostom treats them as if there were no difference.

"Teaching and admonishing one another." It is too much lost sight of how Christians, in singing psalms and hymns which are really scriptural and spiritual, teach and admonish one another at the very time they praise and bless God. Each one who joins in these acts of praise praises God, edifies himself, and admonishes his neighbour. (See my notes on Ephes. v. 19.)

"Singing with grace in your hearts to the Lord." There is to be singing, *i.e.*, the utterance of words in musical tones, with the organs of the human voice; and yet this singing, if it is to be acceptable to God, must be from hearts instinct with the grace of God.

17. "And whatsoever ye do in word or deed, do all in the name of the Lord Jesus," &c. This is not meant to be taken in the strict literal meaning, which would be if we said audibly before doing anything, "In the name of Jesus," for St. Paul, from all that we can gather from his life in the book of the Acts and from his Epistles, did not do this. But we are to do all things relying upon the grace of Christ, Who is our Head, and remembering that His Eyes are upon us, so that we must do all things as in His sight. We must, in fact, constantly set before us Christ in heaven; as we are told in the first verse of this chapter, "Seek those things which are above, where Christ sitteth at the right hand of God." The Christians of Tertullian's time sought to obey this precept as literally as possible by making the sign of the cross whenever they did anything. "In all our travels and movements, in all our coming in

q Rom. i. 8. Eph. v. 20. ch. i. 12. & ii. 7. 1 Thess. v. 18. Heb. xiii. 15.
r Eph. v. 22. Tit. ii. 5. 1 Pet. iii. 1.
s Eph. v. 3.

all in the name of the Lord Jesus, [q] giving thanks to God and the Father by him.

18 [r] Wives, submit yourselves unto your own husbands, [s] as it is fit in the Lord.

---

17. "The Lord Jesus." So B., E., K., 17, 37, most Cursives; but A., C., D., F., G., read, "Jesus Christ."

"And the Father." "And" omitted by ℵ, A., B., C., Sah., Copt., Syriac; but retained by D., E., F., G., K., L., most Cursives, Vulg., &c.

18. "Your own husband." "Own" omitted by ℵ, A., B., C., E**., K.

and going out, in putting on our shoes, at the bath, at the table, in lighting our candles, in lying down, in sitting down, whatever employment occupieth us, we mark our forehead with the sign of the cross" ("De Coronâ," v. 3). And again Cyril of Jerusalem: "Let us then not be ashamed to confess the Crucified. Be the Cross our seal made with boldness by our fingers on our brow and on every thing; over the bread we eat, and the cups we drink, in our comings in and goings out, before our sleep, when we lie down and when we are awake." Let those who blame this ask themselves whether they employ any means of reminding themselves of the Saviour in all that they do. Would St. Paul, do they think, blame this practice because the remembrance was of His Cross and not literally of His Name?

"Giving thanks to God and the Father by Him." As prayer is to be offered to the Father through Christ, so is thanksgiving. He is the Medium through Whom God's blessings come down to us and our praises ascend to Him.

18. "Wives, submit yourselves unto your own husbands, as it is fit in the Lord." We have now the same precepts respecting love and subjection in the family which we had in the Epistle to the Ephesians, but with a very marked difference in the way in which they are enforced. St. Paul dismisses the duties of husbands to their wives, and wives to their husbands, in two short verses, whereas in the parallel places in the Ephesian Epistle, he brings forward the headship of Jesus Christ to the Church as the reason why the wife should submit to the husband, and the husband love and cherish the wife. How is it that in this Epistle there is no dwelling upon, or even mention made, of so very extraordinary an illustration of the duty in either case? It can, I think, only be accounted for in

19 [t] Husbands, love *your* wives, and be not [u] bitter against them.

20 [x] Children, obey *your* parents [y] in all things: for this is well pleasing unto the Lord.

21 [z] Fathers, provoke not your children *to anger*, lest they be discouraged.

[t] Eph. v. 25, 28, 33. 1 Pet. iii 7.
[u] Eph. iv. 31.
[x] Eph. vi. 1.
[y] Eph. v. 24. Tit. ii. 9.
[z] Eph. vi. 4.

---

20. "Unto the Lord." So some Cursives, Copt., Æth.; but ℵ, A., B., C., D., E., F., G., K., L., most Cursives, It., Vulg., Goth., read, "in the Lord." Syriac has *in conspectu Domini nostri.*

21. "Provoke not." So ℵ, A., C., D., E., F., G., K., L.; but B., K., most Cursives, Syriac, &c., read, "irritate not" (ἐρεθίζετε).

this way. If we understand that Col. iv. 16, refers to the Epistle to the Ephesians, a copy of which was brought to the Laodiceans, then St. Paul intended that on this point at least, the one Epistle should be supplemented by the other; and in far greater matters than this these Epistles supplement one another, for in that to the Ephesians we have the election of Christians in Christ, their exaltation in Him, and their oneness under Him as their Head, and in the other, that to the Colossians, the eternal power and Godhead of Him of Whose Body we are members, and His absolutely unique place as the Head of the Unseen Universe.

"As it is fit in the Lord." In the Epistle to the Ephesians the reasons for this fitness are given, in that "the husband is the head of the wife even as Christ is the Head of the Church and he is the Saviour of the Body. Therefore as the Church is subject to Christ, so let the wives be to their own husbands in everything."

19. "Husbands, love your wives, and be not bitter against them." This precept also is treated very briefly by the Apostle here, because he had handled it at much greater length in the Ephesian letter. "Be not bitter," "Behave not harshly,"—in the words of St. Peter (himself a married man), "give honour to the wife as to the weaker vessel,"—put up with weaknesses and even follies.

20. "Children, obey your parents in all things: for this is well pleasing unto the Lord." In the sister Epistle the Apostle gives the Scripture proof that obedience to parents is well pleasing to God in the promise "that thou mayest live long upon the earth" appended to the Fifth Commandment.

21. "Fathers, provoke not your children to anger, lest they be discouraged." "Discouraged," lose heart, go about their task in

22 [a] Servants, obey [b] in all things *your* masters [c] according to the flesh; not with eye-service, as menpleasers; but in singleness of heart, fearing God:

23 [d] And whatsoever ye do, do *it* heartily, as to the Lord, and not unto men;

24 [e] Knowing that of the Lord ye shall receive the reward of the inheritance: [f] for ye serve the Lord Christ.

a Eph. vi. 5, &c. 1 Tim. vi. 1. Tit. ii. 9. 1 Pet. ii. 18.
b ver. 20.
c Philem. 16.
d Eph. vi. 6, 7.
e Eph. vi. 8.
f 1 Cor. vii. 22.

---

22. "Fearing God." So K., most Cursives; but ℵ, A., B., C., D., E., F., G., I., f, g, Vulg. (Amiat.), Syriac, read, "the Lord."

24. "For ye serve." "For" omitted by ℵ, A., B., C., D., E., 17, 47, 71, Vulg., Copt.; but retained by K., L., most Cursives, Syr., Arm., Goth.

a listless, moody, sullen frame of mind. (Lightfoot.) But may it not rather mean discouraged in their Christian course, or even discouraged in embracing the religion which their fathers have embraced, seeing that as yet it has not improved their temper or made them more considerate and forbearing with their own flesh and blood?

22. "Servants, obey in all things your masters according to the flesh, not with eye-service," &c. The Apostle dwells more upon the duties of slaves than he does upon those of husbands, wives, and children. This (by Bp. Lightfoot and Bp. Alexander following him) has been attributed to the fact that about this time he wrote the Epistle to Philemon respecting his slave Onesimus; so that his mind may be supposed to be full of the subject; but may it not have been because of the extreme importance of the matter at that time? for nothing could have gone more against the spread of Christianity among the classes who possessed slaves than any suspicion that the liberty which it proclaimed was one which released slaves from their obligations to their masters.

To this it may be added that from all accounts the Church was largely recruited from the slave class, so that it was doubly important to impress upon slaves that Christ was their true master and that in all their service towards their earthly masters they must set Him before their eyes.

23, 24. "And whatsoever ye do, do it heartily . . . . . ye serve the Lord Christ." The reader will thank me for giving the following extract from a sermon of Bp. Latimer on The Lord's Prayer:

25 But he that doeth wrong shall receive for the wrong

---

25. "But he that doeth wrong." So E., K., L., most Cursives, Syriac; but א, A., B., C., D., F., G., five Cursives, Ital., Vulg, Copt., read, "for" (γὰρ).

"St. Paul would have them (slaves) so live that they may adorn and sanctify the name of God: For that servant that doth the thing whereunto he is called, he doth adorn his estate. That servant is a good gospeller that will not be an eye-servant. There be some servants, who do their duties as long as their master is in sight; but as soon as their master is gone they play the lubbers. Unto such fellows I say 'beware.' For though your bodily master see you not, yet your great Master God seeth you and will punish you."

"'Quod agis, toto pectore agito.' What thou doest, do it from the bottom of thine heart, with a good will. Go not away with the Devil's Paternoster as some do. Do all things with a good mind. For I tell you, you be not forgotten in Scripture; you are much commended in the same. St. Paul speaketh very honourably of you saying, 'Domino Christo servitis,' you serve the Lord Christ. It becometh not you to put a difference what business ye be commanded to do. For whatsoever it be, do it with a good will, and it is God's service. Therefore you ought to do it, in respect that God would have you to do so; for I am no more assured in my preaching that I serve God, than the servant is in doing such business as he is commanded to do; scouring the candlesticks or whatever it be. Therefore for God's sake consider the matter. Some of you think, if Christ were here, you would go with Him and serve Him. I tell you when you follow your service, and do such things as your master and mistress shall command you, you serve Him as well as if He were here bodily."

25. "But he that doeth wrong shall receive for the wrong which he hath done," &c. This does not appear in the corresponding part of the Epistle to the Ephesians. In the parallel passage there is one of promise, "Knowing that whatsoever good thing any man doeth, the same shall he receive of the Lord."

St. Paul here seems to correct himself: he had written as if there was nothing but promise, now he shews the reverse side. "He that doeth wrong," &c. This is written of servants or slaves, and shews that as long as they were in a state of servitude their time and labour belonged to their masters, and if they did not honestly

g Rom. ii. 11. Eph. vi. 9. 1 Pet. i. 17. See Deut. x. 17.

which he hath done: and [g] there is no respect of persons.

---

render it they were guilty of injustice; but it applies with even greater force to masters, for the slaves, if ill-treated, were comparatively helpless, but they would assuredly be some day righted. The words of the wise man apply to all who suffer wrong as well as to the fatherless, "Their Redeemer is mighty, he shall plead their cause with thee." (Prov. xxiii. 11.)

CHAP. IV.

MASTERS [a], give unto *your* servants that which is just and equal; knowing that ye also have a Master in heaven.

a Eph. vi. 9.

2 [b] Continue in prayer, and watch in the same, [c] with thanksgiving;

b Luke xviii. 1. Rom. xii. 12. Eph. vi. 18. 1 Thess. v. 17, 18.

c ch. ii. 7. & iii. 15.

---

1. "Masters give unto your servants that which is just and equal," &c. Some have understood this "equal" (lit. the equality) as if the Apostle meant by it that they should recognize the principle of the equality of all men in their dealings with their slaves, but it seems rather to mean that they should be impartial, not harsh to one and kind to another.

"That ye also have a master in heaven." This, which masters should remember in their dealings with their slaves, we should all remember. God is not only our Father, our Creator, our God, but our Master. "If I then be a Father where is mine honour? and if I be a Master, where is my fear?" (Mal. i. 6.) He has called us unto liberty, but in doing this He has not parted with His claim to our constant service.

2. "Continue in prayer, and watch in the same with thanksgiving." Continue in prayer, means cleave unto prayer. It is the same word as in Acts ii. 42, "And they continued stedfastly in

3 [d] Withal praying also for us, that God would [e] open unto us a door of utterance, to speak [f] the mystery of Christ, [g] for which I am also in bonds:

[d] Eph. vi. 19. 2 Thess. iii. 1.
[e] 1 Cor. xvi. 9. 2 Cor. ii. 12.
[f] Matt. xiii. 11. 1 Cor. iv. 1. Eph. vi. 19. ch. i. 26. & ii. 2.
[g] Eph. vi. 20. Phil. i. 7.

3. "For which also." B., F. (Gr.), G., 9, 71, read, "for whom." ℵ, A., C., D., E., K., L., all Cursives, &c., read, "for which."

the Apostle's doctrine and fellowship." Alford renders it "persevere in prayer."

"Watch in the same." "Watch" may be taken literally. In the early ages of the Church they prayed constantly whilst others were asleep: Thus, in the jail at Philippi, Paul and Silas prayed and sang praises at midnight. Anyhow, it means that prayer is not to be performed listlessly, but after the manner of men who are on the watch to engage the ear of God. Chrysostom (and following him many commentators, as Cornelius a Lapide) gives a prayer of marvellous force and piety: "I know a certain holy man who prayeth thus: he used to say nothing before these words, but thus, 'We give thee thanks for all thy benefits shewn forth upon us the unworthy, from the first day until the present, for what we know, and what we know not, for the seen, for the unseen, for those in deed, those in word, those with our wills, those against our wills, for all that have been bestowed upon the unworthy, even us; for tribulations, for refreshments, for hell,[1] for punishment, for the kingdom of heaven. We beseech thee to keep our soul holy, having a pure conscience; an end worthy of thy loving-kindness. Thou that lovedst us so as to give Thy Only-Begotten for us, grant us to become worthy of Thy love; give us wisdom in Thy word, and in Thy fear, O Only-begotten Christ, inspire the strength that is from Thee. Thou that gavest thy Only-Begotten Son for us, and hast sent Thy Holy Spirit for the remission of our sins, if in aught we have wilfully or unwillingly transgressed, pardon and impute it not; remember all that call upon Thy Name in truth; remember all that wish us well, or the contrary, for we are all men.' Then having added the prayer of the faithful he there ended."

3. "Withal praying also for us that God would open unto us a door of utterance." "Praying for us,"—St. Paul, as if he were the merest

[1] This may seem strange; but if the man who prayed thus had a firm belief in God as a perfect moral governor, and that even hell was indispensable to the moral order of the universe, it may not seem so strange.

4 That I may make it manifest, as I ought to speak.

[h] Eph. v. 15. 1 Thess. iv. 12. [i] Eph. v. 16.

5 [h] Walk in wisdom toward them that are without, [i] redeeming the time.

---

novice in the ministry, asks the prayers of those to whom he wrote. Most of them must have been very inferior to himself in faith and holiness.

"A door of utterance" (lit. "a door of the word"). The corresponding passage in the Epistle to the Ephesians is: "And for me, that utterance (λόγος) may be given unto me, that I may open my mouth boldly to make known the mystery of the Gospel, for which I am an ambassador in bonds." The meaning of each passage, notwithstanding verbal differences, must be the same; and St. Paul must ask these prayers that he may, with all boldness, proclaim that particular mystery which he was especially called to set forth, and which was so unpopular with his countrymen—that the Gentiles should be fellow-heirs and members of the same body (Eph. iii. 6). The door of utterance must be the gift of utterance united with the needful courage. It cannot be the mere opportunity, because he had that (Phil. i. 12-18). If we take it as the door of the word, it corresponds with the door of faith (Acts xiv. 27), and seems to mean a door into the hearts of those that heard the word.

4. "That I may make it manifest, as I ought to speak."

St. Paul seems oppressed with the difficulty of preaching that all men, Jew and Gentile alike, are called to be fellow-heirs and members of the same body. He desired to speak it with all boldness and yet to give no offence—that is, no needless offence in anything. How unlike those who have not the smallest misgivings about themselves lest by their own lack of wisdom and needless offensiveness they hinder the truth.

5. "Walk in wisdom toward them that are without," &c. Say and do what, without compromising the truth, will win the heathen and unconverted Jews to the Gospel rather than drive them from it. Chrysostom adduces as an instance of doing this St. Paul himself, who said to Agrippa, "I think myself happy, because I shall answer for myself this day before thee, ... especially because I know thee to be expert in all customs and questions which are among the Jews" (Acts xxvi. 2, 3). But had he thought it his duty to insult the ruler, he would have spoiled everything. Some have thought that

6 Let your speech *be* alway [k] with grace, [l] seasoned with salt, [m] that ye may know how ye ought to answer every man.

k Eccles. x. 12. ch. iii. 16.
l Mark ix. 50.
m 1 Pet. iii. 15.

---

men should walk in wisdom that they may avoid needless persecution; but must it not rather be, that no obstacles may be thrown in the way of the heathen embracing the Gospel?

"Redeeming the time," making the most of it with the view of employing it for the honour of Christ and for the good of our brethren.

"Redeeming the time," from needless slumber, from vain frivolous conversation, from excess of amusement, from time spent in reading trashy and frivolous books.

In the parallel passage in the Epistle to the Ephesians the Apostle adds "because the days are evil," and the same holds good here. We have so to pass through things temporal that we gain, and lose not, the things eternal.

6. "Let your speech be always with grace." Some consider this to be kindness and pleasantness; others that it is the grace of God which in their intercouse with unbelievers they must constantly invoke from God.

"Seasoned with salt." The same difference of opinion applies to the explanation of what this salt is: some suppose that it is allied to wit and readiness; but it is hard to see how St. Paul can enjoin wit and readiness upon those who by nature have not these things in them. Bishop Alexander, in the "Speaker's Commentary" conceives that it alludes to Sacrificial Salt, "every sacrifice was salted with salt." It was unlawful to offer any sacrifice without it. It signified the purity and incorruption which should attend all offerings to God, "With all thine offerings thou shalt offer salt." (Levit. ii. 13.) The verse is in some respects a difficult one, but it evidently means that their speech should be always attended with that which they can always themselves procure by prayer to God at the moment. The latter clause, "that ye may know how ye ought to answer every man," seems to teach that it refers to intercourse with "them that are without." Solomon says, "A word spoken in due season, how good it is." And again he says, "A word fitly spoken is like apples of gold in pictures of silver." (Prov. xv. 23, xxv. 11.) I have known men who never had a con-

7 [n] All my state shall Tychicus declare unto you, *who is* a beloved brother, and a faithful minister and fellowservant in the Lord:

n Ephes. vi. 21.

o Ephes. vi. 22.

8 [o] Whom I have sent unto you for the same purpose, that he might know your estate, and comfort your hearts;

---

8. "That he might know your estate, and comfort your hearts." So C., E., K., L., most Cursives, f, Vulg., Goth., Syriac; but ℵ, A., B., D*., F. (Gr.), G., P., some eleven Cursives, d, e, g, Arm., Æth., read, "that ye might know our estate, and that he might comfort," &c.

versation with one of their fellow-creatures without offering up a silent prayer to God to order their words.

7, 8. "All my state shall Tychicus declare unto you, who is a beloved brother, &c. . . . comfort your hearts." This Tychicus was one of that large band of faithful disciples and companions of St. Paul, by whose instrumentality he governed the Churches. They were vicars apostolic or archdeacons, whom he was constantly sending about, that they might deliver his letters or traditions to the various Churches, and that through them he might hear of their spiritual state. We first hear of him in Acts xx. 4 ("Of Asia, Tychicus and Trophimus"), then here and in the parallel passage in Ephes. vi. 21; and lastly in the Epistle to Titus, iii. 12 ("When I shall send Artemas unto thee, or Tychicus, be diligent to come to me," &c.)

"A faithful minister and fellowservant in the Lord." "Minister." To whom did he minister? To the Lord or to St. Paul? To both. In serving the one as his fellow-labourer and messenger, he served the Other. For it was the will of God that St. Paul during his life here should not part with his Apostolic authority in the case of any Church, but should rule each one, and watch over it through his disciples or companions.

8. "Whom I have sent unto you for the same purpose . . . comfort your hearts." In our Authorized there seems to be a difference in the purpose for which St. Paul sent Tychicus to Ephesus and to Colosse. To Ephesus he sent him that the Ephesians might know St. Paul's affairs—to the Colossians, that he might know their affairs; but in all the oldest and best MSS. the words to the Colossians are the same as those to the Ephesians, "that ye might know our affairs, and that he might comfort your hearts."

9 With [p] Onesimus, a faithful and beloved brother, who
is *one* of you. They shall make known unto
you all things which *are done* here.
10 [q] Aristarchus my fellow-prisoner saluteth
you, and [r] Marcus, sister's son to Barnabas, (touch-
ing whom ye received commandments: if he come
unto you, receive him;)

p Philem. 10.
q Acts xix. 29. & xx. 4. & xxvii. 2. Philem. 24.
r Acts xv. 37. 2 Tim. iv. 11.

---

9. "With Onesimus, a faithful and beloved brother, who is one of you." This was the former runaway slave of Philemon, to whom he wrote the short, but most instructive and delightful Epistle respecting his reconciliation. This verse shews how completely he had been absolved, and also proves how radically he had been changed.

"They shall make known unto you all things which are done here." That is, all the progress of the Gospel, notwithstanding the hindrances; all the afflictions endured by St. Paul and his companions, and their consolations under them.

10. "Aristarchus my fellow-prisoner, saluteth you." Aristarchus is first mentioned as the companion of St. Paul in Acts xix. 29. "And having caught Gaius and Aristarchus, men of Macedonia, Paul's companions in travel," &c. Then in Acts xx. 4, "And these accompanied him . . . of the Thessalonians, Aristarchus, and Secundus." Then when he was sent to Rome as a prisoner, it is said that one Aristarchus, a Macedonian of Thessalonica, was with him. And now he is with St. Paul as his fellow-prisoner, meaning by this that he was put under some restraint, as being so special a friend and companion of the Apostle, or that he voluntarily put himself under the same restraint, dwelling probably in the same lodging, that he might the better minister unto him.

"And Marcus, sister's son to Barnabas (touching whom ye"), &c. The word ἀνεψιὸς seems properly to mean cousin. The insertion of the direction that they were to receive him is generally taken to mean that notwithstanding his defection at the commencement of the first missionary journey, they were to hold him as having been restored, and therefore as the friend and minister of St. Paul, but the length of time which had elapsed (nearly twenty years) seems to render this meaning unlikely.

11 And Jesus, which is called Justus, who are of the circumcision. These only *are my* fellowworkers unto the kingdom of God, which have been a comfort unto me.

s ch. i. 7. Philem. 23.
|| Or, *striving*.
t Rom. xv. 30.
u Matt. v. 48. 1 Cor. ii. 6. & xiv. 20. Phil. iii. 15. Hebr. v. 14.
|| Or, *filled*.

12 [s] Epaphras, who is *one* of you, a servant of Christ, saluteth you, always || [t] labouring fervently for you in prayers, that ye may stand [u] perfect and || complete in all the will of God.

---

12. "And complete." Rather "fully assured," or "fully persuaded" (Rev.). So ℵ, A., B., C., D., F., G., and six Cursives; but E., K., L., P., most Cursives, Syriac, Arm., read, "complete."

11. "And Jesus, which is called Justus, who are of the circumcision." The words, "who are of the circumcision," seem only to refer to Mark and Jesus, called Justus. It is possible that they also refer to Aristarchus, but the fact that he is three times said to belong to Macedonia or Thessalonica, seems to render it unlikely.

"These only are my fellowworkers unto the kingdom of God." This refers only to those of the circumcision. The majority of the converted Jews in the Roman Church very probably stood aloof from St. Paul, owing to his treating the Gentiles as on an equality with the Jews—perhaps opposed him (Phil. i. 15).

12. "Epaphras, who is one of you, a servant of Christ, saluteth you, always," &c. In the Epistle to Philemon, written at the same time, Epaphras is called by St. Paul his fellow-prisoner in Christ Jesus.

"One of you," that is, of the same city.

"Always labouring fervently for you in prayers." He was likely to do so, because he had been their Evangelist, but it was well that St. Paul should put in this proof that his devotion to their spiritual interests had not slackened.

The oldest and best MSS. read "fully persuaded," rather than "complete," which is perhaps the more likely reading, implying that he prayed earnestly that they might not be moved, or shaken in mind by the false doctrine of the heretical teachers.

13. "For I bear him record that he hath a great zeal for you, and them," &c. Much zeal—perhaps it should be read "much

13 For I bear him record, that he hath a great zeal for
you, and them *that are* in Laodicea, and them in Hierapolis.
14 [x] Luke, the beloved physician, and [y] Demas,
greet you.
15 Salute the brethren which are in Laodicea,
and Nymphas, and [z] the church which is in his
house.

x 2 Tim. iv. 11.
y 2 Tim. iv. 10. Philem. 24.
z Rom. xvi. 5. 1 Cor. xvi 19.

---

13. "A great zeal." So K., L., most Cursives, and Syriac; but א, A., B., C., P., read, "labour" (πόνον), and D., F., G., κόπον.

15. "Nymphas." B. reads, "Nympha," a female name; and "her house."

"Their" (αὐτῶν) read in א, A., C., P. "his;" D., E., F., G., K., L., most Cursives, Syriac, &c.

labour," *i.e.* in prayer. There may be as much labour thrown into prayer, as into the performance of any spiritual duty. It was said by the late Bishop Hamilton, of Salisbury, that no man prays well except he makes a business of it. The cities mentioned here were no great distance from one another, and might well at the first have been evangelized by the same man.

14. "Luke, the beloved physician, and Demas, greet you." Luke the physician, the beloved one, or "my beloved." This is the only place in the New Testament which speaks of Luke as a physician. The Gospel which bears his name, and the book of the Acts of the Apostles, contain many indications of this in the use of medical terms, which are not employed elsewhere in the New Testament. The reader will find a number of the principal instances in an excursus at the end of my volume on the Acts of the Apostles.

The fact that there was a physician amongst the companions of St. Paul, and one who is here specially recognized as one, seems to shew that the miraculous healing of diseases in the early Church was occasional, and after some clear indication from God that certain persons should be healed apart from human means.

"Demas." His desertion took place some time after this. Bishop Lightfoot notices that St. Paul has no affectionate word for him as he has for Luke. He probably exhibited coldness and slackness in the work long before his desertion of the Apostle.

15. "Salute the brethren which are in Laodicea, and Nymphas,' &c. This can hardly be the whole Church of Laodicea, for they

16 And when [a] this epistle is read among you, cause that it be read also in the church of the Laodiceans; and that ye likewise read the *epistle* from Laodicea.

[a] 1 Thes. v. 27.

---

had an epistle sent to them, as we learn from the next verse. Bishop Lightfoot supposes it to be some colony or family of Colossian Christians residing in Laodicea, who assembled in the house of this Nymphas.

As there were no public buildings yet erected for worship, the Christians assembled in large rooms, which could be procured in private houses, and Nymphas had such an assembly in his house. But this is all conjecture. There are various readings: "his," "her," "their," which will be seen in the critical notes.

16. "And when this epistle is read among you, cause that it be read also . . . . ye likewise read the epistle from Laodicea." In all human probability this epistle from Laodicea was the Epistle to the Ephesians. The words "from Laodicea" cannot mean that it was written by the Laodicean Church, but that it was, or would be, sent from Laodicea to Colosse, *i.e.*, received by them from Laodicea,[1] when they sent for it.

The reader will find this matter discussed at great length in

---

[1] As it is unfit that I should assume that the readers of this volume possess that in which I have commentated on the Epistle to the Ephesians, the reader will pardon me if I transcribe from the preface to the Ephesians what follows. "Upon the whole, giving the most ample significance to the difference of reading (the omission of ἐν Ἐφέσῳ), the fact seems to have been that he undoubtedly sent the first letter to the Ephesian Church, inscribed to 'the Saints which are in Ephesus,' but that he gave directions that copies should be sent to the Churches in the neighbourhood; and that from these copies the words ἐν Ἐφέσῳ were omitted, as supposed to be unsuitable; and from some of these copies the omission in the MS. ℵ, and in the copies mentioned by Basil, had its origin. It seems extremely improbable that he should send a letter with so many personal references in it without an inscription, and yet containing the participle τοῖς οὖσιν ("which are"), which seems to demand the name of a place, which place could originally be no other than Ephesus. Another question before we conclude; the Colossian Churches are directed to send the Epistle which St. Paul wrote to them to the Laodiceans, and to receive in turn and read some letter from Laodicea. This could not properly be a letter written by the Laodicean Church, but must have been some letter of St. Paul's. Was it then some letter which has been lost, or was it this Epistle to the Ephesians which had been sent to the Laodicean Church? I believe the latter; Laodicea was comparatively near to Colosse, and both at a considerable distance from Ephesus. It was natural then that if a copy of the Ephesian Epistle had been sent to Laodicea by St. Paul's direction, that he should order the Colossians to send for it, and send theirs to Laodicea."

17 And say to [b] Archippus, Take heed to [c] the ministry
which thou hast received in the Lord, that thou
fulfil it.
18 [d] The salutation by the hand of me Paul.
[e] Remember my bonds. [f] Grace *be* with you.
Amen.

[b] Philem. 2.
[c] 1 Tim. iv. 6.
[d] 1 Cor. xvi. 21. 2 Thes. iii. 17.
[e] Heb. xiii. 3.
[f] Heb. xiii. 25.

¶ Written from Rome to the Colossians by Tychicus and Onesimus.

---

17. "Thou hast received." "Thou didst receive."

Bishop Lightfoot's Notes on the Ephesians, in which he examines the various interpretations of this verse, particularly the theory that an Epistle to the Laodiceans, found in some Latin MSS., is the document alluded to. This theory is dismissed by Jerome in the words, "ab omnibus exploditur." ("De Vir. Illus," 5.)

17. "And say to Archippus, Take heed to the ministry which thou hast received," &c. What this particular ministry was must be left to conjecture. It must have been one of importance, or it would not have had such special notice here. Some suppose that it was the Episcopate of the Colossian Church, which Epaphras, their original Evangelist, being a prisoner at Rome, was unable to exercise. From the earnest—indeed, peremptory—way in which the charge is expressed, it has been conjectured that the Apostle had heard that Archippus had become slack in the exercise of this ministry, and this has been supposed to be the beginning of the exhibition of that lukewarmness for which the angel of the Church of the Laodiceans is so sternly rebuked by the Lord in the Apocalypse.

18. "The salutation by the hand of me Paul. Remember my bonds," &c. St. Paul wrote his letters through an amanuensis, and signed them himself at the end. Thus 2 Thess. iii. 17: "The salutation of Paul with mine own hand, which is the token in every Epistle" (also 1 Cor. xvi. 21).

Remember what I do and suffer for the sake of Christ, and be of the same mind. I do not exhort you without having first set you an example.

THE
EPISTLES TO THE THESSALONIANS.

INTRODUCTION TO THE TWO EPISTLES.

THE genuineness and authenticity of the Epistles to the Thessalonians have never been doubted in the Church of Christ. They are mentioned as St. Paul's in the fragment called the Muratorian Canon. The first Epistle is alluded to or quoted more than once in the Epistle of Polycarp. Thus chap. xi.: "Abstain from every form of evil;" and 2 Thess. iii. 15, in chap. xi.: "Do not count such as enemies, but call them back as suffering and straying members." Justin Martyr clearly alludes to 2 Thess. ii. 3. "The other [advent] in which He shall come from heaven with glory, when the man of apostasy who speaketh strange things against the most High," &c. (Dial cx.).

Both Epistles are quoted by Irenæus. Thus, Against Heresies, v. 6-1: "And for this cause does the Apostle, explaining himself, make it clear that the saved man is a complete man as well as a spiritual man; saying this in the First Epistle to the Thessalonians: 'Now the God of peace sanctify you perfect, and may your spirit, soul, and body,' &c. (1 Thess. v. 23)."

Also Clement of Alexandria: "To this point, says the Divine Apostle. 'For this is the will of God, even your Sanctification,'" &c. (Miscellanies, iv. 12). Also: "Let us not then sleep as do others," &c. (iv. 22). And Tertullian: "The character of these times learn, along with the Thessalonians. For we read 'how ye turned from idols to serve the living and true God, and to wait for his Son,'" &c. On the Resurrection of the Flesh, chap. 24.

CHARACTER OF THE EPISTLE.

The first matter connected with these Epistles which the careful reader of Scripture has to realize is that they are the earliest of the Epistles. But though they are, in point of time, the first of the books of the New Testament written for the instruction of Gentile Christians, they assume that the Church to which St. Paul addressed them was already in the possession of all Christian truth. St. Paul does not teach them, as *ab initio*, one article of the Christian faith. They were acquainted with the fundamentals of all Christian doctrine, either through his own personal instruction, or through that of his companions, Sylvanus, Timotheus, and others.

Glancing over the Epistle, we gather from the very first verse that St. Paul had taught them that they could be "in" God, and "in" Christ. This remarkable way of speaking postulates all that doctrine which pervades such Epistles as those to the Ephesians and Corinthians, that Christians are now in Christ by grace as all men by nature are in Adam.

From the third verse we find that he had taught them the election of God—that they could not have become what they were unless God had chosen them—and the sign of this choice on God's part was that the Gospel came to them "not in word only, but in power, and in the Holy Ghost, and in much assurance." It came to them not with outward miracle only, but in the inward transformation wrought in them by the Spirit of God. This transformation is described in verses 9 and 10 as "turning from idols to serve the living and true God; and waiting for His Son from heaven, Whom He raised from the dead, even Jesus, Who delivered us from the wrath to come." Those two verses, it will be seen, imply instruction in five articles of the creed—in the living and true God, Who is a Father because He has a Son, Whom He gave for us, to deliver us by His Death from the wrath to come. This Son He raised from the dead, and this Son we have to wait for, for He will come again "to judge the quick and the dead." The Thessalonian Church, then, was instructed in those articles of the faith respecting the Son of God incarnate, crucified, risen, ascended, and returning, which we find St. Paul taught everywhere as his Gospel (Rom. i. 1; 1 Cor. xv. 1-15). It was the one faith, of the one Lord, professed at the one Baptism.

Furthermore we learn that they had from the first been instructed in all precepts of goodness and holiness. They had "received of him how they ought to walk and to please God," and all that they required was to be urged to "abound more and more" (1 Epistle, iv. 1-2). Again he appeals to their perfect knowledge of their duty when he writes, "Ye yourselves know how ye ought to follow us."

They were instructed then at the first in all faith and duty. Now it is interesting to note the word by which St. Paul designates this instruction which at the first he delivered to them to keep and observe. He calls it tradition (παραδόσις). "Therefore, brethren, stand fast and hold the traditions which ye have been taught, whether by word, or our Epistle" (2, ii. 15). "We command you, brethren, in the Name of our Lord Jesus Christ, that ye withdraw yourselves from every brother that walketh disorderly, and not after the tradition which he received of us" (2. iii. 6). This word tradition (*paradosis*) is the same which is applied to the false glosses by which the Scribes and Pharisees had evaded the true meaning of the word of God, and shows us that traditions may be good or bad—good if they are in accordance with the revealed will of God, or bad if they make void that will.

There is another matter of great importance connected with the earliness of the writing of these letters. They contain no allusion to Justification by faith as opposed to Justification by the works of the law, or by circumcision, as in the Epistle to the Galatians. They contain no allusion to the Election of the Gentiles, or the Reprobation, or casting away of the Jews with which the Epistle to the Romans is so much occupied. There is, as I have noticed, a reference to the election of the Thessalonian Christians, and to the wrath having come upon the Jews to the uttermost; but the first is rather personal election, and the second is the impending doom on their country and chief city. This shows a very early stage in the conflict with which so much of the life of St. Paul was occupied. Though he was everywhere persecuted by the Jews, yet the Judaizers, *i.e.*, those who desired to bring the Gentiles under the yoke of the law for Justification, had apparently not opposed or thwarted his work as they had done when he wrote his letters to the Galatians and Philippians. Neither had he had yet to contend with those incipient forms of Gnosticism (philosophy and vain deceit) which he refers to in the Epistle to the Colossians.

DATE.

With respect to the date of the first Epistle, we are able to approximate to it tolerably closely by taking into account that it must have been written shortly after the return of Timotheus to St. Paul with good tidings respecting the Church at Thessalonica (1 Thess. iii. 6). St. Paul having departed from Philippi came to Thessalonica (Acts xvii. 1) where he planted a Church. Driven from Thessalonica by the persecution of the Jews, he came to Berea, to which place also the enmity of his countrymen pursued him, and so the brethren there sent him away by sea, and brought him to Athens. The persons who had brought him there received a command to bring to him with all speed Silas and Timotheus, and no doubt they shortly rejoined him at Athens. But whilst at Athens he was in such anxiety respecting the state of the Thessalonian Church that he sent Timothy back again to Thessalonica to bring him word respecting their true state (1 Thess. iii. 1). The first Epistle must have been written very shortly after he received this good account, and as his stay appears to have been very short, probably the first Epistle was written soon after his arrival in Corinth, where Timothy and Silas had rejoined him (Acts xviii. 5) and about 52 or 53 after Christ. There seems to have been no special occasion which caused him to write it, except to remind them of what he had taught them.

It seems to be generally agreed that the Second Epistle was written shortly after the first. It seems to have been written for a special purpose—to warn the Thessalonians that they should not be so "moved" or "shaken in mind" by what he had taught them respecting the nearness of the Second Advent, as to neglect the duties of daily life, which some among them had begun to do.

THE CITY OF THESSALONICA.

It remains to say a word respecting Thessalonica itself. It was anciently known as Therma, and received the name of Thessalonica from Cassander, the son of Antipater, who rebuilt and enlarged it, and named it after his wife Thessalonica, the sister of Alexander the Great. The harbour was well suited for commerce, and under the Romans it had the additional advantage of lying on the Via Egnatia, which led from the western shores of Greece to Byzantium, and the East. Its magistrates were named *πολιτάρχαι*, a peculiar title, and the accuracy of St. Luke in calling them by this name is confirmed by an inscription on an arch of the time of the early Emperors, in which this unique title is given to them. It appears to have had in all times of its history a large population of Jews, and a small number could scarcely have persecuted the Apostles, and made their animosity felt in other cities in the way described by St. Luke.

THE

FIRST EPISTLE TO THE THESSALONIANS.

CHAP. I.

PAUL, and [a] Silvanus, and Timotheus, unto the church of the Thessalonians, *which is* in God the Father and *in* the Lord Jesus Christ: [b] Grace

[a] 2 Cor. i. 19. 2 Thess. i. 1. 1 Pet. v. 12.
[b] Eph. i. 2.

---

1. "Paul, and Silvanus, and Timotheus, unto the church of the Thessalonians," &c. How is it that Silvanus and Timotheus are joined with the Apostle in writing this his first letter? Because, as I have before said, he desired to associate his companions and fellow-helpers with himself, as in some degree sharing his authority. The Epistle is entirely his own, not one word contributed by either of them, and yet as they had frequently to occupy his place in his absence, or when he sent them on messages to the Church, he wished, as far as possible, to invest them with something of Apostolical authority.

Both Silvanus and Timotheus were his fellow-helpers in planting the Church of Thessalonica after his departure from Philippi. Timotheus seems to have joined him at Thessalonica, and when he departed to Athens they were left there (Acts xvii. 14).

Silvanus is always called by St. Luke Silas, but by the Apostle always with the full name. He is mentioned before Timotheus, most probably because he was before him in the Gospel, being a prominent person in the Mother Church of Jerusalem before Timothy became a Christian (Acts xv. 32).

"The church of the Thessalonians, which is in God the Father and in the Lord Jesus Christ." This is the first sentence of St. Paul's writing which has come down to us, and in it we have the

be unto you, and peace from God our Father, and the Lord Jesus Christ.

c Rom. i. 8. Eph. i. 16. Philem. 4.

2 [c] We give thanks to God always for you all, making mention of you in our prayers;

---

1. "From God our Father, and from the Lord Jesus Christ." So ℵ, A., C., D., E., K., L., P., most Cursives, d, e, &c.; but B., F., G., 47, 73, 115, f, g, Vulg., Syriac, &c., omit.

assertion of that which may be called his characteristic doctrine—that as Christians can be in God, so they can be in Christ. They are "in" a Man Who is at the right hand of God, just as they are "in" the God, in Whom we live and move and have our being. That Christ should be thus set forth as containing the Church, just as God contains it, is a very deep mystery, but it is one which the Apostle was raised up to set forth (Ephes. iii. 6). It may be said to underlie the teaching of every Epistle, particularly those to the Romans, the Corinthians, the Ephesians, and the Colossians. "Ye in me, and I in you" "I am the vine, ye are the branches. He that abideth in me and I in him, the same bringeth forth much fruit." This is the way in which the Lord sets forth the mystery, and this Apostle was especially commissioned to take up and dwell upon it, and show how it bears upon all Christian life. So that the Apostle strikes the key note of his teaching in his very first Epistle, and in its first verse.

"Grace be unto you, and peace." "Grace," that is, the power to apprehend God and subdue sin and live holily. "Peace" has especially to do with their dwelling together in unity; and this was, in the eyes of the Apostle, of supreme necessity, for the grace of God could not continue with those who did not love one another, as another Apostle said, "He that loveth his brother abideth in the light" (1 John ii. 10).

2. "We give thanks to God always . . . . making mention," &c. St. Paul almost invariably begins his Epistles with thanks to God for the grace of God manifested in them; thus in Romans i. 8, "I thank my God through Jesus Christ for you all." 1 Corinthians, i. 4, "I thank my God always on your behalf." The only instance to the contrary is that to the Galatians, of whom he has to say, "I am afraid of you, lest I have bestowed upon you labour in vain" (iv. 11). This is a proof quite as clear and cogent as any dogmatic

3 [d] Remembering without ceasing [e] your work of faith, [f] and labour of love, and patience of

[d] ch. ii. 13.
[e] John vi. 29. Gal. v. 6. ch. iii. 6. 2 Thess. i. 3, 11. James ii. 17.
[f] Rom. xvi. 6. Heb. vi. 10.

---

assertion that he recognizes all Christian living as entirely the work of the grace of God.

3. "Remembering without ceasing your work of faith, and labour of love, and patience of hope," &c. Here we have the three great abiding graces mentioned also at the beginning of his teaching: and mentioned in such wise as to show that they never could be alone. Faith, if it be true, must work; love, if it be sincere, must labour; hope, if it is not to be ashamed, must endure with patience. Chrysostom, in expounding this passage, carries the Apostle's remembrances back to the first preaching of the Gospel among them. and the sufferings they then endured: "What is the *work* of faith? That nothing has turned aside your steadfastness. For this is the work of faith. If thou believest, suffer all things: if thou dost not suffer thou dost not believe. For are not the things promised such, that he who believes would choose to suffer even ten thousand deaths. The kingdom of heaven is set before him and immortality and eternal life. He, therefore, that believes will suffer all things. Faith then is shown through his works."

"And your labour of love. Why? what labour is it to love? Merely to love is none at all. But to love sincerely is great labour. For tell me, when many things are stirred up that would draw us from love and we hold out against them all, is it not labour? For what did not these men suffer, that they might not revolt from their love? Did not they that warred on the Gospel go to Paul's host (Acts xvii. 5, 6), and not having found him, drag Jason before the rulers of the city? Tell me is this a slight labour when the seed is not yet taken root to endure so great a storm—so many trials.

"And patience (he says) of hope. For that persecution was not confined to one time, but was continual; and they warred not only with Paul the master, but with his disciples also. For if they were thus affected towards those who wrought miracles, these venerable men, what, think ye, were their feelings towards those who dwelt among them, their fellow-citizens, who had all of a sudden revolted from them?"

hope in our Lord Jesus Christ, in the sight of God and our Father;

|| Or, *beloved of God, your election.*
g Col. iii. 12. 2 Thess. ii. 13.
h Mark xvi. 20. 1 Cor. ii. 4. & iv. 20.
i 2 Cor. vi. 6.

4 Knowing, brethren || beloved, [g] your election of God.

5 For [h] our Gospel came not unto you in word only, but also in power, and [i] in the Holy Ghost,

---

4. "Knowing, brethren beloved, your election of God." Some translate this, "Knowing, brethren beloved of God, your election."

"Patience of hope in our Lord Jesus Christ." What happened to them showed not their fortitude only, but that they believed with full assurance in the rewards laid up for them. It was not human persecution but the power of God that persuaded the souls of the believers.

"In the sight of God and our Father." Their warfare was not before men, but before the heart-searching God. A thing so before unknown in the world, that a man should thus sacrifice life and all things for the love of a crucified and risen Saviour, was not a thing done before men only, but under the eye of God Who had given them grace thus to contend.

4, 5. "Knowing, brethren beloved, your election of God. For our Gospel came not unto you in word only, but also in power," &c. There must have been some deep mysterious reason why the few members of the Church of the Thessalonians had embraced the Gospel, and the surrounding multitude, their neighbours and friends and relations, had not. What was this reason? It was the election, or choice of God, and this was evidenced by the fact that the Gospel had not been to them a mere word, as it was to many around them, but it came to them "in power." It has been made a question whether this power was in the preacher, in his tongue or in his heart, or in the hearers whose hearts were opened by the power of God. In both, we should answer, but especially the latter, for the power of enunciating the truths of the Gospel, and the Holy Ghost enforcing the word spoken with miracles, were outwardly the same to all whose ears heard the word; but that which made the difference was the power of God working in the heart, and drawing them on to belief in Christ (John vi. 44).

Was this election then irreversible, or, as we should say, Calvin-

[k]and in much assurance; as [l]ye know what manner of men we were among you for your sake.

k Col. ii. 2. Heb. ii. 3.
l ch. ii. 1, 5, 10, 11. 2 Thess. iii. 7.

5. "Among you" (ἐν). So B., D., E., F., G., K., L., most Cursives, d, e, f, g. ℵ, A., C., P., Vulg. Amiat., omit ἐν.

istic? No. It was not an election to a place in heaven, without reference to the after-conduct of him whose heart was touched by the Gospel, but an election to be a member of the Church of Christ and to glorify God as such. If a man, from among many applicants, chooses a servant, it is a great thing for that servant to know it, a great incentive for him to do his duty to think that his master has certainly chosen him, and that he must justify his master's choice. And so with the election of God. It postulates two things, outward circumstances as well as inward drawing—the outward calling and all its circumstances, birth in a Christian land, Baptism, Christian training, the Church administering and enforcing the Sacraments. This is the outward calling, but it is as much brought about by the good providence of God as the inward, which is the opening of the man's heart to see the state of grace in which he is, and to recognize in the Church and its ministrations the very kingdom of God which the Redeemer came down to establish.

St. Paul knew then that the persons to whom he wrote could not have embraced the Gospel of themselves, but that God had moved them so to do, and this was a sign not that each and every one would eventually be saved, but that God required their services in His Church. Whether they would answer, or persevere in answering, to this God's call, was another matter (see my Excursus on Election at the end of Notes on the Romans, and also Notes on Ephes. iii.); but each soul must unceasingly commit itself unto God's Holy keeping.

"And in the Holy Ghost." The Holy Ghost is the Spirit of power, both in the heart and out of it. His is the converting power, and His is the power of miracles, and of evidence to show that the doctrine put forth for acceptance is not of man's devising, but by the will of the unseen Father of all.

"As ye know what manner of men we were among you for your sake." If we had preached the Gospel to you, and not exhibited the holiness of the Gospel, ye could hardly have believed our

6 And [m] ye became followers of us, and of the Lord, having received the word in much affliction, [n] with joy of the Holy Ghost:

7 So that ye were ensamples to all that believe in Macedonia and Achaia.

[m] 1 Cor. iv. 16. & xi. 1. Phil. iii. 17. ch. ii. 14. 2 Thess. iii. 9.

[n] Acts v. 41. Heb. x. 34.

---

7. "Ensamples." So ℵ, A., C., F., G., K., L., P., most Cursives; but D. D.*, a few Cursives, d, e, f, v, Vulg., Sah., Copt., Syriac, Arm., Æth., read, "an ensample."

message, for our lives would have belied its power; but so far from this, we exhibited among you that transformation which we pressed upon you. As he says, "Ye are witnesses how holily, and justly, and unblamably we behaved ourselves among you that believe" (ii. 10).

6. "And ye became followers of us, and of the Lord, having received," &c. "Followers," that is, "imitators."

"Of us, and of the Lord." If it seem presumptuous for any mere man to put his own example and that of Christ's side by side, it is to be remembered that the very object of the preaching of the Gospel and of the gift of the Spirit was to produce in men the character and life of Christ, and this could hardly be brought about unless the disciples of Christ so manifested the lineaments of His Divine Character that men might not only hear the word of Christ from their lips, but see His Life in their lives.

But in this case they became "followers," or "imitators" of the Lord in the two matters of receiving the word with much affliction, and with joy of the Holy Ghost. Joy in the midst of suffering was one of the especial marks of the new state of things. In the old state of things, if men obeyed God, "blessed should be their basket and their store." "Blessed shalt thou be in the city, and blessed shalt thou be in the field;" but in the new it is: "Rejoice inasmuch as ye are partakers of the sufferings of Christ, that when his glory shall be revealed, ye may be glad also with exceeding joy" (1 Pet. iv. 13).

7. "So that ye were ensamples to all that believe in Macedonia," &c. Rather "an ensample"—from the readiness with which they received the Gospel, and perhaps from their freedom from the divisions and false doctrine which had disturbed other Churches. The next verse shows how it came to pass that they were so early an ensample.

8 For from you [o] sounded out the word of the Lord not
only in Macedonia and Achaia, but also [p] in every
place your faith to Godward is spread abroad;
so that we need not to speak any thing.
9 For they themselves shew of us [q] what manner
of entering in we had unto you, [r] and how ye
turned to God from idols to serve the living and
true God;

o Rom. x. 18.
p Rom. i. 8. 2 Thess. i. 4.
q ch. ii. 1.
r 1 Cor. xii. 2. Gal. iv. 8.

---

9. "Of us." So B., nearly twenty Cursives, d, e, Sah., Copt.; but all other authorities, "of you."

8. "For from you sounded out the word of the Lord not only in Macedonia," &c. Thessalonica was a great commercial centre and a seaport, and the report of the extraordinary fact that, at the preaching of a handful of unknown men, a considerable number of its inhabitants gave up all belief in their ancestral religion, and embraced a life of self-denial and persecution, spread (to use the vulgar saying) like wild-fire, and paved the way for all Greece—for Macedonia and Achaia comprehended all Greece—at least to listen to the Gospel.

"In every place your faith to Godward is spread abroad; so that," &c. Instead of having to cite you as an example of readiness in receiving the faith we are ourselves told of it by those who have already heard it by common report.

This place is an example of the way in which the report of the success of the Gospel was spread far beyond the range of direct preaching. We are by no means to judge of its effect even on the outside world, by the few and scanty notices in such authors as Tacitus and Suetonius. A parallel instance is to be found in Joshua ii. 9.

9. "For they themselves shew of us what manner of entering in," &c. That is, the inhabitants of the places to which the report of your conversion has reached; so that dwellers in strange cities were the more ready to receive the Gospel.

"What manner of entering in," *i.e.*, what success we had notwithstanding opposition and persecution.

"How ye turned to God from idols to serve the living and true God, and to wait," &c. This is the first account which we have in his own words of what the Apostle preached, and of what his con-

[s] Rom. ii. 7. Phil. iii. 20. Tit. ii. 13. 2 Pet. iii. 12. Rev. i. 7.
[t] Acts i. 11. ch. iv. 16. 2 Thess. i. 7.
[u] Acts ii. 24.
[x] Matt. iii. 7. Rom. v. 9. ch. v. 9.

10 And [s] to wait for his Son [t] from heaven, [u] whom he raised from the dead, *even* Jesus, which delivered us [x] from the wrath to come.

---

verts received. It comprises by sure implication every article of the Creed of Christendom. That there is one God—that the unity of His Godhead does not preclude His having a Son—that He raised this Son from the dead, which demands that He should have come in the flesh in a body capable of death, and should have actually died, or He could not have been raised from the dead—that this Son has delivered us from the wrath to come, which in accordance with all the rest of Scripture He effected by His Death in the first place—in which Death He died to sin and delivered us from the wrath to come, that is, death eternal, by uniting us with Himself in His Death—and for the second coming of this Jesus we have to look, for, "From thence—from the place to which He was raised—He shall come to judge the quick and the dead."

This is the first preaching—the first receiving of the Gospel. It is the Gospel of God—the Gospel of the Son of God—the Gospel of the Death, the Resurrection and the Second Advent—the Gospel of the Supernatural—the Gospel of the deepest mysteries of God.

CHAP. II.

[a] ch. i, 5, 9.

FOR [a] yourselves, brethren, know our entrance in unto you, that it was not in vain:

---

1. "For yourselves, brethren, know our entrance in unto you, that it was not in vain." But we need not dwell upon the testimony of others. Ye yourselves know the extraordinary success which attended our first ministry among you.

2. "But even after that we had suffered before, and were shamefully entreated." When they arrived from Philippi they had the

2 But even after that we had suffered before, and were shamefully entreated, as ye know, at [b] Philippi, [c] we were bold in our God [d] to speak unto you the Gospel of God [e] with much contention.
3 [f] For our exhortation *was* not of deceit, nor of uncleanness, nor in guile:

b Acts xvi. 23.
c ch. i. 5.
d Acts xvii. 2.
e Phil. i. 30. Col. ii. 1.
f 2 Cor. vii. 2. ver. 5. 2 Pet. i. 16.

---

2. "But even after that." ℵ, A., B., C., D., E., F., G., K., L., P., most Cursives, f, g, Vulg., &c., omit. "Even" found only in some Cursives.

marks of their ill-treatment upon them, but were not for a moment deterred from at once preaching the Gospel in Thessalonica.

This their boldness was not mere human obstinacy and determination; but it was "in our God;" inspired by Him, and sustained by His help.

"With much contention," *i.e.*, in vehement striving (*ἀγῶνι*). The Revisers render, "in much conflict." It refers to the conflict described in Acts xvii. 5, "But the Jews which believed not, moved with envy, took unto them certain lewd fellows of the baser sort, and gathered a company, and set all the city on an uproar, and assaulted the house of Jason, and sought to bring them out to the people." Such outward opposition must be attended with great inward struggle and conflict of mind that they should not yield in the least, but that they should contend manfully for that which they knew to be a matter of life and death to all who heard it.

3. "For our exhortation was not of deceit, nor of uncleanness, nor in guile." Here the Apostle is supposed to allude to slanders which were spread respecting him.

"Not of deceit," rather, perhaps, of error.

"Nor of uncleanness." It is difficult to suppose how the Apostle could be accused of impurity. Jowett in his paraphrase interprets it, "of impure motives," and Chrysostom, "It is not for things abominable, as the tricks of jugglers and sorcerers; for this is the meaning of uncleanness."

"Nor in guile." He seems to have been charged in another Church with having made a gain of his converts (2 Cor. xii. 16, 17). Wordsworth supposes that it alludes to adulterating the Gospel.

g 1 Cor. vii. 25. 1 Tim. i. 11, 12.
h 1 Cor. ix. 17. Gal. ii. 7. Tit. i. 3.
i Gal. i. 10.
k Prov. xvii. 3. Rom. viii. 27.
l Acts xx. 33. 2 Cor. ii. 17. & iv. 2. & vii. 2. & xii. 17.
m Rom. i. 9.
n John v. 41, 44. & xii. 43. 1 Tim. v. 17.
o 1 Cor. ix. 4, 6, 12, 18. 2 Cor. x. 1, 2, 10, 11. & xiii. 10. 2 Thess. iii. 9. Philem. 8, 9.
‖ Or, *used authority.*
p 2 Cor. xi. 9. & xii. 13, 14. 2 Thess. iii. 8.
q 1 Cor. ix. 1, 2, 5.

4 But as [g] we were allowed of God [h] to be put in trust with the Gospel, even so we speak; [i] not as pleasing men, but God, [k] which trieth our hearts.

5 For [l] neither at any time used we flattering words, as ye know, nor a cloke of covetousness; [m] God *is* witness:

6 [n] Nor of men sought we glory, neither of you, nor *yet* of others, when [o] we might have ‖ been [p] burdensome, [q] as the apostles of Christ.

---

7. "Gentle" (ἤπιοι). So A., E., K., L., P., most Cursives, Syriac, Sah., Arm., &c.; but ℵ, B., C., D., F., G., some Cursives, d, e, f, g, Vulg., Copt., Æth., read, "babes" (νήπιοι).

4. "But as we were allowed of God to be put in trust with the Gospel," &c. "Allowed," rather "approved" of God. As God has entrusted us, for we have not undertaken this commission at our own will, but by the direct designation of God, and so we speak as those who have to answer to God; not as pleasing men, for, if so, we should not be the servants of God (Gal. i. 10), but as pleasing God, Who above all things requires sincerity in His servants.

5. "For neither at any time used we flattering words as ye know, nor a cloke of covetousness," &c. Chrysostom understands it, "No one can say that we flattered in order to rule, nor that we had recourse to it for the sake of wealth." Of this, which was manifest, he afterwards calls them to be witnesses. Whether we flattered, he said, "ye know." But as to what was uncertain, viz., whether it were in a spirit of covetousness, he calls God to witness.

"Cloke of covetousness." The meaning being that he did not conceal covetousness under a show of better motives.

6. "Nor of men sought we glory, neither of you, nor yet of others . . . apostles of Christ." Glory here seems to be the glory of Apostleship, which also included the right of maintenance. This is specifically mentioned in the next verse but two.

"We might," &c. Silvanus and Timotheus seem to be included

7 But [r] we were gentle among you, even as a nurse cherisheth her children:

8 So being affectionately desirous of you, we were willing [s] to have imparted unto you, not the Gospel of God only, but also [t] our own souls, because ye were dear unto us.

9 For ye remember, brethren, our labour and travail: for [u] labouring night and day, [x] because we would not be chargeable unto any of you, we preached unto you the Gospel of God.

r 1 Cor. ii. 3. & ix. 22. 2 Cor. xiii. 4. 2 Tim. ii. 24.

s Rom. i. 11. & xv. 29.

t 2 Cor. xii. 15.

u Acts xx. 34. 1 Cor. iv. 12. 2 Cor. xi. 9. 2 Thess. iii. 8.

x 2 Cor. xii. 13, 14.

---

9. "For labouring." So E., K., L., most Cursives, Arm.; but ℵ, A., B., D., F., G., H., P., twenty Cursives, d, e, f, g, Vulg., Sah., Copt., Syriac, omit "for."

here as sharing the honour or right, but all through this part of the Epistle St. Paul uses the first person plural even where the words are only strictly applicable to himself; and of course the right of maintenance of his companions in travail and necessary fellow-helpers would be as much asserted, if needful, as his own (see 1 Cor. ix. i, 2, 5, 6).

7. "But we were gentle among you, even as a nurse cherisheth," &c. "We exhibited nothing that was offensive, or troublesome, or displeasing, or boastful. And the expression 'among you' is as if he should say, we were as one of you, not taking the higher place. Does the nurse flatter that she may obtain glory? Does she ask money of her little children? Is she offensive or burdensome to them? Are they not more indulgent to them than mothers?" (Chrysostom).

8. "So being affectionately desirous of you, we were willing to have imparted," &c. Rom. ix. 3 is sometimes cited as a parallel, but it seems too strong; "our own souls" need not, and most probably does not, mean more than our lives. We were ready to die for you, such was our affection.

9. "For ye remember, brethren, our labour and travail." Bishop Wordsworth notices that these words are not synonyms though often joined together. Labour, κόπος, signifies the hewing of wood, from κόπτω; but travail, μόχθος, the carrying it after being hewn. The former indicates energy of action, the latter patience

10 [y] Ye *are* witnesses, and God *also*, [z] how holily and justly and unblameably we behaved ourselves among you that believe:

[y] ch. i. 5.
[z] 2 Cor. vii. 2. 2 Thess. iii. 7.

11 As ye know how we exhorted and comforted and charged every one of you, as a father *doth* his children.

---

in bearing night and day. St. Paul observes the Hebrew sequence ("the evening and the morning were the first day").

"Because we would not be chargeable unto any of you, we preached," &c. Thus early did the Apostle commence labouring on his own account. For what reason? He tells us in 2 Cor. xi. 12: "What I do, that I will do, that I may cut off occasion from them which desire occasion; that wherein they glory they may be found even as we." St. Paul felt that the charge most detrimental to the Gospel which could be made against him was that he preached for gain, and so to repel effectually any such a slander he worked with his own hands for his maintenance (see note on 2 Cor. xi. 9).

It might be objected to this conduct on the part of the Apostle that time was lost in manual labour which might have been spent in the far more precious work of making known the salvation of God; but we are not to take into account in this matter the time only, but the removal of hindrances and the extent to which the example of pure disinterestedness would go in ensuring the acceptance of the message.

10. "Ye are witnesses, and God also, how holily and justly, and unblameably," &c. There are times when men must assert what God by His grace hath enabled them to do and to suffer. The Thessalonians knew well enough that there was not one particle of the spirit of boasting in these words, but that they were said to magnify the grace of God which had enabled Paul and his companions to adorn and commend the Gospel which they preached.

"Holily" looks to purity of heart and life; "justly" looks to righteousness and uprightness in our conduct towards our neighbours; "unblameably" looks to our giving no offence, which even holy and just men may do by want of carefulness, of sympathy, and of consideration.

11. "As ye know how we exhorted and comforted and charged," &c. Literally "we were exhorting," a verb such as "we were"

12 [a] That ye would walk worthy of God, [b] who hath called you unto his kingdom and glory.

13 For this cause also thank we God [c] without ceasing, because, when ye received the word of

[a] Eph. iv. 1. Phil. i. 27. Col. i. 10. ch. iv. 1.
[b] 1 Cor. i. 9. ch. v. 24. 2 Thess. ii. 14. 2 Tim. i. 9.
[c] ch. i. 3.

---

12. "Who hath called." So ℵ, A., a few Cursives (six), Vulg., Goth., Syriac, &c.; but B., D., E., F., G., H., K., L., P., most Cursives, read, "who calleth you."

having to be supplied before the three participles. The use of the participles should be noticed, as it denotes the continuous action. The Revisers render it, "As ye know how we dealt with each one of you . . . . exhorting you, and encouraging," &c. "Exhorted," *i.e.*, "urged upon you," "comforted," *i.e.*, "bid you bear up against all opposition, knowing that it would be but for a little time," in fact, "encouraging you." "Charged," *i.e.*, "witnessed, bore testimony to the power of God's grace." Sometimes the Apostle compares himself, as here, to a father; sometimes to a mother, as in Gal. iv. 19.

"Every one of you." Thus he appeals to the Ephesian elders, Acts xx. 20, "publicly and from house to house."

12. "That ye would walk worthy of God, who hath called you unto his kingdom," &c. Is the kingdom here the present state of grace, and the glory the future glory? It may be so, but we must remember that the present state of grace is, compared to every other state existing in this world, a state of glory. Thus St. Paul, speaking of his kinsmen according to the flesh, says that to them pertained "the glory and the covenants" (Rom. ix. 4), and in comparing the two dispensations in 2 Corinth. iii., he says that the present glory of the new dispensation is such that it altogether eclipsed that of the former one. Though not in the eyes of the world, yet in the sight of God and good angels the present state of Christians—their adoption, their union in the Mystical Body, their possession of the Spirit, their knowledge of Divine things—is all of it glory, so that the calling here on God's part is to a glory as well as to a kingdom.

"Worthy of God," by imitating Him (Ephes. v. 1), by showing forth in yourselves the power of His Spirit.

13. "For this cause also thank we God without ceasing, because, when ye received," &c. This is a repetition or acknowledgment

God which ye heard of us, ye received *it* [d] not *as* the word of men, but as it is in truth, the word of God, which effectually worketh also in you that believe.

[d] Matt. x. 40. Gal. iv. 14. 2 Pet. iii. 2.

14 For ye, brethren, became followers [e] of the churches of God which in Judæa are in Christ Jesus: for [f] ye also have suffered like things of your own countrymen, [g] even as they *have* of the Jews:

[e] Gal. i. 22.

[f] Acts xvii. 5, 13.

[g] Heb. x. 33, 34.

15 [h] Who both killed the Lord Jesus, and

[h] Acts ii. 23. & iii. 15. & v. 30. & vii. 52.

---

of i. 5 ("our Gospel came not unto you in word only, but also in power)."

"We thank God without ceasing." We must remember that this was written shortly after the extraordinary putting forth of God's power in the conversion of the Thessalonians, when it was yet fresh in the Apostle's mind.

"The word of men . . . the word of God." This word was the word preached by the Apostle. If the utterances of St. Paul were thus the word of God, much more that which he wrote with deliberation and purpose and which has been preserved in the Church as her standard of doctrine.

"Which effectually worketh also in you that believe." When they received it, it proved itself to be the word of the living God by the transformation which it wrought in them.

14. "For ye, brethren, became followers of the churches of . . . . Judæa," &c. Why does the Apostle single out the churches of Judæa as those which the Church of Thessalonica so closely followed? Because their persecution was really owing to the Jews; the heathen Thessalonians were incited to harass them, not of themselves, but by the Jews, and they must not expect treatment different from what the Jews accorded to their own flesh and blood in Judæa.

15. "Who both killed the Lord Jesus," &c. "If they have persecuted me, they will also persecute you."

"And their own prophets" (perhaps "the prophets"). The Lord Himself especially designates Jerusalem as the slayer of the prophets. "O Jerusalem, Jerusalem, thou that killest the prophets and stonest them which are sent unto thee" (Matth. xxiii. 37).

[i] their own prophets, and have ‖ persecuted us; and they please not God, [k] and are contrary to all men:

16 [l] Forbidding us to speak to the Gentiles that they might be saved, [m] to fill up their sins alway: [n] for the wrath is come upon them to the uttermost.

17 But we, brethren, being taken from you for a short time [o] in presence, not in heart, en-

i Matt. v. 12. & xxiii. 34, 37. Luke xiii. 33, 34. Acts vii. 52.
‖ Or, *chased us out.*
k Esth. iii. 8.
l Luke xi. 52. Acts xiii. 50. & xiv. 5, 19, & xvii. 5, 13. & xviii. 12. & xix. 9. & xxii. 21, 22.
m Gen. xv. 16. Matt. xxiii. 32.
n Matt. xxiv. 6, 14.
o 1 Cor. v. 3. Col. ii. 5.

15. "Their own prophets." So K., L., most Cursives, Syriac, Goth.; but ℵ, A., B., D., E., F., G., P., eight Cursives, Ital., Vulg., Sah., Copt., Arm., Æth., read, "the prophets."

"And they please not God." Though He had chosen them to Himself as especially His own people, though He had given them the law, and the prophets, and sent His Son as one of themselves to win them back to Him.

"And are contrary to all men." How? Because if we ought to speak to the world, and they forbid us, they are the common enemies of mankind. A heathen writer, Tacitus, notices their sullen alienation from the rest of mankind ("adversus omnes alios hostile odium").

16. "Forbidding us to speak to the Gentiles . . . . for the wrath is come," &c.

"To fill up their sins alway." Remember the Lord's withering denunciation, "Fill ye up then the measure of your fathers" (Matth. xxiii. 32).

"The wrath is come upon them to the uttermost." This must be said in anticipation of the Romans coming and taking away their place and nation. The prophecies of our Lord respecting the destruction of Jerusalem must have been well known to St. Paul, and were so circumstantial that he would consider them as history, and regard what the Lord predicted as already fulfilled.

17. "But we, brethren, being taken from you for a short time, in presence, not in heart," &c. "Taken from you." The original word is much more tender and affectionate, it is "bereaved from you," bereaved in being separated from you, returning as it were

deavoured the more abundantly [p] to see your face with great desire.

[p] ch. iii. 10.

18 Wherefore we would have come unto you, even I Paul, once and again; but [q] Satan hindered us.

[q] Rom. i. 13. & xv. 22.

19 For [r] what *is* our hope, or joy, or [s] crown of ‖ rejoicing? *Are* not even ye in the presence of our Lord Jesus Christ [t] at his coming?

20 For ye are our glory and joy.

[r] 2 Cor. i. 14. Phil. ii. 16. & iv. 1.
[s] Prov. xvi. 31.
‖ Or, *glorying?*
[t] 1 Cor. xv. 23. ch. iii. 13. Rev. i. 7. & xxii. 12.

---

to the idea of the father and his children, only he invests the parent with the feelings of bereavement.

"Endeavoured the more abundantly to see your face with great desire."

18. "Wherefore we would have come . . . . but Satan hindered us." In what way? By what external circumstances Satan or the adversary hindered the accomplishment of his desire we know not. Ancient commentators, as Chrysostom, who lived so much nearer to the time of the Apostles, know nothing of it.

It teaches, however, this important lesson, that God for the furtherance of His all-wise purposes, allows Satan to have some power in controlling events, just as He allows men to work their own will whilst they bring about the furtherance of His designs. The hindrance of Satan is evil, but it is ordered by God to bring about a greater good, just as the very existence of evil itself is.

19, 20. "For what is our hope, or joy, or crown of rejoicing . . . ye are our glory and joy." He might well desire earnestly to come and see them again. For they were his hope—the hope that he had not run in vain or spent his strength for nought; his joy, that God had made him the honoured instrument of so successful a work—his crown of rejoicing, the summit, the very acme of his joy or glory. Thus Cornelia said of her children, when another had been displaying her jewels, "These are my jewels." Looking at them as his spiritual children he might have had in his mind Proverbs xvii. 6, "Children's children are the crown of old men, and the glory of children are their fathers."

CHAP. III.

WHEREFORE [a] when we could no longer forbear, [b] we thought it good to be left at Athens alone;

[a] ver. 5.
[b] Acts xvii. 15.

2 And sent [c] Timotheus, our brother, and

[c] Rom. xvi. 21. 1 Cor. xvi. 10. 2 Cor. i. 19.

1, 2. "Wherefore when we could no longer forbear, we thought it good . . . . to comfort you concerning your faith." "We thought it good to be left at Athens alone." St. Paul yearned to know whether their faith stood firm; and yet he yearned for the company of his disciples and fellow labourers; for no one could endure to wage such a warfare as his was alone and single handed.

This passage tells us of a circumstance which we do not gather from the history in the Acts, that is, of a journey of Timotheus to Thessalonica whilst St. Paul was at Athens. The account of St. Paul leaving Macedonia and arriving at Athens is given in Acts xvii. 13, &c.: "When the Jews of Thessalonica had knowledge that the word of God was preached of Paul at Berea, they came thither also, and stirred up the people. And then immediately the brethren sent away Paul to go as it were to the sea: but Silas and Timotheus abode there still. And they that conducted Paul brought him unto Athens: and receiving a commandment unto Silas and Timotheus for to come to him with all speed, they departed." If we had only the account in the Acts, we should have supposed that his two companions did not join him till he had been some time at Corinth (Acts xviii. 5), but this is quite inconsistent with the earnest wish that they should come to him at Athens "with all speed." Now from this Epistle we gather that they did so join him in Athens as he wished, but the desire to know the spiritual state of the Thessalonians was uppermost in the Apostle's mind, and he sent Timothy back that he might bring him an exact account of matters. It has been asked why did the Apostle say that he thought it good to be left alone when apparently Silas was with him? To which we answer that very probably he had sent Silas away on some other mission.

minister of God, and our fellowlabourer in the Gospel of Christ, to establish you, and to comfort you concerning your faith:

[d] Eph. iii. 13.

[e] Acts ix. 16. & xiv. 22. & xx. 23. & xxi. 11. 1 Cor. iv. 9. 2 Tim. iii. 12. 1 Pet. ii. 21.

[f] Acts xx. 24.

3 [d] That no man should be moved by these afflictions: for yourselves know that [e] we are appointed thereunto.

4 [f] For verily, when we were with you, we told you before that we should suffer tribulation; even as it came to pass, and ye know.

---

2. "And minister of God." So ℵ, B., P., four Cursives, Vulg., Goth., Copt.

"Our fellow labourer." So K., L., most Cursives, Syriac. D. reads "fellow worker with God."

4. "We should suffer." Properly, "we are to suffer."

"Our brother and minister of God, and our fellowlabourer in the Gospel of Christ." He very probably bears this testimony to Timothy, to show that he has sent one who could, if any one could, supply his place to them.

"To establish you and to comfort you concerning your faith." No one could do this so well as Timothy, of whom shortly after the Apostle wrote, "My beloved son and faithful in the Lord, who shall bring you into remembrance of my ways which be in Christ, as I teach every where in every church" (1 Cor. iv. 17). Nothing would so tend to confirm the Thessalonians as the repetition of St. Paul's teaching.

"To comfort you concerning (or in the matter of) your faith."

3. "That no man should be moved by these afflictions; for yourselves," &c. It was almost an article of faith in that age that Christians must partake of the sufferings of Christ. It was part of the faithful saying, "If we suffer we shall also reign with him" (2 Tim. ii. 12). And when Ananias was sent to restore St. Paul at his conversion, the Lord said, "I will show him how great things he must suffer for my name's sake" (Acts ix. 16). Thus also Acts xiv. 32, "confirming the souls of the disciples, and exhorting them to continue in the faith, and that we must, through much tribulation, enter into the kingdom of heaven."

4. "For verily, when we were with you, we told you before that we should suffer," &c. This does not mean that he foretold to the Thessalonians the particular shape which this tribulation would

5 For this cause, [g] when I could no longer forbear, I sent
to know your faith, [h] lest by some means the
tempter have tempted you, and [i] our labour be
in vain.
6 [k] But now when Timotheus came from you
unto us, and brought us good tidings of your faith
and charity, and that ye have good remembrance
of us always, desiring greatly to see us, [l] as we
also *to see* you:

g ver. 1.
h 1 Cor. vii. 5. 2 Cor. xi. 3.
i Gal. ii. 2. & iv. 11. Phil. ii. 16.
k Acts xviii. 1, 5.
l Phil. i. 8.

---

assume, but that he forewarned them that "all that will live godly in Christ Jesus must suffer persecution." They witness against the world and the world will retaliate. Almost, one might say, in the natural order of things, the suffering came to pass.

5. "For this cause, when I could no longer forbear, I sent to know your faith," &c. How was it that the Apostle was so exceedingly anxious, and thus dwells upon his anxiety? Most likely because he was compelled to leave Thessalonica in such haste and upon a sojourn so comparatively short that he had no experience of the steadfastness of the Thessalonians.

"The tempter have tempted you." To fall from the faith through persecution was, in the eyes of the Apostle, treason against Christ. How was it that he said, "and our labour be in vain," when he was sure of his reward? Because he laboured not for reward, but to save souls whom he loved because Christ had loved them so as to give Himself for them.

6. "But now when Timotheus came from you unto us, and brought us good tidings . . . . to see us, as we also to see you." "Of your faith and love." "In Jesus Christ neither circumcision availeth anything, nor uncircumcision, but faith which worketh by love" (Gal. v. 6).

"And that ye have good remembrance of us," &c. Here the Apostle recognizes the ministerial tie—the mutual love of pastor and flock. The Thessalonians could scarcely have been credited with true faith, unless they had good remembrance of him who, under the pressure of extreme danger and toil, had communicated to them this faith by which they had obtained God and Christ and eternal life.

7. "Therefore, brethren, we were comforted over you in all our affliction," &c. If this Epistle was written shortly after the coming

7 Therefore, brethren, [m] we were comforted over you in all our affliction and distress by your faith:

8 For now we live, if ye [n] stand fast in the Lord.

9 [o] For what thanks can we render to God again for you, for all the joy wherewith we joy for your sakes before our God;

10 [p] Night and day [q] praying exceedingly [r] that we might see your face, [s] and might perfect that which is lacking in your faith?

[m] 2 Cor. i. 4. & vii. 6, 7, 13.
[n] Phil. iv. 1.
[o] ch. i. 2.
[p] Acts xxvi. 7. 2 Tim. i. 3.
[q] Rom. i. 10, 11. & xv. 32.
[r] ch. ii. 17.
[s] 2 Cor. xiii. 9, 11. Col. iv. 12.

---

of Silas and Timotheus to the Apostle at Corinth, then the affliction and distress was probably that which he endured through the persecution of his countrymen as related in Acts xviii. 5, 6, 7.

8. "For now we live, if ye stand fast in the Lord." This is a very strong expression indeed. It is not "we are comforted" or "are rejoiced," but "we live" and indeed the success of the cause of Christ, *i.e.*, the winning of souls to Him, and the continuance of such souls in Him, was St. Paul's very life. He lived for it his outward life. He was sustained by it in his inner life. He looked upon it as the chief joy, next to the sight of Christ, of his eternal life.

9. "For what thanks can we render to God again for you, for all the joy," &c. Notice these thanks and this joy. He thanked God not only for them, but for the exceeding joy with which he rejoiced at the thought of their faith, their love, their steadfastness, and this "before our God."

No words can express how, whilst on earth, his soul was in heaven. He dwelt in a heaven contemplating the love of God to souls, and the eternal life of these souls, and God's having made him the instrument in bringing down such blessings on his fellow creatures.

10. "Night and day praying exceedingly that we might see . . . lacking in your faith." He prayed so earnestly to see them in order that he might perfect that which was lacking in them. Personal intercourse goes farther than letters in establishing the weak and wavering.

"That which is lacking." Some have thought that what they particularly lacked was a right view of the state of the departed,

11 Now God himself and our Father, and our Lord Jesus
Christ, ‖ [t] direct our way unto you.
12 And the Lord [u] make you to increase and
abound in love [x] one toward another, and toward
all *men*, even as we *do* toward you:
13 To the end he may [y] stablish your hearts
unblameable in holiness before God, even our
Father, at the coming of our Lord Jesus Christ
[z] with all his saints.

‖ Or, *guide*.
t Mark i. 3.
u ch. iv. 10.
x ch. iv. 9. & v. 15. 2 Pet. i. 7.
y 1 Cor. i. 8. Phil. i. 10. ch. v. 23. 2 Thess. ii. 17. 1 John iii. 20, 21.
z Zech. xiv. 5. Jude 14.

---

13. "Lord Jesus Christ." "Christ" omitted by ℵ, A., B., D., E., K.
"With all his saints," ℵ, A., D., E., five Cursives, d, e, Vulg., Copt., Æth.

but it is very probable that the Apostle alluded to the whole body of their faith, that it required strengthening and settling.

11. "Now God himself and our Father, and our Lord Jesus Christ," &c. Here Jesus Christ is invoked along with the Father to direct St. Paul's way to his converts; implying that the Son of God had along with His Father all the dispensations of providence at His disposal.

12. "And the Lord make you to increase and abound in love one toward," &c. This seems to be an invocation of grace from the Lord Jesus Himself. In every place in this Epistle in which the word "Lord" occurs, it means the Second Person of the Trinity, and in this place especially are we bound so to understand it, because the Lord is invoked to stablish our hearts unblameable before God, even our Father, evidently implying two Persons.

Some suppose that as two of the Three adorable Persons are mentioned afterwards, that by the God of verse 11 (God Himself and our Father), the Holy Ghost is intended, but this is doubtful.

Notice this prayer of the Apostle's. In it he asks for two things, that they may increase in love, and this the love of the brethren; and that they may be established in holiness in the sight of the Searcher of hearts. St. Paul would not allow an unloving man to be a holy man, and so, according to his view, a man to be established in holiness must abound in Christian love.

It is not an association which is commonly inculcated among us in these last days, but it is assuredly deep in the mind of the Apostle, that love cannot be dissevered from holiness, nor holiness from love.

CHAP. IV.

FURTHERMORE then we || beseech you, brethren, and || exhort *you* by the Lord Jesus, [a] that as ye have received of us [b] how ye ought to walk [c] and to please God, *so* ye would abound more and more.

|| Or, *request*.
|| Or, *beseech*.
a Phil. i. 27. Col. ii. 6.
b ch. ii. 12.
c Col. i. 10.

---

1. "How ye ought to walk and to please God." To this ℵ, A., B., D., E., F., G., eight Cursives, d, e, f, g, Vulg. (Amiat.), Goth., Copt., Arm., Æth., add, "as also ye are walking;" but K., L., most Cursives, and Syriac omit.

1. "Furthermore then we beseech you, brethren, and exhort you," &c. Here the hortatory part of the Epistle begins.

Through the whole of this chapter the Apostle seems to have in his mind the prayer which he has just addressed to God on their behalf. That they may abound in love one toward another occupies from the ninth to the twelfth verses. Sanctification is enforced upon them in verses 3 to 8, and the coming of the Lord with the view to which he desires that their hearts should be established in holiness, comes on at verse 8, and occupies the remainder of this chapter and much of the next chapter.

"By the Lord Jesus"—it is rather "in the Lord Jesus." He and they are members of one Body, and he exhorts them not as a philosopher or teacher of general ethical truths, but as one whose place in the mystical Body is to teach and exhort his fellow members.

"As ye have received of us how ye ought to walk and to please God." They received this—they had it delivered to them in the tradition or body of Christian truth which they received at the first. (See 2 Thess. ii. 15 and iii. 6.)

"How ye ought to walk and to please God." To this the oldest Uncials append the sentence, "As ye also do walk." This is thoroughly in St. Paul's manner, to acknowledge the progress they had already made, and to bid them proceed further in the same good way, that is, that "ye would abound more and more."

2. "For ye know what commandments we gave you by the Lord

2 For ye know what commandments we gave you by the Lord Jesus.

3 For this is [d]the will of God, *even* [e]your sanctification, [f]that ye should abstain from fornication:

4 [g]That every one of you should know how to possess his vessel in sanctification and honour;

d Rom. xii. 2. Eph. v. 17.
e Eph. v. 27.
f 1 Cor. vi. 15, 18. Eph. v. 3. Col. iii. 5.
g Rom. vi. 19. 1 Cor. vi. 15, 18.

---

4. "To possess his vessel." See below. Jowett, "Should know how to get himself his own vessel."

Jesus." "Ye know," &c. Ye must have them perfectly in remembrance, they were so distinct, so earnestly delivered, and respecting such obvious duties of daily life.

3. "For this is the will of God, even your sanctification," &c. That each one of you should abstain from having intercourse, not only with harlots, but with any woman who is not his lawful wife. This was not considered a sin amongst the heathen, and so the decree ordained of the Apostles and elders at Jerusalem was that the converted Gentile should abstain from "meats offered to idols and from blood, and from things strangled, and from fornication" (Acts xv. 29).

"This is the will of God, even your sanctification," seems to be a reproduction of "Be ye holy, for I am holy,"—the abstinence from fornication being a chief and necessary part of this.

4. "That every one of you should know how to possess his vessel in sanctification," &c. A singular difference prevails amongst commentators respecting the meaning of this word "vessel." Some (as Professor Jowett) understand vessel to mean "wife," and appeal to some Rabbinical passages, and to 1 Peter iii. 7 ("the weaker vessel"). Also to the primary meaning of possess (*κτᾶσθαι*) which is rather to acquire or get possession of than to use; so that in fact this place really makes celibacy unlawful, and binds strictly upon all men that to avoid fornication each man should acquire and keep his own wife. Others, on the contrary, understand by it the body, which is the instrument of debasing lusts, and appeal to 1 Saml. xxi. 5, "The vessels of the young men are holy."[1]

---

1 "With respect to the sense of κτᾶσθαι, even if it be allowed that it must mean 'to acquire,' yet it includes the meaning of 'having,' as is evident from the boast of the

h Rom. i. 24, 26. Col. iii. 5.
i Eph. iv. 17, 18.
k 1 Cor. xv. 34. Gal. iv. 8. Eph. ii. 12. & iv. 18. 2 Thess. i. 8.
l Lev. xix. 11, 13. 1 Cor. vi. 8.
‖ Or, *oppress*, or, *overreach*.
‖ Or, *in the matter*.
m 2 Thess. i. 8.

5 [h] Not in the lust of concupiscence, [i] even as the Gentiles [k] which know not God:

6 [l] That no *man* go beyond and ‖ defraud his brother ‖ in *any* matter: because that the Lord [m] *is* the avenger of all such, as we also have forewarned you and testified.

Upon the whole it seems best to understand it of the body. Compare Rom. xii. 1, "That ye present your bodies a living sacrifice, holy, acceptable to God."

5. "Not in the lust of concupiscence, even as the Gentiles which know not God." The not knowing God, the not retaining Him in men's knowledge, was the occasion of the frightful lusts of uncleanness reprobated in Rom. i. 26, sq.

6. "That no man go beyond and defraud his brother in any matter," &c. Here the Apostle forbids, not simple impurity or fornication only, but adultery. The adulterer defiles his own body, defiles his neighbour's wife, and grievously, we may say irreparably, injures his neighbour.

"In any matter," is a wrong translation. It should be rendered "in *the* matter," *i.e.*, the matter of injuring a neighbour by committing adultery with his wife.

"The Lord is the avenger of all such." The Lord, *i.e.*, the Lord Jesus at His coming is not only the Judge, but the Avenger, the Redresser of all wrong. Here it is expressly asserted that He will avenge those who have suffered in this way. Nothing, we may be sure, will be allowed to stand in the way of the exercise of retributive justice. Even if the wrong-doer has been converted, and has repented, means will be found even in the next world, by Him Who has all the resources of the Universe at His disposal, that the wronged one shall be righted, and shall have abundant satisfaction for the wrong done to him.

"As we have also forewarned you and testified." "When we first preached the Gospel to you," for an integral part of the Gospel

---

Pharisee, 'I give tithes of all that I possess' (ὅσα κτῶμαι). It is also well said by Theophylact that the Apostle here calls a man's body his vessel, which, when it is tainted by uncleanness, sin takes possession of, and enslaves it, but when it is purified, we ourselves make it our own." (Note in Wordsworth.)

7 For God hath not called us unto uncleanness, [n]but
unto holiness.
8 [o]He therefore that ‖ despiseth, despiseth not
man, but God, [p]who hath also given unto us
his holy Spirit.

n Lev. xi. 44. & xix. 2. 1 Cor. i. 2. Heb. xii. 14. 1 Pet. i. 14, 15.
o Luke x. 16.
‖ Or, *rejecteth.*
p 1 Cor. ii. 10. & vii. 40. 1 John iii. 24.

---

8. "Who hath also given." So A., K., L., most Cursives, Vulg., &c.; but א, B., D., E., F., G., seven Cursives, read, "who also giveth."

of St. Paul is that a day is coming when God will judge the secrets of men (Rom. ii. 16).

7. "For God hath not called us unto uncleanness, but unto holiness." The literal rendering is "For God hath not called us for uncleanness but in holiness." God hath not called us that we should live after the flesh, indulging sinful, and worldly lusts; but *in* holiness—in fact, in Christ, in Whom we have sanctification.[1]

8. "He therefore that despiseth, despiseth not man, but God who hath also," &c. "He therefore that despiseth," *i.e.*, despiseth the precepts of holiness, or the state of holiness in which we are called; or rather despiseth and maketh naught of the purity of family life; despiseth not man, *i.e.*, the being for whose moral welfare marriage was ordained, or perhaps the man whom he has wronged or desires to wrong.

"But God." God has ordained chastity to be the principle of the relations between the sexes. He has ordained marriage, without which social purity is impossible.

"Who hath also given unto us his holy Spirit," *i.e.*, as the Sanctifier. Some translate this as in the Authorized, "Who hath also given to us," in which case it forms one of those many passages in which God is supposed to give some portion of the Holy Spirit to all in His Church. Thus, 1 Corinth. vi. 19-20; xii. 7-11; Gal. v.

---

1 "The preposition ἐπὶ in such expressions wavers between the senses of object and condition; ἐν signifies the state in which men are called (comp. Gal. i. 6) or which results from their calling. It often happens that modes of thought vary without corresponding variations of meaning; the same Christian grace may be represented indifferently as a condition, or an object, or a state, or a result. There is no need, therefore, to make an antithesis between ἐπὶ and ἐν, the inversion of which would not have involved any change in the sense. The appearance of antithesis arises partly from the love of variety natural to all language, partly from an awkwardness in the use of language, in a late and rhetorical age, by a writer who was imperfectly master of it." (Jowett, *in loco.*)

q ch. v. 1.
r Jer. xxxi 34. John vi. 45. & xiv. 26. Heb. viii. 11. 1 John ii. 20, 27.
s Matt. xxii. 39. John xiii. 34. & xv. 12. Eph. v. 2. 1 Pet. iv. 8. 1 John iii. 11, 23, & iv. 21.
t ch. i. 7.
u ch. iii. 12.

9 But as touching brotherly love [q] ye need not that I write unto you: for [r] ye yourselves are taught of God [s] to love one another.

10 [t] And indeed ye do it toward all the brethren which are in all Macedonia: but we beseech you, brethren, [u] that ye increase more and more;

25; Tit. iii. 6. It may be rendered in the present "Who giveth us," "Who constantly gives the Holy Spirit."

In resisting or despising the presence of the Holy Spirit we despise God, Who is in the Church by the Spirit. Thus Ananias and Sapphira, in lying to the Apostles, the organs of the Spirit, lied not unto men, but unto God.

9. "But as touching brotherly love ye need not that I write unto you: for ye yourselves," &c. Brotherly love here is philadelphia, not the same word as the charity of 1 Cor. xiii., but philadelphia leads to love or charity, the highest and best of Christian graces. Thus the Apostle writes, "add to you brotherly kindness (philadelphia), charity."

These words, "Ye are taught of God," imply that the most prominent teaching of the words of Christ is the love of one another, for if men are taught the words of Christ at all, they must be taught some such words as "A new commandment I give unto you, that ye love one another as I have loved you." The sermon on the Mount, the precepts of forgiveness, the parable of the unmerciful servant, the visions of Judgment of Matth. xxv., the whole example of the Saviour, and every miracle teach us that we are to love one another. And it is equally so if we understand the words "taught of God" as meaning "taught inwardly by His Spirit," for the first sign of spiritual life is the love of the brethren. "We know that we have passed from death unto life, because we love the brethren." (1 John iii. 14.)

10. "And indeed ye do it toward all the brethren which are in all Macedonia." This implies that the Gospel had spread with great rapidity, and that churches had been formed, or were being formed, everywhere, and also that these churches received material assistance from the members of the mother Church of Thessalonica.

11 And that ye study to be quiet, and [x] to do
your own business, and [y] to work with your own
hands, as we commanded you;
12 [z] That ye may walk honestly toward them
that are without, and *that* ye may have lack || of
nothing.

[x] 2 Thess. iii. 11. 1 Pet. iv. 15.
[y] Acts xx. 35. Eph. iv. 28. 2 Thess. iii. 7, 8, 12.
[z] Rom. xiii. 13. 2 Cor. viii. 21. Col. iv. 5. 1 Pet. ii. 12.
|| Or, *of no man.*

"That ye increase more and more." There is no end of progress in the Divine Life, for it is the life of Christ and of God, and as the Divine Life is made up of different virtues and graces, so, if we increase in the whole life of God, we increase in each particular grace or virtue.

11. "And that ye study to be quiet, and to do you own business," &c. The word translated "study" is remarkable. It is that ye "be ambitious," that ye "contend to be quiet," as if there were some unwonted difficulty in the way of their being so, and from several intimations in the Second Epistle we gather that there must have been such. (See 2 Thess. iii. 6-12.)

"And to do your own business, and to work with your own hands," &c. The phrase "to do your own business," both in Greek and English, implies that the persons to whom it is spoken yielded to the temptation of meddling in the concerns of others.

The temptation to be busybodies and to neglect their own proper employments is supposed to have arisen from the fact that the whole Church was unhinged by the impression which had got hold of them of the immediate appearance of the Lord, and there is much in the Second Epistle which would lead us to believe this: but each community of Christians would have its special idiosyncrasies.

12. "That ye may walk honestly towards them that are without," &c. We should gather from this that the restlessness and meddlesomeness of some in the Thessalonian Church had been a cause of scandal to the surrounding heathen.

"And that ye may have lack of nothing." Comparing this with the somewhat similar precept in Ephes. iv. 28, it comprises under the head of "lack" ability to give to the relief of others, "rather let him labour, working with his hands the thing which is good, that he may have to give to him that needeth."

13. "But I would not have you to be ignorant, brethren, con-

13 But I would not have you to be ignorant, brethren, concerning them which are asleep, that ye sorrow not, [a] even as others [b] which have no hope.

a See Lev. xix. 28. Deut. xiv. 1, 2. 2 Sam. xii. 20.
b Eph. ii. 12.

13. "But I would not." So a few Cursives, Syriac; but א, A., B., D., E., F., G., K., L., most Cursives, d, e, f, g, Vulg., Goth., Æth., read, "we would not."

cerning," &c. It seems that they had sent him a question respecting the state of the departed, or that Timothy, or some one, had told him that they were in some perplexity respecting the state of those who had fallen asleep before the coming of Christ, whether they would be in an inferior state to those who would be alive and would be transformed when Christ should come.

"Concerning them which are asleep" (or are falling asleep). After Lazarus was dead the Lord said, "Our friend Lazarus sleepeth, but I go that I may awake him out of sleep," John xi. 11. And of St. Stephen it is said that when he had prayed, "Lord, lay not this sin to their charge," he fell asleep [1] (Acts vii. 60).

"That ye sorrow not, even as others which have no hope," *i.e.*, as the heathen, who had no well-grounded hope of a life beyond the grave. Nature is not allowed by God to teach this directly. She is only permitted to give us parables or suggestive illustrations. The great spirits among the heathen could not be said to believe it; and a series of passages are quoted by Bishop Wordsworth and by Jowett, in which it is denied. As, for instance, Theocritus: "The living have hopes, but the dead are without hope." Catullus: "When once our brief time of light has failed us we have to sleep in one perpetual night;" and Lucretius, "No one awakes and lives who has once been overtaken by the chilling end of life." It is Christ alone Who has abolished death, and brought life and immortality to light through the Gospel. (2 Tim. i. 10.)

But the Apostle forbids not sorrowing on the prospect of a dear friend being taken away. He says, respecting Epaphroditus, "God had mercy upon him, and not on him only, but on me also, lest I should have sorrow upon sorrow." (Phil. ii. 27.) But our sorrow is to be the lawful sorrow over those who have gone a journey, and

1 See also Matth. xxvii. 52; Acts xiii. 36; 1 Cor. xi. 30, xv. 6, 18, 20, 51.

14 For [c] if we believe that Jesus died and rose again, even so [d] them also which sleep in Jesus will God bring with him.

15 For this we say unto you [e] by the word of the Lord, that [f] we which are alive *and* remain unto the coming of the Lord shall not prevent them which are asleep.

c 1 Cor. xv. 13.
d 1 Cor. xv. 18, 23. ch. iii. 13.
e 1 Kings xiii. 17, 18. & xx. 35.
f 1 Cor. xv. 51.

---

are parted from us for a time, not as for those who are parted from us for ever.

14. "For if we believe that Jesus died and rose again, even so them also," &c. The Resurrection of Jesus and of the members of His Body is inseparable. "If there be no resurrection of the dead then is Christ not risen." "If Christ be not raised your faith is vain." "If the dead rise not then Christ is not raised." "By man came the Resurrection of the dead." "Now is Christ risen from the dead, and become the firstfruits of them that slept" (1 Cor. xv.).

"Even so them also which sleep in Jesus will God bring with him." Some render this "through" Jesus, as through the power of Jesus. By the Death and Resurrection of Jesus their death is abolished and become a sleep from which they must awake. Jesus has composed them to sleep. "As all things are said to be in Christ, so they may also be said to be through Christ." Jowett.

"Will God bring with him." Chrysostom explains it. "But the expression, 'He shall bring with him,' shows that they are brought from many places." "Bring," a tender word used of the living. It denotes bringing with one as a companion. It is remarkable that this coming of the Lord *with* his saints is the subject of the very first prophecy uttered after those at the Fall. "And Enoch also, the seventh from Adam, prophesied of these, saying, Behold, the Lord cometh with ten thousand of His Saints." (Jude 14.)

15. "For this we say unto you by the word of the Lord, that we which," &c. By the word of inspiration; not by any words which Christ spake when on earth, but as the Prophets were wont to begin their prophecies with "Thus saith the Lord," so I, in the Spirit of God, say "that we which are alive and remain," &c.

"We which are alive and remain unto the coming of the Lord," *i.e.*, we who are the quick or living when the Lord comes.

"Shall not prevent them which are asleep." This is rendered

16 For [g] the Lord himself shall descend from heaven with a shout, with the voice of the archangel, and with [h] the trump of God: [i] and the dead in Christ shall rise first:

g Matt. xxiv. 30, 31. Acts i. 11. 2 Thess. i. 7.
h 1 Cor. xv. 52.
i 1 Cor. xv. 23, 52.

---

by the Revisers "Shall in no wise precede them that are fallen asleep." This was probably the cause of distress to the Thessalonian Christians. They believed that the Lord would come quickly, and that they should see Him and be with Him; but they were not so assured of the condition of those who died in the interim between the Gospel being first preached to them and the Second Advent.

16. "For the Lord himself shall descend from heaven, with a shout," &c. The shout as of one giving command. Is it the voice of the Archangel summoning the hosts of heaven to attend the assize of the Son of man? or is it that of the Son of man according to His word, "All that are in the graves shall hear his voice, and shall come forth" (John v. 28)? We know not. Only we know that we shall hear it.

"With the voice of the archangel, and with the trump of God." This is the reminiscence of the Lord's words, Matth. xxiv. 31, "And they shall see the Son of man coming in the clouds of heaven with power and great glory. And he shall send his angels with a great sound of a trumpet," &c. In this place only is the presence of the Archangel mentioned. It is probable from this that St. Paul received an independent revelation of the circumstances of the coming of the Lord from the Lord Himself, as he did respecting the institution of the Eucharist.

"And the dead in Christ shall rise first." This evidently means that the Resurrection of the dead in Christ will precede the change in the bodies of those who are caught up to meet the Lord.

A question arises on these words, "the dead in Christ shall rise first." Does St. Paul, or does the Holy Spirit, mean by this the first resurrection of Revel. xx. 5, 6? It is to be remarked that both here and in 1 Corinth. xv., St. Paul speaks only of the Resurrection of those in Christ, and ignores altogether the Resurrection of the whole body of the dead, or of the wicked. It is impossible to say; for prophecy very seldom so reveals the sequence of events, that we can treat it as if it were history. If this be the

17 [k] Then we which are alive *and* remain shall be caught up together with them [l] in the clouds, to meet the Lord in the air: and so [m] shall we ever be with the Lord.

18 [n] Wherefore ‖ comfort one another with these words.

k 1 Cor. xv. 51.
l Acts i. 9. Rev. xi. 12.
m John xii. 26. & xiv. 3. & xvii. 24.
n ch. v. 11.
‖ Or, *exhort*.

---

first resurrection of Rev. xx., then a thousand years (or an indefinite time), may intervene between the two: but what is this when we have St. Peter writing respecting the last things, telling us that "one day is with the Lord as a thousand years, and a thousand years as one day" (2 Pet. iii. 8)?

17. "Then we which are alive and remain shall be caught up together with them in the clouds," &c. "The wicked will remain beneath (perhaps not raised till afterwards) while the righteous being absolved shall be assessors with their Lord in the judgment" (Wesley).

"In the air." Not in heaven, not in some sphere infinitely remote from the world, but into the upper regions of this lower atmosphere, whence His Saints, according to the prophecy of Enoch, will return with Him. As they ascend to meet Him their bodies will be changed from natural into spiritual bodies, which being fashioned after the likeness of His glorious body will be able to endure the brightness of His presence, which those yet in flesh and blood could not (Rev. i. 17).

"And so shall we ever be with the Lord." "Where I am there shall also my servant be." And again, "I will come again and receive you unto myself, that where I am there ye may be also" (John xiv. 3). And again He prays, "Father, I will that those whom thou hast given me be with me where I am" (John xvii. 24).

"With the Lord." Where? If in an infinitely distant heaven beyond the furthest star, if He be there so shall we be. If in the New Jerusalem which descends out of heaven from God we shall be there.

18. "Wherefore comfort one another with these words." Lay aside all fears respecting those that have fallen asleep in Christ, and comfort one another with the thought that not one soul in Christ is lost, not one is missing, not one is not clearly discerned by Him now, and its place in His presence appointed.

CHAP. V.

[a] Matt. xxiv. 3, 36. Acts i. 7.
[b] ch. iv. 9.
[c] Matt. xxiv. 43, 44. & xxv. 13. Luke xii. 39, 40. 2 Pet. iii. 10. Rev. iii. 3. & xvi. 15.

BUT of [a] the times and the seasons, brethren, [b] ye have no need that I write unto you.

2 For yourselves know perfectly that [c] the day of the Lord so cometh as a thief in the night.

1, 2. "But of the times and the seasons . . . . yourselves know perfectly that," &c. He has no need to write to them, because it would be folly to prophesy the exact time of events which God has hidden from us for the very intent that not knowing when they shall happen we are ever to be looking for them.

The words of the Lord Himself, just before He was taken up, are nearly the same: "It is not for you to know the times or the seasons which the Father hath put in his own power" (Acts i. 7).

"For yourselves know perfectly." This seems to imply that they knew it independently of his own teaching, and it would be so, if they had some accounts of the words of the Lord such as the Logia of St. Matthew. St. Paul could scarcely be said to preach Christ unto them unless he spoke to them of the words and miracles of Christ, and in any account which they had of the words of Christ there must have been some report of His great prophecy respecting things to come which the first preachers would refer to and enforce upon them; so that they must know it perfectly.

"That the day of the Lord so cometh as a thief in the night." On two separate occasions the Lord likeneth His coming to that of a thief. Once as recorded in Luke xii. 39, "And this know, that if the goodman of the house had known what hour the thief would come, he would have watched, &c. . . . Be ye therefore ready also, for the Son of man cometh at an hour when ye think not." And again in His last prophetical discourse, Matth. xxiv. 43, 44. Six times in the New Testament is the Second Advent likened unto the coming of a thief.[1]

---

[1] Matth. xxiv. 43; Luke xii. 39; 1 Thess. v. 2; 2 Pet. iii. 10; Rev. iii. 3, and xvi. 15.

3 For when they shall say, Peace and safety; then [d] sudden destruction cometh upon them, [e] as travail upon a woman with child; and they shall not escape.

4 [f] But ye, brethren, are not in darkness, that that day should overtake you as a thief.

5 Ye are all [g] the children of light, and the children of the day: we are not of the night, nor of darkness.

d Isa. xiii. 6-9. Luke xvii. 27, 28, 29. & xxi. 34, 35. 2 Thess. i. 9.
e Jer. xiii. 21. Hos. xiii. 13.
f Rom. xiii. 12, 13. 1 John ii. 8.
g Eph. v. 8.

---

3. "For when they shall say." So K., L., P., Vulg.; but ℵ, A., F., G., 17, 44, 47, 179, d, e, f, g, Goth., Syriac, omit "for." B., D., E., Copt., read, "but" (δὲ).

4. "As a thief." A., B., Copt., read, "as thieves."

5. "Ye are all." ℵ, A., B., D., E., F., G., L., P., more than twenty Cursives, Ital., Vulg., Goth., Syriac, read, "for ye are all." K. omits "for."

3. "When they shall say, Peace and safety, then sudden destruction," &c. Our Lord represents the ungodly as saying to themselves "Peace and safety," when He describes their carelessness in such terms as, "As it was in the days of Noe, so shall it be also in the days of the Son of man. They did eat, they drank, they married wives, they were given in marriage, until the day that Noe entered into the ark." (Luke xvii. 26, 27.)

4. "But ye, brethren, are not in darkness, that that day should overtake you as a thief. Ye are all the children of light, and the children of the day." They were not in darkness, they were all the children of light because they had the light of the Apostolic teaching, which reproduced to them, as in this case, the words of Christ. They had the light of the Spirit inwardly and vividly bringing home such truths as that of the Advent to their hearts. They had also a more sure word of prophecy, 2 Pet. i. 19, for the old Testament Scriptures had many and striking predictions of the glories and terrors of the Second Coming.

This is one of those many places in the Pauline Epistles which assume that all in the Church have received enlightening grace. Not "some of you may be enlightened," but "ye are all the children of light." They all had something from God on which St. Paul desired to build. Similar places are 1 Cor. iii. 10; vi. 15-19; xii. 7-14; Gal. iii. 26, 27; Ephes. iv. 7. I need not say that in all her offices the Church of England proceeds on this assumption.

6. "Therefore let us not sleep, as do others; but let us watch

h Matt. xxv. 5.
i Matt. xxiv. 42. & xxv. 13. Rom. xiii. 11, 12, 13. 1 Pet. v. 8.
k Luke xxi. 34, 36. Rom. xiii. 13. 1 Cor. xv. 34. Eph. v. 14.
l Acts ii. 15.

6 [h] Therefore let us not sleep, as *do* others; but
[i] let us watch and be sober.
7 For [k] they that sleep sleep in the night;
and they that be drunken [l] are drunken in the
night.
8 But let us, who are of the day, be sober,

---

and be sober." This sleep is, of course, the sleep of sin, which is the image of death, and which, if men are not awakened from it, will end in death. Ephes. v. 14. The "others" may be the heathen, or fallen Christians, who have slidden back into the condition of the heathen.

"Let us watch and be sober." The same words are used by St. Peter with respect to being on the watch against Satan. 1 Pet. v. 8. Let us watch for the coming of our Lord, and against our external adversary, and our internal corruptions. Let us be sober, not only in the matter of eating and drinking, but of the gratification of all lawful desires. Let us be sober minded, not led away by every new thing, by every blast of false doctrine. Our Lord Himself constantly enjoins this "watching" and "being sober." "Watch ye therefore, and pray always, that ye may be accounted worthy to escape all these things that shall come to pass, and to stand before the Son of Man." (Luke xxi. 36.) And again, as to being sober, Luke xxi. 34, "Take heed unto yourselves, lest at any time your hearts be overcharged with surfeiting, and drunkenness, and cares of this life, and so that day come upon you unawares."

7. "For they that sleep sleep in the night; and they that be drunken," &c. Here we must understand the Apostle as using the habits of the men of the world as a parable. The night is their time for both sleep and debauchery. But we are not of the world, we are enlightened by the light of the Sun of righteousness, so we must be awake, and live in the light of the true Life; we must be sober, as having no night in which to shroud evil deeds.

8. "But let us, who are of the day, be sober." Sober in every gratification and in every pursuit. Let us not be fanatical in our religion even, but serve God with a quiet and even, and yet with a resolute and courageous mind.

[m] putting on the breastplate of faith and love; and for an helmet, the hope of salvation.

9 For [n] God hath not appointed us to wrath, [o] but to obtain salvation by our Lord Jesus Christ.

10 [p] Who died for us, that, whether we wake or sleep, we should live together with him.

m Isa. lix. 17. Eph. vi. 14, 16, 17.
n Rom. ix. 22. ch. i. 10. 1 Pet. ii. 8. Jude 4.
o 2 Thess. ii. 13, 14.
p Rom. xiv. 8, 9. 2 Cor. v. 15.

"Putting on the breastplate of faith and love; and for an helmet," &c. Here, in this part of his Epistle, we have the figurative use of the soldier's equipment, which culminates in the passage in the last chapter of the Ephesians, one of the latest of the Apostle's letters. There is a difference, however, which it is important to note. In the letter to the Ephesians it is the breastplate of righteousness, and love is not mentioned as a part of the armour: here we have the breastplate of faith and love. This shows us that the exact figurative meaning of each part of the armour is not to be pressed. The parts are all defensive, and in the spiritual equipment may be interchanged.

9. "For God hath not appointed us to wrath, but to obtain salvation," &c. This is an outcome of the last piece of Christian armour alluded to, "For an helmet the hope of salvation." We ought, indeed, to have a well-assured hope of salvation, seeing that God has done so much to purchase it for us, and to make it ours. He desires all men to be saved. May nothing hinder Him having His desire in each one of us.[1]

10. "Who died for us, that, whether we wake or sleep, we should live." "Whether we wake," *i.e.*, whether we live this present life; "or sleep," *i.e.*, whether we rest in our graves, we should live together with Him. This is the salvation of which we are to put on the helmet, that, whether alive or dead, we should live with Christ. If we live in the flesh we are to live by the faith of the Son of God; we are to live by His grace, under His protection, in His Body. If we die, we die unto Him, and in some way He

---

1 It is one of the most singular things in the history of Christian opinion, that the exact contrary to this statement of the Apostle's—viz., that God hath appointed the greater part of mankind to wrath—should have been actually erected into a dogma. I shall have more to say upon this when I come to consider 1 Tim. ii. 4.

11 [q] Wherefore || comfort yourselves together, and edify
[q] ch. iv. 18. one another, even as also ye do.
|| Or, *exhort.*
[r] 1 Cor. xvi. 18. Phil. ii. 29. 1 Tim. v. 17. Heb. xiii. 7, 17.
12 And we beseech you, brethren, [r] to know
them which labour among you, and are over you
in the Lord, and admonish you;
13 And to esteem them very highly in love for

---

reveals Himself as nearer to us than when we live here. Thus the Apostle says, "To depart and to be with Christ is far better." (Phil. i. 23. See also Rom. xiv. 8-9.)

11. "Wherefore comfort yourselves together, and edify one another, even as also ye do." This enjoins mutual comfort and edification over and above the mere ministerial teaching and exhortation of the next verse.

12. "And we beseech you, brethren, to know them which labour among you." Those who are over them are the ministers of the Church, the elders whom, at a previous period, they had ordained in every city, the bishops or overseers of Phil. i. 1. Three duties of these elders, or overseers, are given. "Labours," no doubt house to house visitation, of which the Apostle himself set them an example (Acts xx. 20)—superintendence, "over you," but "in the Lord," having no secular authority, and teaching and admonishing you.

Let the reader remember that this exhortation to the flock to know, *i.e.*, to respect their ministers, is in the first Epistle which the Apostle wrote. This shows that ministerial oversight is not an accident, but of the very essence of a Church; and, in fact, no community can exist as a community without it. The angels in heaven, the heavenly hosts, are not an unofficered army, but under "principalities and powers." (Ephes. i. 21; iii. 10, &c.) If it be asked is this oversight presbyterian or episcopal, we answer, both. The oversight of the faithful in each city was in the presbyters, but the oversight over these presbyters and the whole flock was always kept by the Apostle in his own hands.

13. "And to esteem them very highly in love for their work's sake." Chrysostom has some most pertinent remarks upon the difficulty of this passage: "He who is convicted and reproved, be he what he may, is sure to cease from being thankful, and to become an enemy. In like manner he will act who is admonished and exhorted. If, therefore, I should say, empty out wealth on the

their work's sake. [s] *And* be at peace among yourselves. [s] Mark ix. 50.

14 Now we ‖ exhort you, brethren, [t] warn them ‖ Or, *beseech*. [t] 2 Thess. iii. 11, 12.

---

needy, I say what is offensive and burdensome. If I say, chasten thine anger, quench thy wrath, check thine inordinate desire, cut off a small portion of thy luxury, all is offensive and burdensome. And if I should punish one who is slothful (or wilful), or should remove him from the Church, or exclude him from the public prayers, he grieves, not because he is deprived of these things, but because of the public disgrace."

And again, hinting at the word "standing up for" (rendered in our translation, "over you"): "If a man stand up for thee before a man, thou doest anything, thou confessest thyself much indebted; but he stands up for thee before God, and thou dost not own the favour. And how does he stand up for me? thou askest. Because he prays for thee, because he ministers to thee the Spiritual gift that is by Baptism, he visits, he admonishes, he warns thee, he comes at midnight if thou callest for him. . . . Again, he who loves Christ, whatever the priest may be, will love him, because through him he has obtained the awful mysteries."

"For their work's sake" means, not merely for the way in which they have performed their work, but for the work itself, which is always the setting forth of Christ, whether in preaching or in the Eucharist.

"Be at peace among yourselves." This follows naturally upon the exhortation to esteem these ministers for their work. The ministry is ordained to bind the whole mystical body together in one. See Ephes. iv. 11, 12, 13. So that it should be not only in peace, but in unity.

14. "Now we exhort you, brethren, warn them that are unruly." Some suppose that this, following upon the two verses respecting ministers, is a precept for the rulers of the Church; but though it is for the rulers to exercise Godly discipline, it is for the whole Church, and for each member in particular, as far as lies in him, to repress disorders. By this the restraining power of the ministry is indefinitely increased. Each man, then, should warn his neighbour if he acts disorderly, *i.e.*, if he sets at naught the rules which must bind every community, if it is to live and progress harmo-

|| Or, *disorderly*.
u Heb. xii. 12.
x Rom. xiv. 1. & xv. 1. Gal. vi. 1, 2.
y Gal. v. 22. Eph. iv. 2. Col. iii. 12. 2 Tim. iv. 2.

that are || unruly, [u] comfort the feeble-minded, [x] support the weak, [y] be patient towards all *men*.

---

niously. The "unruly" are in all probability those alluded to in chap. iv. 11, 12, and in the Second Epistle, iii. 6.

"Comfort the feeble-minded." This also pertains to each member of the Church, that with the comfort wherewith God hath comforted him he also should comfort his brother (2 Cor. i. 4-6).

"Feeble-minded." Literally, those of small souls as distinguished from the great souls, or great hearts—those who are full of complaints, distressed with trifles, inverting the order of things, making much of that which is in comparison little, making little of that which is in comparison much.

"Support the weak." St. Paul elsewhere speaks of the weak as the over-scrupulous (Rom. xiv. 2), but he evidently means here those who are weak in all Christian grace, especially in faith. Chrysostom has some most pertinent remarks on this verse: "'Comfort the feeble-minded, support the weak, be patient towards all men.' For he who is rebuked with harshness, despairing of himself, becomes more bold in contempt. On this account it is necessary by gentle warning to render the medicine sweet. But who are the disorderly? Those, surely, who do what is contrary to the will of God. For this order of the Church is more harmonious than the order of an army, so that the reviler is disorderly, and the drunkard is disorderly, and the covetous, and all who sin. For they walk not orderly in their rank, but out of the line, wherefore also they are overthrown. But there is also another kind of evil, not such as this indeed, but itself a vice. And what is this? Little-mindedness. For this is destructive equally with sloth. He who cannot bear an insult is feeble-minded. He who cannot endure trial is feeble-minded. This is he who is sown upon a rock. There is also another sort, that of weakness. 'Support the weak,' he says, speaking of those who are weak in faith. For with respect to that also there is a weakness. But observe how he does not permit them to be despised. And elsewhere in his Epistles he says, 'Those that are weak in the faith receive ye.' For in our bodies too we do not suffer the weak member to perish. 'Be patient toward all men,' he says. What, then, even to the

15 [z] See that none render evil for evil unto any *man;* but ever [a] follow that which is good, both among yourselves, and to all *men.*
16 [b] Rejoice evermore.

z Lev. xix. 18. Prov. xx. 22. & xxiv. 29. Matt. v. 39, 44. Rom. xii. 17. 1 Cor. vi. 7. 1 Pet. iii. 9.
a Gal. vi. 10. ch. iii. 12.
b 2 Cor. vi. 10. Phil. iv. 4.

---

disorderly? Yes, certainly. For there is no medicine equal to this, especially for the teacher, none so suitable to those who are under rule. It can quite shame and put out of countenance him that is fiercer and more impudent than all men." (Chrysostom.)

15. "See that none render evil for evil unto any man," &c. Some suppose that this is a direction for ministers; but this is impossible, for it is in the most general language—see that *no* one—to *any* man. Our Lord's words are stronger, "Resist not evil." "Do good to them that hate you." "Pray for them that despitefully use you."

It is remarkable that St. Paul, and the same is true of his brother Apostles, never reproduces the Lord's words, "Love your enemies." He comes very near it in Romans xii., but the words of the Lord are very short. They are the most decisive words, one may say, in Scripture. If St. Paul knew any words of the Lord, he must have known these. Perhaps, however, he thought that he reproduced them practically by his precept, "If thine enemy hunger, feed him," for it is by obeying precepts such as these that we can get to love our enemies.

"But ever follow that which is good, both among yourselves and all men." Lit. "pursue the good"—both towards yourself, *i.e.*, the Church, and towards all men, *i.e.*, to those who are without, the unconverted, the heathen, even though they persecute you.

16. "Rejoice evermore." The Apostle frequently repeats this, especially with respect to God and Christ, "We joy in God through our Lord Jesus Christ, by whom we have received the atonement" (Rom. v. 11). "We are the Circumcision who .... rejoice in Christ Jesus" (Phil. iii. 4). "Rejoice in the Lord always, and again I say, rejoice." The reader need not, I trust, be reminded that this is the rejoicing of holy souls in the fact that God through His Son redeems them from sin and breaks its yoke from off their necks. Rejoicing in God and having pleasure in sin cannot possibly exist together in any soul. If they do, such rejoicing is vain.

c Luke xviii. 1. & xxi. 36. Rom. xii. 12. Eph. vi. 18. Col. iv. 2. 1 Pet. iv. 7.
d Eph. v. 20. Col. iii. 17.

17 [c] Pray without ceasing.

18 [d] In every thing give thanks: for this is the will of God in Christ Jesus concerning you.

"Evermore." Even in tribulations. Perhaps no word of mere man can so well describe this "rejoicing evermore," as those of this Apostle: "I take pleasure in infirmities, in reproaches, in necessities, in persecutions, in distresses, for Christ's sake; for when I am weak, then am I strong" (2 Corinth. xii. 10). St. James also by the same spirit was enabled to say, "Brethren, count it all joy when ye fall into diverse temptations." "There were giants in the earth in those days."

17. "Pray without ceasing." We are tempted to say that this cannot be obeyed literally, because we must have sleep, and there are certain occupations which take up, for the time, all our attention, but there have been, and doubtless are, Christians who obey this almost to the letter. We cannot pray when asleep, but is it not well to have a rule whenever we wake in the night to have some short prayers commending to God our waking moments, for such are often dangerous ones. And with respect to some engrossing business, multitudes of Christians never engage in any business without a short commendation of it to God. I have known one who whenever he was visited by any one would retire for a moment, or pause, or do something which his friends knew to be a short but conscious putting of himself into the presence of God. Then Nehemiah ii. 4, "So I prayed to the God of heaven, and said unto the King." It is not sufficient to say we should be always in the spirit of prayer. The spirit of prayer is only known by constant secret acts of prayer.

18. "In every thing give thanks." To give thanks for all things, in every thing, under all circumstances, is a more important Christian duty than at first sight appears, for it is our acknowledgment to God that He overrules all things for the best—that no matter what evil there is He intends to bring good out of it, and for that good He is to be thanked. Many have reason to thank Him for sicknesses, many for trials and disappointments, many for the loss of friends, many for losses in property and straitened means, for such things bring men to themselves and make them know God.

19 [e] Quench not the Spirit.
20 [f] Despise not prophesyings.
21 [g] Prove all things; [h] hold fast that which is
good.

[e] Eph. iv. 30. 1 Tim. iv. 14. 2 Tim. i. 6. See 1 Cor. xiv. 30.
[f] 1 Cor. xiv. 1, 39.
[g] 1 Cor. ii. 11, 15. 1 John iv. 1.
[h] Phil. iv. 8.

---

21. "Prove all things." So ℵ, A., a very few Cursives, Copt., Syriac; but B., D., E., F., G., K., L., sixty Cursives, d, e, f, g, Vulg., Goth., &c., read, "but prove all things."

19. "Quench not the Spirit." When the influences and graces of the Spirit are extinguished in the soul by constant resistance, He is provoked to depart and to leave the soul to itself. If St. Paul here, as some think, refers to what we call the miraculous gifts, prophecy, tongues, &c., they may be quenched by want of use, or by want of due use, if, for instance, they are used for purposes of vain glory; but in his references to the gifts of the Spirit, in 1 Corinth. xii., he appends no caution against neglecting to use them, and so it seems better to understand this verse of the ordinary gifts of the Spirit, the gifts of enlightening and sanctifying the heart. These unquestionably may be quenched, even to the withdrawal of the Spirit Himself (Psalm li. 11). Thus Isaiah lxiii. 10, "They rebelled, and vexed his holy Spirit." Thus St. Stephen, "Ye do alway resist the Holy Ghost" (Acts vii. 51). Ephes. iv. 30, "Grieve not the Holy Spirit of God."

The word "quench" refers, no doubt, to the Holy Spirit as symbolized by fire.

20, 21. "Despise not prophesyings, (but) prove all things." How was it, when it was well known that certain persons were gifted by the Spirit to utter prophesyings, that the Thessalonians should need a caution not to despise them? Probably because the Holy Spirit did not choose to bestow the gift of prophecy on the educated only, but sometimes on those who were less refined; and they must learn to recognize and reverence the gift when the gifted person was less honourable or learned. Some suppose that they were under the temptation to despise a comparatively homely gift like prophecy in comparison with a more showy gift, as that of speaking with tongues.

"Prove all things." The preponderance of ancient authority is in favour of joining this sentence with the last verse, "Despise not prophesyings, but (δὲ) prove or try all that is uttered." The

[i] ch. iv. 12. 22 [i] Abstain from all appearance of evil.
[k] Phil. iv. 9. 23 And [k] the very God of peace [l] sanctify you
[l] ch. iii. 13. wholly; and *I pray God* your whole spirit and

---

spirits of the prophets are subject to the prophets. There were those who had from God the spirit of discernment, and these pronounced upon certain supposed utterances of the Spirit whether they were really from the Holy Spirit or the outcome of the mere human spirit. St. John makes it a duty to try the spirits where he says, "Beloved, believe not every spirit, but try the spirits whether they are of God: because many false prophets are gone out into the world" (1 John iv. 1).

"Hold fast that which is good." This may mean, "Remember and ponder over and practise whatever good remains after the prophecy has been examined," but it is surely a maxim of universal application. That which the Holy Spirit, acting on your enlightened reason, aided by those who have the gift of spiritual discernment, pronounces to be good, that retain and realize.

22. "Abstain from all appearance of evil." This is rendered "abstain from every kind or form of evil." Still it is a truth that we have to abstain from all that appears evil to our brethren, lest we offend them, and make the religion we profess odious to them.

23. "And the very God of peace sanctify you wholly; and I pray God your whole spirit and soul and body," &c. "Wholly," *i.e.*, entirely, in every part; and he goes on to specify the parts of human nature which should partake of the sanctification—the spirit, the soul, and the body.

Most commentators believe that St. Paul here refers to the threefold division of man into body, soul, and spirit—the body a framework of organs, admirably adapted to carry out the will of the thinking or immaterial part within it, and this thinking part also divided into two parts—the soul and the spirit; the soul, that which we have in common with the animal world, which has affections, which can remember, and love, and hate, which can, to a certain extent, reason and calculate, and even repent, but only with reference to things in its own sphere; whilst the characteristic attribute of the spirit seems to be the faculty of apprehending another and a higher sphere, the sphere in which dwells God and Christ

soul and body [m] be preserved blameless unto the coming of our Lord Jesus Christ.

[m] 1 Cor. i. 8.

---

and the Holy Spirit, the sphere of sin and righteousness, faith, hope of a future life, redemption, judgment.

Some, as Professor Jowett, seem to deny, or to be very doubtful whether St. Paul alludes to psychological distinctions. "Had he," the Professor asks, "a distinct thought attached to each of these words? Probably not. He is not writing a treatise on the soul, but pouring forth from the fulness of his heart a prayer for his converts." Yes, we answer, but this prayer mentions not two, but three things, whereas, if he had mentioned only two, he would have avoided exciting a world of speculation. This same Apostle most clearly distinguished between the two parts of our inner man, the psuchicos and the pneumaticos, in 1 Cor. ii. 14. The natural man is the Psychical man, the man under no higher influence than his animal soul, though that soul may have its intellectual or rational, as well as its sensual side. The spiritual man is the man in whom the spirit, his noblest part, does not lie buried under the weight of the animal, or merely mental or intellectual, but is alive to God, and takes in the things of God.

Many commentators and divines write as if the pneuma was lost at the Fall, and was restored in Baptism, but surely the old saints of God, though not baptized, had each a spirit. Surely Abraham, Moses, Joshua, David, had spirits as well as souls, or how could they have been so receptive of the Holy Spirit? Perhaps we may be wrong in speaking of the "soul" and "spirit" as two parts. The spirit may be, perhaps, rather a function of the inner man, which is receptive of a revelation from God. Canon Mason (on Thessalonians in "Cassell's Bible"), has some admirable remarks. "The soul includes the intellect, the affections, and the will, and it is of the very essence of the Gospel to force sharply upon man the distinction between it and the spirit. (Hebrews iv. 12, 'Piercing even to the dividing asunder of soul and spirit.') Low-living men may have soul, *i.e.*, intellect, affection, will in abundance, but their spirit falls into complete abeyance (Jude 19). The souls belong altogether to the lower nature, so that when St. Paul uses the two-fold division, body and spirit, the soul is reckoned as part of the body, and when St. Paul describes the works of the flesh, he includes among them such distinctly *soul* sins as heresies. (Gal. v. 20.)"

n 1 Cor. i. 9. & x. 13. 2 Thess. iii. 3.

24 n Faithful *is* he that calleth you, who also
will do *it*.

o Col. iv. 3. 2 Thess. iii. 1.

25 Brethren, o pray for us.

p Rom. xvi. 16.

26 p Greet all the brethren with an holy kiss.

|| Or, *adjure*. q Col. iv. 16. 2 Thess. iii. 14.

27 I || charge you by the Lord that q this epistle
be read unto all the holy brethren.

---

25. "Pray for us." B., D., add "also."

27. "The holy brethren." So A., K., L., P.; but ℵ, B., D., F., G., a few Cursives, d, e, f, g, omit "holy."

"Unto the coming of our Lord Jesus Christ." Rather at, or in, the coming of our Lord Jesus Christ. Compare Ephes. v. 27: "That he might present it to himself a glorious Church, not having spot, or wrinkle, or any such thing." And again, (iii. 13), "To the end, that he may establish your hearts unblamable in holiness before God and our Father, at the coming of our Lord Jesus Christ with all His saints."

24. "Faithful is he that calleth you, who also will do it." He will do it if you continue to desire it and to pray for it. His having called you to holiness is a pledge of His desire for your complete sanctification, but you must continue to meet and further His desire.

25. "Brethren, pray for us." Some MSS. read "for us too." We are not above your prayers. Remember Phil. i. 19, "I know that this (that Christ is preached every way), shall turn to my salvation through your prayer, and the supply of the Spirit of Jesus Christ."

26. "Greet all the brethren with an holy kiss." This was not a kiss to be given in private, but in all probability a part of the solemnity of the Eucharistic celebration. (See my notes on Rom. xvi. 16, and 1 Cor. xvi. 20.)

27. "I charge you by the Lord that this epistle be read unto all the holy brethren." This is far stronger in the original. It is, "I adjure you, I put you on your oath before the Lord that this Epistle be read," &c.

We should scarcely have supposed that they needed so very solemn an appeal on such a matter, but the fact that St. Paul saw fit to use such an adjuration is very suggestive. He would not have done so unless he had been thoroughly assured that the contents of

28 [r] The grace of our Lord Jesus Christ *be* with you. Amen. [r] Rom. xvi. 20, 24. 2 Thess. iii. 18.

¶ The first *epistle* unto the Thessalonians was written from Athens.

---

his letter was the inspiration of the Holy Spirit. Bishop Wordsworth makes two valuable remarks. 1. That the fact that he so solemnly ordered his own letter to be read in their public assemblies as if it were Scripture, seems to necessitate that he should have supplied them with some account of the words and actions and Death and Resurrection of our Lord to be similarly read, and 2, that the command to read such a document from the first was a guarantee of its genuineness. It will suffice to convince all reasonable persons that the Epistles which we have in our hands bearing the Apostle's name, cannot well have been tampered with, and that these Epistles, as a whole, and every part of them, are what they profess to be, the writings of the blessed Apostle St. Paul, for unless this Epistle had been undoubtedly his, when it was included amongst the canonical writings the Thessalonian Church would have protested that they never had had such a document read in their midst.

28. "The grace of our Lord Jesus Christ be with you." The Epistle ends with an Invocation of Grace from Jesus Christ, the Son of God, and it is a sure proof of the Lord's Godhead, for from whom could grace be invoked except from One Who was in His own Person the Giver of Grace?

THE

SECOND EPISTLE TO THE THESSALONIANS.

CHAP. I.

PAUL, [a] and Silvanus, and Timotheus, unto the church of the Thessalonians [b] in God our Father and the Lord Jesus Christ:

[a] 2 Cor. i. 19.
[b] 1 Thess. i. 1.
[c] 1 Cor. i. 3.

2 [c] Grace unto you, and peace, from God our Father and the Lord Jesus Christ.

[d] 1 Thess. i. 2, 3. & iii. 6, 9. ch. ii. 13.

3 [d] We are bound to thank God always for you,

---

1. "Paul, and Silvanus, and Timotheus, unto the church of the Thessalonians," &c. From this we gather that these three were together, as at the writing of the first Epistle. This proves, according to Mason, that this Epistle was written before the end of the second missionary journey, *i.e.*, before the events narrated in Acts xviii. 19-22; for we do not read of Silvanus being in the company of Paul after this time.

1, 2. "Unto the Church . . . God our Father and the Lord Jesus Christ." This is the same salutation as at the beginning of the first Epistle. There can be no doubt respecting the retention of the words, "From God our Father and from the Lord Jesus Christ" here, though some editors out of deference to some MSS. of the neutral text, omit them in the first Epistle.

3. "We are bound to thank God always for you, brethren, as it is meet, because," &c. "We are bound to thank God . . . as it is meet." Why should St. Paul so earnestly give thanks on their behalf? Because they would be his hope and joy, and crown of rejoicing at the coming of Christ: but even putting any personal considerations, however exalted and holy, out of the question, it is a matter

brethren, as it is meet, because that your faith groweth exceedingly, and the charity of every one of you all toward each other aboundeth;

4 So that [e] we ourselves glory in you in the churches of God [f] for your patience and faith [g] in all your persecutions and tribulations that ye endure:

[e] 2 Cor. vii. 14. & ix. 2. 1 Thess. ii. 19, 20.
[f] 1 Thess. i. 3.
[g] 1 Thess. ii. 14.

---

of thanksgiving to a holy creature to see the manifestation of the glory of God in the triumph of good and the eradication of evil: thus in the Gloria in Excelsis we say, "We give thanks to Thee for Thy great glory, O Lord God, heavenly King, God the Father Almighty."

"Because that your faith groweth exceedingly." Here again are faith and love mentioned together as if inseparable. Faith made them discern in every brother who endured persecution patiently the triumph of God's grace, and so it grew, because it had so many examples to nourish it; and the sympathy which was engendered by the sight of such heroic examples of endurance made their love to abound.

"The charity of every one of you." From this we gather that St. Paul had not only a general knowledge of the state of the Church, but a particular knowledge of the patient endurance of each one. Let the reader remember Acts xx. 31, where with respect to, as we should suppose, a much larger Church, he says that he "ceased not to warn every one night and day with tears."

4. "So that we ourselves glory in you in the churches of God for your patience." He spoke of their patience and faith in the Church of Corinth and the neighbourhood, in every church which he visited in Macedonia and Achaia.

"For your patience and faith." He does not say for their patient faith, but he speaks of the two as distinct Christian graces; but the one upheld the other; the patience strengthened the faith, because it was faith in exercise (and a limb by exercise grows stronger); and the faith strengthened the patience, because it (the faith) was the evidence of the unseen reward of endurance. Persecution and tribulation are not the same. Persecution implies active, powerful, personal enemies. Tribulation may be inflicted by no enemy, but may be entirely from within.

5 *Which is* [h] a manifest token of the righteous judgment of God, that ye may be counted worthy of the kingdom of God, [i] for which ye also suffer:

6 [k] Seeing *it is* a righteous thing with God to recompense tribulation to them that trouble you;

7 And to you who are troubled [l] rest with us, when [m] the Lord Jesus shall be revealed from heaven with † his mighty angels,

h Phil. i. 28.
i 1 Thess. ii. 14.
k Rev. vi. 10.
l Rev. xiv. 13.
m 1 Thess. iv. 16. Jude 14.
† Gr. *the angels of his power.*

---

5. "Which is a manifest token of the righteous judgment of God." This place brings out wonderfully clearly the faith which St. Paul had in God as a righteous judge. If for a time the wicked were permitted to triumph, if God was just, it would only be for a time, and such permission of a short-lived triumph of evil must be for a good purpose which is here expressed by "that ye may be counted worthy of the kingdom of God for which ye also suffer." "Being counted worthy of the kingdom," means, of course, that they were made really and truly worthy of it. In the kingdom of a heart-searching God they who are accounted worthy must answer to that which they are accounted to be.

That they were persecuted was a manifest token—a proof—that in the all-ruling providence of God their enemies will some day (the day of the Lord) be punished. It cannot be otherwise if God is a righteous God; and so he says:

6. "Seeing it is a righteous thing with God to recompense tribulation," &c. The great principle involved here is applicable to all cases of persecution and injustice, no matter by whom inflicted, or by whom endured. It is a righteous thing with God to render just retribution, and even if so-called believers have persecuted unbelievers, they must receive retribution just as others, for they have exhibited conduct which is not only contrary to Christianity but is always a serious hindrance to its success.

7. "And to you who are troubled rest with us, when the Lord Jesus," &c. It is to be remarked how the Apostle makes the rest to date, not from the falling asleep with Jesus, but from the Second Coming. Death is ignored, and all hope, even of rest, fixed on the Second Advent, "When the Lord Jesus shall be revealed from heaven with His mighty angels."

8 [n] In flaming fire ‖ taking vengeance on them [o] that know not God, and [p] that obey not the gospel of our Lord Jesus Christ:

n Hebr. x. 27. & xii. 29. 2 Pet. iii. 7. Rev. xxi. 8.
‖ Or, *yielding.*
o Ps. lxxix. 6. 1 Thess. iv. 5.
p Rom. ii. 8.

---

8. "Jesus Christ." So ℵ, A., F., G., most Cursives, d, e, f, g, Vulg., Goth., Syriac; but B., D. (Gr.), E. (Gr.), K., L., P., 17, about thirty Cursives, omit "Christ."

8. "In flaming fire taking vengeance on them that know not God," &c. Notice how the angels which will form, as it were, His body-guard, are His angels, as well as the Father's. He is the Lord of angels. Thus when the Son of man comes in power and great glory, He shall send His angels, and they shall gather together His elect (Matth. xxiv. 31). The question has been asked, "Is the flaming fire here an adjunct of the glory of His appearance, or is it the instrument of His Vengeance?" We should think the former. Whenever God visibly manifests Himself, it is in the brightness of fire. Thus Psalm xviii. 8, 12, 13; also Psalm l. 3, and Daniel (vii. 9, 10), "His throne was like the fiery flame, and His wheels as burning fire. A fiery stream issued and came forth from before Him." And yet we have "There shall go a fire before Him and burn up His enemies on every side" (Ps. xcvii. 3).

"Taking vengeance on them that know not God and that obey not the Gospel," &c. Here it seems there are two classes; those who "know not God," and those who "obey not the Gospel." The first of these seems all-comprehensive. The heathen have some power of knowing God. The Apostle says of them, "When they knew God, they glorified Him not as God," so that the ignorance of God which will be punished, is a wilful moral ignorance, a turning away from some measure of light from God, a shutting their eyes to what they might know of Him.

"And that obey not the gospel of our Lord Jesus Christ." This is not, as by some, to be limited to the Jews who rejected the Gospel. It also is a place of the widest application. Each and every part of the Gospel is given that it should be obeyed. Even the great atoning feature, the Crucifixion, is to be obeyed; it is only obeyed by them who "crucify the flesh with its affections and lusts." And so the Incarnation, even in its humiliation, is to be obeyed. "Let this mind be in you which was also in Christ Jesus."

q Phil. iii. 19. 2 Pet. iii. 7.

r Deut. xxxiii. 2. Isai. ii. 19. ch. ii. 8.

9 q Who shall be punished with everlasting destruction from the presence of the Lord, and r from the glory of his power;

So is the Resurrection, "If ye be risen with Christ, seek those things which are above." So is the Ascension into heaven. We pray that "we may in heart and mind thither ascend, and with Him continually dwell."

9. "Who shall be punished with everlasting destruction from the presence," &c. Commentators dwell upon the question, "Is this destruction annihilation, or is it what is commonly known as everlasting punishment?"

Annihilation cannot well be considered as retributive, for retribution almost of necessity implies consciousness of the retribution. There seems to me no getting over the intimations of eternal or aionian punishment; but even good men have revolted from the consideration of it, because of the incredible harshness with which it has been dealt out to all who differ from the self-constituted judge, who usurps the place of the Judge of all. By the Lord the Judge it is categorically assigned only to the selfish, to those who have lived and died unmindful of the wants of their fellow-creatures (Matth. xxv. 31). He seems also to assign it, but by implication, to those who have not cut off the right hand of evil doing, or plucked out the right eye of evil desire (Mark ix. 43). It seems incredible to think that such a host of Christian writers have assigned it to those who have had, as they suppose, mistaken views in the matter of imputed or imparted righteousness. Among such I have myself been educated.

However, leaving this, it is a fact that this is the only place in the Epistles of St. Paul where everlasting destruction is mentioned. It is mentioned here, but here only, so that in mercy to souls, we cannot leave it unmentioned, and yet the constant dwelling upon it may have exactly the contrary effect to what we intend. When a man is under the pressure of temptation he thrusts away the terrors of future punishment, with the hope that God will give him, sometime before his death, repentance—that God will save him in his sins—that God will take into account the strength of his temptation, his natural proneness to fall under such or such incentives to gratify evil inclinations.

10 [s]When he shall come to be glorified in his saints, [t]and to be admired in all them that believe (because our testimony among you was believed) in that day.

[s] Ps. lxxxix. 7.
[t] Ps. lxviii. 35.

It seems clearly wrong in so invaluable an expositor of the New Testament as Chrysostom to write "Let us not remember the kingdom so much as hell. For fear has more power than the promise. And I know that many would despise ten thousand blessings, if they were rid of the punishment." Judged by the one single mention of this by the Apostle he is clearly wrong, but his words are weighty indeed, and much to be pondered over by those of us who profess to preach the word of God, when he asks, "But dost thou fear the offensiveness of such words? Hast thou then, if thou art silent, extinguished hell? or if thou speakest of it hast thou kindled it? Whether thou speakest of it or not the fire will boil forth. Let it be continually spoken of, that thou mayest never fall into it. It is not possible that a soul anxious about hell should readily sin."

In leaving this awful subject it is to be remarked that St. Paul looks upon the loss of the presence of Christ as the real punishment. It is not simply destruction, but "destruction from the presence of the Lord, and from the glory of His power." This he said because "to him to live is Christ." This he said because he could say, "I live, yet not I, but Christ liveth in me, and the life which I now live in the flesh I live by the faith of the Son of God." (Gal. ii. 20.) To him the greatest imaginable deprivation was to be deprived of the presence of Christ.

"And from the glory of His power; when He shall come to be glorified in His Saints."

This glory of the Lord's power from which the wicked are to be excluded is the glorification of His Saints, or rather of Himself in His saints, in the renovation of their souls after His image, and in the resurrection of their bodies incorruptible and glorious, according to the words, "He shall come to be glorified in His saints." He is glorified in them because what they will be at His coming will be brought about by His being formed in them.

"And to be admired in all them that believe." "Through them He is shewn to be admirable. For when He brings to so much splendour those who were pitiable and wretched, and who had suf-

11 Wherefore also we pray always for you, that our God would ‖ [u] count you worthy of *this* calling, and fulfil all the good pleasure of *his* goodness, and [x] the work of faith with power:

12 [y] That the name of our Lord Jesus Christ

‖ Or, *vouchsafe.*
u ver. 5.
x 1 Thess. i. 3.
y 1 Pet. i. 7. & iv. 14.

---

fered unnumbered ills, and had believed, then His power is shewn." (Chrysostom.)

"Because our testimony among (or unto) you was believed." This seems to be thrown in to assure the Thessalonian sufferers, that because of their belief in the testimony of the Apostles to the Person and Work of Christ they had a part in this glorification of Christ in His Church. Their having, by God's grace, been enabled to accept the testimony whilst others had rejected it, was a sure sign that God intended to make—indeed had made them, "vessels of honour prepared before to glory."

11. "Wherefore also we pray always for you that our God would count you," &c. "Of this calling"—rather "of the calling"—the calling at the last day to enter into the joy of their Lord. They and all Christians are called at their conversion or repentance unto life, or through their Christian instruction, but this calling has to be made sure, and if, by God's grace, they make this calling sure, then it is equivalent to their being counted worthy of the final calling.

"And fulfil all the good pleasure of his goodness, and the work of faith," &c. The good pleasure of God respecting any creature is that he may be made as good and holy and happy as he is capable of being. This most benevolent design of good he too often frustrates, because of his free will, which is free to entertain evil as well as good, and here the Apostle seems to pray that the good pleasure of God may have free course in each one of his converts.

"And the work of faith with power." The faith of the creature, owing to the flesh, being weak, the Apostle seems to pray that God may overcome or strengthen this weakness by His power, so that the fruits of faith in each may not be few and partial, but abundant—that in fact the word sown in each heart may bear fruit an hundredfold.

12. "That the name of our Lord Jesus Christ may be glorified in you." The name of the Lord is the substance of His glorious attri-

may be glorified in you, and ye in him, according to the grace of our God and the Lord Jesus Christ.

---

butes. The power, the goodness, the holiness, the mercy, the love of Christ are glorified in the Christian because he shews forth the operation of all these in his life and character.

"And ye in Him." We are glorified not in ourselves, but in Him, because all our goodness is through our union with Him.

Chrysostom gives another shade of meaning, true in itself: "How is He glorified in us? Because we prefer nothing before Him. How are we glorified in Him? Because we have received power from Him so that we do not yield at all to the evils which are brought upon us."

"According to the grace of our God and the Lord Jesus Christ." All that the Christian has, and is, is from grace. It is also according to grace—according to the measure with which Almighty Wisdom meets out grace, and also gives grace to continue in it, and improve it. And this is the grace of God and Christ conjointly, the Father and the Son working together in every good gift which the creature enjoys.

CHAP. II.

NOW we beseech you, brethren, [a] by the coming of our Lord Jesus Christ, [b] and *by* our gathering together unto him,

[a] 1 Thess. iv. 16.
[b] Matt. xxiv. 31. Mark xiii. 27. 1 Thess. iv. 17.

---

1. "Now we beseech you, brethren, by the coming of our Lord Jesus Christ." "By the coming," is not an adjuration, but should rather be rendered "with reference to." The Revisers translate it, "touching the coming." The matter, however, is of such importance that he asks them earnestly, he beseeches them, so that they may not misunderstand it.

"And by our gathering together unto Him." This is inseparable in his mind from the Advent. He comes to be glorified in His saints. Those that are asleep in Him will God bring with Him.

2 [c] That ye be not soon shaken in mind, or be troubled, neither by spirit, nor by word, nor by letter as from us, as that the day of Christ is at hand.

3 [d] Let no man deceive you by any means: for

c Matt. xxiv. 4. Ephes. v. 6. 1 John iv. 1.
d Matt. xxiv. 4. Ephes. v. 6.

2. "Day of Christ." ℵ, A., B., D., E., F., G., L., P., It., Vulg., Syr., read, "of the Lord."

2. "That ye be not soon shaken in mind:" lit., "that ye be not soon shaken from your mind—from your right mind."

"Or be troubled, neither by spirit, nor by word, nor by letter as from us." "By spirit," that is by some spiritual revelation or manifestation; this seems to imply that there might be spiritual revelations or utterances, which were not according to the truth of things: thus St. John writes, "Believe not every spirit, but try the spirits whether they are of God."

"Nor by word," *i.e.*, by word of preaching, or exhortation, or argument.

"Nor by letter as from us." Many have taken this to mean "as by some forged letter," but it seems very unlikely that any one should take the trouble to forge a letter from the Apostle urging men to look too earnestly for the coming of Christ. Taking all things into account, it seems to mean, do not allow any letter, even one from us, as our former epistle, to upset your minds on this matter.

"As that the day of Christ is at hand." This means immediately at hand—that it would come in a few days or weeks. St. Paul always taught that Christians were to be on the watch for Christ; in doing this he followed the teaching of Christ Himself, Who before He departed taught His disciples to "watch and pray always that they might escape those things which should come to pass, and to stand before the Son of Man." (Luke xxi. 36.) But this was a different thing from being utterly unhinged in mind as if they saw His sign in the Heavens. And besides this the Lord would not come till certain events had taken place—the Apostasy, and the Revelation of the Anomos. They must be on their guard against both of these or they might be drawn into the vortex of the one, and seduced by the other.

3. "Let no man deceive you by any means, for that day will not come," &c. For it will not be except the falling away come first—

that day shall not come, [e] except there come a falling away first, and [f] that man of sin be revealed, [g] the son of perdition;

4 Who opposeth and [h] exalteth himself [i] above all that is called God, or that is worshipped; so that he as God sitteth in the temple of God, shewing himself that he is God.

e 1 Tim. iv. 1.
f Dan. vii. 25. 1 John ii. 18. Rev. xiii. 11, &c.
g John xvii. 12.
h Isai. xiv. 13. Ezek. xxviii. 2, 6, 9. Dan. vii. 25. & xi. 36. Rev. xiii. 6.
i 1 Cor. viii. 5.

---

3. "Man of sin." So A., D., E., F., G., K., L., P., most Cursives, &c.; but ℵ, B., ten Cursives, &c., read, "man of lawlessness."

4. "As God." So E., F. (Gr.), G., K., L., most Cursives, Syriac; but ℵ, A., B., D., d, e, f, Vulg., &c., omit.

not a falling away, as if it were an ordinary Apostasy, but *the* falling away—the Apostasy—respecting which I warned you so fully when I was present with you. To this no doubt the Lord refers when He asks, "Nevertheless, when the Son of man cometh shall He find *the* faith on the earth?" (Luke xviii. 8.)

"And that man of sin be revealed, the son of perdition." Other men are sinners. This is *the* "man of sin"—one in whom rebellion against God and opposition to the law of God culminates.

"The son of perdition"—one for whom in a deeper and more fearful sense than can be predicated of any other human being, perdition is reserved.

4. "Who opposeth and exalteth himself above all that is called God, or that is worshipped." Putting together the two words "opposeth" and "exalteth himself above," we should gather that he will desire to concentrate all worship upon himself, not tolerating any other. So that in him would be literally fulfilled the words of Daniel: "He shall speak great words against the Most High, and shall wear out the saints of the Most High" (vii. 25); and again: "He shall exalt himself, and magnify himself above every God, and shall speak marvellous things against the God of Gods" (xi. 36).

"Or that is worshipped." The word is only found here, and in Acts xvii. 23, and signifies "objects of worship."

"So that he as God sitteth in the temple of God, shewing himself that he is God." What is this temple in which the Man of sin sits as God? Some suppose it to be the Jewish temple rebuilt and

5 Remember ye not, that, when I was yet with you, I told you these things?

|| Or, *holdeth.*

6 And now ye know what || withholdeth that he might be revealed in his time.

k 1 John ii. 18. & iv. 3.

7 For [k] the mystery of iniquity doth already

---

reconsecrated. Others that it is some Christian church, which may be taken to be the typical Church of Christendom, as St. Peter's at Rome. Others that it is the spiritual building in which the man of sin usurps the Headship of Christ.

I shall consider the question as to whom the Man of sin or Anomos is in an excursus. I shall merely now assert, in passing, that no man or body of men, or succession of men, has yet appeared in Christendom which in the least degree answers to this account given us by the Apostle.

5. "Remember ye not, that, when I was yet with you, I told you these things?" If the Apostle gave them a true account, so far as inspired man can know them, of the circumstances of the Lord's coming, he must have warned them, as I have said, respecting the two things which would precede it—the Apostasy and the Man of Sin.

6. "And now ye know what withholdeth that he might be revealed," &c. "What withholdeth," *i.e.* "what hindereth," "what restraineth," "what holdeth down the final outburst of lawlessness." The Apostle speaks to them as well aware of what this "withholding power" was, but he seems to shrink from naming it. This accords well with the fact that the restraining power was that of Imperial Rome, but we shall afterwards have to consider in what capacity, as it were, or by what mode of action Rome was the Catechôn, the hindering power.

7. "For the mystery of iniquity doth already work: only he that now letteth," &c. From this we learn that Antichrist, or rather the Spirit of Antichrist, was already in the world, or rather in the Church; but that already the withholding power was doing its work. Many gather from this that the Revelation of the Anomos must have been in the time of the Apostle himself, and identify him with Caligula, or Nero, or Simon Magus, or some extremely wicked man of the period; but this we shall see is a great mistake, and arises from not considering what is the real

work: only he who now letteth *will let*, until he be taken out of the way.

8 And then shall that Wicked be revealed, [l] whom the Lord shall consume [m] with the spirit of his mouth, and shall destroy [n] with the brightness of his coming:

9 *Even him*, whose coming is [o] after the working of Satan with all power and [p] signs and lying wonders,

[l] Dan. vii. 10, 11.
[m] Job iv. 9. Is. xi. 4. Hos. vi. 5. Rev. ii. 16. & xix. 15, 20, 21.
[n] ch. i. 8, 9. Heb. x. 27.
[o] John viii. 41. Eph. ii. 2. Rev. xviii. 23.
[p] See Deut. xiii. 1. Matt. xxiv. 24. Rev. xiii. 13. & xix. 20.

---

8. "The Lord." So B., K., L., most Cursives; but ℵ, A., D., E., F., G., It., Vulg., Copt., Syr., read, "the Lord Jesus."

"Shall consume." So E., K., L., most Cursives; but A., B., read, "consumeth."

nature of the hindrance or letting which prevents the bursting forth of the Lawless One.

"Until he be taken out of the way." We may be labouring under a great mistake if we suppose the Catechôn to be a dynasty or succession of emperors. The same power of restraint may be as effectually exercised by many kingdoms as by one; but of this hereafter.

8. "And then shall that Wicked [that lawless one, that Anomos] be revealed, whom the Lord shall consume," &c. There seems to me no room for doubt but that the Apostle holds the Anomos to be a real man, the leader of all rebellion and wickedness, who shall be destroyed at the Second Advent.

9. "Even him, whose coming is after the working of Satan with all power," &c. No one has, as far as I can read history, ever appeared on its stage with pretensions like these. To cite certain miracles of healing performed by bones or relics of saints as the fulfiment of this prophecy seems as if it were invented to make some of the gravest statements of Scripture ridiculous. This sign of Antichrist is foretold by the Lord where He says, "For there shall arise false Christs and false prophets, and shall shew great signs and wonders, insomuch that, if possible, they shall deceive the very elect" (Matt. xxiv. 24). This is not predicated by the Lord, it is true, of one Antichrist, but of several; and this is not unlikely, for it is scarcely probable that the Antichrist should be absolutely alone, and without ministers or disciples to whom he may impart some of his evil power.

10 And with all deceivableness of unrighteousness in [q] them
that perish; because they received not the love of
the truth, that they might be saved.
11 And [r] for this cause God shall send them
strong delusion, [s] that they should believe a lie:
12 That they all might be damned who believed
not the truth, but [t] had pleasure in unrighteousness.

[q] 2 Cor. ii. 15. & iv. 3.
[r] Rom. i. 24, &c. See 1 Kin. xxii. 22. Ezek. xiv. 9.
[s] Matt. xxiv. 5, 11. 1 Tim. iv. 1.
[t] Rom. i. 32.

---

10. "Deceivableness of unrighteousness;" rather "deceit of unrighteousness."
11. "Strong delusion." "An energy of error or delusion."
12. "Damned." "Condemned."

10. "And with all deceivableness of unrighteousness in them that perish, because," &c. The deceivableness is connected with unrighteousness, and signifies that it is in every way calculated to deceive, and so "in them that perish" should rather be rendered, "for them that are perishing." The Revisers translate it "with all deceit of unrighteousness for them that are perishing."

"For them that perish (are perishing)." It is not by an arbitrary decree of God that they perish, but, as the Apostle proceeds to say, because "they received not the love of the truth that they might be saved." The truth has not only to be received intellectually, but received so as to be loved.

It is the love of the truth, the embracing of it, as it were, which saves.

11, 12. "And for this cause God shall send them strong delusion . . . . had pleasure in unrighteousness." No teacher and no system has yet appeared in Christendom of which it could be said that it attracted to it all who believed not the truth, but had pleasure in unrighteousness, and by consequence repelled all who believed the truth and had pleasure in righteousness. The Romish system has multitudes of adherents who believe every word of what God has given to us respecting His Son, and are indefatigable in preaching righteousness, though this may be associated with much superstition, and those who, on the Continent particularly, reject the Romish system, do this on avowedly infidel grounds.

As I have shewn in my Excursus on Election, in Notes on the Romans, God in carrying out His purposes reserves to Himself the

13 But [u] we are bound to give thanks alway to God for
you, brethren beloved of the Lord, because God
[x] hath [y] from the beginning chosen you to salvation [z] through sanctification of the Spirit and belief
of the truth:

14 Whereunto he called you by our gospel, to
[a] the obtaining of the glory of our Lord Jesus
Christ.

[u] ch. i. 3.
[x] 1 Thess. i. 4.
[y] Ephes. i. 4.
[z] Luke i. 75. 1 Pet. i. 2.
[a] John xvii. 22. 1 Thess. ii. 12. 1 Pet. v. 10.

---

13. "God hath from the beginning chosen you." So ℵ, A., D., E., K., L., most Cursives, d, e, g, Syr., Copt., Arm.; but B., F., G. (Gr.), P., a few Cursives, Vulg., read, "chosen you as first fruits."

14. "He called you." So A., B., D., E., K., L., most Cursives, d, e, Cop., Æth.; but ℵ, F., G., P., f, g, Vulg., read, "he also called you" (καὶ).

"You." So ℵ, E., F., G., K., L., P., most Cursives, &c.; but A., B., D., read, "us."

right of making use of evil men and evil spirits, who are permitted (after men have gone to a certain length in wickedness) to harden them still further. After they have deluded themselves he "chooses their delusions" to lead them on still further in the direction which they have chosen. They hate the truth and have pleasure in unrighteousness. They secretly desire to be confirmed in their evil course, and so God sends them that which confirms them.

"A lie" is rather "the lie"—the lie which promises them immunity from future judgment.

13. "But we are bound to give thanks alway . . . . belief of the truth." He desires not to discourage or intimidate them by these awful warnings; and so he sets before them again God's evident purpose in having chosen them from the beginning. This may be from all eternity, or it may be from the beginning of the preaching of the Gospel to them; it is probably the latter, for since they had effectually received the Gospel God had supported them through manifold persecutions, and every present deliverance from distress and every gift of patience under it was from God, and a token of His continuing love. Some MSS., however, read, "chosen you as the first fruits."

14. "Whereunto he called you (to sanctification and belief) by our gospel, to the obtaining," &c. This is a repetition of what he had before written. "God hath not appointed us to wrath, but to obtain salvation by our Lord Jesus Christ." All the acts of God's

15 Therefore, brethren, [b] stand fast, and hold [c] the traditions which ye have been taught, whether by word, or our epistle.

16 [d] Now our Lord Jesus Christ himself, and God, even our Father, [e] which hath loved us, and hath given *us* everlasting consolation and [f] good hope through grace,

b 1 Cor. xvi. 13. Phil. iv. 1.
c 1 Cor. xi. 2. ch. iii. 6.
d ch. i. 1, 2.
e 1 John iv. 10. Rev. i. 5.
f 1 Pet. i. 3.

---

16. "God, even our Father." MSS. differ between "God, even our Father," "God our Father," "our God and Father."

providence on their behalf, the bringing them within the sound of the Gospel—the disposing of their hearts to receive it—the Church and its ordinances and Sacraments, their being upheld to persevere amidst so much opposition—all set forth the desire of God that they should obtain the glory of the Lord Jesus—that when He should appear they should appear with Him in glory.

15. "Therefore, brethren, stand fast, and hold the traditions which ye," &c. How strange this must sound to the partially instructed reader—"ye have been called to share the glory of the Lord, therefore stand fast and hold the traditions." But the difficulty vanishes when we consider what these traditions were. They were the teachings or instructions of the Apostle respecting the Christian faith. Now the faith embraced the Second Coming of the Lord, a thing for which all men were to look, and in order that they might look aright, and not be deceived, they were to remember that there were dangers to their faith, a fearful apostasy, and an extraordinary revelation of a most specious evil personality, and if they were deceived the Lord would appear to them not to salvation but to judgment. "If then," he says, "ye would stand before the Lord and welcome His appearing, remember my first teaching, remember what I first delivered to you respecting the dangers as well as the hopes before you."

16, 17. "Now our Lord Jesus Christ Himself, and God, even our Father," &c. Here again we have the Father and the Son united as the One Giver of everlasting salvation and good hope, and this through the grace of which they are the joint Fountain, which grace must be taken to be the Holy Spirit.

"Comfort your hearts." Under your present persecutions, and your liability to undergo future dangers.

17 Comfort your hearts, [g] and stablish you in every good word and work.

g 1 Cor. i. 8. 1 Thess. iii. 13. 1 Pet. v. 10.

"And stablish you [or them, *i.e.*, your hearts,] in every good word and work." God, Who is spoken of under many titles as the author of the Gospel, has this one especially in the writings of St. Paul, that He is the God of all consolation (Rom. xv. 5; 2 Cor. i. 3).

"Stablish you in every good work." Strengthen you in doing, and make you to persevere in doing all good works—all prayer, all thanksgiving, all works of kindness, sympathy and long-suffering.

"Stablish you in every good word." In all God's promises, in all God's revelations of the great truths of the Gospel—in every good precept—in every needful warning.

CHAP. III.

FINALLY, brethren, [a] pray for us, that the word of the
Lord † may have *free* course, and be glorified, even as *it is* with you:
2 And [b] that we may be delivered from † un-

a Eph. vi. 19. Col. iv. 3. 1 Thess. v. 25.
† Gr. *may run.*
b Ro. xv. 31.
† Gr. *absurd.*

---

1. "Finally, brethren, pray for us, that the word of the Lord may have," &c. "Pray for us." He had prayed earnestly for them; now he asks them to pray for him and his companions, for if they prayed for him, then it was more certain that the word of the Lord would have free course, *i.e.*, not creep along, but run (τρέχῃ).

"Even as it is with you.' He was now labouring in Corinth, where he had much encouragement (Acts xviii. 8), but there was also much opposition, and so he writes,—

2. "And that we may be delivered from unreasonable and wicked men," &c. He seems here to allude to the Jews, for they were more unreasonable than the heathen, because they so pertinaciously resisted the appeals of the Apostle to Scripture, and the miracles which he wrought in attestation of his mission.

c Acts xxviii. 24. Rom. x. 16.
d 1 Cor. i. 9. 1 Thess. v. 24.
e John xvii. 15. 2 Pet. ii. 9.
f 2 Cor. vii. 16. Gal. v. 10.
g 1 Chron. xxix. 18.
|| Or, *the patience of Christ*, 1 Thess. i. 3.

reasonab[illegible] men: [c] for all *men* have
not faith[illegible]

3 But [illegible]ful, who shall stablish
you, and [e] ke[illegible]

4 And [f] we ha[illegible] the Lord touch-
ing you, that ye bo[illegible] do the things
which we command you.

5 And [g] the Lord direct [illegible]ts into the
love of God, and into || the p[illegible]ting for
Christ.

"For all men have not faith." He seems here, however, to allude to some in the Church, and his first Epistle to the Corinthians shews that some had no firm hold on the doctrine of the Resurrection, which St. Paul looked upon as a virtual rejection of Christ.

3. "But the Lord is faithful, who shall stablish you, and keep you from evil." The Lord here is the Son of God, Who along with the Father works every good work in Christians, and guards them from every adversary.

"And keep you from evil." Literally from "the evil" or the "evil one" (ἀπὸ τοῦ πονηροῦ). Some think that there is here a reminiscence of the Lord's Prayer; others, that ὁ πονηρός is the man of sin, of whom he had just been speaking, and whose coming was to be expected before the day of Christ.

4. "And we have confidence in the Lord touching you." "In the Lord." Both ye and we are in Christ, and so as Christ has given us a good hope concerning you, and ye are continuing to abide in Him, we have the best ground for trusting that His grace will enable you to obey always, and in all things.

"The things which we command you." The Apostle could say with all confidence in his own inspiration and calling to be an Apostle: "If any man think himself to be a prophet, or spiritual, let him acknowledge that the things that I write unto you are the commandments of the Lord" (1 Cor. xiv. 37).

5. "The Lord direct your hearts," *i.e.*, the Lord Jesus. This is a prayer to Christ.

"The patient waiting for Christ." The literal rendering is "the

6 Now we command you, brethren, in the name of our Lord Jesus Christ, [h]that ye withdraw yourselves [i]from every brother that walketh [k]disorderly, and not after [l]the tradition which he received of us.

7 For yourselves know [m]how ye ought to follow us: for [n]we behaved not ourselves disorderly among you;

8 Neither did we eat any man's bread for

h ver. 14. Rom. xvi. 17. 1 Tim. vi. 5. 2 John x. 10.
i 1 Cor. v. 11, 13.
k 1 Thess. iv. 11. & v. 14. ver. 11, 12, 14.
l ch. ii. 15.
m 1 Cor. iv. 16. & xi. 1. 1 Thess. i. 6, 7.
n 1 Thess. ii. 10.

---

6. "He received." B. reads, "ye received." ℵ, A., D., E., K., L., P., most Cursives, "they received."

patience of Christ." By some this is taken to be the patience which Christ Himself shewed, and which should be reproduced in the Christian; by others, patience in working and suffering for the cause of Christ.

Chrysostom notices these differences of meaning and seems to prefer that which is contained in our version. "What is the patient waiting? That we should endure even as He endured, or that we should do those things (as He did). With patience also we should wait for Him, that is, that we should be prepared. For since He has promised many things, and Himself is coming to judge the quick and the dead, let us wait for Him and let us be patient."

6. "Now we command you, brethren, in the name . . . . that ye withdraw," &c. Does St. Paul here urge the excommunication of those who walked disorderly? I think not. It seems that he urged upon the church the application of a discipline which might, by God's blessing, save those disorderly persons from the extreme measure of excommunication. The language is very different from that used in 1 Cor. v. 3, 4, 5, and 1 Tim. i. 20, and seems to order, at first at least, a social withdrawal.

In our present want of discipline in the Church of England it would be well if earnest and serious minded persons would, without respect of persons. similarly place a ban upon irregular livers. I have known instances in which a very feeble attempt at this has produced an unlooked-for good effect.

7, 8. "For yourselves know how ye might . . . chargeable to any of you." The tradition evidently was a very stringent forbidding of

nought; but [o] wrought with labour and travail night and day, that we might not be chargeable to any of you:

9 [p] Not because we have not power, but to make [q] ourselves an ensample unto you to follow us.

10 For even when we were with you, this we commanded you, [r] that if any would not work, neither should he eat.

11 For we hear that there are some [s] which walk among you disorderly, [t] working not at all, but are busybodies.

o Acts xviii. 3. & xx. 34. 2 Cor. xi. 9. 1 Thess. ii. 9.
p 1 Cor. ix. 6. 1 Thess. ii. 6.
q ver. 7.
r Gen. iii. 19. 1 Thess. iv. 11.
s ver. 6.
t 1 Thess. iv. 11. 1 Tim. v. 13. 1 Pet. iv. 15.

---

idleness, and this not merely by the word, but by the example of the Apostle, who refused to receive that which he was entitled to that he might set them an example of industry, for he proceeds to say,—

9. "Not because we have not power but to make ourselves an ensample," &c. The setting an example was not always the reason. In the case of the Corinthian Christians it was to take away the ground from under the false teachers, that wherein they boasted, they might be found even as he and his companions. (2 Cor. xi. 12.)

10. "For even when we were with you, this we commanded you," &c. This seems to imply that assistance was rendered out of Church funds to those who from age, illness, or any other honest cause, were unable to work. It is probable from 1 Cor. xi. 21, 22, that the agapé was used for this purpose, as some who came were hungry and were disappointed because they had no share of the provisions. It must refer to relief from Church funds, for in the natural order of things if a poor man would not work he would starve.

11. "For we hear that there are some which walk among you," &c. When he first taught among them he found reason to warn them against this sin of idleness, but since then he has heard that during his absence the evil had increased.

"Working not at all, but are busybodies." There is a remarkable paranomasia, or play upon words, in the original: not working

12 [u] Now them that are such we command and exhort by our Lord Jesus Christ, [x] that with quietness they work, and eat their own bread.

13 But ye, brethren, [y] || be not weary in well doing.

14 And if any man obey not our word || by this

u 1 Thess. iv. 11.
x Eph. iv. 28.
y Gal. vi. 9.
|| Or, *faint not.*
|| Or, *signify that man by an epistle.*

---

12. "By our Lord Jesus Christ." So K., L., most Cursives, Syriac, Æth.; but ℵ, A., B., D., E., F., G., P., d, e, f, g, Vulg., Goth, Copt., read, "in our Lord Jesus Christ."

at all is ἐργαζομένους—busybodies is περιεργαζομένους. The nearest rendering in English is, to employ a paraphrasis—not rightly busy, but busy to no purpose; the idle man mostly employing himself in scandal and interference in what belongs to others—busy only with what is not his own business. (Jowett.)

12. "Now them that are such we command and exhort by our Lord Jesus Christ," &c. It was a very serious matter, this idleness. It would contribute more than any thing else to turn away from Christianity the heathen among whom they lived.

"With quietness they work, and eat their own bread." "Quietness;"—this may allude to calmness of mind respecting the Lord's coming. "Their own bread," earned by their own honest labour and not got by begging or relying on funds intended for those unable to work.

13. "But ye, brethren, be not weary in well doing." Theodoret understands this as, "Let not their improbity—their want of well-doing—overcome your munificence." Persevere in well-doing, notwithstanding the ill-doing of those around you. Chrysostom says, "Withdraw yourselves from them and reprove them; do not, however, suffer them to perish with hunger." It seems not to be a general precept but one which is suggested by the particular ill-conduct which he is now reproving.

14. "And if any man obey not our word by this epistle, note that man," &c. "By this (the) epistle." This shews that the letter was read in the Church, and that when it thus became known to all, it became the law in the Church as coming from one who in the Spirit spake for Christ.

Some translate this—"Note that man by an Epistle"—*i.e.*, "send his name to me in your next communication;" but this is not at all

epistle, note that man, and [z] have no company with him, that he may be ashamed.

15 [a] Yet count *him* not as an enemy, [b] but admonish *him* as a brother.

16 Now [c] the Lord of peace himself give you peace always by all means. The Lord *be* with you all.

z Matt. xviii. 17. 1 Cor. v. 9, 11. ver. 6.
a Lev. xix. 17. 1 Thess. v. 14.
b Tit. iii. 10.
c Ro. xv. 33. & xvi. 20. 1 Cor. xiv. 33. 2 Cor. xiii. 11. 1 Thess. v. 23.

---

16. "By all means" (ἐν παντὶ τρόπῳ). So ℵ, B., E., K., L., P., almost all Cursives, Syr.; but A., D., F., G., d, e, f, g, Vulg., read, "in every place" (τόπῳ).

likely to be right, for St. Paul is giving them directions how to deal with him at once on the spot.

"Have no company with him, that he may be ashamed." If the man has any true Christian feeling nothing is likely to do him more good than being shunned by his fellow members—nothing is more likely to bring him to a better mind than this informal excommunication.

15. "Yet count him not as an enemy, but admonish him as a brother." "Count him not," &c.: for, if so—if you shew by your bearing towards him that you consider him to be an enemy to Christ and the Church—you drive him away from the Gospel. The principle here inculcated is that recommended by the Lord in Matth. xviii. 15.

There were, of course, the overseers or elders, whose duty it was to admonish, but every man under the new covenant, just as every man under the old, was bound not to suffer sin upon his brother. (Levit. xix. 17.)

16. "Now the Lord of peace Himself give you peace always by all means." This is a special benediction of peace because the action of those busybodies, whom he felt it necessary to denounce, was least of all conducive to peace in the Church.

Mark the repetition for the sake of emphasis, "always"—"by all means."

"Always," for constantly occasions of discord were cropping up.

"By all means"—in every way. If there is to be genuine and continued peace, many things must help together—the grace of God—the striving together to be of one heart and mind—each one bearing and forbearing—each one doing his duty in his own particular calling.

17 [d]The salutation of Paul with mine own hand, which is the token in every epistle: so I write.

18 [e]The grace of our Lord Jesus Christ *be* with you all. Amen.

d 1 Cor. xvi. 21. Col. iv. 18.
e Rom. xvi. 24.

¶ The second *epistle* to the Thessalonians was written from Athens.

---

17. "The salutation of Paul with mine own hand." Here the Apostle takes the pen out of the hand of his secretary or amanuensis and subscribes with a hand well known to them,—

18. "The grace of our Lord Jesus be with you all." Not that this salutation was always the same to the letter. In the Epistle to the Colossians it was "grace be with you." In that to the Galatians it was "the grace of our Lord Jesus Christ be with your spirit." But it was a solemn invocation of grace which St. Paul always wrote with his own hand. With this invocation of grace he begins and with this he ends. For the one thing which he held that all sinners needed to make them holy and happy here and hereafter was Grace.

EXCURSUS

ON THE ANTICHRIST OR ANOMOS.

The first step in endeavouring to ascertain the meaning of St. Paul's words respecting the man of sin is to understand the bearing of the teachings of the two Epistles to the Thessalonians upon one another. There seems to be considerable misunderstanding upon this point.

The first Epistle undoubtedly teaches that the coming of the Lord was at hand when it was written. Thus in i. 9, 10, he writes in praise of the Thessalonians that they turned from idols to serve the living and true God and to wait for His "Son from Heaven." Again in chap. iv. 15 and 17, he speaks of himself as being amongst those who should be alive and remain when the Lord returned. This he says twice. And in v. 2, he speaks of the day of the Lord so coming as a thief in the night, and he praises them as if they were perfectly alive to this fact and so were "not in darkness that that day should overtake them as a thief."

Now when we come to the Second Epistle we find that without in the least degree withdrawing or modifying the truth of what he had written respecting the Day of the Lord being at hand, he endeavours to correct a wrong inference which he finds that they were drawing from what he had written to them. They were "shaken in mind" and "troubled" as if the Lord would come at once, and were so unhinged by the thought of His awful nearness that they neglected the duties of their daily life, and St. Paul strives to correct this by assuring them that two portentous signs must be fulfilled before He would come—there must be a widespread apostasy, and the "man of sin," the "Anomos," must be revealed.

With respect to this latter he implies that the spirit of it (1 John, iv. 3) was even then actively at work: "The mystery of iniquity doth already work;" and more than this, he tells them that it (or he) was prevented from breaking out by something which was *then* restraining or letting: so that so far from the Second Epistle postponing the Lord's Advent to some period far distant in the future, it teaches us that St. Paul himself discerned the signs of its being at hand, though not so immediately at hand that men should be upset in mind by the thought.

The Apostle, then, evidently expected that the coming of Christ would not be long delayed, and apparently he was mistaken, for 1800 years have passed and the Lord has not returned.

This is brought forward by Rationalistic critics as an argument against the inspiration of the Apostle, that on a fact of such importance he was mistaken. "How could he be inspired," it is asked, "if he could believe that an event would occur in his own lifetime, and in that of many of his Thessalonian converts, which has not yet taken place?

Now the answer to this is of the utmost importance. St. Paul believed that the second coming of Christ was soon to be expected, because Christ intended him so to believe. All the teaching of Christ is at one on this point, that from the time of His departure He might return at any moment, and He has left the time of His return absolutely uncertain in order that each successive generation of Christians might look for it and prepare to meet Him—not merely be prepared to be taken to Him by death—of this He says absolutely nothing, but to watch for Him as coming to them whilst they were living in the world.

The Lord sets forth this most explicitly in His words in Mark xiii. 32. "Of that day and that hour knoweth no man, no, not the angels which are in heaven, neither the Son, but the Father. Take ye heed, watch and pray: for ye know not when the time is. For the Son of man is as a man taking a far journey, who left his house, and gave authority to his servants, and to every man his work, and commanded the porter to watch. Watch ye therefore: for ye know not when the master of the house cometh, at even, or at midnight, or at the cock-crowing, or in the morning: lest coming suddenly he find you sleeping. And what I say unto you I say unto all, Watch."

Now all this St. Paul accepted to the letter, and so he lived in the faith of it as if it was really true. The Lord had given him authority and had assigned to him "his work," and in addition to the diligence with which he was to fulfil his work, the Lord commanded him, as He commanded all His servants, to watch and be ready to welcome Him, and this was what the Apostle was actually doing. If the Apostle had believed that the Lord would come late in the ages, as, for instance, at the time indicated by the cock-crowing, or in the morning, both which represent a season very distant from His Ascension, there would have been no need for him to watch, but if he believed that the Lord might return "in the evening," that is, very shortly after his departure, it was needful for him to watch. And so he did, for he said respecting the Second Advent, "we which are alive and remain." The Lord had laid it upon His people not only to believe, but to watch, not only to love, but to watch, not only to obey, but to watch—in fact, to be in that state of mind which is described in the parable of the Ten Virgins: and this state St. Paul was in by the operation of the Holy Spirit. The teaching, then, of the Second Epistle in no way undoes that of the first. It simply asserts that Christians must not only look for the Lord, but be on their guard against two dangers which will precede it.

St. Paul, then, if he looked for the Lord, must have been alive to the fact that two signs at least must precede it, and that the appearance of one of these signs must be delayed or hindered by what was then in operation—which he does not describe, in fact, he seems to be careful not to commit himself about it—but which he tells them that they knew, for he had himself taught them about it.

It is clear, then, that if St. Paul looked for the coming of Christ he must be expecting the development of that which must precede it, and he says that he does.

What is this hindering or restraining thing?

The Fathers almost universally understand it of the Roman Empire, and when that Empire would be destroyed they conceived that the hindrance to the development of the Anomos would be removed, and that he would immediately be revealed.

Now what was the hindering cause or principle in the Roman Empire, and when was it removed? This is important, because upon the answer to this depends whether the restraint exercised by the power was an arbitrary enactment, as if a certain dynasty continued in the world till another dynasty of much the same character as itself took its place, or whether the restraining power embodied a principle which, as it were naturally, restrained the outbreak or revelation of a contrary principle. No doubt the latter. If the man of sin was the Anomos, the lawless one, what must restrain him except "law," nomos? Now this was the spirit of the Roman Power. It was law—cruel, iron, inflexible law, but still Law so far good that the Apostle could speak of those who ministered it, even though they persecuted him and his fellow Christians, as "the minister of God to us for good." (Rom. xiii. 4.)

And the due consideration of this will serve to shew that the cessation of any Roman dynasty need not at all be the cessation of Roman rule, considered as a principle.

When was that which let, or hindered, or restrained, taken out of the way? If this restrainer be any dynastic succession of Roman governors, it must have been removed at one of two times. The Roman Empire in the East collapsed in 1453, and the Empire in the West nominally ceased under Romulus Augustulus in 476, and was, till it expired, in a state of extreme weakness, and was succeeded in the course of a century or two by such an empire as that of Charlemagne, which in its time was divided into the German and French kingdoms or empires. Now I have nothing to do with the history of these or any other divisions of the great Roman Empire except this, that these empires and kingdoms maintained Law. None of them for a moment attempted to act the part of an Anomos—least of all him whom the Protestant world has united in dignifying with this title. Granting fully that during this period, whilst the Roman Empire in Southern Europe was breaking up, and the great kingdoms of Northern Europe were consolidating themselves into what became in process of time the monarchy of France and the Empire of Germany—granting, I say, that during three centuries the Bishops of Rome gained temporal sovereignty over the middle of Italy, and established a system of ecclesiastical tyranny over the Western Church, this may have been, as doubtless it was, very bad: but to say that this Papal system was the fulfilment of the prophecy of the Apostle, that it was the revelation of the man of sin, who opposeth and exalteth himself above all that is called God or worshipped, and who is to be revealed immediately after the removal of the restraining power, *i.e.*, in A.D. 476, and is to be destroyed, not by a lingering atrophy, but quickly, as in a moment, by the brightness of the Lord's coming, seems to me an interpretation of a prophecy as opposite to the terms of the prophecy itself as any two things can be. But in addition to this, if we look for the fulfilment of this prophecy of the hindering power being removed and the Anomos revealed when the Western Empire came to an end, we must find some one who about that period performed such miracles that the true elect of God were on the point of being deceived by them; and that such was the power of these signs and wonders that for above a thousand years they have literally judged the world; those who accepted the ecclesiastical rule of the Bishop of Rome being universally those led away by deceivableness of unrighteousness—all of them ordained to perdition, not one of them receiving the love of the truth that they might be saved; every man who submitted to the Papal claims, doing so that he might be damned on account of his believing not the truth, but having pleasure in unrighteousness.

I assure the reader (indeed he may read and judge for himself) that I am not in the least degree exaggerating this. The Apostle describes one whom out of the whole body of sinful men he calls *the* man of sin—whom out of the whole body of lawless men he calls *the* lawless one. In this man all evil seems to converge. He opposeth and exalteth himself above all that is called God or worshipped. He assumes to be God. He deceives all the unrighteous. He attaches to himself all who deserve eternal damnation. He deludes all who have pleasure in unrighteousness. He comes at a particular time in the world's history, either in 475 or thereabouts, or in 1450. The latter is much too late in the ages, so we must take the former: but if so we can find nothing at all answering to the picture drawn by the Apostle. The spiritual or ecclesiastical pretensions of the Bishop of Rome had been growing for centuries before he acquired temporal power, and the acquisition of temporal power, which was only consolidated in the time of Innocent III. (1200) added no one feature of resemblance to the prophetical picture drawn by the Apostle.

But another most extraordinary fact remains to be stated. All Protestants hold that at the time of the Reformation God raised up Luther and other reformers to proclaim that the Bishop of Rome was Antichrist. Now the line taken by Luther in opposition to the Bishop of Rome was mainly this, that the Pope upheld a legal system. Instead of being the Anomos, he was the very incarnation and embodiment of law—law of course as non-justifying, but still of law. And so far as the reign of law was concerned—I mean its divine and sin-restraining nature—Luther before he died had to confess, and abundantly confess—confess with wailing—that under his own preaching, and that of those associated with him, crime and ungodliness of every kind had fearfully increased; the fervent and intense faith manifested at the first period of the so-called Reformation speedily grew cold, and has been growing colder and colder ever since, and now instead of faith in the Person and Work of Christ being characteristic of the Reformed bodies, it is absolutely the contrary. In bodies of Christians once Lutheran or Calvinistic there is the most extensive denial of the supernatural in any shape. Fewer and fewer believe in the Lord's Godhead. The very cathedrals in their hands, as at Geneva and Berne, are closed from Sunday to Sunday, and the Churches of the Roman obedience only are those in which you can hear "Thou art the King of Glory, O Christ, Thou art the everlasting Son of the Father."

Looking at the state of religion on the Continent at this moment nothing can be further from the fact that those who love not the truth are attracted to the Bishop of Rome, and those who love it and have pleasure in righteousness adhere to the bodies who protest against his claims.

But another significant fact also must be plainly stated. The obvious meaning of St. Paul's prophecy is that Antichrist is in the plentitude of his power when the Lord comes and consumes him with the breath of His mouth, but if we take the Papacy to be

Antichrist then we find that for several centuries his power has diminished and is still diminishing. Bunyan, in the seventeenth century, in his celebrated allegory represents him as decaying and becoming rapidly effete.

Now this decadence of Papal power has taken place, not by anything which can possibly be called the brightness of Christ's coming, but by the dissemination of what are called liberal opinions in religion and politics, and this is daily progressing. The ruling spirit or principle amongst the educated classes in France, Spain, and Italy is not Roman Catholicism, but Scepticism.

Since the time of the last Roman Emperor to the present time there has arisen nothing which corresponds to St. Paul's picture of the Antichrist, or Man of Sin, or Anomos. The papacy, no doubt, is, in the eyes of us of the Church of England, the embodiment or representation of certain very evil exaggerations or corruptions. It exaggerates the leadership accorded by Christ to St. Peter that he should be the first to open the kingdom to the Jews, and the first to open it to the Gentiles. It exaggerates it so that it virtually abolishes Episcopacy throughout that part of Christendom which is subject to the Roman Obedience. All healthy independence even of thought in the rest of the Episcopate, or Presbyterate, is crushed out, and there is but one Bishop.

Then there is the evil exaggeration of Mariolatry and saint worship. This is an exaggeration of the honour which God put upon the Holy Virgin when He chose her to be the instrument through which He brought about the Incarnation of His Son, and a natural exaggeration of the honour in which all right-minded Christians hold the memory of the martyrs and confessors of the Church.

Then the denial of the Cup to the laity, or rather to all except the celebrant, is a monstrous exaggeration of the reverence due to one of the consecrated elements, but was established in the Church centuries after the latest date which can be assigned to the removal of the restraining power. Now all these evil traditions are exaggerations of what was, or is, in its own nature, good—they are, or profess to be, not antagonistic to God, but the carrying out of His will. They all may be very bad, and the system which binds them upon so large a part of the Church tyrannical and cruel, but they are not the evil predicted in this prophecy of the Anomos, or anything like it. They are evil of a different kind; they are, so to speak, in a different sphere of evil. They may, as all evil may, work towards the Anomos, and prepare for him, but, to say that they are the characteristics of the Anomos is to say what is, on the face of it, contrary to the truth and reality of the prophecy.

And lastly, the Anomos, or Antichrist, is an infidel power. St. John describes him as denying the Incarnation. "Every spirit that confesseth not that Jesus Christ is come in the flesh is not of God, and this is that Spirit of Antichrist whereof ye have heard that it should come," &c. (1 John iv. 3.) And St. Paul's description, "Who opposeth and exalteth himself," &c., is that of a rampantly infidel power—indeed, seems incompatible with any belief in God whatsoever. Now the Papal dynasty, evil though it is, is neither Antichristian in the sense of denying the Godhead of Christ, nor Atheistic. The Pope is the principal administrator of a system which requires that it should be said daily in every Parish under his obedience, "I believe in one God the Father Almighty, Maker of heaven and earth, and of all things visible and invisible, and in one Lord Jesus Christ, the only begotten Son of God, begotten of His Father, before all worlds, ... Who for us men and for our Salvation came down from heaven," &c. And what is more, in the parishes not under his rule, words confessing, as these do, the Godhead of Christ, are not said daily, and not even weekly, for the bodies apart from Roman Catholicism in the greater part of Europe are most extensively permeated with Socinianism and the denial of the supernatural.

Nothing, then, can be clearer than this, that in the whole history of Christendom the breaking up of no dynasty has been followed by any such portentous form of evil as that prophesied of by St. Paul.

So that the revelation of the Anomos must be yet future. But how does this accord with the removal of the Roman restraining power? We answer, It has never been removed. It exists to this moment, parcelled out among the law-abiding kingdoms of Europe. Simultaneously with the breaking up of the effete Roman dynasty there appeared a monarchy, that of Clovis, which inherited the power of Rome over a large part of northern Europe. A century or two after there arose the Empire of Charlemagne. Then that was divided between the German and French monarchs, who, whatever they did, maintained law and upheld the worship of God, the worship which they thought most acceptable to Him. And that has continued to this day.

Supposing that the Roman empire, in its dissolution, was broken and parted into any number of kingdoms, say ten, these all inherited much, if not all, of its nomos, its law-power, and so inherited its power of restraining the Anomos.

Now, in order to make what I have said the clearer, let us remember that in the time of our fathers, *i.e.*, in the last decade of the last century, there was as near an approach to the state of things which we should suppose the man of sin will bring about in the world, as we can well conceive. The following is a description of what occurred in France at this period, from one who wrote in 1838. "In the capital of that powerful nation these things took place, as we all well know, within the last fifty years, an open apostasy from Christianity; not from Christianity only, but from every kind of worship which might retain any semblance or pretence of the great truths of religion. Atheism was absolutely professed; yet, in spite of this, it seems a contradiction in terms to say it, a certain sort of worship, and that, as the prophet (Daniel) expresses it, "a strange worship," was introduced. Observe what this was. They avowed on the one hand atheism. They prevailed upon an unhappy man, whom their proceedings had forced upon the Church as an Archbishop, to come before them in public, and proclaim that what he had hitherto taught was a fable. They wrote over the burial places that death was an eternal sleep. They closed the churches, they seized and desecrated the gold and silver plate belonging to them. They formed mock processions, clad in priestly garments, and singing profane hymns. They annulled the Divine ordinance of marriage, resolving it into a mere civil contract to be made and dissolved at pleasure. Having broken away from all restraint towards God and man, they gave a name to the reprobate State itself into which they had thrown themselves, and exalted their very negatives of religion, or rather, this real and living blasphemy, into a kind of god. They called it LIBERTY, and they literally worshipped it as a divinity. After abjuring our Lord and Saviour, and blasphemously declaring Him to be an impostor, they proceeded to decree, in the public assembly of the nation, the adoration of Liberty and Equality as divinities, and they appointed festivals besides in honour of Reason, the country, the constitution, and the Virtues. Further, they determined that tutelary gods, even dead men, may be canonized, consecrated, and worshipped; and they enrolled in the number of these some of the most notorious infidels and profligates of the last century. The remains of the two principal of these were brought in solemn procession into one of their churches, and placed upon the holy altar itself; incense was offered to them, and the assembled multitude bowed down in worship before one of them—before what remained on earth of an inveterate enemy of Christ."

Surely our fathers and grandfathers who saw this might say, This must be the end; no outbreak of irreligion or wickedness can come near to this; but they were mistaken, the end was not yet. An autocrat arose, who assumed the powers of the Cæsars, professed to restore the Roman Empire, called a son that was born unto him the king of Rome, and so on. We detest his memory, because he threatened our existence, but, nevertheless, he restored worship, he restored order, he re-established law, and so for a time restrained, or held back, the Anomos, the Antichrist.

The Antichrist prophesied of by Daniel, by the Lord, by St. Paul, by St. John, is yet to come, and he must be near. It is of infinite importance that we expect him from the quarter in which all prophecy points to his appearance, in the quarter of direct antagonism to God, direct denial of the person and work of Christ, absolute abolition of all restraint on the evil passions of men. That such a development of evil may come is surely possible. Much in the history of our own time should teach us that there are fires smouldering beneath, which, unless restrained, are ready to burst forth and destroy all in their way.

"Such meditations as these may be turned to good account. What a curb upon our self-willed, selfish hearts, to believe that a persecution is in store for the Church, whether or not it comes in our days! Surely, with this thought before us, we cannot bear to give ourselves up to thoughts of ease and comfort, of making money, settling well, and rising in the world. Surely, with this thought before us, we cannot but feel that we are, what all Christians really are, in the best estate (nay, rather, would wish to be, had they the will, if they be Christians in heart), *pilgrims*, watchers waiting for the morning, waiting for the light, eagerly straining our eyes for the first dawn of day, looking out for our Saviour's coming, His glorious Advent, when He will end the reign of sin and wickedness, accomplish the number of His Elect, and perfect those who at present struggle with infirmity, yet in their hearts love and obey Him.

"May He perform all this in His own good time, according to His infinite mercies! May He give us strength according to our day, and peace at the last." "Tracts for the Times, 83. Advent Sermons on Antichrist."

NOTE.

I have written the above quite conscious of the fact that almost all, if not all, the Divines of the Reformation period held the Bishop of Rome to be Antichrist. Taking into account their Theology, which in the best of them had a strong leaning towards Zwinglianism, and the line of politics into which they were forced, it was scarcely possible for them to do otherwise.

I shall take, as a fair example of their mode of treating this subject, Bishop Jewel's notes on the second chapter of the second epistle to the Thessalonians. It is not too much to say that history has entirely disproved his arguments.

He writes as any other man would who held the Roman system, not only to be the greatest evil of his time, but the greatest of all possible evils at any time. He had no idea that there could be such an outbreak of Atheism, dogmatic and persecuting, as broke out nearly one hundred years ago, and deluged Europe with blood.

He wrote under the conviction that Romanism would be an increasingly persecuting power, and it never entered into his mind that Romanists could be persecuted by Atheists. He believed that the Empire, *i.e.*, the Empire of Charles the Fifth, was coming to an end, and that it alone restrained the Pope from being the temporal as well as spiritual autocrat of all Europe, whereas he knew not, as we know now, that the Empire, in its two divisions of Germany and Austria, is stronger than ever, that Italy is united under one sovereign, who considers it treason to assert the right of the Pope to temporal sovereignty, and that the power of the Pope has been diminishing ever since his (Jewel's) time. He believed that the Spirit of the Lord's mouth, which was to destroy the Pope, was the proclamation of the Gospel, as held by Zwingle and Calvin, whereas, if he had lived in our time, he would have seen with dismay the continental Protestants preach a doctrine from which all reference to the Godhead and Atonement of Christ is excluded, indeed, in which, in an increasing number of pulpits, all that can be called supernatural in Christianity is denied.

I have also written the above with the full knowledge of what the late excellent Bishop Wordsworth has written in his learned commentary. It will be sufficient to say that he holds the views of the Divines of the sixteenth century in seemingly total unconsciousness that he himself was not living in the reign of Elizabeth, but that since her time there have been three centuries of European life—religious and political—which have rendered most of the views of the Reformation Period, respecting the Antichrist, simply impossible.

THE EPISTLES TO TIMOTHY.

INTRODUCTION.

TESTIMONY OF THE FATHERS.

IN ascertaining the genuineness of any Epistle which claims to be written by an Apostle, we have first of all to look to the testimony of the Church, which is the keeper and expounder of Holy Writ. If any Gospel or Epistle has from the first been quoted or appealed to as the writing of such a man as St. Paul, such a testimony must outweigh a thousand times over the conjectures or surmises of those who, living nearly 1,800 years later, appeal to certain features which they for the first time in the history of Christendom have discovered, as proving the writing in question to be a forgery.

Now this is the case with the Pastoral Epistles. They were accepted as genuine, and appealed to, in the same way as he appealed to the acknowledged books of Scripture, by a writer of the first century, Clemens Romanus.

Thus (ch. xxix), "Let us draw near to him with holiness of Spirit, *lifting up pure and undefiled hands* unto him." So 1 Tim. ii. 8, "lifting up holy hands without wrath and doubting;" also "ready to every good work," from Titus iii. 1. Again, ch. xxi., "without preferring one before another" (1 Tim. v. 21).

Again, Polycarp in the beginning of the second century, in his Epistle, ch. iv. "But the love of money is the root of all evil. Knowing, therefore, that we brought nothing into the world, so we can carry nothing out" (1 Tim. vi. 7, 10).

Tertullian, and Clement of Alexandria, flourishing at the end of the first century, quote these Epistles far more frequently than most modern writers do, the former about one hundred, the latter more than fifty times.

But the most striking testimony is that of Irenæus. He begins his great work, "Against Heresies," with a quotation from the first Epistle to Timothy, "Inasmuch as certain men have set the truth aside, and bring in lying words, and vain genealogies, which, as the Apostle says, minister questions rather than 'Godly edifying which is in faith,'" &c. But this is by no means all the testimony of Irenæus. It appears that Eusebius gives the full title of Irenæus's work as "Refutation and subversion of knowledge falsely so called,"[1] so that Irenæus incorporates a phrase or short sentence from 1 Timothy, vi. 20, into the title of his work.

Let the reader consider the significance of this. Here is a writer whose memory of Church matters (for he was a Christian by birth) extended to at the least A.D. 130, so that he could have conversed with men not very old who were contemporaries of St. Paul in his last years. Is it to be supposed that he could have accepted as St. Paul's writing a forgery of A.D. 110 or 120, or even later? He came from the East, and his birthplace was supposed to be Smyrna, or some neighbouring city. If then any one as early as even A.D. 100, had published a spurious Epistle as one written by such a man as St. Paul to such a man as Timothy, would he not have been cognizant of the fact—was there nobody to tell him that the Church was deceived in receiving certain letters as St. Paul's which never saw the light till perhaps half a century after St. Paul's death, so that he should be saved from the mistake of beginning his great work with a citation from an Epistle which a very little examination would show was not written by St. Paul? If there had been the smallest doubt about the matter of their Pauline origin, a man who devoted so much of his time to the history of contemporary religious thought, could not have been so deceived.

DATE OF WRITING.

It is difficult to understand how there can have been two opinions upon this matter. The history of the Acts closes with the account of St. Paul in Rome, dwelling "two whole years in his own hired house, and receiving all that came in unto him, preaching the Kingdom of God, and teaching those things which concern the Lord Jesus, with all confidence, no man forbidding him." Now it is impossible to suppose that the close of these two years

[1] Ἐλέγχου καὶ ἀνατροπῆς τῆς ψευδωνύμου γνώσεως. (Eus. v. 7.)

was the close of St. Paul's life by martyrdom. All history, both that of the New Testament, and that of the earliest Church historians is against it. Before the conclusion of this imprisonment and from his place of detention, St. Paul writes two letters, one to the Philippian Church, in which he expresses his confidence that "he shall abide and continue with them all" (i. 25, 26), and that he will come to them shortly (ii. 24); the other to Philemon, in which he asks him to prepare him a lodging (22). That his expectation was fulfilled, the three Pastoral letters are a proof, and this whether they be genuine or whether they be forged. If they be genuine, then there is an end of the matter, for one of them was written on the eve of his martyrdom, at the conclusion of a second imprisonment, and the other (1st Epistle) contains certain references which show that he was taking journeys for which no ingenuity can make room (as regards time) in the period covered by the narrative of the Acts. If, on the contrary, they are forgeries, then the forger must have believed that St. Paul's life did not end with his first imprisonment, that he must have been imprisoned twice, and this because he makes St. Paul write a letter in which he daily expected martyrdom, a letter in the greatest contrast with the letters written during his first imprisonment, when he daily expected deliverance. Now why does the supposed forger assume that St. Paul was liberated after the detention of two years in his hired house? Because it was a well-known fact, upon which there could be no difference of opinion in the first century, for St. Paul's life was not that of a man who lived in a corner. He was the best known man, the best loved man, and the most hated man of his day.

The fact, then, that the forger placed his two forgeries after the first imprisonment is, because he had no other time in which to put them, and he could not have assigned them to the period after this first imprisonment, had not the whole Christian world known that it existed.

His liberation from his first imprisonment is referred to by Clement of Rome, in the words: "Owing to envy, Paul, who obtained the reward of patient endurance, after being seven times thrown into captivity (2 Cor. xii. 23, 'in prisons more frequent') compelled to flee, and stoned. After preaching both in the East and West, he gained the illustrious reputation due to his faith, having taught righteousness to the whole world, and come to the extreme limit of the West, and suffered martyrdom under the prefects" (Tigellinus and Sabinus, as is generally supposed, in the last year of the Emperor Nero).

Upon this I will only remark that "the extreme limit of the West" cannot mean Rome, and St. Paul, till the termination of his first imprisonment, was never further west than Rome.

It is remarkable that the journey of St. Paul to Spain, after, of course, his first imprisonment, seems to be mentioned in the Muratorian fragment, "Sed et profectionem Pauli ab urbe [Rome] ad Spaniam proficiscentis."

Eusebius also mentions his liberation after his first imprisonment. "Luke, that wrote the Acts of the Apostles, after showing that Paul passed two whole years at Rome as a prisoner at large, and that he preached the Gospel without restraint, brings his history to a close. After pleading his cause, he is said to have been sent again upon the ministry of preaching, and after a second visit to the city that he finished his life with martyrdom."

OBJECTIONS MADE AGAINST THE GENUINENESS OF THESE EPISTLES.

We now come to the objections which have been raised by German critics, and partially allowed by some English ones to the genuineness of these Epistles.

These have been brought by Dean Alford in his "Prolegomena on the Pastoral Epistles," under three heads.

1. The historical difficulty of finding a place for the writing of the three Epistles during the lifetime of St. Paul.

2. The apparent contact with various matters and persons who (or which) belong to a later age than that of the Apostle, and—

3. The peculiarity of expressions and modes of thought, both of which diverge from those of St. Paul's recognized Epistles.

(1). With respect to the first, the difficulty of finding a place for the writing of these letters in the lifetime of the Apostle. This assumes the fact (contrary to all history) that St. Paul's life ended with his first imprisonment. One writer (in Smith's "Dictionary of the Bible") writes, "Of these conjectures, A and B (the one of which makes the journey from Ephesus to Macedonia in the two years' work at Ephesus, the other identifies it with the journey of Acts xx. 1), have the merit of bringing the Epistle within the limit of the authentic records of St. Paul's life." But why merit? If St. Paul lived and worked and suffered for some years after his first imprisonment, these Epistles have the greater merit of giving us some small accounts of his later history; how he served his Master faithfully to the very last, how he served the Churches faithfully by making provision for their order after his final departure. If, however, he was martyred at the close of his first imprisonment, then the fact must have been known all over Christendom, and we have the enormous difficulty of supposing that the forgers of these Epistles added several years to the Apostle's life, which the whole Church must have known to have never existed. The difficulty, then, of finding a place for these Epistles during the period embraced by the Acts is a difficulty which in the nature of things can have no existence except in the imagination of modern critics.

(2). The second reason alleged for the forging of these Epistles at a much later date than the time of the Apostle, is the apparent contact with various matters and persons who belong to a later age than that of the Apostle.

The first of these matters is that the Gnosticism opposed in these Epistles is of a much later development than that of St. Paul's time. Now it would be a sufficient answer to this, that we are in absolute ignorance of the early history of Gnosticism. We know from Irenæus the names of the authors of some of the Gnostic sects, and their tenets, but nothing more. We are totally ignorant of its origin and early development. For instance, we are told that the Essenes adopted certain tenets of angelology. From whom did they get these? certainly not from Judaism proper. Did they adopt them from Babylonian mythology, or from the ancient Persian speculations? Undoubtedly, we should say, from the latter, but whether these were the outcome of their sojourn in Babylon, or whether the Zoroastrian speculations invaded the Eastern mind and so got to the Essenes and Simon Magus we know not.

However, we will give all the references to false teaching of all sorts which we find in these Epistles, and then put it to the reader whether they belong to an early or to a late development of Gnosticism.

1 Tim. i. 3-4. "Charge some that they teach no other doctrine, neither give heed to fables and endless genealogies which minister questions," &c.

I. 7. "Desiring to be teachers of the law, understanding neither," &c.

I. 20. "Of whom is Hymenæus and Alexander, whom I have delivered unto Satan," &c.

IV. 1, 3, 4. "Seducing spirits and doctrines of devils. Speaking lies in hypocrisy . . . forbidding to marry, and commanding to abstain from meats. . . . Every creature of God is good, and nothing to be refused," &c.

7. "Profane and old wives' fables."

8. "Bodily exercise (or training) profiteth (a) little, but godliness," &c.

VI. 5. "Perverse disputings of men of corrupt minds and destitute of the truth, supposing that gain is godliness."

20. "Avoiding profane and vain babblings, and oppositions of science (gnosis or knowledge) falsely so called."

2 Tim. i. 15. "All they which are in Asia are turned away from me, of whom are Phygellus and Hermogenes."

II. 14. "That they strive not about words to no profit, but to the subverting of the hearers."

16. "Shun profane and vain babblings, for they will increase to more ungodliness, and their word will eat as doth a canker, of whom is Hymenæus and Philetus, who concerning the truth have erred, saying that the Resurrection is past already," &c.

23. "Foolish and unlearned questions avoid, knowing that they do gender strifes."

III. 6. "Of this sort are they which creep into houses, and lead captive silly women laden with sins . . . ever learning and never able . . . Now as Jannes and Jambres withstood Moses, so do these also resist the truth. . . . But they shall proceed no further."

IV. 3. "The time will come when they will not endure sound doctrine; but after their own lusts . . . shall be turned unto fables."

Titus i. 10. "Many unruly and vain talkers and deceivers, specially they of the circumcision . . . who subvert whole houses," &c.

14. "Not giving heed to Jewish fables and commandments of men that turn from the truth."

III. 9. "But avoid foolish questions, and genealogies and contentions and strivings about the law, for they are unprofitable and vain."

These are all the references to false teachers and their teaching. Now let the reader observe that the greater part of these false teachings are Jewish and not Gnostical. The Jews had fables in abundance, they had also genealogies which they mysticized and perverted to the furtherance of their superstitions; but it is impossible to suppose, if Gnosticism was either fully developed, or on the way of being so (as in the beginning of the second century) that the Apostle, or supposed Apostle, would have principally warned the Church against *Jewish* errors. Jewish errors, however noxious, must contain some substratum of truth respecting the unity of God, respecting the creation of the world, respecting His sending Moses and the prophets, and so on. Whereas Gnosticism, long before its full development, denied the God of Moses and the prophets to be the true God, and placed a number of successive intermediate beings between God and man.

Again, the only absolutely certain reference to Gnosticism is the one place where it is expressly mentioned as Gnosis, "science (or gnosis) falsely so called." The references to genealogies in 1 Tim. i. 3-4, and Tit. iii. 9, cannot, I am persuaded, refer to successions of æons, for St. Paul, much less a person who forged his name, and who wrote to oppose developed Gnosticism, would never speak of these blasphemies which ousted the Creator from His creative glory and made Christ a being with many æons intervening between Him and God, in so mild and feeble a way.

Now let any of my readers who can get access to a copy of Irenæus peruse his first and second books, and read the strange tissue of intellectual folly and blasphemy, totally inconsistent with any form of Judaism, as well as any form of Christianity, and then say whether any forger, desiring to use St. Paul's name and authority to oppose such things, would content himself with the very mild terms in which the Apostle is supposed to denounce it. But it is said that the later Judaizers became more and more infected with Gnosticism. It may have been so, but surely one desirous of opposing growing Gnosticism would not look upon it as less dangerous than Judaism, and yet almost all these cautions against false doctrine are directed rather against Judaizing than Gnosticism.

Lastly it will be observed that the writer of these Epistles does not scruple to name the leading false teachers, Phygellus and Hermogenes, Hymenæus and Philetus. Now supposing that he had lived at the end of the century, would he have singled out these comparatively obscure and forgotten persons? would he not, for instance, have named Cerinthus, who was certainly the leader of Gnosticism at the close of the first century?

I assert, then, from the passages cited above that the principal ground of fear in the eyes of the Apostle or the forger was Judaism. It may have begun to be mixed up with or allied with Gnosticism, but it was the Judaism of Paul's declining years, not the Gnosticism of fifty or sixty years afterwards.

Then in the next place the Church regimen of these Epistles is said to be that of a later date than that of the end of St. Paul's career. We assert, on the contrary, that so far as the local Church government of Ephesus, or the various congregations in it were concerned, the regimen is that of Acts xx., bishops or overseers and elders being as yet identical in name: and that of Phil. i. 1, where bishops (or elders) and deacons constitute the Church staff of officers, the only difference being that St. Paul in this Epistle delegates to Timothy that Apostolic supervision which he himself exercised in person in his interview with the Ephesian elders (or bishops or overseers, ἐπίσκοποι, of verse 28), as narrated in Acts xx.

3. Then in the last place the diction of these Epistles is said not to be that of St. Paul, which means that he uses certain words and phrases in these Epistles which he does not use in other letters which he wrote.

Now, if the reader will calmly consider this, he will acknowledge it to be one of the most irrefragable proofs of the genuineness of these Epistles; for if a forger had set before his mind the necessity of combating certain errors, and using the name of St. Paul, he would have taken care that every word which he used in the Pseudo-Pauline documents should be Pauline—that is, used by the Apostle elsewhere. I believe that would be his first consideration. If, then, on examining these Epistles, we found no words, or very few words, which St. Paul had not used in the Epistles commonly ascribed to him, we should account it a very suspicious circumstance indeed. For the occasion of the writing of these letters is different from that of all others of the Apostle's: for in all other Epistles he writes to the Churches themselves—that is, to bodies of men—and in not one of them does he say one word about their government, whereas in these three he writes to pastors respecting the government of the Churches he had committed to them.

Now, if we look at the words used in these Epistles, and not in others, we shall find that a considerable number of them refer to the particular phases of error he is combating: thus, fables (μύθοι); genealogies (γενεαλογίαι); old wives' (γραώδεις); wholesome as regards doctrine or teaching (ὑγιής). The longer he lived the more he saw the connection between sound doctrine and a healthy religious mind. Thus also vain jangling (ματαιολογία), so also κενοφωνίαι, and ψευδωνύμος. Take the last—he constantly uses the word γνῶσις, but he has never had occasion to speak of that which beyond all else claimed to be gnosis, and was absolutely false, so he uses for the first time ψευδωνύμος in connection with it.

And take another illustration. In his Epistle to the Galatians he had to oppose the Judaizers, but on quite different grounds to those which he takes in the Pastoral Epistles. The Galatians were led away by Judaizers demanding that the converts should be circumcised in order to be justified, and so he mentions no "old wives' fables," but sternly tells them that if they submit to the law for justification, they fall from Christ. But in these Epistles that phase of error seems to have passed away, and he has to warn them about myths, genealogies, perverse disputings, profane and vain babblings, and such things.

There is, however, one phrase occurring several times in these Epistles which requires notice. In no other Epistles have we the "faithful sayings." "This is a faithful saying, and worthy of all acceptation, that Christ Jesus came into the world to save sinners" (1 Tim. i. 15). "This is a faithful saying" (rendered in the authorized "true") (1 Tim. iii. 1). "This is a faithful saying, and worthy of all acceptation" (iv. 9). "It is a faithful saying" (2 Tim. ii. 11). How is it that St. Paul quotes four of these faithful words in his later Epistles and not elsewhere? Evidently because in his later years a number of sayings or short sentences had become proverbial, and were in everyone's mouth: and so St. Paul appealed to three or four of these in support of what he was writing. It is simply an interesting circumstance, but critics must be very hard up for arguments to use it as a reason for rejecting these Epistles.

In considering the authenticity of these Epistles (or rather the two to Timothy) I have assumed that they cannot have been written seven or eight years apart from one another as they must have been if one had been written before the first imprisonment and the other after. "On every account they must stand or fall together. Their style and diction, the motives which they furnish, the state of the Church and of heresy which they describe, are the same in all three, and to one and the same period must we assign them." (Alford.)

There is another argument which to me is overwhelming. These Epistles are the only writings in the New Testament in which we have any directions respecting ministerial life and conduct. Is it possible to imagine that the God of truth would permit these precepts to be given to the Church through the intervention of an untruthful man, which the writer must have been, if he commended his works to the Church under a false title?

HISTORY OF TIMOTHY.

The first notice of this companion of St. Paul in the Scriptures is in Acts xvi. 1. "Then came he to Derbe and Lystra; and behold, a certain disciple was there named Timotheus, the son of a certain woman who was a Jewess, and believed; but his father was a Greek. Which was well reported of by the brethren that were at Lystra and Iconium. Him would Paul have to go forth with him, and took and circumcised him because of the Jews which were in those quarters, for they knew all that his father was a Greek" (Acts xvi. 1, 2).

Next we find that he was with the Apostle in Macedonia, for he was left at Berea by Paul when he went to Athens. He joined St. Paul at Athens, and was sent by him on a special message to ascertain the state of the Thessalonian Church (1 Thess. iii. 2); after this he rejoined St. Paul in Corinth (Acts xviii. 5).

Then he was sent by the Apostle from Ephesus along with Erastus to Macedonia (xix. 22.) Then he accompanied Paul as far as Troas, or rather reached the city before him, and tarried there for him (xx. 4, 5). This is the last notice of him in the Acts, so that it is not probable that he accompanied St. Paul to Jerusalem, or was for any length of time with him in Cæsarea, and certainly not on his voyage to Rome. During the Apostle's detention in Rome he rejoined him there, and was present with him when he wrote the Epistles to the Philippians and Colossians. In the former of these

Paul expresses his trust that he will be able to send him to them (Phil. ii. 19).

In the first Epistle to Timothy we find that he was again travelling in the company of the Apostle, who left him at Ephesus when he was journeying to Macedonia (1 Tim. i. 3); and in the second, written from prison in Rome, the Apostle bids him use all diligence that he may come to him, for he had scarcely a friend left to comfort him (2 Tim. iv. 9, 10).

With respect to his Christian character it must have been very lovely and very holy, for of all St. Paul's companions and fellow-helpers he seems to have been not only the best beloved, but the most trusted by him. Thus he writes to the Philippians: "I have no man likeminded who will naturally care for your state. For all seek their own, not the things which are Jesus Christ's. But ye know the proof of him that as a son with the father he hath served with me in the Gospel" (Phil. ii. 20). And he had written in the same spirit respecting him long before (1 Cor. iv. 17).

Some have surmised from the repeated charges to be strong, to be faithful, to fight bravely, and to do his duty, that he was weak, and inclined too much to give way to opposition, and so on, but in reading these we must remember that the writer had an extraordinary high standard of faith and love and zeal, and that it is certain that he would write in the same style to any bishop or parish priest now living in England; and we must also remember that the charges and exhortations and warnings of these Pastoral Epistles were not written for the sake of Timothy alone, but for all ministers of Christ, from his time to the present; so that, if we would be good ministers of Christ, we must "put the brethren in mind of these things"—we must expect "to suffer reproach, because we trust in the living God," we must be "examples to the believers in word, in conversation," &c. We must "neglect not the gift that is in us," but stir it up by prayer and reading of the word. We must "meditate upon these things, and give ourselves wholly to them." We must "take heed to ourselves and to the doctrine." We must "do nothing by partiality;" we must "keep ourselves pure," we must "fight the good fight of faith." We must be very particular in warning those who are earnest in making money, as well as those who have money, of the danger of riches. We must "stir up the gift of God received at our Ordination," we must "hold fast the form of sound words," we must be "strong in the grace that is in Christ

Jesus." We must "endure hardness," we must "study to show ourselves approved unto God." We must "follow after righteousness, faith, charity, peace." We must "preach the word, and be instant in season and out of season."

So that we should study these Epistles well—we should read them very frequently, and remember that the words of exhortation with which they abound belong to the lowest grades of the ministry as well as to the highest.

INTRODUCTION TO FIRST EPISTLE TO TIMOTHY.

Little need be added respecting the particular features of these two Epistles respectively.

The first begins with the Apostle addressing Timothy as his own son in the faith. It proceeds to bid him oppose certain false teachers, whose doctrine was corrupted Judaism. It cites the faithful saying that "Christ Jesus came into the world to save sinners," and names two heretics whom he had excommunicated.

In the next chapter he proceeds to speak about public prayers, and that women should not be allowed to teach or speak in the Church assembly.

Then in the third chapter he lays down the moral qualifications to be required in candidates for the episcopate or eldership, for the diaconate, and for the order of deaconesses.

Then he sets forth the mystery of Godliness.

Then he warns against heresies which would crop up in the last times, and after some words of precept and warning addressed to Timothy himself, he enters upon the matter of the distribution of the alms of the Church to the widows.

Then he speaks of the elders—very solemnly warns Timothy against partiality in dealing with those he was called upon to judge, and warns him against hastily admitting men into the ministry.

Then he speaks about the duties of slaves, and the iniquity of those false teachers who (apparently), under the pretext of Christian liberty, would encourage them in disobedience; and the few remaining verses are occupied with the danger of desiring riches, and the Epistle seems to end with a sublime doxology, but he appends a sort of postscript, again speaking of the danger of riches, and again exhorting Timothy to keep diligently the doctrine committed to him, and avoid science, or rather gnosis, falsely so called.

There is but one historical allusion in the Epistle, in i. 3, where the Apostle reminds him how he besought him to abide still in Ephesus, when he (the Apostle) went into Macedonia. But this is important as another reason, and indeed a chief one, for fixing the date after the first imprisonment, for in the Acts of the Apostles St. Paul is said to have been twice at Ephesus. On the first occasion he stayed but a short time, leaving Aquila and Priscilla there, and then departed not to Macedonia, but to Jerusalem (Acts xviii. 19-22). On the second occasion he stayed in Ephesus above two years, but determined to pass through Macedonia and Achaia on his way to Jerusalem, "he sent into Macedonia two of them that ministered unto him, Timotheus and Erastus, but he himself stayed in Asia for a season" (Acts xix. 22), so that he could not have left Timothy at Ephesus on either occasion.

INTRODUCTION TO SECOND EPISTLE.

The second Epistle to Timothy was written from Rome shortly before the martyrdom of the Apostle. It was written chiefly to urge Timothy to come to him, all his other companions in the service of Christ (except Luke) being away. One, Demas, had deserted him, others, as Tychicus, he had sent away. But though apparently sent for the purpose of urging Timothy to come to him quickly, it contains the most precious exhortation to him, and through him to all ministers, "to make full proof of their ministry," and this it does in the words of a dying man, who was "ready to be offered and the time of his departure at hand." Whatever special onslaughts of the evil one were yet in store for him, we have his expression of faith that God would carry him triumphantly through all: "The Lord shall deliver me from every evil work, and will preserve me unto His heavenly kingdom."

THE FIRST EPISTLE TO TIMOTHY.

CHAP. I.

PAUL, an apostle of Jesus Christ [a] by the commandment [b] of God our Saviour, and Lord Jesus Christ, [c] *which is* our hope;

a Acts ix. 15. Gal. i. 1, 11.
b ch. ii. 3. & iv. 10. Tit. i. 3. & ii. 10. & iii. 4. Jude 25.
c Col. i. 27.

---

1. "Of Jesus Christ." So A., K., L., most Cursives, Vulg. (Amiat.), Syr., Arm., Æth.; but ℵ, D., F., G., P., d, f, g, Cop., read, "Christ Jesus."

1. "Lord Jesus Christ." "Jesus Christ," ℵ, K., L., most Cursives, Copt., Arm., Æth.; but A., D., F., G., P., some Cursives, d, f, g, Vulg. (Amiat.), read, "Christ Jesus;" also A., D., F., G., P., d, f, g, Vulg., Goth., Syr., omit "Lord."

1. "Paul, an apostle of Jesus Christ, by the commandment of God our Saviour," &c. Though this is a friendly letter, almost we might say a private one, primarily intended for the instruction not of a Church but of an individual, yet it begins with the assertion of St. Paul's apostleship—not that Timothy could have any doubt whatsoever about it, as the Galatian Churches had, but that he might consider the commands in it, not as coming from a dear friend, a father in Christ, his teacher in the Lord, but as from Christ Himself, Whose Apostle Paul was, and to the Apostles Christ said, "As my Father sent me, so send I you."

"By the commandment of God our Saviour." When was this commandment given? It might have been in the Divine counsels, as the Lord says of the chosen, "Thine they were and thou gavest them me." It might have been at his conversion (Gal. i. 15), or at his ordination, when the Holy Ghost said, "Separate me Barnabas and Saul for the work whereunto I have called them" (Acts xiii. 2).

"God our Saviour." This is God the Father. He is the Saviour, because all the work of His Son for sinners was ordered

d Acts xvi. 1. 1 Cor. iv. 17. Phil. ii. 19. 1 Thess. iii. 2. e Tit. i. 4. f Gal. i. 3. 2 Tim. i. 2. 1 Pet. i. 2.

2 Unto [d] Timothy, [e] *my* own son in the faith: [f] Grace, mercy, *and* peace, from God our Father and Jesus Christ our Lord.

---

by Him. In the Pastoral Epistles alone this title is given to the Father; elsewhere (as in Luke ii. 11; John iv. 42; Acts v. 31, &c.), it is usually applied to Jesus Christ. This is one of the most irrefragable proofs of the Godhead of Jesus, that a name which Jehovah claims as His only (Isaiah xliii. 11) should be applied to His Incarnate Son.

"And Jesus Christ, which is our hope." Properly "Jesus Christ our hope." This is a title claimed by the One God. Thus Jer. xiv. 8, "O the hope of Israel;" l. 7, "Even the Lord the hope of their fathers;" and yet Christ is "in us the hope of glory" (Col. i. 27). He is our Hope, not only because by His work and merits all that is in the way of our salvation is removed, but because through His Resurrection we look for the Resurrection, when our vile bodies shall be raised in the likeness of His glorious Body.

2. "Unto Timothy, my own son in the faith: Grace, mercy, and peace." "My own son in the faith." St. Paul writes to the Corinthians, a very mixed Church, with the words, "as my beloved sons I warn you," and to the Galatians, another Church which was giving him much trouble, "My little children, of whom I travail in birth again till Christ be formed in you" (Gal. iv. 19). He held, then, that all whom he had converted to Christ were his spiritual children, but Timothy was peculiarly his, always loving, always obedient, always attentive. As such he distinguishes him as "his own," *i.e.* very, true, proper son, unique amongst many sons: "in the faith," not because they had a common element of faith in their souls, but because the Apostle, through God's grace, engendered in Timothy the same faith which he himself had in Christ Incarnate, Crucified, Risen, and Ascended, so that as both were in the one Body and in the one Spirit, they were also in the one Lord and in the one faith, partaking of the One Baptism.

"Grace, mercy, and peace." In all other Epistles the opening salutation is "grace and peace," omitting mercy. In the opening of the Pastoral Epistles mercy is added between grace and peace. Why this most significant addition? Is it because of all Christian people Christ's ministers most need mercy, inasmuch as they

3 As I besought thee to abide still at Ephesus, [g] when I went into Macedonia, that thou mightest charge some [h] that they teach no other doctrine,

[g] Acts xx. 1, 3. Phil. ii. 24.
[h] Gal. i. 6, 7. ch. vi. 3, 10.

---

represent Christ, and, humanly speaking, their deficiencies, the deficiencies of the best, in representing such an One as Christ, must be very great? We know not. Only this place in its invocation of mercy reads a very strong lesson to many professors of religion in these latter days (Plymouth Brethren, Plymouth Sisters). We have those amongst us who openly and dogmatically assert that they have no need of mercy—they are, as they say, "saved," they *may* have once needed it, but now, as they say, they need it no longer; it would be an insult to God's goodness in having saved them to ask mercy at His hands. But it is extremely unlikely that, notwithstanding all this self-confidence, they are in a higher position before God than this "own son" of the great Apostle, and yet the Apostle invokes mercy from God and Christ upon Timothy. It seems wonderful that we should have to expose so impudent an assumption.

3. "As I besought thee to abide still at Ephesus, when I went into Macedonia." Does St. Paul here allude to some journey to Macedonia from Ephesus previous to his first imprisonment, or does he refer to some journey after his return from his first imprisonment? No doubt the latter. Only three journeys of St. Paul to Macedonia are recorded in the Acts, in none of which does he leave Timothy in Ephesus. In his first journey (Acts xvii. 14, xviii. 5) he took Timothy with him. Before his second journey he had sent Timothy into that country (Acts xix. 22), and he rejoined Timothy in Macedonia (2 Cor. i. 1). In his third journey he took Timothy with him, and with him he sailed beyond Ephesus on his way to Jerusalem (Acts xx. 4). Besides, it was very unlikely that St. Paul, in the full vigour of life and work, as he then was, should commit a newly planted Church in so important a place as Ephesus to a subordinate. Such action on his part was far more likely when he had become "Paul the aged," and the Ephesian Church only required to be reminded of his instructions, which Timothy was above all men able to do (1 Cor. iv. 17).

"That thou mightest charge some that they teach no other doctrine."

l ch. iv. 7. & vi. 4, 20. 2 Tim. ii. 14, 16, 23. Tit. i. 14. & iii. 9.
k ch. vi 4.

4 [l] Neither give heed to fables and endless genealogies, [k] which minister questions, rather than godly edifying which is in faith: *so do.*

---

4. "Godly edifying." So D., d, f, g, Vulg.; but א, A., F., G., K., L., P., read, "economy of God" or "administration of God."

4. "Neither give heed to fables and endless genealogies, which minister questions," &c. "Charge," *i.e.*, "command." Here is the Apostolical authority. For who else could command the teacher in a large city and district to teach nothing else but what he had taught them? By thus charging them, he showed that he considered that there was no authority in the presbyters gathered together in a synod, much less in each separate congregation, to set at naught what he laid down.

"Fables and endless genealogies." These fables were most probably Jewish fables, of which all Rabbinical writings are full. There is more doubt respecting the "endless genealogies." Some suppose that they are Gnostical speculations of successions of æons; but this is very unlikely, for the æons, though many, could scarcely be described as endless. A parallel passage in the Epistle to Titus would lead us to believe that these teachings were Jewish, "not giving heed to Jewish fables and commandments of men that turn from the truth." A passage also in Ignatius' Epistle to the Magnesians would lead us to the same conclusion: "Be not deceived with strange doctrines nor with old fables, which are unprofitable. For if we still live according to the Jewish law, we acknowledge that we have not received grace." (Epistle to Magnesians, ch. viii.) Philo, whose writings were well known to the Jews long before this, took the genealogies of the Old Testament in a mystical sense, and the Apostle in all probability refers to some such absurd opinions.

This place has been used by those who wish to get rid of the authenticity of this Epistle, to prove that it was not written till the middle of the next century, as the "endless genealogies" refers to a form of Gnosticism more developed than any in St. Paul's time; but if the reader will look to my remarks on the heresy of the Colossian Church in the introduction to that Epistle, he will see that the root of all Gnostical speculation respecting successions of æons is to be found in a book far older than the New Testament—in the

5 Now [l] the end of the commandment is charity [m] out of a
pure heart, and *of* a good .conscience, and *of*
faith unfeigned:
6 From which some ‖ having swerved have
turned aside unto [n] vain jangling;
7 Desiring to be teachers of the law; [o] under-
standing neither what they say, nor whereof they
affirm.

l Rom. xiii. 8, 10. Gal. v. 14.
m 2 Tim. ii. 22.
‖ Or, *not aiming at.*
n ch. vi. 4, 20.
o ch. vi. 4.

Zend Avesta. If the reader will also look to the accounts of Gnostical heresies in the early books of Irenæus, he will see that the Apostle would never designate such anti-Christian and blasphemous systems by such a mild term as "endless geneaolgies, which minister questions."

"Which minister questions rather than godly edifying, which is in faith." "Questions," that is, controversies, or disputes upon nnprofitable matters.

"Godly edifying." Instead of edifying, most Uncials, and almost all Cursives, read "æconòmy," or "dispensation"—the dispensation of God, which is by faith rather than by questionings and disputings.

5. "Now the end of the commandment is charity out of a pure heart," &c. The commandment, *i.e.*, the will of God as revealed in the Gospel, for our practical guidance, is charity or love. Thus he elsewhere says: "All the law is fulfilled in one word, even in this, thou shalt love thy neighbour as thyself" (Gal. v. 14).

"Out of a pure heart," &c. This distinguishes the love of the Gospel from mere friendship, or from unholy animal passion. It is out of a pure heart, a heart cleansed by God's Spirit, so that we may love God—a pure conscience, a conscience void of offence, a conscience which judges and pronounces according to right—faith unfeigned, a sincere belief in the Person and Work of the Son of God.

6. "From which some having swerved, have turned aside," &c.

7. "Desiring to be teachers of the law . . . whereof they affirm." "Having swerved." Having missed the mark of true teaching, which must always be practical, not employing itself with aimless and useless trifles.

"Have turned aside unto vain jangling." Such vain talking describes the miserable disputations into which the Jews had fallen

p Rom. vii. 12. 8 But we know that [p] the law *is* good, if a man use it lawfully;

q Gal. iii. 19. & v. 23. 9 [q] Knowing this, that the law is not made for

---

respecting the law—such as, which of any two commandments was the greater, and not unfrequently so handling it as to relieve men of its obligations, as in their treatment of the fifth commandment, denounced by our Lord in Matth. xv. 4, 5, 6.

It seems to me abundantly clear from these verses that the "endless genealogies" were not gnostical speculations which degraded the Son of God into an æon of some later emanation, but the perversions of Judaism with which the Apostle had all his life to contend.

"Understanding neither what they say, nor whereof they affirm." They talked at random, and had no firm hold of the principles embodied in the law; they clung to its letter, which seemed to afford them an easy righteousness in which they could boast, rather than to its spirit, which would have brought them in guilty before God.

8, 9. "But we know that the law is good if a man use it lawfully. Knowing this, that the law," &c. When does a man use the law unlawfully? when he uses it as the means of justification, which it is not because it is a mere command without carrying with it the power to fulfil the command. He also uses it unlawfully when either in his teaching or in the regulation of his own spirit he confines himself to its letter. A man, *i.e.*, a teacher or a layman uses it lawfully, when he regards it in its spiritual aspect, as the Lord has taught him to do in the sermon on the Mount. Then the law is good, as elsewhere (in Rom. vii. 12, 14), "Wherefore the law is holy, and the commandment holy, and just, and good." Also, "we know that the law is spiritual."

9. "Knowing this, that the law is not made for a righteous man," &c. The law, the Decalogue, was given to the children of Israel, when, immediately after their deliverance from Egypt, they were in a very low state both of Divine knowledge and of morality. With the exception of the last commandment it is all directed against gross sins, murder, adultery, theft. Now, so far from the righteous man needing the seventh commandment, he is in agony if an unclean thought has been allowed in his mind a moment.

a righteous man, but for the lawless and disobedient, for the ungodly and for sinners, for unholy and profane, for murderers of fathers and murderers of mothers, for man-slayers,

10 For whoremongers, for them that defile themselves

Still, notwithstanding this, the outward literal law is the foundation of the spiritual. It is needful that we should understand that murder and adultery are contrary to the will of God, if we would realize the sin of the murderous or adulterous thought.

"For the lawless." Not those who have grown up under no law, but those who have cast aside the restraints of law.

"And disobedient." Those who are not under any control, human or Divine.

"For the ungodly and for sinners." This pair of evils seem to denote opposition to God, of Whose will the law is the expression. "Ungodly" signifies impious, irreverent, having no respect for unseen and eternal things. "Sinners" in connection with this seems to indicate sinners against God.

"For unholy and profane." With respect to their bodies, not regarding them as holy. "Profane" does not signify profane in our sense of the word. It is translated "contaminatis" in the Vulgate.

"For murderers of fathers and murderers of mothers." It is singular that the Apostle should notice so extreme a violation of the fifth commandment; but this is not uncommon among the heathen who remove their parents out of the way when they become old and infirm. I know from the account of a missionary (Bishop Horden) that this crime is usual among unconverted North American Indians.

10. "For whoremongers, for them that defile themselves with mankind," &c. "For whoremongers," comprehending also adulterers, for Sodomites, for the worst sort of thieves, *i.e.*, for men-stealers. It is to be remembered that slavery by no means depends upon men-stealing. Slavery was lawful among the Israelites, but with respect to man-stealing Moses writes, "If a man be found stealing any of his brethren of the children of Israel, and maketh merchandise of him or selleth him, then that thief shall die, and thou shalt put evil away from among you" (Deut. xxiv. 7).

with mankind, for menstealers, for liars, for perjured persons, and if there be any other thing that is contrary [r] to sound doctrine;

11 According to the glorious gospel of [s] the blessed God, [t] which was committed to my trust.

[r] ch. vi. 3. 2 Tim. iv. 3. Tit. i. 9. & ii. 1.
[s] ch. vi. 15.
[t] 1 Cor. ix. 17. Gal. ii. 7. Col. i. 25. 1 Thess. ii. 4. ch. ii. 7. 2 Tim. i. 11. Tit. i. 3.

"For liars, for perjured persons." Both these are comprehended under the ninth commandment. This is the reason why in the duty towards our neighbour lying is placed between evil speaking and slandering, as a breach of the ninth commandment.

"And if there be any other thing which is contrary to sound doctrine." This must sound strange to some of us who associate "doctrine" with such matters as imputed righteousness, election, reprobation, and such things; but does it not teach us that we should descend at times very low in our teaching, and that we should preach against crimes? Those who receive confessions will tell us that some of the most evil things in the above list are not quite so uncommon as we think. Fornication is in our Gospel-professing country scarcely considered a sin. Bastardy is fearfully on the increase in some of the large Protestant capitals of continental Europe as well as in the Romish ones. Let us remember that Christ's redemption is from all these great sins. The wholesome doctrine of the Cross and Resurrection can deliver from the worst sins, the grossest as well as the most refined.

11. "According to the glorious gospel of the blessed God." The Gospel of the glory of the blessed God is in all its parts directed against all sin. "He gave himself for us that he might redeem us from all iniquity, and purify unto himself a peculiar people, zealous of good works." (Tit. ii. 14.) Is His crucifixion a part of the gospel? then they that are Christ's have crucified the flesh with its affections and lusts. Is His Resurrection a part of the Gospel? then we believe that "in that he died, he died unto sin once: but in that he liveth, he liveth unto God. Likewise reckon ye also yourselves to be dead indeed unto sin, but alive unto God." Rom. vi. 10, 11.

"Which was committed to my trust." This entrustment of the Gospel to the Apostle is constantly referred to by him. Thus

12 And I thank Christ Jesus our Lord, [u] who hath enabled me, [x] for that he counted me faithful, [y] putting me into the ministry;

13 [z] Who was before a blasphemer, and a persecutor, and injurious: but I obtained mercy, because [a] I did *it* ignorantly in unbelief.

u 2 Cor. xii. 9.
x 1 Cor. vii. 25.
y 2 Cor. iii. 5, 6. & iv. 1. Col. i. 25.
z Acts viii. 3. & ix. 1. 1 Cor. xv. 9. Phil. iii. 6.
a Luke xxiii. 34. John ix. 39, 41. Acts iii. 17. & xxvi. 9.

---

12. "Who hath enabled me." So A., D., F., G., K., L., P.; but ℵ reads, "doth enable me."

1 Cor. ix. 17, "A dispensation of the gospel is committed to me." Thus 1 Thess. ii. 4, &c.

12. "And I thank Christ Jesus our Lord, who hath enabled me, for that," &c. "Enabled me," *i.e.*, strengthened me.

"For that he counted me faithful, putting me into the ministry." "How," it is asked, "could the Lord have counted St. Paul faithful?" Some, as Alford, considered that it was because of his foreseen faith; others, with more probability, refer to his many years of probation before he was finally set apart to the Apostleship at Antioch (see Gal. i. 16-22). This may have been, according to some, thirteen years. It is true that during this period he preached in the synagogues, but that was accorded to unordained persons as a regular custom.

"Putting me into the ministry." The diaconia. This sentence could not have been written so late as some wish to date this Epistle. It could only have been written when the distinctions in the ministry were as nothing to the ministry itself. I think that no one after St. Paul's death would have designated his Apostleship as simply a diaconia.

13. "Who was before a blasphemer, and a persecutor, and injurious." Thus he recounts with bitterness the sins of his unconverted state. He felt that that the fact of God's having forgiven him was no reason why he should forgive himself.

"I obtained mercy because I did it ignorantly in unbelief." This assertion of the Apostle is in one sense very valuable, because it shows us that God will deal with us in accordance with that sense of justice which he has implanted in us. A truly just man would make the fullest allowances for the ignorance of those who have offended. It is quite true that the law of a human kingdom

[b] Rom. v. 20. 1 Cor. xv. 10.
[c] 2 Tim. i. 13.
[d] Luke vii. 47.
[e] ch. iii. 1. & iv. 9. 2 Tim. ii. 11. Tit. iii. 8.

14 [b] And the grace of our Lord was exceeding abundant [c] with faith [d] and love which is in Christ Jesus.

15 [e] This *is* a faithful saying, and worthy of all

---

takes no account of ignorance of the law because all are presumed to know it, but God, the reader of hearts, knows exactly the state of men's minds in the matter of ignorance, and will act accordingly. There have been long periods in the history of our Church, and of the continental reformed bodies, when to have made such an assertion as this would have been held to be the rankest heresy, and would have deprived the man who made it of his means of subsistence.

14. "And the grace of our Lord was exceeding abundant with faith and love," &c. The faith and love, the fruits of the grace of Jesus Christ seem to be mentioned in contrast with his former unbelief and hatred of the Church. He could not but be conscious that whereas he had held our Lord to be a false Christ and a blasphemer, now he held Him to be the Son of God, the Saviour of the world; and he was equally conscious that he once had hated the Church and persecuted its members to the death, but now spent his life and strength in building up its fabric and enlarging its borders.

15. "This is a faithful saying, and worthy of all acceptation." The expression "this is a faithful saying" is used only in the Pastoral Epistles. It is supposed to introduce some aphorism which by constant repetition had become a household word amongst Christians. It is used only once besides this with the adjunct "worthy of all acceptation" (1 Tim. iv. 9). Once there is appended to it, "These things I will that thou affirm constantly" (Tit. iii. 8). Once it appears to be used with reference to a matter of not much importance, as in the remaining place in 1 Tim. iii. 1, where Chrysostom supposes that it must be joined with the last words of the preceding chapter.

The reader will remember that this is one of the comfortable words in our Eucharistic Office. It seems, then, to teach that no remembrance of past sin should keep us from approaching to receive the highest pledge of God's mercy, and that the Body and Blood of Christ, like His other gifts, are not for the righteous, but for sinners; not for the righteous who feel no need, and come in a

acceptation, that [f] Christ Jesus came into the world to save sinners; of whom I am chief.

[f] Matt. ix. 13. Mark ii. 17. Luke v. 32. & xix. 10. Rom. v. 8. 1 John iii. 5.

---

self-righteous spirit, but for those who feel sin, even though forgiven, to be a disgrace.

"Came into the world to save sinners." "I came not to call the righteous, but sinners to repentance." "Come unto me all ye that labour, and are heavy laden, and I will give you rest."

He came into the world to save all sinners, no matter how gross their sin has been, if they repent. When He uttered the words, "I came not to call the righteous, but sinners to repentance," He was surrounded by very gross sinners—by publicans, who had led lives of extortion and fraud, and by harlots, who had led lives of impurity and adultery; and when He was asked why He did so, He gave the memorable answer, of which the Apostle's words are the reproduction.

So that the teacher of religion has the greatest confidence in applying these words to every sinner who is grieved and wearied with the burden of his sins.

It has been asked, how could St. Paul say that he was the chief of sinners? How did he know this? He would not say unreal words, and yet he spoke with evident sincerity, with evident assurance of its truth. The reader has doubtless heard the solution of this. He knew the aggravation of his own sins—how in persecuting the members of Christ's Body he came across instances of faith in God, of trust in Him in life and death, of patience, of longsuffering, of love for persecutors, even of prayer for their forgiveness, such as he had never seen before. These, as no other sermons could have done, preached to him the truth of Christ's mission, for the God of Truth would not have accredited with such signs as these the words and works of a false Christ. He was fully convinced how long and patiently the Son of God had borne with his obstinacy and wilful quenching of the light. All these, with their aggravations owing to wilful unbelief, he knew, and he knew that there was no palliation for them. He could not urge before God one extenuating circumstance; but though he knew and realized the aggravation in his own case, he knew not, and so could not realize the extenuations in the case of others. He felt that he was bound to exercise toward them—even the chief priests, the scribes, the

16 Howbeit for this cause [g] I obtained mercy, that in me first Jesus Christ might shew forth all longsuffering, [h] for a pattern to them which should hereafter believe on him to life everlasting.

17 Now unto [i] the King eternal, [k] immortal, [l] invisible, [m] the only wise God, [n] *be* honour and glory for ever and ever. Amen.

g 2 Cor. iv. 1.
h Acts xiii. 39.
i Ps. x. 16. & cxlv. 13. Dan. vii. 14. ch. vi. 15, 16.
k Rom. i. 23.
l John i. 18. Hebr. xi. 27. 1 John iv. 12.
m Rom. xvi. 27. Jude 25.
n 1 Chron. xxix. 11.

---

16. "Jesus Christ." So א, K., L., P., most Cursives, Syr., Copt. Arm., Æth.; but A., D., read, "Christ Jesus."

17. "Only wise." So K., L., P., most Cursives; but א, A., D., F., G., d, f, g, Vulg., Sah., Copt., omit "wise."

elders, whose willing tool he had been—the charity which thinketh no evil, and which hopeth all things, and so comparing himself even with these men he pronounced himself the chief of sinners.

Bishop Jackson, in the "Speaker's Commentary," remarks: "The tense is instructive; of whom I *am* chief, not I *was*. A pardoned sinner is a sinner still."

16. "Howbeit for this cause I obtained mercy, that in me first Jesus Christ might show forth all long-suffering," &c. Notice here that to Jesus Christ is ascribed the divine attribute of long-suffering in dealing with sinners. God is long-suffering. And His Son, Who inherits all the divine attributes, inherits this same long-suffering.

"All long-suffering," lit., "the all-long-suffering, the infinite long-suffering which appertains to Him."

"For a pattern to them which should hereafter believe on him." So that sinners who had sinned after the pattern of St. Paul in persecuting those whom they had every reason to believe to be in the right, might yet hope for mercy on their repentance and faith. Another turn, however, has been given to this sentence. The pattern has been supposed to be given to believers that they in their turn should exercise the same long-suffering which Christ had done, that as He had pardoned and received into favour His worst enemies, so should they. The first meaning, however, seems the more natural one.

17. "Now unto the King eternal, immortal, invisible, the only wise God," &c. Having thus expressed his view of the mercy of God in Christ in sending His Son to save sinners, he breaks forth into

18 This charge [o] I commit unto thee, son Timothy, [p] according to the prophecies which went before on thee, that thou by them mightest [q] war a good warfare:

o ch. vi. 13, 14, 20. 2 Tim. ii. 2.
p ch. iv. 14.
q ch. vi. 12. 2 Tim. ii. 3. & iv. 7.

---

a doxology to God the Father, the King of the ages, invisible, *i.e.*, whom no man hath seen or can see. It is a similar outburst of praise to that in the last chapter of this Epistle. The principal Uncials omit "wise," so that we read "the only God." [1]

18. "This charge I commit unto thee, son Timothy, according to the prophecies," &c. What charge? Some say the charge is contained in verse 3, but this interposes a great distance between that very short charge and what he calls here "this charge." I believe that it refers not to a word or two which comes before, but to the whole of what follows to the end of the Epistle, all which may be called an Apostolic charge. The charge really commences with chap. ii. 1, the short reference to Hymenæus and Alexander being a digression thoroughly in St. Paul's style.

"According to the prophecies which went before on thee." Therefore to elevate him, and prepare him to be sober and watchful, he reminds him by Whom he was chosen and ordained, as if he had said, "God hath chosen thee. He gave thee thy commission, thou wast not made by human vote." The occurrence was probably somewhat similar to that which brought about the ordination of St. Paul himself, where it is written, "There were

---

[1] Chrysostom has some very good remarks on the Father being here called the only God. Speaking of the Father, he says, "*To the only God.* Is the Son then not God? The only immortal. Is the Son then not immortal? Or does He not possess that Himself which hereafter He will give to us? Yes, they say, He is God and immortal, but not such as the Father is. What then, is He of inferior essence, and, therefore, of inferior immortality? What then is a greater and a less immortality? For immortality is nothing else than the not being subject to destruction. For there is a greater and a less glory; but immortality does not admit of being greater or less. . . . . For a thing must be destructible or altogether indestructible. . . . . Why then do you make the difference? Because the Father is made such as He is by no other: but the Son is what He is from the Father. This we also confess, not denying that the Son is generated from the Father incorruptibly. And we glorify the Father, he means, for having generated the Son such as He is. Thus you see the Father is most glorified when the Son hath *done* great things. For the glory of the Son is referred again to Him. And since He generated Him omnipotent, and such as He is in Himself, it is not more the glory of the Son than of the Father that He is self-sufficient and self-maintained and free from infirmity."

19 [r] Holding faith, and a good conscience; which some having put away concerning faith [s] have made shipwreck:

20 Of whom is [t] Hymenæus and [u] Alexander;

r ch. iii. 9.
s ch. vi. 9.
t 2 Tim. ii. 17.
u 2 Tim. iv. 14.

---

certain prophets to whom the Holy Ghost said, Separate me Barnabas and Saul," &c. (Acts xiii. 1-3).

But probably the prophecies made known to the Church the peculiar fitness of Timothy for what we may call the sub-apostolate which he was to exercise under the great Apostle.

"Mightest war the good warfare." If the Christian's life is that of a soldier, much more the minister's life. All the warfare of the more secular, the layman's Christian life, is concentrated in the pastor's. Let every pastor learn from this that his life is more emphatically a fight and a struggle. If the pastor does not realize this, he should ask himself whether he is fighting at all, whether he is not a renegade, a deserter.

19. "Holding faith and a good conscience." See verse 5: "A pure heart, a good conscience, and faith unfeigned." Holding faith is not merely holding intellectually some doctrine of the power of faith, or its place in the matter of justification and sanctification, but having a firm hold through faith of the great Object of all faith, even the Son of God.

"And a good conscience." In the words of the Apostle, "Exercising ourselves to keep a good conscience, void of offence towards God and towards men."

"Which some having put away (*i.e.*, not having been careful respecting holy living) concerning faith have made shipwreck." "Faith," rather "the faith," is a great gift of God, and He is not likely to maintain those in it who are careless in obeying their monitor within them. Conscience is the chart of the Christian life, which, if a man follows, he will keep clear of the rocks and quicksands of unbelief and heresy.

20. "Of whom is Hymenæus and Alexander; whom I have delivered unto Satan," &c. Hymenæus is mentioned as a teacher of falsehood in 2 Tim. ii. 17, 18, his heresy being that the Resurrection is past already. Alexander bears the same name as the man whom in the tumult in Ephesus, described in Acts xix. 33, the Jews put forward as their leader, and many assume him to be the same person.

whom I have [x] delivered unto Satan, that they may learn not to [y] blaspheme.

[x] 1 Cor. v. 5.
[y] Acts xiii. 45

"Whom I have delivered unto Satan." We are naturally led to consider this an act of excommunication of the same fearful character as that mentioned in 1 Corinth. v. 5. It was, apparently, not only a cutting off from Church privileges, especially the Eucharist, but was attended with some temporal disorder which would end in death. (Compare 1 Cor. xi. 29, 30.)

Such a judgment inflicted on notorious evil doers was apparently reserved to the Apostles, by whom it was exercised on Ananias and Sapphira (Acts v. 1-11), on Elymas (Acts xiii. 11), on the incestuous Corinthian (1 Cor. v. 5), and on the persons here mentioned.

Here, however (and in 1 Cor. v.), it was remedial. It was inflicted on these heretics not to avenge the cause of God's truth, but "that they might learn not to blaspheme."

CHAP. II.

I || EXHORT, therefore, that, first of all,

|| Or, *desire*.

1. "I exhort, therefore, that, first of all, supplications, prayers, intercessions," &c. A question arises upon this Apostolic exhortation, why it is with such apparent emphasis placed *first* of all? The third chapter contains the character of those who are to be appointed to the ministry; the fourth contains some important warnings against false teachers who came under the garb of self-denial and asceticism; the fifth, regulations respecting widows and the due administration of Church funds. Now, how is it that this precept respecting public prayers and intercessions is put *first of all*? We should have imagined that if they had (and we know that they had) public worship at all, they would have prayer for all men, and need not to be reminded of this *in the first place*.

supplications, prayers, intercessions, *and* giving of thanks, be made for all men;

Then there is another matter bearing upon this. St. Paul had given to the Corinthian Church minute directions or traditions respecting public worship (1 Cor. xi. 1, 2), at least so far as it was Eucharistic, and he had promised that when he returned he would complete what he had given (1. Cor. xi. 34): "The rest will I set in order when I come." So that the celebration of the Eucharist would be constant among all the Churches which he or his disciples or fellow-helpers had planted. I cannot help thinking that this matter of intercession had not the fulness in the ancient draughts of Liturgy which it ought to have had, and which it had afterwards. And I cannot help being confirmed in this belief by a singular circumstance which I think has not been sufficiently noticed, which is this: that in the most ancient types of Liturgy the Prayer for Kings and all in authority seems evidently founded upon this enactment of St. Paul's; for in each is reproduced the particular words of St. Paul which follow. Thus in the oldest type of Liturgy of all (the Clementine), in the solemn intercession just after the prayer of consecration, we have, "Further, we call upon Thee, O Lord, for the King, and all that are in authority, for the success of the army, that they may be kindly disposed towards us; that leading our whole life in peace and quietness, we may glorify Thee through Jesus Christ our hope." In that of St. Mark, "King of Kings, and Lord of Lords, defend Thy servant our king . . . . Incline his heart to be favourable and gracious to Thy Holy Catholic and Apostolic Church: and to all Christian people; so that in his peace we may enjoy peace, and live quietly in all Godliness and honesty." St. Chrysostom's, "For our Emperors . . . . in the faith and love of Christ, for the court and camp, give them, O Lord, a peaceable reign, that in their peace we may also lead a quiet and peaceable life in all Godliness and honesty." The same nearly verbatim in the Liturgy of St. Basil.

I cannot help, then, regarding the intercessory prayers for all men in the ancient services as brought about by this direction of St. Paul.

"Supplications, prayers, intercessions, and giving of thanks." Various shades of meaning have been given to these four kinds of

2 [a] For kings, and [b] *for* all that are in ‖ authority; that we may lead a quiet and peaceable life in all godliness and honesty.

[a] Ezra vi. 10. Jer. xxix. 7.
[b] Rom. xiii. 1.
‖ Or, *eminent place.*

---

devotion. "Supplications" imply need, and we ask the supply of that need. "Prayers" (προσευχαὶ) seem to look to our devotions as performed to God and God only.

"Intercessions" implies interpellations, when we accuse others and pray to God to be righted, or when we pray on behalf of others. The latter is of course incomparably the more frequent, but still we have the example of the importunate widow (Luke xviii. 1) and of the saints under the altar (Rev. vi. 10).

"Giving of thanks" is Eucharistia. And though we must not, as some seem to do, confine it to the Eucharist, yet unquestionably the Eucharist, as setting forth Redemption and thanking God for it, is *the* giving of thanks.

"Be made for all men."

2. "For kings, and for all that are in authority; that we may lead a quiet and peaceable life," &c. "For all men," for all sorts and conditions of men, and for all their needs, public and private, spiritual and temporal. No form of supplication can be conceived fuller (and yet not descending to ridiculous particulars) than our Litany. Should not those who cannot come to join in it on the three appointed days of the week use it in private? Those who repudiate its use omit the mention of many persons for whom as Christians they are bound to intercede. I once asked a godly dissenter who never (or seldom) joined in it, whether in all the prayers he had heard during his life, he had ever heard a petition for "our enemies, persecutors, and slanderers." He turned round, looked me full in the face, and answered, "No, I never did."

"All that are in authority." The governor of a distant province might do infinite harm to Christians in the part he ruled over, and never be called to account for it.

"That we may lead a quiet and peaceable life," &c. Since the soul of some Christian might be slow at hearing this, and reject the exhortation if, at the celebration of the Holy Mysteries, it was necessary to offer prayers for a heathen king, he shows them the advantage of it, thus, at least, to reconcile them to the advice,

[c] Rom. xii. 2. ch. v. 4.
[d] ch. i. 1. 2 Tim. i. 9.
[e] Ezek. xviii. 23. John iii. 16, 17. Tit. ii. 11. 2 Pet. iii. 9.
[f] John xvii. 3. 2 Tim. ii. 25.

3 For this *is* [c] good and acceptable in the sight [d] of God our Saviour;

4 [e] Who will have all men to be saved, [f] and to come unto the knowledge of the truth.

"that we may lead a quiet and peaceable life," as much as to say, "Their safety is a security to us." (Chrysostom.)

3. "For this is good and acceptable in the sight of God our Saviour." That is the spirit of intercession. The sense of our own needs would prompt us to pray for ourselves, but the sense of universal redemption, the realization of the truth that all men are one brotherhood, would make us intercede for all, and this God will regard as the fruits of His grace and holy Spirit within us. It shows the working of grace when men pray for themselves, but it shows more grace when men pray sincerely for all men, for unbelievers, that God would gather them into the fold, for our enemies, that God would turn their hearts. In this we follow the guidance of the Lord where he exhorts, "Pray for them that despitefully use you, and persecute you. That ye may be the children of your Father which is in heaven, for he maketh his sun to rise on the evil and on the good, and sendeth rain on the just and on the unjust" (Matth. v. 44, 45).

4. "Who will have all men to be saved, and to come unto the knowledge of the truth." This is not so strong as in the original, "Who willeth that all men should be saved." How is it, then, that He does not bring about His Will by the instantaneous conversion of every sinner? Because He has decreed that the sinner must accept His salvation, and the acceptance of salvation is the acknowledgment on the sinner's part that he desires present deliverance from sin, and the life of God within him. But sinners will not—multitudes of them, that is—accept this salvation. As the Lord says, "Ye will not come unto me, that ye might have life." And so God, owing to the infinite justice of His character, and owing to His respect for the freedom with which He has endowed His intelligent creatures, does not allow Himself to have His Will. A human king would often pardon rebels who have not submitted to the terms of his grace, but for the sake of the law, for the sake of the order of his kingdom, for the sake of the cause of

5 [g] For *there is* one God, and [h] one mediator between God and men, the man Christ Jesus;

g Rom. iii. 29, 30. & x. 12. Gal. iii. 20.
h Heb. viii. 6. & ix. 15.

---

righteousness, he feels he must not. (See my notes on Christ weeping over Jerusalem, on St. Luke, p. 503).

"And to come unto the knowledge of the truth." This depends in a measure upon the Church, that she is alive to her duty of making known the Gospel to the world. A Church which cares not for missions, cares not for carrying out the Will of God, just as a soul which cares not to come to Christ and receive Him, cares not for carrying out the Will of God as regards itself.

5. "For there is one God, and one mediator between God and man," &c. "For." What is the connection? It may either be "pray for all men," for there is one God and One Mediator for all to second your prayers; or, God our Saviour desires all men to be saved, and the assurance of this is, that He has constituted the man Christ Jesus to be the Mediator between Himself and all mankind. But the two converge and unite. For the fact that God "desires all men to be saved and to come to the knowledge of the truth," is known to us by the corresponding fact that God has put One Mediator between Himself and the race, Who has first done the principal work of a mediator by reconciling man to God through His Sacrifice, and yet carries on the work of reconciliation by pleading with God for those (all) whom He has redeemed, according to His words, "Whatsoever ye shall ask the Father in my name, he will give it you" (John xv. 16).

"For there is one God, and one mediator between God and men, the man Christ Jesus." How is it that the Godhead, or Divine nature of the Lord Jesus is not asserted? Because such a Mediatorship as is ascribed to Christ necessitates all Divine attributes. For just as it requires the Infinity, the Omnipresence, and Omniscience of God to hear the prayers of each particular sinner—so it belongs to the Infinity, the Omnipresence, and Omniscience of the Mediator, the Son of God, to plead the cause of each sinner with His Father, and intercede for him. Thus St. John, "If any man sin (ἐάν τις ἁμάρτῃ) we have an advocate with the Father, Jesus Christ the righteous, and he is the propitiation for our sins." The same is implied in Rom. viii. 34, "Who is he that condemneth? It is Christ that died . . . who also maketh intercession for us." From

6 [l] Who gave himself a ransom for all, [k] ‖ to be testified [l] in due time.

l Matt. xx. 28. Mark x. 45. Eph. i. 7. Tit. ii. 14.
k 1 Cor. i. 6. 2 Thess. i. 10. 2 Tim. i. 8.
‖ Or, *a testimony.*
l Rom. v. 6. Gal. iv. 4. Eph. i. 9. & iii. 5. Tit. i. 3.

---

these places we learn that the Lord intercedes for each sinner in particular. The Son of God can say of every sinner who perseveres in the Life of God, "I have prayed for thee, that thy faith fail not."

We must remember that the mediatorship of the Son is at the appointment of the Father. It is not as if the Father was angry and implacable in Himself, but rather in the Divine economy of Redemption, foreseeing the needs of the universe of intelligent creatures, He has Himself appointed the Son to be the Mediator. We need not also add that the Son possesses all the infinite qualifications to intercede for each one of an innumerable number of creatures, because, by His eternal generation, He receives from His Father all His Divine attributes.

"The man Christ Jesus." His manhood is specifically mentioned, because He partakes with us in it. He is our perfect Mediator, because He is not only our God to hear every word, and read every thought, but because He is our brother, bone of our bone, and flesh of our flesh, and so can fully sympathize, and so fully represent our case to God.

6. "Who gave himself a ransom for all." This was His great act of Mediatorship. He was the Priest and the Victim for the race. He gave Himself in sacrifice, and He continues to present His sacrifice, for He appears in heaven not merely as a king on His throne, but as a "Lamb standing as slain" (Rev. v. 6). It is surprising that notwithstanding two such assertions of Universal Redemption as we have here, and in 1 John ii. 2, we of the Church of England were once in imminent danger of having the monstrous assertion forced upon us as an article of faith, that Christ died for a comparatively few. I allude to the attempted imposition of the Lambeth articles on the Church in Queen Elizabeth's time. If the reader wishes to see an account of this extraordinary transaction, I would refer him to Dean Hook's "Ecclesiastical Biography," article, Baro.

"To be testified in due time." After natural religion, Judaism and philosophy had been tried and found wanting, then the Son of God was revealed. Not at the first, for then there would have

7 [m] Whereunto I am ordained a preacher, and an apostle, ([n] I speak the truth in Christ, *and* lie not;) [o] a teacher of the Gentiles in faith and verity.

m Eph. iii. 7, 8. 2 Tim. i. 11.
n Rom. ix. 1.
o Rom. xi. 13. & xv. 16. Gal. i. 16.

---

been many who would have said, that if men had been left to themselves they would have righted themselves. They were left to themselves, and it is said of God that "he saw that there was no man, and wondered that there was no intercessor; therefore his own arm brought salvation unto him, and his righteousness it sustained him" (Is. lix. 16).

Some, however, understand the testimony (τὸ μαρτύριον) as being an implied reference to the ark of the testimony, others that Christ giving Himself a ransom in His Death, was the testimony of God that He desired all men to be saved, but I think the meaning which I have given is the more likely. Chrysostom, however, writes: "His suffering was a testimony, he says, for He came, it is meant, to bear witness to the truth."

7. "Whereunto I am ordained a preacher and an apostle, (I speak the truth in Christ, and lie not)," &c. "Preacher" here is a herald (κήρυξ). The person and work of the Son of God had to be declared publicly, heralded in fact, and this was the first duty of an Apostle, as one sent to proclaim Jesus to be a Prince and a Saviour.

But why does he put in a parenthesis the words "I speak the truth and lie not"? Evidently because there were some who persistently denied his Apostleship, and in such a city as Ephesus there would be some, perhaps many of these, and the fact was so constantly present to the Apostle's mind, that he naturally interjects here this asseveration.

This is one of the many proofs that this Epistle is the genuine writing of the Apostle. It seems impossible to imagine that any forger should insert such a thing. Very shortly after his death there would be no ground for any such insertion. It would be gratuitous folly.

"In faith and verity." "In faith" because he set forth Christ to be believed in; "in verity" because he called upon men to believe in no cunningly devised fable, but in the truth.

8. "I will therefore that men pray every where, lifting up holy

p Mal. i. 11. John iv. 21.

8 I will therefore that men pray [p] every where,

---

hands." "That men," properly "the men;" men is indicative of the sex, ἀνὴρ always signifying the male, the husband, whilst the other word (ἄνθρωπος) signifies the human being. St. Paul apparently introduces the subject here because some women, relying on the equality of the sexes in the sight of God, and emboldened perhaps by the example of the women who ministered to the Lord, and by the position in the Church of such women as Dorcas, Priscilla, and others, had taken upon themselves to exercise priestly functions. Some of the Corinthian women had done this, and had also laid aside the badge of subjection in the covering of their heads, and these he rebukes sharply in his first Epistle to that Church (1 Cor. xi. 1-16; xiv. 34, 35).

"Pray every where." This is supposed by Chrysostom to assert the ability of Christians to pray in all places in contrast with the Jews who were only permitted to pray in one place. But this is said in forgetfulness of the fact that the Greek Jews had synagogues and also *proseuchæ* in all parts (Acts xvi. 13.) The meaning probably is that Christians might meet for prayer everywhere, but if they did the men were to pray aloud, leading the congregation, and not the women. Bishop Wordworth has (for him) a remarkable comment on this: "Here is a holy work enjoined to all men, the work of prayer. This is a function of that priesthood which appertains to all, and which all ought to discharge." It seems to me very unfortunate that owing to the revulsion of feeling at the time of the Restoration against the unbounded license which prevailed during the Commonwealth, the liberty of Church people in this matter of prayer was restricted to such an extent that all access to God everywhere was virtually confined to the words of the Book of Common Prayer, to consecrated buildings and to the priesthood. It is not so amongst Romanists, who are supposed to be far more sacerdotal than we are. I have seen a layman conducting a Litany service on the steps of the high altar in Vienna Cathedral, and I have seen two others performing the same function in the cathedral at Mayence. In our colonies laymen are licensed to say the whole Daily Office and Litany, except such a part as the Absolution. Unfortunately many of our laymen belong to a school which despises all prayer except what is called extempore, and desire to display their gift of fluency before the people. This is most

[q] lifting up holy hands, without wrath and doubting. [q Ps. cxxxiv. 2. Isai. i. 15.]

9 In like manner also, that [r] women adorn themselves in modest apparel, with shamefaced- [r 1 Pet. iii. 3.]

---

disastrous. I have known persons of the utmost power and rapidity of utterance who were habitual drunkards, and I have known humble-minded Christians living most closely to God who have scarcely been able to put two words together in public prayer.

"Lifting up holy hands." To lift up the hands was a Jewish custom; thus Psalm lxiii. 4, "I will lift up my hands in thy name." Also Psalm cxxxiv. 2, "Lift up your hands in the sanctuary." Tertullian in his treatise on prayer says, "We not only lift up our hands, but spread them out too, and disposing them after the manner of the Lord's Passion, and praying confess Christ" (Treatise on Prayer. XI.)

"Holy hands." This verse seems to have been in the mind of Clement of Rome when he wrote, "Let us then draw near to him with holiness of spirit, lifting up pure and undefiled hands unto him."

"Without wrath and doubting." Thus our Lord, "When ye stand praying, forgive if ye have aught against any."

"And doubting." So St. James, "Let him ask in faith nothing wavering."

9. "In like manner also, that women adorn themselves in modest apparel." This is by many commentators supposed to allude exclusively to their adornment in public worship, but the Apostle seems to intend worship which may be offered in every place, so that women should be clad always as if at any time they might be called upon to join in, or to be present at, prayer. The word "apparel" is supposed by some to include not only dress but demeanour. Wetstein refers to a passage in Plutarch apparently much to the point where καταστολὴν περιβολῆς signifies "modesty of dress."

"With shamefacedness and sobriety." Almost all expositors draw attention to the fact that in our Authorized the original rendering was "shamefastness," but was altered in 1611 to "shamefacedness," but "shamefastness" is an utterly obsolete word.

ness and sobriety; not with ‖ broided hair, or gold, or
‖ Or, plaited. pearls, or costly array;
s 1 Pet. 3, 4. 10 [s] But (which becometh women professing godliness) with good works.
11 Let the woman learn in silence with all subjection.
t 1 Cor. xiv. 34. 12 But [t] I suffer not a woman to teach, [u] nor
u Eph. v. 24. to usurp authority over the man, but to be in silence.

'Αιδώς signifies reverence, as in Heb. xii. 28 (it may not, however, be the proper reading in this last place). "Shamefastness" is an old English word signifying steadfastness.

"Not with broided hair, or gold, or pearls, or costly array." So 1 Pet. iii. 3.

10. "But (which becometh women professing godliness) with good works." "Professing godliness," professing to be Christians.

"With good works." The religious ordering of their households, visiting the sick, making clothes for the poor and destitute, teaching in schools, and, if they have opportunity, nursing.

11, 12. "Let the woman learn in silence . . . to be in silence." The Apostle in writing to the Corinthians had forbidden the women even to ask questions in the public assembly. "If they will learn anything let them ask their husbands at home, for it is a shame for women to speak in the Church" (1 Cor. xiv. 35). It is surprising how, notwithstanding that these prohibitions are formally acknowledged to be the words of one who spake by the Holy Ghost, this forwardness on the part of some Christian women to intrude into that which was to them a forbidden office, lingered amongst professing Christians, even in the Church. Tertullian, speaking of the way in which heretics were puffed up, says "That the very women are bold enough to dispute, to lead, to enact exorcisms, to undertake healings, and even to baptize" ("Prescription against Heretics," xli.). In the Apostolic Constitutions, certainly not later than the beginning of the third century, and containing matter much earlier, we find injunctions to women, who are subject to men, not to perform the office of a priest. "In a much later age tendencies toward the usurpation of sacerdotal functions

13 For [x] Adam was first formed, then Eve.
14 And [y] Adam was not deceived, but the
woman being deceived was in the transgression.
15 Notwithstanding she shall be saved in child-

x Gen. i. 27. & ii. 18, 22. 1 Cor. xi. 8, 9.
y Gen. iii. 6. 2 Cor. xi. 3.

---

14. "Being deceived." Rather, "being utterly deceived" (ἐξαπατηθεῖσα). ℵ, A., D., F., G., P., &c.; but K., L., and most Cursives, read simply "being deceived."

were shown by those who held positions of authority in conventual houses. Charlemagne issued an edict to bishops in A.D. 789, in which he says, "It has come to our ears that certain abbesses, contrary to the custom of God's holy Church, veil virgins with priestly benediction, which thing you, holy fathers, are to understand to be entirely forbidden in your dioceses." (Blunt.)

How scandalously this apostolical injunction is contravened in these days is well known. Even in our Church attempts have been made to give sanction to public instruction, or indeed preaching, on the part of women.

"Silence" is softened by the Revisers and others into "quietness," but the Apostle evidently means actual silence, so that their voices are not heard. He considers that teaching by women, no matter how gently performed, is usurping authority, and he forbids it.

13, 14. "For Adam was first formed, then Eve . . . in the transgression." Two reasons are given for the subordinate place of women in the matter of Church functions. One, that the man Adam was created before his wife, the other that it was not the man, but the woman who yielded to the tempter.

Was Adam then not deceived? Not by Satan, for he probably was persuaded by his wife, not deceived as she had been.

15. "Notwithstanding she shall be saved in childbearing, if they continue," &c. This, as the reader probably knows, is a very difficult passage. The Revisers translate it, "she shall be saved through the childbearing, or through her childbearing." The most literal translation of *διὰ τῆς τεκνογονίας*, is "through the childbearing."

There have been various meanings given to "through" (*διὰ*). One is "through the childbearing." There is one childbearing by the side of which no other can be named, *i.e.*, the childbearing with which the New Testament opens. But even Romanists such as Cornelius à Lapide, do not recognize this as being in the mind

bearing, if they continue in faith and charity and holiness with sobriety.

---

of the Apostle. Bernardine à Piconio paraphrases the verse, "Salvabitur autem mulier, per piam liberorum educationem, si permanserit constans in fide, in charitate, in sanctitate, et morum sobrietate."

Upon the general meaning of the place, I would remark, first that it cannot well refer to any temporal salvation in childbearing —for such is contrary to fact. Neither can it refer to the reversal of the primal curse, for as long as the present state of things exists, it is and will be true of all women, "In sorrow thou shalt bring forth children" (Gen. iii. 16). And I do not think it is right to bring in education, for that takes place long after the childbirth, and is, as far as I can see, in no way connected with it. The best exposition I have seen is in a note by Dr. Hammond, given in Bishop Wordsworth's commentary. "The woman, that is, Eve (v. 14) being deceived was in the transgression, that is, was first guilty of eating the forbidden fruit, but rescued from the punishment by the promised seed—that is by her childbearing—by the Messiah which was to be born of a woman, and so to redeem that nature which He assumed, but this not absolutely, but on condition of faith and charity, and holiness, and sobriety, and continuing in all these."

CHAP. III.

THIS [a] *is* a true saying, If a man desire the office of a [b] bishop, he desireth a good [c] work.

[a] ch. i. 15.
[b] Acts xx. 28. Phil. i. 1.
[c] Eph. iv. 12.

---

1. "This is a true saying, If a man desire the office of a bishop," &c. The words, "This is a true saying," are exactly the same as those in verse i. 15, "This is a faithful saying." How is it that the same phrase should be applied to two things so very different? In the first place, it is probable that there were a considerable number of short aphorisms introduced by the words "faithful is

2 [d] A bishop then must be blameless, [e] the hus- [d] Tit. i. 6, &c. [e] ch. v. 9.

---

the saying," common in the earliest days of the Church; and, secondly, we must remember that to desire the office of a bishop or overseer at that time was to desire an office which, in addition to its other anxieties, entailed far more danger than the ordinary profession of the Faith. In some of the first years of Christianity to desire any prominent office in the Church was to desire persecution, imprisonment, and martyrdom.

"The office of a bishop," that is of overseership. For "bishop" simply signifies overseer. The officer was apparently indifferently called "elder" or "bishop," see Acts xx. 17, 28, Titus i. 5, 7. Respecting the office and its relations to other offices of the Christian ministry, see an Excursus at the end of this volume.

2. "A bishop then must be blameless." Bishop Jackson well remarks, "It has been objected that the qualifications here required for a bishop are too commonplace; only, for the most part, what should be found in every consistent Christian. The answer is that it is precisely the consistency of his previous conduct and character, and his excellence in the relations of social and domestic life, which guarantees the fitness of one who desires the office for the work of a bishop."

"The husband of one wife." So many questions can be raised on the meaning and limits of this injunction that I must (in order not to break unduly the sequence of these notes) postpone the examination of it to a note at the end of this chapter. Suffice to say at present that many think it lays down that a bishop must not have married twice, have not taken to himself a second wife after the decease of his first one; but whether this restriction was intended to be a permanent canon of the Catholic Church, or only for "the present distress" (1 Cor. vii. 26) requires further consideration.

"Vigilant," translated by Revisers "temperate." Chrysostom, however, whose vernacular was Greek, explains it as what we usually mean by vigilant. "Vigilant," he says, "that is, circumspect, having a thousand eyes about him, quick-sighted, not having the eyes of his mind dimmed. For many things occur which permit not a man to see clearly, to see things as they are. For care and troubles, and a load of business on all sides press upon him. He must therefore be vigilant, not only over his own con-

‖ Or, *modest.*
f 2 Ti. ii. 24.
g ver. 8. Tit. i. 7.
‖ Or, *Not ready to quarrel, and offer wrong, as one in wine.*
h 2 Ti. ii. 24.
i 1 Pet. v. 2.
k 2 Ti. ii. 24.

band of one wife, vigilant, sober, ‖ of good behaviour, given to hospitality, [f] apt to teach;

3 [g] ‖ Not given to wine, [h] no striker, [i] not greedy of filthy lucre; but [k] patient, not a brawler, not covetous;

---

3. "Not greedy of filthy lucre." Omitted by ℵ, A., D., F., G., K., L., P., many Cursives, Vulg., Syr., &c.; not found in any Uncial.

cerns but over those of others. He must be well awake, he must be fervent in spirit, and as it were breathe fire, he must labour and attend upon his duty by day and by night, even more than a general upon his army, he must be careful and concerned for all."

"Sober," self-restrained. Revisers translate it "sober-minded."

"Of good behaviour." Revisers "orderly," vulg. "ornatum," "modest."

"Given to hospitality." Probably a large portion of the Church revenues were assigned to him, as is the case now with respect to diocesan bishops, for this express purpose.

"Apt to teach." This is important as showing that the bishop or pastor must never lay aside his original work of teaching ("some pastors and teachers." Ephes. iv. 11). It also implies that the bishop should have a firm grasp of the subject he taught, and that he should have had experience in instructing others, or he would not be "apt to teach."

3. "Not given to wine," &c. This seems to mean, not given to drunkenness: the Greek word pointing to a man who becomes beside himself with wine, and not to the mere drinking of wine in moderation. So apparently Chrysostom: "Here he does not so much mean intemperate, as insolent and impudent."

"No striker." We must remember that in this early age Christianity could scarcely have become the civilizing influence it was afterwards. This word gives an instructive view of the impulsive vehemence of the Oriental character, by which St. Paul himself was a sufferer at the hands of the Asiatic Jews (Acts xxi. 27-31), and of the difficulties with which Christianity had to contend in curbing its impetuosity. Chrysostom extends this to undue severity and harshness in rebuke: "'No striker,' this, too, does not mean a striker with the hand. What means then 'no striker?'

4 One that ruleth well his own house, [l] having his children in subjection with all gravity;

[l] Tit. i. 6.

5 (For if a man know not how to rule his own house, how shall he take care of the church of God?)

6 Not ‖ a novice, lest being lifted up with pride [m] he fall into the condemnation of the devil.

‖ Or, *one newly come to the faith.*

[m] Isa. xiv. 12.

Because there are some who unseasonably smite the consciences of their brethren, it seems to be said with reference to them."

"Not greedy of filthy lucre." The Greek word (*αἰσχροκερδῆ*) is probably spurious here. It is fully represented by "not covetous." "Patient," gentle, perhaps.

"Not a brawler." Not pugnacious or quarrelsome. Vulg. *litigiosum.* "Not covetous," not a lover of money.

4, 5. "One that ruleth well his own house, having his children in subjection," &c. Here is the great principle of episcopal rule, whether the episcopus rules a diocese of many congregations, or one only. It is to be paternal, and yet absolute; the children in the one case, the family in the other, are not to govern themselves, but to be governed, to be under authority, in subjection. Whether this principle can be carried out in the nineteenth century, as it was intended to be by the Apostle in the first, is another matter; but if the Episcopate of the Church is analogous to that of a family, it is natural, and has its roots in family life, whereas all other government is more or less artificial.

The Apostle here, of course, speaks the language of common sense. By ruling well the household the man is fitted for ruling well the Church.

"With all gravity." With all decency of deportment. Vulg. "with all chastity or purity."

6. "Not a novice, lest being lifted up with pride he fall into the condemnation," &c.—*i.e.*, not one newly converted. "If before he had well been a disciple he should at once be made a teacher, he would be lifted up into insolence."

The only hint which we have in Scripture respecting the nature of the fall of Satan is in the Epistle of St. Jude, "the angels which kept not their first estate, but left their own habitation" (v. 6). They must have left their first estate in order to compass some higher

n Acts xxii. 12. 1 Cor. v. 12. 1 Thess. iv. 12.
o ch. vi. 9. 2 Tim. ii. 26.
p Acts vi. 3.

7 Moreover he must have a good report [n] of them which are without; lest he fall into reproach [o] and the snare of the devil.

8 Likewise *must* [p] the deacons *be* grave, not

---

one, and this must have been through ambition or pride. This, too, was the temptation by which the evil one assaulted our first parents—to exalt themselves above the estate in which God had placed them.

7. "Moreover, he must have a good report of them that are without," &c.—*i.e.*, of the heathen and unconverted Jews.

"Lest he fall into reproach and the snare of the devil." It is difficult, I confess, to catch the Apostle's meaning. "Such persons—that is, those who have not a good report from the heathen without—would be exposed to the taunts of ungodly men, disparaged as unworthy of their position, and, conscious of this, would probably be tempted to do things which would entangle them in Satan's net of unseemly wranglings or dangerous relationships."

This is saying something, but it is very far fetched. This is a much more important place than many seem to think, for is it meant that the door of the ministry is to be shut against all who have not lived virtuously as heathen? If so, what becomes of the words of St. Paul speaking of gross sinners in their heathen state? "Such were some of you, but ye have been washed, sanctified, justified, in the name of the Lord Jesus, and by the Spirit of our God" (1 Cor. vi. 11). Is it possible that the Apostle may mean slander by the snare of the devil? They who were for some good reason in evil odour with the heathen might be more than others exposed to slander (*διαβολή*), and bring an evil name on the whole Christian community.

8. "Likewise must the deacons be grave, not double-tongued, not given," &c. The deacons are mentioned only by name (in our English version) here, and in Phil. i. 1, "with the Bishops and deacons." In Acts vi. we have the appointment of the seven, but they are not there called deacons, though the Church is almost unanimous in considering that they were the first deacons. In Acts xiii. 5 we have, "They (Paul and Barnabas) had John to their minister," *i.e.*, "deacon" in the Greek. Some suppose them to be the helps (*ἀντιλήψεις*) of 1 Cor. xii. 28, but this is doubtful.

doubletongued, [q] not given to much wine, not greedy of filthy lucre;

9 [r] Holding the mystery of the faith in a pure conscience.

q ver. 3. Lev. x. 9. Eze. xliv. 21.
r ch. i. 19.

Rom. xii. 7, "Or ministry, let us wait on our ministering," may be rendered "or diaconate, let us wait on our diaconate:" but this also is doubtful. It may be taken to mean any ministry. Throughout the Epistles of Ignatius they are associated with the bishops and priests as a permanent order of the Church, to whom, along with the other two orders, obedience is due from the body of the faithful. In Justin Martyr, 1st Apol. 67, they are said to convey the Eucharistic element to those who are absent. I shall consider this function more at large in the Appendix on the Christian Ministry.

"Grave," *i.e.*, serious. The word σεμνός is often rendered "reverend" in the sense of worthy of reverence.

"Not double-tongued" (διλόγος). Only used in this place, and means, not saying one thing to one person and another to another. They were probably that part of the ministry which, having much to do with the distribution of alms, were most in contact with all classes and needed such an injunction.

"Not given to much wine, not greedy of filthy lucre." The same requirements as were looked for in the bishops or presbyters. All who in any sense bore the vessels of the Lord were to be clean, *i.e.*, "holy" (Is. lii. 11).

9. "Holding the mystery of the faith in a pure conscience." It has been suggested that this qualification is required because the deacons had the instruction of the Catechumens for Baptism; but why should it not be because it was one of their functions to preach? One at least of the seven, Stephen, was eminent as an Evangelist and preacher. Another was an Evangelist (Acts xxi. 8).

But very probably the stress is to be laid on the last clause, "in a pure conscience." The mystery of the faith was the common creed. It was the one faith held by all, the faith of the Son of God Incarnate, Crucified, Risen, and Ascended. It was held (at least outwardly professed) by many who were not careful about their Christian life. The mystery is the same in substance as that of the mystery of Godliness of verse 16.

10 And let these also first be proved; then let them use the office of a deacon, being *found* blameless.

a Tit. ii. 3. 11 a Even so *must their* wives *be* grave, not slanderers, sober, faithful in all things.

---

11. "Their wives." Generally understood as the women—the deaconesses.

10. "And let these also first be proved; then let them use the office," &c. Some suppose that they were to be proved by having some inferior work committed to them as a sort of probation; others that this "proving" was a searching examination into their qualifications: also that the names of candidates should be read in the congregation after the manner of our "si quis." The word "also" should be noticed. It is as if there was a probation, or strict examination into the qualifications of the bishops or presbyters, but the Apostle had omitted to enjoin it as taking it for granted, but here he mentions it with respect to the diaconate, hinting, however, by this also, that they were not the only ones "proved." Chrysostom considers it as parallel to the words "not a novice" of verse 6. Here he requires, though in other words, that he be not a novice, when he says, "Let these also first be proved, when the conjunction 'also' is added, as connecting this with what had been said before of bishops, for nothing intervenes between, and there is the same reason for the 'not a novice' in that case. For would it not be absurd, that when a newly-purchased slave is not entrusted with anything in a house till he has by long trial given proofs of his character, yet that one should enter into the Church of God from a state of heathenism, and be at once placed in a station of preeminence."

11. "Even so must their wives be grave, not slanderers," &c. There can be no doubt that the word "wives" should be rendered "women," and that it does not refer to the wives of the deacons, but to the women who held the office of deaconesses in the Church. Thus Chrysostom: "Some have thought that this is said of women generally, but it is not so, for why should he introduce anything about women to interfere with his subject? He is speaking of those who hold the rank of deaconesses. The qualifications of the wives of bishops are not alluded to, why should those of the wives of deacons?" The institution of deaconesses, or women ministering to

12 Let the deacons be the husbands of one wife, ruling
their children and their own houses well.
13 For [t]they that have ‖ used the office of a
deacon well purchase to themselves a good degree,
and great boldness in the faith which is in Christ
Jesus.

[t] See Matt. xxv. 21. ‖ Or, *ministered*.

---

the Church, was far older than this, for in Rom. xvi. 1, 'Phœbe our sister' is a deaconess of the Church which is at Cenchrea.

"Not slanderers." Having much to do with the female part of the Church, they should by their example be a reproof of tale-bearing.

"Faithful in all things." No higher qualification can be required, or even imagined.

12, 13. "Let the deacons be the husbands of one wife . . . great boldness in the faith," &c. This, which is the same direction as that which the Apostle had given respecting presbyters, shows that the lower offices require the same moral qualifications as the higher.

13. "For they that have used the office of a deacon well purchase," &c. This has been understood by some as referring to personal religion—they procure for themselves a good firm step, or standing, in the Divine Life; but it seems rather to indicate that they procure for themselves a right and due qualification for a higher step in the ministry—that into the higher grade of the episcopate, or eldership. It is difficult to suppose that the lower grade—that of a deacon—was intended to be permanent. If it was so, the great Christian institution would be much inferior to many others of this world. If the presbyterate of any place required recruiting, which it constantly would, who would be more fit to be chosen into it than those who had discharged well the functions of the lower office?

"Great boldness (or confidence) in the faith which is in Christ Jesus," *i.e.*, confidence in declaring it or making it known. This confident, bold, unhesitating declaration of the faith, was much in the Apostle's mind. He felt that even he required it for himself. Thus he bids the Ephesians pray: "For me, that utterance may be given to me, that I may open my mouth boldly, to make known the mystery of the Gospel." (Ephes. vi. 19.)

14. "These things write I unto thee, hoping to come unto thee shortly." We do not know whether this hope was fulfilled. Pro-

14 These things write I unto thee, hoping to come unto thee shortly:

15 But if I tarry long, that thou mayest know how thou oughtest to behave thyself [u] in the house of God, which is the church of the living God, the pillar and || ground of the truth.

u Ephes. ii. 21, 22. 2 Ti. ii. 20.

|| Or, *stay*.

---

bably not. Still this is instructive, for it shows us that St. Paul had not yet parted with his Apostolical authority over Ephesus, but retained it till his martyrdom. He wrote because his coming might be delayed. "Shortly" (τάχιον) means rather "soon."

15. "But if I tarry long, that thou mayest know how thou oughtest to behave thyself," &c. Some understand this as not intended to give direction to Timothy personally, but to all who have to regulate the affairs of the Church of God: thus the Revisers translate, "that thou mightest know how men ought to behave themselves in the house of God."

"The house of God, which is the church of the living God." The "house of God, the Church," is, of course, the building of spiritual stones. It here refers to that part of the great spiritual building which existed in Ephesus, in which Timothy was called upon to exercise oversight, direction, apostolical rule.

"To behave" is not an adequate word. In the vulgate it is translated *conversari*, and might be rendered "to act, to fulfil one's place, or position in."

"The pillar and ground of the truth." The Church, *i.e.*, the Church Catholic, the one Church existing at all times and in all places, which we confess in our creed when we say, "I believe in one Catholic and Apostolic Church," the Church holding fast to the Godhead, the Incarnation, the Death, Resurrection, and Ascension of the Eternal Son of God, is the pillar and ground of the truth, as it exists among men, and is confessed by them. In some of its branches this Church may be too superstitious, in others it may be too secular, but still the history of Christendom proves that the Churches which retain the Creeds and the Apostolic government, and the Divine Liturgy of the Eucharist, support the truth which they have received, and in its historical aspect and continuity furnish a basis for it in this world. The history of Christendom proves this. The Christian bodies which, since the Reformation, have put

16 And without controversy great is the mystery of godliness: [x] God was † manifest in the flesh,

x John i. 14. 1 John i. 2.

† Gr. *manifested.*

16. For differences of reading see critical note at the end of this chapter.

themselves outside the Church of the succession because of its superstitions and additions to what is primitive, have extensively declined from the faith, and this decline is going on, and nothing seems capable of arresting it. Certainly God has given it to the Church of England to be the pillar and ground of the truth in this land. She does not so much witness to what is subjective, as to what is objective, especially to the truth, the truth of truths, of God manifest in the flesh; and the coming of the Eternal Son amongst us is the only ground of what is subjective, it is the only ground of faith and hope and love, in the Christian sense of the words.

16. "And without controversy great is the mystery of godliness: God was manifest in the flesh." Almost all critics and expositors have given up the reading of our English Bible, "God," Θεὸς, and have adopted that of the principal Uncials, the relative pronoun, ὃς. So that, if this be adopted, the translation literally is, "Great is the mystery of godliness, who was manifest in the flesh." Now here, in one of the most important passages of the New Testament, we have an imperfect, ungrammatical sentence, beginning with a relative with no antecedent.

Now accepting the reading ὃς (who), what must be—not what may be, but what must be—its antecedent? It must be something which involves a deep mystery. We are told (by Alford and Ellicott), that it is Christ; but this is no answer at all, for there is no mystery about the manifestation of Christ, unless He have some superior nature manifest in the flesh. If Christ be the Messiah which the Jews expected, a man only, the descendant of David, then there is no mystery about the manifestation. It would be the merest truism to say that the best or wisest of men was "manifest in the flesh." It pertains to all men—indeed, to all creatures that are born into the world—to be manifest in the flesh. There is no special mystery about it. That the mystery of Godliness should be a mystery at all, implies that He Who was manifest in the flesh should be of a superior nature, and this nature can be only that of God, or of an angel. No one contends for the latter, so that we can only choose the former. And in choosing the former we are following the

[y] justified in the Spirit, [z] seen of angels, [a] preached

y Mat. iii. 16. John i. 32, 33. & xv. 26. & xvi. 8, 9. Rom. i. 4. 1 Pet. iii. 18. 1 John v. 6, &c.

z Mat. xxviii. 2. Mark xvi. 5. Luke ii. 13. & xxiv. 4. John xx. 12. Eph. iii. 10. 1 Pet. i. 12.

a Acts x. 34. & xiii. 46, 48. Ro. x. 18. Gal. ii. 8. Eph. iii. 5, 6, 8. Col. i. 27, 28. ch. ii. 7.

---

leading of the parallel passages, for this passage is not by itself, it is one of many; it must be associated with "The Word was made flesh;" "I came down from heaven;" "Before Abraham was I am;" "Of whom, as concerning the flesh, Christ came, who is God over all;" "Who, being in the form of God, thought it not robbery to be equal with God, but emptied himself, being formed in fashion as a man;" "The Second Man is the Lord from heaven;" "Our hands have handled of the Word of Life, for the Life was manifested."

The matter is, as the Apostle says, amongst true believers, not a matter of controversy, but is confessed and acknowledged on all hands (Alford) to be a great—the greatest of mysteries.

Still if we ask how it is that this most important enunciation begins so strangely with a relative, and where are we to look for the actual antecedent, I answer that the passage is in all probability an extract; perhaps, as most suppose, from a hymn, or from some liturgical formula; perhaps from a faithful saying longer than the others cited in this Epistle.

Bishop Wordsworth conjectures that the "living God," of verse 15, is the real antecedent, and that we must understand the words, "without controversy great is the mystery of godliness," as thrown in parenthetically, as is not unusual with the Apostle.

"Justified in the Spirit." This is also difficult to explain, and depends upon the meaning of "Spirit." If it means "by the Holy Spirit," as in Rom. i. 3, then it refers to the Resurrection, and to the miracles which were wrought by Himself and His Apostles, and the descent of the Spirit at Pentecost. If it means His own Spirit, the higher part of His human nature answering to the spirit of man in us, then it seems to allude to His being proved in all things to be the just One—He was fully justified, from the accusations of His enemies, and from His rejection by His own people; but I much prefer the former explanation.

"Seen of angels." From the position of this article of faith between His Resurrection, which was His great justification, and the preaching of Him to the Gentiles, or among them, it would seem to

unto the Gentiles, [b] believed on in the world, [c] received up into glory.

[b] Col. i. 6, 23.
[c] Luke xxiv. 51. Acts i. 9. 1 Pet. iii. 22.

---

refer to His appearance to angels after His Resurrection. St. Paul dwells far more on the glories and mysteries of the angelic world than we do, who profess to believe in his inspiration. It seems to have been a mystery in his eyes that He should be seen first of angels whom He came not to redeem, and not by men whose nature He had assumed in order to redeem them.

"Preached unto the Gentiles"—that the Gentiles should have Christ preached unto them, so that if they accepted Him they should be on an equality in God's sight with His ancient people, was "the mystery hid from ages and generations" (Coloss. i. 26). It was the especial mystery committed to St. Paul, that he should make it known, and insist upon the inferences which God intended men to draw from it.

"Believed on in the world." This was also a wonderful fact, that the Gospel of a despised and abhorred race—of a Jew crucified, risen, and ascended, should be believed on in the world for its salvation—that a new era should date from it, a new life be infused amongst men from it, a new standard of goodness and holiness begin with it. Let us throw ourselves back in the ages, and imagine what we should have thought if we had been called upon to believe for everlasting life on an unknown Galilean Who had suffered the vilest of deaths—nothing but miracles would have induced us so much as to listen to it—nothing but grace would have led us to accept it.

"Received up into glory." This is also an inconceivably great thing—that the Crucified should take His seat at the right hand of God, and have all worlds and all their powers, angelic, terrestrial, and infernal, under His supreme command.

2. "THE HUSBAND OF ONE WIFE."

Several questions arise upon the meaning of this injunction.

(1.) Polygamy was then practised. It was allowed to the Jews to have more wives than one (see note in Blunt).

(2.) Divorce was permitted and was common both among Jews and heathen. It may be, then, that St. Paul forbade anyone who had had two wives at the same time, or who had ever divorced one of his wives, to be admitted to the pastorate. Certainly it would seem that there could be no doubt about their unfitness for an office which demands more than ordinary purity and self-denial.

But the earliest fathers who mention this place undoubtedly held it to allude to those who had contracted a second marriage after the first wife was dead. Thus Tertullian (Ad Uxorem, ch. vii.), "Præscriptio Apostoli digamos non sinit præsidere." Thus Origen (Hom. 17 in Luc.), "Neque Episcopus, nec Presbyter nec Diaconus nec vidua possunt esse digami" (from note in Wordsworth, who also refers to fourth "Council of Carthage," c. lxix., Epiphanius, Apostolic Canons, Jerome and Ambrose, but does not quote). It is, however, to be remembered that the two authorities nearest to the time of St. Paul held extreme opinions on this matter. One (Tertullian) wrote a treatise, addressed to his wife, that she should not contract a second marriage after his death; the other (Origen) took to the letter our Lord's words in Matt. xix. 12, and mutilated himself.

Taking into account that polygamy and divorce were practised among the Jews, from whom the Church was largely recruited, it seems most reasonable to suppose that St. Paul means what we should naturally suppose, a man who had only one wife when he was a candidate for the ministry. But was there, in the Apostle's eyes, anything morally wrong or impure in a second marriage after the first wife or husband was dead? He expressly lays down that there is not: "If the husband be dead she is loosed from the law of her husband" (Rom. vii. 2, 3). If then a second marriage is allowed to the layman, on what grounds is it forbidden to the clergyman? It must be on the grounds not of legality, but of expediency; and if the Apostle by "the husband of one wife" means one who has only been married once, it must be because of the "distress" to which for several centuries the Christians were always subject. One branch of the Catholic Church, the Church of England, has not prohibited the ordination of a widower who has contracted a second marriage, nor has she prohibited a clergyman who is a widower from marrying again.

16. "GOD WAS MANIFEST IN THE FLESH."

There are three readings which claim attention. (1.) Θεός, God, as in the Authorised. (2.) ὅς, who (not He Who, but simply Who). (3.) ὅ, the reading of D. and of the Latin.

(1.) God (Θεός) is read indisputably in K., L. (both belonging to ninth century); almost all Cursives, Arab. (Polygl.) Slav.; Chrysostom (Chrysostom's words are, "God was manifest in the flesh. The Creator was seen incarnate"), Theodoret, Euthalius, Damascene, Theophylact, Æcumenius, Ignatius, Epist. to Ephes. 19 ("God himself being manifested in human form for the renewal of eternal life.")

(2.) Ὅς is read in ℵ (a correction of a much later date has appended θε in very small letters to Ὅς). It is read apparently in A., though this is denied. A. has $\overline{\Theta C}$, but the stroke at the top and the small stroke in the Θ are in a later hand, and in later or different ink, which has almost faded away. Bishop Ellicott and Wordsworth, who have both examined it, are convinced that OC is the true reading. It is also read in C. (a facsimile of the passage is given in the plates in Scrivener's third edition of "New Testament Criticism"). B. does not contain the Pastoral Epistles. Ὅς is also read in F., G., in Cursives 17, 73, 181, Sah., Copt.

(3.) ὅ is found in D., d, f, g, Vulg., and most Latin Fathers.

We shall not dwell upon this latter, but confine our remarks to the comparative probability of Θεός or Ὅς. If Θεός be the original reading, it is difficult to see how Ὅς could have been substituted for it, because the Godhead of the Lord Jesus occupies a far more prominent position in the theology of the early Church than in that of this age—one has only to look at Ignatius and Justin Martyr to be convinced of this. So that it is impossible to imagine how a reading which directly declares the Godhead of the Saviour could be exchanged for one which only indirectly declares it. And, again, it is equally difficult to imagine how early copyists could have exchanged a nominative case, Θεός, for such a remarkable instance of a relative with no antecedent. We have every reason to think then that the original reading was Ὅς: but then we are to remember that the MSS. which read Θεός are not wrong, but supply the only possible antecedent. They *read* what, if we are true Christians adoring the Son, we must understand to be meant.

It is lamentable to see the cool and unconcerned way in which commentators who profess the Catholic faith are content to leave the matter after they have decided against the reading, "God." Is the faith once delivered to the Saints of no concern to them that they should make no effort to show to the ignorant or semi-believing reader that it is required by the sense? The sense of the words "great is the mystery of Godliness" requires a mystery. It absolutely requires that a superior nature or a being not originally in the flesh should be seen in the flesh (1 John i. 1, 2). So that the substitution of the word Christ for God as the antecedent, is simply surrendering the Lord's Godhead, for an increasing number of persons are refusing to believe that there is anything supernatural in the Person of Christ.

If the reader wishes to study further the criticism on this passage, I refer him to Tischendorf's note in his eighth edition, to Scrivener's note, page 637 of his third edition of "Introduction to Criticism of the New Testament," and to the notes in Bishop Ellicott and Wordsworth.

CHAP. IV.

NOW the Spirit [a] speaketh expressly, that [b] in the latter times some shall depart from the

[a] John xvi. 13. 2 Thess. ii. 3. 2 Tim. iii. 1, &c. 2 Pet. iii. 3. 1 John ii. 18. Jude 4, 18.
[b] 1 Pet. i. 20.

---

1. "Now." "But," Revisers.

1. "Now the Spirit speaketh expressly, that in the latter times some," &c. "Now," this is properly "but" (δὲ). The Apostle had been speaking of the mystery of godliness—how it was confessed universally by Christians. Now he warns Timothy, and the Church through him, that, notwithstanding this present holding of the truth, there will be a great apostasy.

"Speaketh expressly." He alludes probably to such particular declarations of the Spirit as that which he had many years before this made known to the Thessalonians, in his Second Epistle to that Church, that in the latter times some shall depart from the faith, *i.e.*, from the one Faith—the Faith once for all delivered to the saints.

"From the faith" means "the faith," the articles of which he had just set forth in his account of the mystery of Godliness, especially

c 2 Tim. iii. 13. 2 Pet. ii. 1. Rev. xvi. 14.
d Dan. xi. 35, 37, 38. Rev. ix. 20.
e Matt. vii. 15. Rom. xvi. 18. 2 Pet. ii. 3.
f Eph. iv. 19.

faith, giving heed [c] to seducing spirits, [d] and doctrines of devils;

2 [e] Speaking lies in hypocrisy; [f] having their conscience seared with a hot iron;

---

2. "Through the hypocrisy of men that speak lies, branded in their own conscience as with a hot iron," Revisers.

the Incarnation. Thus his brother Apostle, St. John, writes: "Many false prophets are gone out into the world. Hereby know ye the Spirit of God. Every spirit that confesseth that Jesus Christ is come in the flesh is of God, and every spirit," &c. (1 John iv. 3).

"Giving heed to seducing spirits, and doctrines of devils." St. Paul here gives us plainly to understand that doctrines which cause men to apostatize from the Faith once delivered to the saints are not the product of the minds of mere men. They are the inspirations of evil spiritual beings—of demons. Now does he mean by this to affirm that all false doctrine comes from evil spirits? To this we answer all falsehood must come from beneath—all teaching which obscures the truth, which perverts the truth, which unduly exalts one necessary truth at the expense of another, must have an evil source. To this we must add all teaching which divides unnecessarily one Christian from another, and prevents the Church uniting as one man against every form of evil. But are not men to be allowed to differ? We are not to prevent them, except by the exhibition of the One Faith, and by bringing forward what is in the Holy Scriptures as it has been interpreted from the first; but it should be a matter of very serious consideration to every one who brings forward what is seemingly a new opinion, whether he has been taught it by the Holy Spirit, or by some other spirit.

The consideration that we may be under the influence of seducing spirits in what we teach should make us exceedingly watchful, wary, careful, prayerful. It is our best wisdom to distrust ourselves, and to pray that by the Spirit we may adhere to the old paths.

2. "Speaking lies in hypocrisy." Rather "through the hypocrisy of those who speak lies."

"Having their conscience seared with a hot iron." This is

3 [g] Forbidding to marry, [h] *and commanding* to abstain from meats, which God hath created [i] to be received [k] with thanksgiving of them which believe and know the truth.

g 1 Cor. vii. 28, 36, 38. Col. ii. 20, 21. Heb. xiii. 4.
h Rom. xiv. 3, 17. 1 Cor. viii. 8.
i Gen. i. 29. & ix. 3.
k Rom. xiv. 6. 1 Cor. x. 30.

---

translated by Bishop Ellicott, "men bearing a brand on their own conscience." The allusion is doubtful. It may refer to the searing nature of the brand, or it may allude to the cauterization, branding them as the slaves of sin.

3. "Forbidding to marry, and commanding to abstain from meats." This is said, according to Chrysostom, of the "Manicheans, the Encratites, and the Marcionites, and the whole of their tribe, that they should hereafter depart from the faith." Some commentators (amongst them Bishop Wordsworth) treat this as said in anticipation of the enforcement of celibacy on the clergy by the Church of Rome; but though the denial of family life to the clergy of all Western Christendom under the Roman Obedience may be very evil, yet it is not enforced on the blasphemous principles that this was—viz., the belief that matter is intrinsically evil, and was not created by the God Who is the Giver of all good things. The Roman celibacy is rather based upon what is said by St. Paul in 1 Corinth. vii. 32: "I would have you without carefulness. He that is unmarried careth for the things that belong to the Lord, how he may please the Lord." It seems monstrous, however, to cite these words of the Apostle as applicable to all the clergy, when he lays down that bishops and deacons are to be the husbands "of one wife," thereby assuming it to be the normal state of things that they should be married.

"Which God hath created to be received with thanksgiving of them which believe," &c. All the good things which God has created are to be received with thanksgivings, and, of course, with moderation. Is not luxury forbidden? Certainly it is. But why, if good things are created to be received? Because He created bread, and yet too much is forbidden. And wine also, and yet excess is forbidden. And we are not commanded to avoid dainties, as if they were unclean in themselves, but because they corrupt the soul by excess. Some sect of the Encratites refused to receive the Eucharist in the element of wine, accounting it unclean. It is noteworthy that

4 For [1] every creature of God *is* good, and nothing to be refused, if it be received with thanksgiving:

5 For it is sanctified by the word of God and prayer.

[1] Rom. xiv. 14, 20. 1 Cor. x. 25. Tit. i. 15.

---

some amongst ourselves have fallen into this error—not understanding that wine is as much a creature of God as water, and though its exhilarating qualities are produced under a different law, that law is equally the law of God. And perhaps on account of the danger which there is of taking it to excess, and so men should scornfully reject it, it is emphatically declared in Scripture to be a gift of God (Psalm civ. 15, John ii. 3-10).

"Of them which believe and know the truth." Such are mentioned here because they only can render to God the true and devout thanksgiving which He looks for.

"For every creature of God is good, and nothing to be refused, if it be received," &c. "What, then, is not swine's flesh unclean? By no means, when it is received with thanksgiving, and with the seal; nor is anything else. It is your unthankful disposition to God that is unclean" (Chrysostom).

5. "For it is sanctified by the word of God and prayer." What is this "word of God"? It has been variously interpreted. I think it most probably alludes to such a word of God as that spoken by God in Acts x. 15: "What God hath cleansed, that call not thou common." All created things were at the first pronounced to be good, and therefore clean. God afterwards withdrew certain of His creatures from the use of His chosen people under the first dispensation, and then restored the same to them under the second, in such words of God as those I have quoted, and those in Mark vii.: "Do ye not perceive that whatsoever thing from without entereth into the man, it cannot defile him?"

"By prayer." All "graces" or thanksgiving before meals are prayer.

In the Apostolical Constitutions we have the following grace: "Blessed be thou, O Lord, Who hast fed me from my youth, Who givest food to all flesh. Fill our hearts with joy and gladness, that having always all sufficiency, we may abound unto all good works, in Christ Jesus our Lord."

6. "If thou put the brethren in remembrance of these things,

6 If thou put the brethren in remembrance of these things, thou shalt be a good minister of Jesus Christ, [m] nourished up in the words of faith and of good doctrine, whereunto thou hast attained.

7 But [n] refuse profane and old wives' fables, and [o] exercise thyself *rather* unto godliness.

m 2 Tim. iii. 14, 15.

n ch. i. 4. & vi. 20. 2 Tim. ii. 16, 23. & iv. 4. Tit. i. 14.

o Heb. v. 14.

---

thou shalt be," &c. "These things"—*i.e.*, not only what he says respecting every creature of God being good, but also of the mystery of Godliness, and of the Apostasy of the later times.

"In the words of faith"—rather "of the Faith," the great truths of Christ Incarnate, Crucified, Risen, and Ascended.

"Whereunto thou hast attained"—rather, "which thou hast closely followed." As if he said, "I lay nothing new upon thee, but what thou hast already profited in. Thou art well acquainted with the words in which the faith is embodied, and the good practical teaching which springs from them."

7. "But refuse profane and old wives' fables." These words allude to the absurd stories which abounded in the Jewish traditionary lore, and cannot well be applied to the Gnostical speculations which were διδασκαλίαι δαιμονίων, doctrines of devils, rather than silly old women's stories.

"And exercise thyself rather unto godliness." By increasing in that in which thou hast been instructed from a child, the knowledge of the Scriptures, by prayer and devout meditation, by what thou knowest of the Lord's Life and actions and Divine words. "Exercise thyself" must refer to learning something which is most opposite to the profane old wives' fables; and this at that time could only be the Scriptures (Old Testament) or the Gospels.

"Exercise thyself rather unto godliness." He now speaks of the need of spiritual exercise (such as prayer and fasting) for spiritual health. The word by which he describes these exercises, γυμνάζω, shows that the spiritual exercises are to be regular, and that they require effort, and suppose spiritual mortification and wrestling. The Apostle compares the Spiritual Life to training in a ghostly gymnasium. Compare 1 Cor. ix. 24, where he likens its religious exercises to those of an athlete, and says (v. 27) ὑπωπιάζω μοῦ τὸ σῶμα, "I beat under my own body (μοῦ, emphatic), not the body of

p 1 Cor. viii. 8. Col. ii. 23.
|| Or, *for a little time.*
q ch. vi. 6.
r Ps. xxxvii. 4. & lxxxiv. 11. & cxii. 2, 3. & cxlv. 19. Matt. vi. 33. & xix. 29. Mark x. 30. Rom. viii. 28.

8 For p bodily exercise profiteth || little: q but godliness is profitable unto all things, r having promise of the life that now is, and of that which is to come.

---

8. "Profiteth little." Rather "profiteth a little."

another, as this world's athletes do; I contund myself, my own flesh, as if it were my enemy" (Bishop Wordsworth).

8. "For bodily exercise profiteth little: but godliness is profitable unto all things." This verse arises out of the latter part of the former, in which the Apostle had bidden Timothy *exercise* himself unto godliness, and then bearing in mind the utterly profitless, rather the evil exercising, involved in the forbidding to marry, and commanding to abstain from meats, both which were merely bodily, he reverts to the training for the games—the races, the wrestlings, with which they were so familiar. And so he says: "Bodily exercise—training after such a sort—profiteth a little, but that is very insignificant when compared with the spiritual training; the bodily training is good for winning a temporal crown, the spiritual is good for this life and also for the future and eternal one."

Two things are to be borne in mind together to enable us to enter into the Apostles' meaning.

(1.) He would on no account commend in the least degree the false Jewish or Gnostical asceticism of verse 3. He would never describe it as profiting a little, for it was a doctrine of seducing spirits or demons.

(2.) He would not say a word in discouragement of what he had inculcated in the two Epistles to the Corinthians (1 Cor. ix. 27): "Keeping under his body, and bringing it into subjection;" or, "Crucifying the flesh with its affections and lusts" (Gal. v. 24). So that we are on no account to take this verse as militating against that fasting which the Lord commends in His Sermon on the Mount (Matt. vi. 16), or that which he, together with others, practised at his own ordination to the Apostolate (Acts xiii. 2).

"Godliness is profitable unto all things, having promise of the life that now is." Godliness has promise of the life that now is because it abounds in that which alone secures the true enjoyment of

9 [s] This *is* a faithful saying and worthy of all acceptation. [s] ch. i. 15.

10 For therefore [t] we both labour and suffer reproach, because we [u] trust in the living God, [x] who is the Saviour of all men, specially of those that believe.

[t] 1 Cor. iv. 11, 12. [u] ch. vi. 17. [x] Ps. xxxvi. 6. & cvii. 2, 6, &c

---

10. "We both labour." "Both" omitted by ℵ, A., C., D., retained by F., G.

10. "Suffer reproach." So D., L., P., most Cursives, d, f, g, Vulg., Goth., Syr., Copt. Arm.; but ℵ, A., C., F., G., K., and seven Cursives, read, "we contend" or "strive."

life, and that is contentment (Phil. iv. 12). Being reconciled to God, and living as His children, we can rely upon our Father for His blessing and protection in everything—the world, life or death, things present or things to come, all are his who possesses godliness (1 Cor. iii. 22); besides he has such direct promises as "the eyes of the Lord are over the righteous, and his ears are open to their prayers" (Ps. xxxiv. 12). "Your heavenly Father knoweth that ye have need of these things; all these things shall be added unto you" (Matt. vi. 32, 33).

And, of course, it has the promise of that which is to come. "My sheep hear my voice, and I know them, and they follow me, and I give unto them eternal life, and they shall never perish, neither shall any man pluck them out of my hand" (John x. 27).

9. "This is a faithful saying and worthy of all acceptation." This refers to what has just been said respecting godliness—that it is profitable for both the present and the future life.

10. "For therefore we both labour and suffer reproach [or strive], because," &c. We "labour and strive" (see Critical Notes) because we trust in the living God, Who has the ordering of both the present and the future, and so orders all things for good to them that love Him. We have every confidence in striving to work out our salvation, because we know that it is God that worketh in us both to will and to do (Phil. ii. 13).

"Who is the Saviour of all men, specially of those that believe." He is the Saviour of all men because He gave His Son to be the propitiation "for the sins of the whole world" (1 John ii. 2). That His Spirit should make so absolute a declaration as this, that He should be the Saviour of those who have never heard of Him, teaches us not universal salvation, but that God will make every

y ch. vi. 2. z 1 Cor. xvi. 11. Tit. ii. 15. a Tit. ii. 7. 1 Pet. v. 3.

11 [y] These things command and teach.
12 [z] Let no man despise thy youth; but [a] be

---

allowance for the want of faith and defective lives of those who have never heard the Gospel. It cannot possibly mean that He is the Saviour of all men because He saves their animal or natural lives from death, for this He does not do. The vast majority of men die before they have attained to the natural term of life: it must be because He has, in a sense, saved all by the sacrifice of His Son. He has even cleansed them by the same sacrifice (Acts x. 15, and note), and we doubt not that He will find ways of having mercy upon them which we know not.

"Specially of those that believe," because by believing they accept His mercy and honour Him for it, and plead the all-sufficient Sacrifice. Of such He will assuredly be the Saviour. He will save such to the uttermost. Chrysostom, looking back upon those ages of persecution, gives a somewhat different turn, "How is He the Saviour of the faithful? Had He not been so, they must long since have been destroyed, for all men have made war upon them."

11. "These things command and teach." Observe, it is not "these things suggest and recommend," but these things "command." This is because St. Paul committed to him as much apostolical authority as, not being an actual Apostle, he could receive.

He was to command the bishops and deacons to do and teach because he acted by the authority of the Apostle. There was no inherent authority in any presbytery to sit in judgment upon what he commanded.

12. "Let no man despise thy youth." Timothy was no doubt a young man when he joined the Apostle, and both his father and mother seem then to have been living. This was about ten or twelve years before the writing of this letter, so probably he was now thirty-six or thirty-eight. This we should not account young, but it was very natural that the aged Apostle should so account it. I mention this because some sceptical writers have said that it was contrary to reason to speak of Timothy as if he was always young, but it is at the utmost a matter of ten years, and if we take 1 Cor. xvi. 11 as referring to his youthful appearance, scarcely a matter of six years.

thou an example of the believers, in word, in conversation, in charity, in spirit, in faith, in purity.

13 Till I come, give attendance to reading, to exhortation, to doctrine.

14 [b] Neglect not the gift that is in thee, which [b] 2 Tim. i. 6.

---

12. "In spirit." Omitted by א, A., C., D., F., G., eight Cursives, d, f, g, Vulg., Copt., Syriac; but K., L., P., and most Cursives, retain it.

"Be thou an example of the believers, in word." "In word" signifies either in the preaching and teaching of the Word, or in the words he employs in his intercourse with the believers, that they should be grave and sober, befitting one who remembers that for every word he speaks he shall be called to give account.

"In conversation," that is in his habitual deportment and intercourse.

"In charity," in love, and kindness, and sympathy.

"In spirit," omitted by principal uncials.

"In faith," in holding firmly to the great truths of the Gospel, in living as if he believed them.

"In purity," not only in what is commonly accounted purity, but in purity of doctrine and of motives—what we should call unworldliness.

13. "Till I come, give attendance to reading." Give attendance, attention, heed.

"To reading," *i.e.*, to "the reading," most probably the reading of the Scriptures in the public assembly.

"To exhortation, to doctrine." Exhortation, as distinguished from doctrine, may be appeals to the feelings. "Doctrine" is instruction both in the faith and in morals. "Give attendance to reading the Divine writings, to exhortation of one another, to teaching of all."

14. "Neglect not the gift that is in thee." "The gift in thee," "prophecy," the "laying on of hands." All these three things suggest questions which cannot now be, in all respects, satisfactorily answered.

"The gift in thee" was this the gift of the Holy Spirit which was given to him at his first ordination, to enable him to fulfil the common work of the ministry? or was it the Gift given to him when he was set apart to the especial work of overseeing the Church

c ch. i. 18.
d Acts vi. 6. & viii. 17. & xiii. 3. & xix. 6. ch. v. 22. 1 Tim. i. 6.
‖ Or, *in all things.*

was given thee [c] by prophecy, [d] with the laying on of the hands of the presbytery.

15 Meditate upon these things; give thyself wholly to them; that thy profiting may appear ‖ to all.

---

of Ephesus, or some other apart from these? We cannot say, only that in the strictly parallel passage in 2 Tim. i. 6, we read, "I put thee in remembrance that thou stir up the gift of God which is in thee by the putting on of my hands." This gift seems to be interpreted in the next verse as that of "power and love, and of a sound mind."

Again, what is the prophecy through which, as in some sense a medium, the gift was bestowed? Is it the prophecy alluded to in Acts xiii. 1, 2, "In the Church that was at Antioch, certain prophets and teachers, as Barnabas and Simeon. . . . As they ministered to the Lord and fasted, the Holy Ghost said, Separate me," &c.? Most probably it was. If some prophet or prophets singled out Timothy from among the mass of believers for the presbyterate or episcopate, or apostolic vicariate, it must have been by the inspiration of the Holy Ghost, or St. Paul would not have cited it, but the exact form which it outwardly took has not come down to us, other, of course, than the laying on of hands.

Then the "laying on of the hands of the presbytery." This was certainly not any presbytery of Ephesus. Was Barnabas one of them? No, because he and Paul had parted company before Timothy was known to Paul. Was Silvanus one? In all probability he was. It is scarcely possible to suppose that this Presbytery was that of some local Church. It stands to reason that it must have been one composed of the immediate disciples or fellow-helpers of St. Paul. That St. Paul was himself one of them is evident from his words in 2 Tim. i. 6.

15. "Meditate upon these things; give thyself wholly to them." "These things." What things? Upon the mystery of godliness, upon the dangers of the latter days, upon exercising himself and others with godliness, upon the Living God being the Saviour of all men, of being an example to the believers, &c., upon the gift through prophecy, and the laying on of hands, &c.

"Give thyself wholly to them." The words of the original are

16 [e] Take heed unto thyself, and unto the doctrine; continue in them: for in doing this thou shalt both [f] save thyself, and [g] them that hear thee.

e Acts xx. 28.
f Ezek. xxxiii. 9.
g Rom. xi. 14. 1 Cor. ix. 22. James v. 20.

---

much stronger, "Be in these things" (ἐν τούτοις ἴσθι). Bengel says of this, "He who *is* in them will be less in worldly companies, in other kinds of pursuits, in collecting books, shells, coins, in which many pastors unconsciously spend a great part of their time" (quoted by Dr. Fairbairn). If Bengel had lived in England he would probably have added horses, hounds, guns, tennis lawns, hot-houses, &c.

"That thy profiting may appear to all." This of course does not mean that he is to make a display of religion, but that he is to be careful to remember that the life of a pastor is narrowly watched, and that he must unconsciously show no decline, but rather progress in the Divine Life.

16. "Take heed unto thyself, and unto the doctrine; continue in them," &c. "Thyself and unto the doctrine." Take heed that thou continue in the doctrine, that thou adorn the doctrine in thy life, that thou defend it against gainsayers, that thou preach it unweariedly, and teach it thoroughly, and realize it in thine own spiritual life.

"For in doing this thou shalt both save thyself and them that hear thee." If ever man was in a saved state—a state of salvation —it was this son of the Apostle, and yet even to him salvation was future, and depended, under God's grace, on his exertions. If he was to be saved at the great day of account, he must take heed unto himself and to the doctrine; he must continue in what he had been taught. The work of Christianity is woven in with the right discharge of the office of the ministry. "Many ministers can say that if they had not been ministers, they had in all appearance lost their souls. The subject of the minister's work is the same with that of a Christian, and above all men should he be careful of his heart and intentions, that all be pure and spiritual. No man is under so strict a necessity of dependence on the influence and assistance of the Holy Ghost, both for gifts and grace. And are not all these great helps to one's own salvation?" (Trail, quoted in Fairbairn.)

CHAP. V.

REBUKE [a] not an elder, but intreat *him* as a father; *and* the younger men as brethren;

[a] Lev. xix. 32.

2 The elder women as mothers; the younger as sisters, with all purity.

[b] ver. 5, 16.

3 Honour widows [b] that are widows indeed.

---

1. "Rebuke not an elder, but intreat him as a father." The elder here is called πρεσβυτερὸς, or presbyter, the same word as is employed for the designation of the ministerial office in Tit. i. 6, 7. Most commentators, however, seem to be agreed in considering that the Apostle alludes to elders in years, elderly persons, who would be likely to resent a rebuke from one much younger than themselves, and be discouraged or perhaps alienated by it.[1]

"The younger men as brethren." Let your bearing towards young men be that of a brother, an equal, rather than of a dignified superior.

2. "The elder women as mothers; the younger as sisters, with all purity." Mark the words which the Apostle throws in, as it were, when speaking of church or social intercourse with the female part of the flock, "with all purity." What miserable scandals would have been avoided in all ages if this had been constantly remembered. In this, more than in any other respect, a young priest has to abstain from all appearance of evil. If Timothy was thus advised, let others consider what sort of conduct is required of them, that they should give no ground of suspicion, no shadow of pretext to those who wish to calumniate.

3. "Honour widows that are widows indeed." It has been much disputed whether these widows are persons who have devoted themselves to certain duties in the Church, or Christian body, or

---

[1] Still, it is well to remember that the word presbyter is almost invariably used in the New Testament of Jewish or Christian ecclesiastical officers. According to Mr. Blunt, "it is used sixty-four times in the New Testament, thirty-one times in the Gospels and Acts to denote the Jewish elders, once in the sense of ancestors (Heb. xi. 2), thirty-one times in the Acts and Epistles and the Revelations as the name given to ordained men."

4 But if any widow have children or nephews, let them learn first to shew || piety at home, and [c] to requite their parents: [d] for that is good and acceptable before God.

|| Or, *kindness*.
c See Gen. xlv. 10, 11. Matt. xv. 4. Eph. vi. 1, 2.
d ch. ii. 3.

---

4. "Good and acceptable." "Good and" omitted by ℵ, A., C., D., F., K., L., P., most Cursives, Ital., Vulg., Syriac, &c.; no authority for the retention of these words.

whether they are widows in the ordinary sense of the word without any Church obligations.

I am inclined to think the latter. In times of persécution many widows would require support or assistance from the Church funds who were simply persons in need, and who could not devote their time to Church work. St. Paul meets the cases of such persons in this and the few next verses, and then in verse 9 passes on to the case of those widows who were enrolled in a Church guild, or society, and who afterwards became the order of deaconesses.

Honour means not only to pay deference to, but materially contribute to the support of such.

"Widows indeed," that is, utterly destitute and desolate—having no relations who were under obligations to maintain them.

4. "But if any widow have children, or nephews, let them learn first to shew piety at home." This seems to be capable of but one application. "If any widow have children, or grandchildren, let them, *i.e.*, the children, or grandchildren, learn first to show piety at home, and to requite their progenitors, that is, the widows, their mothers or grandmothers." If the Church takes upon herself the burden of maintaining widows who have descendants capable of supporting them, by relieving them of this duty she injures these persons. An extraordinary explanation, however, has been given to this by some ancient and modern commentators (*e.g.*, Chrysostom and Wordsworth), which is that it is the widow who by bringing up her children well requites her own ancestors, not her children who by supporting her in her declining years requite her. I will give it in the words of the former: "*To requite* their parents. How? For bringing them up and educating them. As if he should say: 'Thou hast received from them (thy ancestors) great care. They are departed. Thou canst not requite them. For thou didst not bring them forth or nourish them. Requite them in their descendants, repay the debt through the children.'"

5 [e] Now she that is a widow indeed, and desolate, trusteth in God, and [f] continueth in supplications and prayers [g] night and day.

6 [h] But she that liveth || in pleasure is dead while she liveth.

e 1 Cor. vii. 32.
f Luke ii. 37. & xviii. 1.
g Acts xxvi. 7.
h James v. 5.
|| Or, *delicately*.

But this seems a very roundabout way of inculcating a plain duty. If the widow has children and grandchildren her first duty, which nature itself as well as revelation teaches, is to them. She is not even to take upon herself Church work which would interfere with her duty to her children.

"That is good and acceptable before God." As the fifth commandment, and the words of our Blessed Lord (Matth. xv. 1-6) in vindicating its sanctions, teach us.

5. "Now she that is a widow indeed, and desolate, trusteth in God, and continueth," &c. Do, then, all distressed and desolate widows trust in God? If they have real religion they do. St. Paul is here directing by implication that the Church alms should not be given to irreligious, but to religious persons, and the true widow, who alone was worthy of help, was one whose afflictions and bereavements had brought her near to God, and so she trusted in God, Who had taken from her her earthly supports that she might be nearer Him.

"And continueth in supplications and prayers."

St. Paul must have had his disciple's account of Anna in his mind, "who departed not from the temple, but served God with fastings and prayers night and day." St. Polycarp in his Epistle seems to refer to this place: "Teach the widows to be discreet as respects the faith of the Lord, praying continually for all, being far from all slandering, evil speaking, false witnessing," &c.

6. "But she that liveth in pleasure is dead while she liveth." Though the Apostle says this of widows it is of course capable of the widest application. The man who devotes himself to pleasure is dead. If the current of his thoughts runs upon amusement, no matter how innocent as an occasional recreation, upon eating and drinking, upon costly dishes and choice wines, upon collecting, in fact, upon any worldly thing so that he may be said to live in it, and to be thinking about it more than about the things of God—such an one is dead, and requires that he should hear the call, "Awake thou that sleepest, and arise from the dead."

7 And these things give in charge, that they may be
blameless.

8 But if any provide not for his own, and specially [k] for those of his own house, || he hath denied the faith,[m] and is worse than an infidel.

9 Let not a widow be || taken into the number

i ch. i. 3. & iv. 11. & vi. 17.
k Isa. lviii. 7. Gal. vi. 10.
|| Or, *kindred.*
l 2 Tim. ii. 5. Tit. i. 16.
m Matt. xviii. 17.
|| Or, *chosen.*

And this applies with tenfold force to those who are living in sinful pleasures, such as fornication and drunkenness; they are dead indeed—in fact, the Second Death seems to have begun in them.

The word "liveth in pleasure" (σπαταλῶσα) we are told by Archbishop Trench combines the notion of luxurious self-indulgence with that of prodigality. It is used elsewhere only in James v. 5, where it is rendered, "ye have been wanton."

7. "And these things give in charge, that they may be blameless." Give in charge to the presbyters, or pastors, that they may instruct the widows who have children, and the children, whose natural duty it is to support their widowed mothers, that they may be blameless, for this is a matter closely connected with the fair fame of Christianity itself, for he proceeds to say,—

8. "But if any provide not for his own, and specially for those of his own house," that is, his own parents, or children. What is the difference between his own, and those of his own house? The former seems to have a wider application, and to include all near relatives, the latter means his parents, or children.

"He hath denied the faith." The faith is given to raise and regulate the life. If a man professes to believe in Christ, and neglects his family, gives them no godly education, and leaves others to provide for them, he acts as if he did not believe in God and in Christ. Men will naturally ask how can he believe in a Saviour Who had given Himself for him to redeem him from all iniquity, when he sets at naught the plainest obligations of nature and of human society? He is worse than the heathen, for some heathen nations have been particularly careful respecting the duties of family life.

9. "Let not a widow be taken into the number under threescore years old." There is much difference of opinion as to the widows to whom the Apostle here refers. The Revisers translate it: "Let none be enrolled as a widow," &c. The question is, were these

n Luke ii. 36. ch. iii. 2. under three-score years old, [n] having been the wife of one man,

---

widows merely recipients of Church alms, or were they set apart to do certain Church work? Some call them Presbyteral widows, and suppose that they were entrusted with certain duties towards the female part of the Church.

It is difficult to suppose that the Apostle here lays down the qualifications of those widows who were to be supported by the Church, for surely there must have been (in times of persecution especially) widows in the greatest straits, and who had no children to help them long before they had attained to the age of sixty years. And many would be entitled to alms on the score of distress and want who had not the qualifications laid down in verse 10.

Bishop Ellicott gives a very likely explanation, first suggested by Grotius, and then ably expounded by Mosheim, and followed by De Wette, and others, that an order of widows is referred to whose duties apparently consisted in the exercise of superintendence over, and the ministry of counsel and consolation to the younger women, whose office in fact was, so to say, presbyteral (*πρεσβύτιδες*) rather than diaconic. The external evidence for the existence (though not necessarily the special ecclesiastical organization) of such a body, even in the earliest times, is so fully satisfactory, and so completely in harmony with the internal evidence supplied by verse 10, *sq.*, that on the whole we should adopt this view.

"Having been the wife of one man." Not having been divorced and remarried, and many suppose not having been widowed and married a second time. Chrysostom's remarks are worthy of notice, both with reference to this and chap. iii., 2 and 12. "But why does he discourage second marriages? Is the thing condemned? By no means. That is heretical. Only he would have her henceforth occupied in spiritual things, transferring all her care to virtue. For marriage is not an impure state, but one of much occupation. He speaks of them having leisure, not of them being more pure by remaining unmarried. For marriage certainly implies much secular occupation. If you abstain from marriage that you may have leisure for the service of God, and yet do not so employ that leisure, it is of no advantage to you (if you do not use your leisure) to perform all services to strangers and to the saints.

10 Well reported of for good works; if she have brought up children, if she have [o] lodged strangers, if she have [p] washed the saints' feet, if she have re-

[o] Acts xvi. 15. Hebr. xiii. 2. 1 Pet. iv. 9.
[p] Gen. xviii. 4. & xix. 2. Luke vii. 38, 44. John xiii. 5, 14.

If you do not, then you abstain from marriage not for any good end but as though you condemned the state."

10. "Well reported of for good works; if she have brought up children, &c." The qualifications here enumerated seem to shut us up to the conclusion that the widows here were church officials, who to command respect must have been foremost in the performance of the duties for which women are looked up to.

"Well reported of for good works." These, or some of them, are now enumerated, to show that they are peculiarly the duties which belong to women; for instance, diligence in teaching or expounding Scripture is not included.

"If she have brought up children." This is mentioned the first, because it is the first duty of women. If it be asked were these her own children? Certainly, we answer, if she had had any, but if a Christian woman had not, she would probably be a kind mother to some orphans, and this would be the first qualification. Bishop Jackson, in "Speaker's Commentary," puts "Those of others, especially orphans, besides her own."

"If she have lodged strangers." The strangers here are any strangers, but, of course, Christian ones especially. It has been asserted that this implies that she had some means, but, as one says, "If she has a house, she can at least afford shelter."

"If she have washed the saints' feet." It is singular to observe the difference between the treatment of this clause by the ancients and by the modern commentators. With the moderns it is a metaphorical washing. Bishop Wordsworth and Blunt take no notice of the place; nor does Dr. Fairbairn. Bishop Jackson explains as "Paid the kind duties of hospitality in an especial manner to Christians as distinguished from strangers." Bishop Ellicott writes: "An act not only connected with the rites of Eastern hospitality, but demonstrative of her humility" (1 Sam. xxv. 41). It was commonly a servant's office. Augustin says, "Nec dedignetur quod fecit Christus facere Christianus." Chrysostom: "The saints' feet are holy, though they are poor men; but not even the head of the

lieved the afflicted, if she have diligently followed every good work.

11 But the younger widows refuse: for when they have begun to wax wanton against Christ, they will marry;

---

profane is honourable. Such efficacy is there in the feet of the saints that when they shake off the dust of their feet, they inflict punishment. When a saint is amongst us, let us not be ashamed of anything that belongs to him. And all are saints who unite a holy life with a right faith; and though they do not work miracles, nor cast out devils, still they are saints."

Of course it would now be impossible to revive this custom, but it may be some consolation to remember that the deaconesses who work in our hospitals, and our nursing sisterhoods, do work far more menial than this.

"If she have relieved the afflicted." The words imply much more than merely relieving by alms.

"If she have diligently followed every good work." Many are the good works which the Christian can do to his fellows besides these. So St. Paul, by these words, would sanction the admission of a widow who had devoted herself to any good work for the sake of Christ and His Church.

11. "But the younger widows refuse: for when they have begun to wax wanton," &c. "Refuse"—*i.e.*, decline to put on the roll of Church widows. This can scarcely mean "refuse to give any assistance to them in the time of their distress."

What would the Apostle have thought of a system which requires young women, sometimes very young women, to devote themselves to a so-called religious life, which, in order to prevent them giving scandal, virtually imprisons them for life?

We cannot but gather from this that those who were enrolled (or taken into the number) were to be considered as dedicated to God in an especial way; and if they declined from this life, and went again back into the world, they occasioned great scandal, and on this very account St. Paul lays down that all marriageable young widows—in fact, all young women—were to be be refused entrance into a society in which it would be a scandal—a breach of promise—if they married, as a dereliction of duties which were by him considered only compatible with a single life.

12 Having damnation, because they have cast off their first faith.

13 [q] And withal they learn *to be* idle, wandering about from house to house; and not only idle, but tattlers also and busybodies, speaking things which they ought not. q 2 Thess. iii. 11.

14 [r] I will therefore that the younger women r 1 Cor. vii. 9.

---

12. "Damnation;" *i.e.* "condemnation."
14. "Younger women;" perhaps "widows."

"To wax wanton against Christ" is explained by Chrysostom to become scornful and luxurious.

12. "Having damnation." Damnation is not eternal damnation, but rather judgment in the sense of condemnation. "Being condemned, because they have," &c.

"Because they have cast off their first faith." Most commentators explain this in the sense of "because they have violated their first pledge of remaining in widowhood, in order that they may the better further the work of Christ." It cannot well mean because they have apostatized from the Gospel they received at the first. Faith must here mean fidelity to a promise or trust.

13. "And withal they learn to be idle, wandering about from house to house." Thus he commands not only men but women also to work. For idleness is the teacher of all sin. What, then, happens where the care of the husband is withdrawn, and the care to please God does not restrain them? They naturally become idlers, tatlers, and busybodies. For he who attends not to his own concerns will be meddling with those of others, even as he who minds his own business will take no account of, and have no care about the affairs of another (Chrysostom).

14. "I will therefore that the younger women marry, bear children." Here we have this great teacher of religion laying down what he wills or desires respecting these young women, and it is that they should lead domestic lives. But is this all? May not a woman lead a very domestic life without reference to Christ? Certainly; and, of course, what the Apostle wills is that what he has taught elsewhere respecting domestic duties should be taken into full account here. He had taught respecting servants that

marry, bear children, guide the house, [s] give none occasion to
[s] ch. vi. 1. Tit. ii. 8. the adversary † to speak reproachfully.
† Gr. *for their railing.* 15 For some are already turned aside after Satan.
16 If any man or woman that believeth have
widows, let them relieve them, and let not the
[t] ver. iii. 5. church be charged; that it may relieve [t] them
that are widows indeed.

---

16. "If any man or woman that believeth have widows." So D., K., L., most Cursives; but ℵ, A., C., F., G., P., three Cursives, Vulg. (Amiat.), Copt., Arm., read, "If any woman that believeth hath widows."

what they did they should do it heartily, as to the Lord, and not unto men. And so here he undoubtedly desires that wives should submit themselves unto their own husband as unto the Lord—*i.e.*, Christ, "for the husband is the head of the wife even as Christ is the Head of the Church, and He is the Saviour of the body" (Ephes. v. 23).

"Bear children"—that is, not out of a perverse asceticism live in the married state as if they were in the single state.

"Guide the house," as if it was a part of Christ's great household, the Church.

Giving "none occasion to the adversary to speak reproachfully" —*i.e.*, to compare them with virtuous heathen women to their disadvantage, or on account of their reviling or slandering, a sin which idle, gadding women were almost sure to fall into.

15. "For some are already turned aside to Satan." And yet in the censures he had passed upon these widows he had mentioned no crime, nor anything which we should at this day account a serious fall. Perhaps, however, by these words he means to indicate there had already been serious falls, perhaps from the profession of the faith, perhaps from the faith itself, perhaps from purity.

16. "If any man or woman that believeth have widows, let them relieve them"—that is, have near relations that have lost their husbands, and are in a state of distress, and they (the believing relatives) are able to support them. The Church fund is to be

17 [u] Let the elders that rule well [x] be counted worthy of double honour, especially they who labour in the word and doctrine.

u Rom. xii. 8. 1 Cor. ix. 10, 14. Gal. vi. 6. Phil. ii. 29. 1 Thess. v. 12, 13. Heb. xiii. 7, 17.
x Acts xxviii. 10.

---

carefully husbanded, or it will not be able to support those who have no other means of support.

17. "Let the elders that rule well be counted worthy of double honour." The words "that rule well" rather mean "that preside well," and refer to the standing before the congregation, and conducting the service of the Church. We need be in no doubt about this, because the worship of the Christian congregations is described by Justin Martyr (A.D. 150) in these terms: "Having ended the prayers, we salute one another with a kiss. There is then brought to the president of the brethren (*ἔπειτα προσφέρεται τῷ προεστῶτι τῶν ἀδελφῶν ἄρτος*, &c.) bread and a cup of wine mixed with water, and he taking them gives praise and glory to the Father of the universe, through the name of the Son and of the Holy Ghost, and offers thanks at considerable length for our being counted worthy to receive these things at his hands," &c. (Justin, Apol. i. 65).

This gives a perfectly adequate explanation. It has generally been explained as if there were a body of elders, all equal, some of whom ruled, and some did not; and that some of those who ruled laboured in the word and doctrine, and some did not; and those who united both qualifications were to have double honour (as some explain, a double honorarium); but there is not the smallest evidence that the body of elders were thus divided. If anyone takes the trouble to look into any of the most ancient types of Liturgy (*i.e.*, of Eucharistic Liturgy) which have come down to us, he will see that to render such acts of prayer and praise and thanksgiving well would be no easy task, especially as it is very probable that they were transmitted orally, rather than written. For further remarks on this I desire to refer the reader to my note on Rom. xii. 8, and to an Excursus on Apostolic Traditions at the end of the volume of notes on the Epistles to the Corinthians. The meaning I have given solves the difficulty of there having been two sorts of elders in one college, one ruling, and the other not, of which institution not a trace has come down to us, whereas, in a large city like Ephesus, there must have been numerous small congregations (for the Chrisy Deut. xxv. 4. 1 Cor. ix. 9.

z Lev. xix. 13. Deut. xxiv. 14, 15. Matt. x. 10. Luke x. 7.

18 For the Scripture saith, [y] Thou shalt not muzzle the ox that treadeth out the corn. And, [z] The labourer *is* worthy of his reward.

---

18. "Treadeth out." "Whilst he is treading out."

tians must have then worshipped in the larger rooms of private houses), each of which would require its προεστὼς for its worship.[1]

"Especially they who labour in the word and doctrine." The best explanation I have seen is that of Chrysostom: "These are the men whom he wishes to be honoured most of all, and he adds the reason—for they sustain great labour. For when one is neither watchful nor diligent, but merely sits in his stall, easy and unconcerned, whilst another wears himself out with anxiety and exertion, especially if he is ignorant of profane literature, ought not the latter to be honoured above all others, who more than others gives himself up to such labours? For he is exposed to numberless tongues. One censures him, another praises him, a third mocks him, another finds fault with his memory and his composition; and it requires great strength of mind to endure all this."

18. "For the Scripture saith, Thou shalt not muzzle the ox that treadeth," &c. This is a citation of Deut. xxv. 4, and is quoted by the Apostle in 1 Corinth. ix. 9, where see note.

"And the labourer is worthy of his reward." This is a saying of the Lord's, and is probably quoted by St. Paul from St. Luke's Gospel (x. 7). It has been alleged that a Gospel would not at so early a date as this be called "Scripture," but would it not be Scripture? Was not the inspiration of St. Luke as great a gift to the Church as that of Moses?[2] We have noticed how such a passage as Coloss. iii. 16 presupposes that St. Paul's converts were acquainted with one at least of the Gospels, probably St. Luke's; anyhow it is clear that long before this the converts were acquainted with many of the sayings of Christ. If this saying of Christ will be acted upon

---

[1] The above explanation is equally consonant with the sort of worship which prevails amongst Presbyterians now. If there was united worship of any sort, there must be some one to conduct it, and that was the *proestos*.

[2] Again in 2 Pet. iii. 16, the epistles of St. Paul are classed as Scripture, where it is said that "evil men convert them as they do the other Scripture to their own destruction." Many, however, suppose that the words were a proverbial saying, and used by our Lord as signifying a commonly acknowledged truth.

19 Against an elder receive not an accusation, but ‖ [a] before two or three witnesses.

20 [b] Them that sin rebuke before all, [c] that others also may fear.

‖ Or, *under*.
a Deut. xix. 15.
b Gal. ii. 11, 14. Tit. i. 13.
c Deut. xiii. 11.

---

20. "Them that sin." So ℵ, K., L., P., most Cursives, Vulg., Copt., Syr., &c.; but A., D., d, f, g, read, "but them that sin" (δὲ).

in the day of judgment, as assuredly it will, what will become of those who have given nothing for the sustentation of their own ministers, as well as nothing for the sustentation of those who have devoted themselves to that first duty of the Church, to preach the Gospel to every creature.

19. "Against an elder receive not an accusation, but before two or three witnesses." An elder most probably means a presbyter, not an elderly person. Here again the Apostle quotes Deut. xix. 15: "At the mouth of two witnesses, or at the mouth of three witnesses, shall the matter be established." But ought not the same precaution against false accusation be taken with everyone, whether elder or not? To which we reply that Timothy was not to be the judge of every individual, but of the clergy; and the same rule was to be observed with respect to accusations against them, as God by Moses had commanded with respect to all others. The Apostle deprecates a severer rule against them, which some might have advocated with the intention of keeping the ministry purer.

St. Chrysostom, however, understands it of elder men, not of the presbyters.

20. "Them that sin rebuke before all, that others also may fear." This would seem to allude to the presbyters or overseers, notwithstanding the words, "Rebuke not an elder."

Of course the sin alluded to must be open sin, and from the participle used it is not some sudden fall but a continued habit. Wordsworth and others suppose that it is heresy, citing part of St. Paul's address to the Ephesian elders in Acts xx. 29, 30, "Also of your own selves shall men arise, speaking perverse things;" and St. Paul would undoubtedly consider this as sinful, as he writes to Titus (iii. 10, 11), "A man that is an heretic, after the first and second admonition, reject. Knowing that he that is such is subverted, and sinneth, being condemned of himself." Still I cannot help thinking that if the Apostle had meant heresy, or indeed in-

21 [d] I charge *thee* before God, and the Lord Jesus Christ, and the elect angels, that thou observe these things ‖ without preferring one before another, doing nothing by partiality.

d ch. vi. 13. 2 Tim. ii. 14. & iv. 1.
‖ Or, *without prejudice.*

---

21. "The Lord Jesus Christ." ℵ, A., D., G., 17, 31, 73, d, f, g, Vulg., Sah., Copt. omit "Lord;" but K., L., P., &c., retain.

cluded heresy under the word "sinneth," he would have plainly said so.

The rebuke before all is a public rebuke before the Church. As Augustine says, "Therefore those sins are to be reproved before all which are committed before all, but they are to be reproved more secretly which are committed more secretly."

21. "I charge thee before God, and the Lord Jesus Christ, and the elect angels," &c. This place is important, as showing the extraordinarily high place in his theology which the Apostle attaches to the presence of angels, not only in heaven but in the Church. It is parallel to what he said in 1 Corinth. xi. 10, "For this cause ought the woman to have power (rather a sign of subjection) on her head because of the angels;" and that we "have come to Mount Zion . . . and to an innumerable company of angels" (Heb. xii. 22), and that one of the articles of the mystery of godliness was that Christ was "seen of angels." We may not understand all about what is said of these ministering spirits, but one thing we are taught very plainly, which is, that the Apostle held them not to inhabit an infinitely distant heaven, but to be in our assemblies upon earth, so that if our eyes, like those of the servant of the prophet, were opened, we should see these wonderful beings bright like fire on every side of us (2 Kings vi. 17).

The "elect" angels—those who stood under some temptation with which God suffered them to be assailed, and from that time have been His chosen—*i.e.*, His elect servants. He chose them because they stood in the fiery trial and fell not away.

It is perfectly certain that St. Paul considered them to be present, and so witnesses of his charge or adjuration.

"That thou observe these things without preferring one before another," that thou deal impartially and equally between those who are upon trial, and are to be judged by thee, that no one may preoccupy thy mind, or gain thee over to his side beforehand.

22 [e] Lay hands suddenly on no man, [f] neither be partaker of other men's sins: keep thyself pure.

23 Drink no longer water, but use a little wine [g] for thy stomach's sake and thine often infirmities.

e Acts vi. 6. & xiii. 3. ch. iv. 14. 2 Tim. i. 6.
f 2 John xi.
g Ps. civ. 15.

22. "Partaker of." "Partaker in."

How strong all this is against preference on any ground except that of merit; against preference because of party considerations, or family ties, or prejudice, which would prevent a Bishop looking on all sides, and taking every circumstance into account.

22. "Lay hands suddenly on no man, neither be partakers of other men's sins," &c. This has been explained by the ancient interpreters, and most of the modern ones, as referring to ordination. He was not to ordain any one hastily, or without very searching examination as to his previous life and conduct. What is suddenly? Not upon a first, nor a second, nor a third trial, but after frequent and strict examination and circumspection. I need hardly remind the reader that in one of our Ember prayers we pray that the bishops may observe this rule, that they may "lay hands suddenly on no man, but faithfully and wisely make choice of fit persons to serve in the sacred ministry of God's Church."

Some have supposed the place to refer to an ancient custom of laying on of hands in absolution, but if so, it would seem out of place here.

"Neither be partakers of other men's sins." Which he would be if he admitted to holy orders men of unsound doctrines, or of evil life. "It is an affair of no common peril. For thou wilt be responsible for the sins committed by him, as well his past as his future sins, because thou hast delegated to him this power."

"Keep thyself pure." Taking what goes before into account, this seems to mean, "In ordaining men to the ministry, keep thyself pure from unworthy motives. Look not upon the sins of those whom thou ordainest carelessly but as in some real way defiling thee if thou hast not used every precaution to ascertain their fitness." Chrysostom says that he writes this with reference to chastity. This seems at first unlikely, but we are to remember the "with all purity" of verse 2.

23. "Drink no longer water, but use a little wine for thy

24 [h] Some men's sins are open beforehand, going before to judgment; and some *men* they follow after.

[h] Gal. v. 19.

---

stomach's sake." This should be rendered, "Be no longer a water drinker," *i.e.*, a total abstainer; which, apparently from this, St. Timothy had hitherto been. If his frequent infirmities occasioned his inability at times to fulfil the work of his ministry, it was clearly his duty to use that gift of God, which God himself had given, to make glad the heart of man; that is, to save it from undue depression, which would hinder him in fulfilling his vocation.

It has been asked, seeing that the application to men's bodies of the handkerchiefs or aprons which had merely touched the body of the Apostle healed sickness and disease, why did not the Apostle by his power of healing keep Timothy for the Church's sake in perfect health? To which we answer, such was not the will of God. The gifts of healing, as most other gifts, were for the sake of unbelievers, that seeing them, or experiencing them, they might be compelled to listen at least to the Gospel; and it is probable that in all cases those who had gifts of healing had secret intimations from God on whom to exercise them and on whom not. Thus in Phil. ii. 27, we learn that Epaphroditus was sick "nigh unto death," and was restored to health not by miracle, but in the course of the ordinary providence of God.

24. "Some men's sins are open beforehand, going before to judgment," &c. The sins of some are so gross and palpable, conducting, as it were, to condemnation, that no minute or searching investigation is required, but the sins of others, who are evidently unfit for the ministry, are not so palpable. They do not publicly proclaim the unworthiness of those guilty of them, but must be investigated. Chrysostom treats this as following closely on verse 22 (verse 23 being in a sort of parenthesis), "He had said, 'Be not partakers of other men's sins.' But what, he might say, if I be ignorant of them? Why, 'Some men's sins are open before,' &c. Some men's, he means, are manifest because they go before whilst others are unknown, because they follow after." It seems to me clear that the sins which 'follow after' manifestly deteriorate the character of the candidate for ordination, but what they are actually may not be known, but, if possible, must be found out.

25 Likewise also the good works *of some* are manifest beforehand; and they that are otherwise cannot be hid.

---

25. "Likewise also the good works of some are manifest beforehand," &c. As it is with sins, so with good works. They are manifest beforehand, and so prove the fitness of him who seeks admission into the ministry; and they that are otherwise—that is, are not so openly manifest—will yet soon come to light.

Blunt says, on this latter clause: "In the same way the 'good works' of some are conspicuous, and of those which are not so they cannot be hid from a Bishop who takes measures for ascertaining the character of those who come to him for ordination."

CHAP. VI.

LET as many [a] servants as are under the yoke count their own masters worthy of all honour, [b] that the name of God and *his* doctrine be not blasphemed.

[a] Eph. vi. 5. Col. iii. 22. Tit. ii. 9. 1 Pet. ii. 18.
[b] Is. lii. 5. Rom. ii. 24. Tit. ii. 5, 8.

---

1. "Let as many servants as are under the yoke count their own masters," &c. Again the Apostle returns to the subject of the duties of servants, or rather slaves, taking no notice, as in the Epistles to the Ephesians and Colossians, of the duties of children. The reason, no doubt, is contained in the words, "that the Name of God and his doctrine be not blasphemed." Nothing would bring more scandal on Christianity than the thought that the liberty of all Christians in Christ emancipated Christian slaves from their duties to their masters.

"Let as many servants (slaves) as are under the yoke count," &c. This seems to imply that some were under the yoke, and some not, whereas it should be translated (as Revisers) "as many as are slaves under the yoke."

"Count their own masters worthy of all honour." There was especial danger that this would be neglected in a society like the

2 And they that have believing masters, let them not despise *them*, [c] because they are brethren; but rather do *them* service, because they are ‖ faithful and beloved, partakers of the benefit. [d] These things teach and exhort.

3 If any man [e] teach otherwise, and consent

[c] Col. iv. 1.
‖ Or, *believing.*
[d] ch. iv. 11.
[e] ch. i. 3.

Church, which in so many places had its roots in the synagogue, for, as Bishop Wordsworth shows, "their Rabbis taught that it was a sinful thing to own any mortal master, and to be bondservants to heathen. The Apostle, therefore, had a difficult task to perform—in vindicating on the one side the great doctrine of Christian liberty against some of the Judaizers, and in asserting and upholding the duty of Christian subjection, on the other hand, against those of the same class, who abused the sacred name of liberty into a plea for licentiousness."

2. "And they that have believing masters, let them not despise them," &c. It would be a great temptation to a slave brought under the redemption of Christ, and therefore into the liberty of the Gospel, to regard himself as now upon an equality with his master in matters of this world; but it must not be, Christianity had not yet abolished slavery, and would not for a thousand years and many more; so that still the slave was the property of his master; and no one more nobly realized this than St. Paul, as we see from his letter to Philemon: "Whom," he says, respecting Onesimus, "I would have retained, that in thy stead he might have ministered unto me in the bonds of the Gospel. But without thy mind I would do nothing, that thy benefit should not be as it were of necessity, but willingly" (verses 14, 15).

"But rather do them service, because they are," &c. This should rather be translated, as Revisers, "but let them serve them the rather, because they that partake of the benefit are believing and beloved." What is the benefit? Some suppose it to be the beneficial labour of the slaves, others the benefits of Christ's redemption.

3. "If any man teach otherwise, and consent not to wholesome words, even the words," &c. "Teach otherwise," teach that Christianity raises all men to a dead level of equality in this world, "and consent not to wholesome words."

[f] not to wholesome words, *even* the words of our Lord Jesus Christ, [g] and to the doctrine which is according to godliness;

4 He is || proud, [h] knowing nothing, but || doting about [i] questions and strifes of words, whereof cometh envy, strife, railings, evil surmisings,

f ch. i. 10. 2 Tim. i. 13. & iv. 3. Tit. i. 9.
g Tit. i. 1.
|| Or, *a fool.*
h 1 Cor. viii. 2. ch. i. 7.
|| Or, *sick.*
i ch. i. 4. 2 Tim. ii. 23. Tit. iii. 9.

"The words of our Lord Jesus Christ." Not necessarily meaning those which were spoken by Him—for in His discourses which have come down to us there is little or nothing respecting the relative duties of masters and slaves—but such as bear upon them the stamp of His authority: along with His own, therefore, those also of His divinely commissioned Apostles and Evangelists. (Fairbairn.)

It is noteworthy, however, and it may be that the Apostle means this, that all the words of the Lord are on the side of submission, even to human authority. Thus He speaks of the submission of servants, or slaves, as a matter of course, in His parable in Luke xvii. 7. But it is mostly on the negative side of what has come down to us of His teaching that its "wholesomeness" is apparent; thus He was always denouncing the worldliness and irreligion of the rich, even to the extent of saying, "How hardly shall a rich man enter into the kingdom of God;" He was ever exposing the false pretensions of the Scribes and Pharisees, and yet there is nothing revolutionary in His teaching, in fact nothing approaching to such a thing—a man who accepted it would take the lowest place, knowing that it was only at the Second Coming that the Judge would say to him, "Friend, go up higher."

4. "He is proud, knowing nothing, but doting about questions and strife of words," &c. "He is proud"—his teaching proceeds from out of himself, and is the reflection of himself, and so is self-asserting, not deeming for a moment that he has, or can have, any superior.

"Knowing nothing" (that is, having no right judgment of anything) as he ought to know it.

"Doting about questions and strifes of words, whereof cometh envy, strife," &c. If a man's mind is full of small questions and distractions about minor matters, it cannot have a due and proper

k 1 Cor. xi. 16. ch. i. 6.
|| Or, *Gallings one of another.*
l 2 Tim. iii. 8.
m Tit. i. 11. 2 Pet. ii. 3.
n Rom. xvi. 17. 2 Tim. iii. 5.

5 [k] || Perverse disputings of [l] men of corrupt minds, and destitute of the truth, [m] supposing that gain is godliness: [n] from such withdraw thyself.

---

5. "From such withdraw thyself" omitted by א, A., D., F., G., d, f, g, Vulg., &c.; but retained by K., L., P., and most Cursives.

grasp or hold of the great articles of the Faith, such as the Person and work of the Eternal Son, His Incarnation, Atonement, and Headship over His mystical Body: for the dwelling upon these dwarfs all other things. And then such contemplation humbles the mind. Such amazing revelations convince the mind of its own littleness and abase it so that there is no room in it for envy, strife, railings, and evil surmisings. Such things are engendered by the dwelling upon what is comparatively little, not upon what is infinitely great.

5. "Perverse disputings of men of corrupt minds, and destitute of the truth." "Perverse disputings." Some translate this "stubborn contention," others (as Revisers) "wranglings." The marginal reading is "gallings one of another."

"Destitute of the truth, supposing that gain is godliness." "Being destitute of the truth, more especially of the Truth Incarnate, they suppose that godliness is gain. The translation, "gain is godliness," is given up by all, and indeed it is contrary to the truth, for no one has ever supposed, or could suppose, that gain—the making of money—was godliness, but St. Paul considers that all false teachers of his day held that godliness was gain, and might be lawfully used to gain wealth and worldly advantage. Bishop Wordsworth very ingeniously connects this with the "teaching otherwise," or teaching different doctrines to the obedience inculcated in the first and second verses: "The false teachers ingratiated themselves with slaves and other dependents, by flattering them that because all men are equal and brethren in Christ, therefore they need not be subject to their masters; or that if they were subject they had a claim to greater temporal advantage than they enjoyed; and thus they excited slaves to disobedience, and made the profession of the Gospel to be a matter of secular traffic and worldly lucre."

6 But [o] godliness with contentment is great gain.

7 For [p] we brought nothing into *this* world, *and it is* certain we can carry nothing out.

8 And [q] having food and raiment let us be therewith content.

o Ps. xxxvii. 16. Prov. xv. 16. & xvi. 8. Heb. xiii. 5.
p Job i. 21. Ps. xlix. 17. Prov. xxvii. 24. Eccles. v. 15.
q Gen. xxviii. 20. Heb. xiii. 5.

---

7. "And it is certain." So K., L., P., most Cursives; but ℵ, A., F., G., g, Vulg., Sah., read, "because" (ὅτι).

6. "But godliness with contentment is great gain." He had said of these evil teachers that they supposed that godliness is gain, and lest they should mistake him he now tells them that there is a true and blessed sense in which godliness is gain. It is gain when united with contentment, for the godly man considers that all his life is allotted to him by God, so that he knows "how to be abased, and how to abound." In all things he is instructed "both to be full and to be hungry, to abound and to suffer need" (Phil. iv. 12). Whatever his heavenly Father gives he receives with thankfulness; whatever He withholds he believes it to be for some good purpose.

7. "For we brought nothing into this world, and it is certain we can carry nothing," &c. That is, we can carry nothing out into the eternal world which we keep during our lives, but whatever we part with for some good and holy purpose, as to the poor for Christ's sake, *that* we carry out with us, or else we should not be able to lay up treasures in heaven, as the Lord commanded. The Revisers translate, "we brought nothing into this world, for neither can we carry anything out." This has little sense, but has been accepted as being the more difficult reading. "Taking the passage as it stands in the best supported form (that is, that of the Revisers), the Apostle not merely says that we both enter and leave the world in a state of destitution as to worldly goods, but that the one is ordered with a certain respect to the other—thus having a lesson embodied in our very birth, in order that we might keep in view the solemn exemplification it was to find at the hour of death" (Fairbairn).

8. "And having food and raiment let us be therewith content." There seems here a reminiscence of the Lord's words in the Sermon on the Mount. "Therefore I say unto you, Take no thought for

9 But [r] they that will be rich fall into temptation [s] and a snare, and *into* many foolish and hurtful lusts, [t] which drown men in destruction and perdition.

10 [u] For the love of money is the root of all evil: which while some coveted after, they have || erred from the faith, and pierced themselves through with many sorrows.

r Prov. xv. 27. & xx. 21. & xxviii. 20. Matt. xiii. 22. Jam. v. 1.
s ch. iii. 7.
t ch. i. 19.
u Ex. xxiii. 8. Deut. xvi. 19.
|| Or, *been seduced.*

---

your life, what ye shall eat, or what ye shall drink; nor yet for your body, what ye shall put on . . . . Your heavenly Father knoweth that ye have need of all these things" (Matth. vi. 25).

9. "But they that will be rich fall into temptation and a snare," &c. This must be translated, "They that desire to be rich: they who wish to be rich." Not those who are rich, as Chrysostom says, but they who wish to be. For a man may have money, and make a good use of it, not overvaluing it, but bestowing it upon the poor.

"Fall into temptation and a snare," that is, to increase what they have by unlawful means (in our day, to gamble with it) and to "withhold from him to whom it is due."

"And into many foolish and hurtful lusts, which drown men in destruction," &c. "Destruction and perdition." The first of these has been said to refer to the destruction of the body, the last to everlasting perdition, but without any reason being given. Ὄλεθρος is joined by the Apostle in 2 Thess. i. 9 with *αἰώνιος*.

10. "For the love of money is the root of all evil." This seems to ascribe too much to the love of money, and so it is noticed that "root" has no article, and is therefore rendered by many "The love of money is a root of all evil." Alford renders it "the love of money is the root of all manner of evil," but I think we may venture to understand it as meaning covetousness, which is evil desire, which is unquestionably *the* root of all evil. It was the covetous desires of our first parents which brought sin into the world. The Apostle's words are to be taken not so much literally as naturally. He had been laying down that certain false teachers supposed godliness to be gain. The Apostle asserted that it was gain when united with contentment. This leads him to say that the truly godly man will

11 [x] But thou, [y] O man of God, flee these things; and follow after righteousness, godliness, faith, love, patience, meekness.

[x] Rom. ii. 22.
[y] Deut. xxxiii. 1. 2. Tim. iii. 17.

---

be contented with very little. This naturally leads him to speak of the danger of the inordinate desire for riches, and his mind being full for the time of this form of evil desire, he says it is the root of all evil. And if the love of money is taken to represent that evil desire of which it is the most prominent sort or species, it may be taken to be as no one other evil thing in man is, the root of all evil. There is certainly no root of bitterness which has occasioned so much misery. Undue sexual desire has, in most cases, its remedy, but covetousness seems to be all-pervading. The Apostle has now rising before him the cases of a vast number of spiritual mariners who have been wrecked on this shoal—some have erred from the faith, others, who may have come short of such a fall, have lost contentment, and with it all happiness of this life. With respect to the latter, the "piercing themselves through with many sorrows," Chrysostom says, "To learn how true this is, the only way is to sojourn with the rich, to see how many are their sorrows, how bitter their complaints."

11. "But thou, O man of God, flee these things; and follow after righteousness," &c. In the words, "Thou, O man of God," does St. Paul speak to Timothy, as being, as it is supposed, a prophet, and therefore worthy of the designation, "man of God," so frequently given to the prophets; or does he not rather speak perfectly generally, and exhort every one who professed godliness to flee coveteousness? I should have thought the latter; but the second part of the next verse is evidently addressed to Timothy personally.

"Follow after righteousness, godliness, faith, love, patience, meekness." It is to be noticed that here, as in several other places, in this list of virtues or graces, faith is not put the first—it occupies here the third place; in 2 Tim. ii. 22, the second; in Gal. v. 22 it is the seventh out of nine. Now why is this, for St. Paul evidently held it to be the means of justification; and in the next verse, the Christian contest is called the "fight of faith"? Evidently because St. Paul was not under the bondage of that modern Evangelical system which makes a man an offender for a word; which

[a] 1 Cor. ix. 25, 26. ch. i. 18 2 Tim. iv. 7.
[a] Phil. iii. 12, 14. ver. 19.
[b] Heb. xiii. 23.

12 [a] Fight the good fight of faith, [a] lay hold on eternal life, whereunto thou art also called, [b] and hast professed a good profession before many witnesses.

---

treats him as unsound and unsaved, if he puts sanctification or love first. Now the Apostle had no care for these niceties, and he was right, for supposing that a man was sincerely desirous to please God, and so began, without due regard to the claims of faith, to pursue righteousness, one of the first things that God would teach him would be that it was unattainable except through a living faith in the Son of God, in His Person and Work, and by that he would lay hold on Christ's strength.

12. "Fight the good fight of faith, lay hold on eternal life." Faith, rather *the* faith (Revisers). Fight the good fight of *the* faith—*i.e.*, the Christian deposit. The one faith in the One Lord, professed at the one Baptism, has to be contended for. "Earnestly contend for the faith once for all delivered to the saints" (Jude), and never in the history of the Church has it more earnestly to be contended for than at this time.

The faith is not a mere abstraction, but the faith of, the believing in, the holding fast to certain facts—the Incarnation, Death, and Resurrection, and Second Coming of the Eternal Son. There is always some attack being made upon these. Men of eminence as Christian officials, insinuate that the Incarnation and Resurrection may be according to natural laws. They proclaim openly that Redemption and its consequences are part of the natural order of things; they say that so-called believers will not be judged for the things done in the body, they more than hesitate about the Death as atoning in any special sense. So that we must fight—fight by prayer and argument and bold confession of the truth—for the Faith.

"Lay hold on eternal life." But had not Timothy laid hold on eternal life long before this? Did he not lay hold on it when he was converted? Was it not assured to him, when he was baptised, if his baptism was like that of his fellow Christians, a Death, Burial, and Resurrection with Christ? Yes; but the laying hold on eternal life is constant, is continuous. Timothy, if any man ever was, was saved when St. Paul wrote to him: "In doing this thou *shalt* both save thyself and them that hear thee."

13 [c]I give thee charge in the sight of God, [d]who quickeneth all things, and *before* Christ Jesus, [e]who before Pontius Pilate witnessed a good || confession;

14 That thou keep *this* commandment without

c ch. v. 21.
d Deut. xxxii. 39. 1 Sam. 2, 6. John v. 21.
e Matt. xxvii. 11. John xviii. 37. Rev. i. 5. & iii. 14.
|| Or, *profession.*

---

13. "Quickeneth." So ℵ, K., L., most Cursives; but A., D., F., G., P., and six Cursives, read, "keepeth alive."

"Whereunto thou art also called." When he first heard the Gospel.

"And hast professed a good profession before many witnesses." Either at his baptism, at which we know, from 1 Pet. iii. 21, there was always made the answer of a good conscience towards God, or at his Ordination.

It is not *a* good profession, but *the* good profession, as if it was one well known in the Church.

13. "I give thee charge in the sight of God, who quickeneth all things," &c. God Who quickens all things at the last day, and will then render to good confessors the reward of their profession in the face of bonds and death.

"And before Jesus Christ, who before Pontius Pilate," &c. "Before" may either mean "in the presence of," or "during the time of." If the former, it was that He was a king—a king Whose kingdom was not of this world—that in this capacity He bore witness to the truth, the eternal truth of God, Whose word was pledged to bring in a kingdom of righteousness.

Or if it means "in the time of Pontius Pilate," then it includes all which Christ said of Himself as the Son of God—the Way, the Truth, and the Life, the Redeemer and Judge of all; and particularly we may single out His confession before the chief Priest and rulers: "Art thou the Christ, the Son of the Blessed?" "I am, and ye shall see the Son of Man sitting on the right hand of power, and coming in the clouds of heaven" (Mark xiv. 62). It was this confession which enabled them to crucify Him.

14. "That thou keep this commandment without spot, unrebukeable, until," &c. "This commandment" may either be the commandment to flee from covetousness, and fight the good fight of faith, which was of the utmost importance, because covetousness

spot, unrebukeable, [f] until the appearing of our Lord Jesus
Christ:

[f] Phil. i. 6, 10. 1 Thess. iii. 13. & v. 23.

15 Which in his times he shall shew, *who is*
[g] the blessed and only Potentate, [h] the King of
kings, and Lord of lords;

[g] ch. i. 11, 17. [h] Rev. xvii. 14. & xix. 16.

16 [i] Who only hath immortality, dwelling in
the light which no man can approach unto;

[i] ch. i. 17.

---

and cowardice in fighting the good fight would destroy all Timothy's power and usefulness; or some take "commandment" to mean the whole Gospel, which is all in the nature of a command to crucify sin, and love God.

As I have frequently mentioned, each and every part of the Gospel has not only to be believed, but to be obeyed. For instance, the obedience to the doctrine of the Cross is not only that we believe in its atoning virtue, but that we "crucify the flesh with its affections and lusts" (Gal. v. 24).

"Until the appearing of our Lord Jesus Christ." Not until the day of thy death, but until the coming of the Lord from heaven.

15, 16. "Which in his times he shall shew, who is the blessed and only Potentate." These titles are, it seems to me, ascribed to God the Father; for it is He only of the Persons of the adorable Trinity of Whom it can be said, "Whom no man hath seen or can see" (John i. 18); and yet it is one of the most irrefragable proofs of the Godhead of the Son, for of the Son it is said that He is "King of Kings and Lord of Lords" (Rev. xvii. 14, xix. 16). "Thou only, O Christ, with the Holy Ghost, art most high in the glory of God the Father."

"Who only hath immortality"—that is, inherent endless life. The Son hath life, because as the Father hath life in Himself, so hath He given to the Son to have life in Himself (John v. 26). The Holy Ghost is the Lord, the Life-Giver, because He proceedeth from the Father and the Son.

"Dwelling in the light which no man can approach unto." All accounts which the Holy Scriptures give us of God unite in this, that He dwelleth in light, and reveals His peculiar presence by light—not light intellectual, or light moral only, but light of which that which illuminates the world is a sort of feeble image. Thus God is said to clothe Himself with light as with a garment (Ps.

[k] whom no man hath seen, nor can see:[l] to whom *be* honour and power everlasting. Amen.

17 Charge them that are rich in this world, that they be not highminded, [m] nor trust in † [n] uncertain riches, but in [o] the living God, [p] who giveth us richly all things to enjoy;

k Ex. xxxiii. 20. John vi. 46.
l Eph. iii. 21. Phil. iv. 20. Jude 25. Rev. i. 6. & iv. 11. & vii. 12.
m Job. xxxi. 24. Ps. lii. 7. & lxii. 10. Mark x. 24. Luke xii. 21.
† Gr. *uncertainty of riches.*
n Prov. xxiii. 5.
o 1 Thess. i. 9. ch. iii. 15. & iv. 10.
p Acts xiv. 17. & xvii. 25.

---

17. "The living God." So D., E., K., L., most Cursives; but "in God" (omitting "the living") in א, A., B., C., P., seven or eight Cursives, &c.

civ. 2). The symbol of His presence is a pillar of fire; and no created thing, if, indeed, that which beams from Him can be called created, can be greater than the light in which He enshrouds Himself.

"Whom no man hath seen, or can see." So John i. 18: "No man hath seen God at any time." So John vi. 46: "Not that any man hath seen the Father, save he which is of God, he hath seen the Father."

"To whom be honour and power everlasting."

17. "Charge them that are rich in this world," &c. We should have thought that the Epistle had ended with this doxology; but here it seems that the Apostle suddenly remembered that there were among the Ephesian converts many who possessed riches without having coveted them. They had inherited wealth, or God had, contrary to their expectations, blessed their trade, and the increase of their fields; and so he says a word to their chief pastor respecting these. They may have become rich, or grown rich, without evil desire; but still there was, as the Lord had constantly warned men, very great danger in riches—in the mere possession of them. Their natural effect was to make men high minded. The world defers to those who possess its good things, and so, seeing that all around, after a sense, worshipped them, they would begin to think themselves worthy of this worship, and be proud and disdainful.

"Nor trust in uncertain riches." Riches naturally make us trust in them. If we have fixed incomes secured to us by the law, we naturally think that we do not depend upon the good providence of God for our daily bread. So that the poor man who feels

18 That they do good, that [q] they be rich in good works, [r] ready to distribute, ‖ [s] willing to communicate;

19 [t] Laying up in store for themselves a good

q Luke xii. 21. ch. v. 10. Tit. iii. 8. Jam. ii. 5.
r Rom. xii. 13.
‖ Or, *sociable.*
s Gal. vi. 6. Heb. xiii. 16.
t Matt. vi. 20. & xix. 21. Luke xii. 33. & xvi. 9.

---

that he depends from day to day on the direct hand of God, has a daily lesson in faith which the rich man has not; and faith, being constantly exercised, grows and strengthens.

We are reminded by many commentators that the words of the Apostle, literally translated, are "in the uncertainty of riches;" but after all it must mean uncertain riches, for we cannot consciously trust in an uncertainty.

"The living God, who giveth us richly all things to enjoy." Throughout the vast area of the world, excepting such small parts of it as the Arctic regions and the deserts, there is a profusion of things fitted for food and raiment to men who will moderately work. God has laid it upon man to work for man's own sake; for if the human race could live in idleness, they would be given over to the worst vices. But, if he works, man has literally a profusion of things wherewith to feed and clothe himself. Of course there may be such things as over-population, restrictive laws, and the like; but though certain countries may be over-peopled, the earth, if properly divided and cultivated, would sustain an infinitely greater population than the present one; and if man makes laws which interfere with the due course of nature, he has no right to say that God does not richly give us all things to enjoy.

18. "That they do good, that they be rich in good works, ready to distribute," &c. All these refer to the distribution of wealth; other duties, of course, remain as they are, and cannot make up for the lack of this use of riches. Neither can they be made up for by seeming liberality. No giving of superfluities will enable an unchaste or dishonest man to enjoy the rewards of the kingdom of God.

19. "Laying up in store for themselves a good foundation against the time to come." This is a remarkable verse. Many, if they found it in the pages of any other book except the Bible, would denounce it as false doctrine, and they who wrote it as unenlightened; but it is the mere reflection of very many sayings of

foundation against the time to come, that they may [u] lay hold on eternal life.

[u] ver. 12.

20 O Timothy, [x] keep that which is committed

[x] 2 Tim. i. 14. Tit. i. 9. Rev. iii. 3.

---

19. "On eternal life;" rather, "on the life which is life indeed." So Revisers, after ℵ, A., D., E., F., G., nine Cursives, d, e, f, g, Vulg., Syriac, &c.; K., L., P., most Cursives, "eternal."

our Lord, as "Blessed are the merciful, for they shall obtain mercy." "When thou doest thine alms, let not thy left hand know what thy right hand doeth." "Thy father which seeth in secret shall reward thee openly." "Do good and lend, hoping for nothing again, and your reward shall be great in heaven." "They (the poor) cannot recompense thee, but thou shalt be recompensed at the resurrection of the just."

But are we not justified by faith? Yes, we are; but those who have believed in God are expressly told that they are to be careful to maintain good works (Titus iii). And there is great need of remembering this, for many think they are right in the sight of God on the score that they understand thoroughly the doctrine of grace, and trust entirely on the grace of God through Christ, and yet have no charity, no liberality—they are not rich in good works—they are very unready to distribute, very unwilling to communicate. I myself have now before me one of large means, great respectability, much looked up to as a neighbour and a magistrate, a great upholder of salvation by faith, and yet he gave next to nothing even to the societies which he patronized, and nothing to the poor—at least nothing that was known or heard of. And in this state he went before the Judge, Who says that He will say at the last, "Inasmuch as ye did it to one of the least of these, my brethren, ye did it unto me. Inasmuch as ye did it not to one of the least of these, my brethren, ye did it not to me." Can we preach Christ faithfully unless we preach Him as the Judge of Quick and and Dead, rendering to every man as his work shall be?

"That they may lay hold on eternal life." So that eternal life is laid hold on not only by prayer, by faith, by watchfulness, but by charity—by giving to Christ in His Church and in His poor.

20. "O Timothy, keep that which is committed to thy trust." O Timothy, guard the deposit. What is this but the Catholic faith—the one faith, the faith once for all delivered to the saints,

[y] ch. i. 4. 6. & iv. 7. 2 Tim. ii. 14, 16, 23. Tit. i. 14. & iii. 9.

to thy trust, [y] avoiding profane *and* vain babblings, and oppositions of science falsely so called:

[z] ch. i. 6, 19. 2 Tim. ii. 18.

21 Which some professing [z] have erred concerning the faith. Grace *be* with thee. Amen.

¶ The first to Timothy was written from Laodicea, which is the chiefest city of Phrygia Pacatiana.

---

the faith of which the Lord asks so seriously, when He says, "Nevertheless, when the Son of man cometh, shall he find the faith on the earth?"

"Avoiding profane and vain babblings, and oppositions of science falsely so called." There must have been some great danger to Timothy from these, for the Apostle writes this short postscript to warn him against what he had already cautioned him about in 1 Tim. i. 4, and iv. 4, and vi. 5, 6. As a Jew, he might be in danger from the babblings; as an intellectual person, he might require cautioning against the antitheses of the falsely-named knowledge or gnosis.

21. "Which some professing have erred concerning the faith." The Gnostical blasphemies, even in their earliest developments, must have upset the faith, for they made out that God was not the author of matter, and they put other mediators between God and us besides the Man Christ Jesus.

THE SECOND EPISTLE TO TIMOTHY.

CHAP. I.

PAUL, [a] an apostle of Jesus Christ by the will of God, according to [b] the promise of life which is in Christ Jesus,

2 [c] To Timothy, *my* dearly beloved son: Grace, mercy, *and* peace, from God the Father and Christ Jesus our Lord.

[a] 2 Cor. i. 1.
[b] Eph. iii. 6. Tit. i. 2. Heb. ix. 15.
[c] 1 Tim. i. 2.

---

2. "And Christ Jesus our Lord." So A., D., E., F., G., K., L., most Cursives, Vulg., &c.; but א reads, "Lord Jesus Christ our Lord."

1. "Paul, an apostle of Jesus Christ by the will of God," &c. In the First Epistle it is by the "commandment of God our Saviour," here it is by the "will of God." The will of God issues in His commandment, the commandment of God issues in the establishment or bringing about of the thing which He commands. In this case it was the effectual apostleship of St. Paul.

"According to the promise of life which is in Christ Jesus." He was an Apostle "according to the promise of life," because he was sent and one commissioned especially to proclaim the promise of life in Christ's Resurrection ("Go speak to the people all the words of this life," Acts v. 20). And he now speaks of his Apostleship being "according to the promise of life," because, as never before, he had the sentence of death upon him, "The time of my departure is at hand." So that it was indeed true of him, "In the midst of death he was in life."

2. "To Timothy, my dearly beloved son." My own son in the faith, and therefore my dearly beloved son.

"Grace, mercy, and peace, from God the Father," &c. Observe

d Rom. i. 8. Eph. i. 16.
e Acts xxii. 3. & xxiii. 1. & xxiv. 14. & xxvii. 23. Rom. i. 9. Gal. i. 14.
f 1 Thess. i. 2. & iii. 10.
g ch. iv. 9, 21.
h 1 Tim. i. 5. & iv. 6.

3 [d] I thank God, [e] whom I serve from *my* forefathers with pure conscience, that [f] without ceasing I have remembrance of thee in my prayers night and day;

4 [g] Greatly desiring to see thee, being mindful of thy tears, that I may be filled with joy;

5 When I call to remembrance [h] the unfeigned faith that is in thee, which dwelt first in thy

---

how again to Timothy he invokes mercy from God upon him. (See note on 1 Tim. i. 2).

3. "I thank God, whom I serve from my forefathers." This seems to imply that some degree of personal piety had been transmitted from one forefather to another, as it was in the case of Timothy.

"With a pure conscience." Remember his words on the temple stairs, "Taught according to the perfect manner of the law of our fathers, and zealous towards God;" and before the council, "I have lived in all good conscience before God to this day."

"That without ceasing I have remembrance of thee in my prayers," &c. Why does he thank God that he unceasingly prays for Timothy? Because he looked upon God as One Who always answers prayer, and he believed that God would not have put into his heart to pray thus continuously for Timothy, unless He had intended to keep him continually in His grace, and make His word effectual in Timothy's mouth.

4. "Greatly desiring to see thee, being mindful of thy tears," &c. These tears were probably shed when he parted with Timothy, when he was arrested and sent to Rome as a prisoner.

"That I may be filled with joy." At seeing thee again, and being able to strengthen and establish thee. Some think that St. Paul was not perfectly assured of Timothy's steadfastness in enduring the fiery trial which was before them both; but this, I think, is scarcely reconcilable with the expressions in the next verse.

5. "When I call to remembrance the unfeigned faith that is in thee, which dwelt," &c. If Timothy was converted in A.D. 53 or so, it was quite possible that both his grandmother and mother received the faith many years before; for Timothy became a Christian and the follower of St. Paul about twenty years after Pentecost. His grand-

grandmother Lois, and [i] thy mother Eunice; and I am persuaded that in thee also.

6 Wherefore I put thee in remembrance [k] that

[i] Acts xvi. 1.

[k] 1 Thess. v. 19. 1 Tim iv. 14.

---

mother, if she was not then among the εὐλαβεῖς in Jerusalem, might have received the account from "those of Asia" or "of Phrygia" (Acts ii. 9), and being a pious Jewess, might have, through God's grace, accepted it, and found that all which she heard of Jesus of Nazareth was according to the prophecies of the Messiah in the Scriptures. I think this is more likely than supposing that Lois was an holy woman under the law, who had only believed in a Christ to come, whilst Eunice and Timothy believed in a Christ which was come.

"And I am persuaded that in thee also." "It is not a conjecture he means, it is my persuasion; I am fully assured of it. If, therefore, from no human motive thou hast embraced it, nothing will be able to shake thy faith" (Chrysostom).

6. "Wherefore I put thee in remembrance that thou stir up the gift," &c. "That thou stir up the gift of God." The metaphor is taken from the act of reviving a fire which is almost out. We gently stir it, or we blow into it, and the cold ashes are soon glowing with heat. Had St. Paul discerned anything in the way of coldness in Timothy that he thus spake to him? Most probably not, for the precept is of universal application in the Church. Whatever means of grace we receive only once in our lives, such as Baptism, Confirmation, and Ordination, we must in after life constantly stir up the gift which we have received in it, for it may lie dormant. And I need not say that if Timothy needed to be so reminded, much more do we. God assigns grace to those who even unworthily receive Baptism, Confirmation, and Ordination, which are only administered to us once in our lives. This grace we must revive and strengthen by acts of faith and prayer. We must make an act of faith in God's grace to us at our baptism. We must say such words as, "Lord, thou didst graft me into Thy Son's body in baptism; Thou didst therein cause me to die and to be buried, and to be raised again in Him. Revive in me Thy grace. Renew in me, most loving Father, whatsoever hath been decayed by the fraud and malice of the devil, or by my own carnal will and frailty." Some men say that grace cannot lie dormant in the soul, which is as much as saying that there can be no dormant faculties

thou stir up the gift of God, which is in thee by the putting on of my hands.

l Rom. viii. 15.
m Luke xxiv. 49.
Acts i. 8.

7 For [l] God hath not given us the spirit of fear; [m] but of power, and of love, and of a sound mind.

---

in any man's soul, to refute which need scarcely be seriously attempted. Chrysostom considers it to be the grace of the Spirit which Timothy had received for presiding over the Church, for the working of miracles, and for every service. "For this grace it is in our power to kindle or to extinguish. Wherefore he elsewhere says, 'Quench not the Spirit.' For by sloth and carelessness it is quenched, and by watchfulness and diligence it is kept alive. For it is in thee indeed, but do thou render it more vehement, that is, fill it with confidence, with joy, and delight. Stand manfully."

"By the putting on of my hands." Was this the same as the putting on of the hands of the presbytery of 1 Tim. iv. 14? If it was, then St. Paul considered that the laying on of his own hands, as those of an Apostle, conferred the real ordination. He certainly assumed that the laying on of the hands of all the rest was as nothing compared to the laying on of his hands. At an English ordination of priests, the presbyters present assist the bishop, but if the bishop's hands alone were laid on the candidate in default of the presence of presbyters, would it not be a valid ordination?

7. "For God hath not given us the spirit of fear; but of power, and of love," &c. "Fear," this fear is explained by almost all as the spirit of timidity or cowardice, or shrinking from danger; whereas He has given us rather power or might of spirit ("strengthened with all might according to his glorious power," Coloss. i. 11); some, however, take it to be the powers of the ministry, some of which were of a supernatural character.

"And of love." Love to the sheep of Christ and His lambs, so as to brave all dangers, to feed and pasture them ("Simon, son of Jonas, lovest thou me? feed my sheep").

"And of a sound mind," *i.e.*, of a prudent mind, not inclined to be led away by fanaticism, or false doctrine, or novelties. Some, as revisers, translate it (a spirit) of discipline, a spirit that fears not to rebuke and censure; others, as simply self-control.

8. "Be not thou therefore ashamed of the testimony of our

8 [n] Be not thou therefore ashamed of [o] the tes-
timony of our Lord, nor of me [p] his prisoner:
[q] but be thou partaker of the afflictions of the
gospel according to the power of God;
9 [r] Who hath saved us, and [s] called *us* with an
holy calling, [t] not according to our works, but

n Rom. i. 16.
o 1 Tim. ii. 6. Rev. i. 2.
p Eph. iii. 1. Phil. i. 7.
q Col. i. 24. ch. iv. 5.
r 1 Tim. i. 1. Tit. iii. 4.
s 1 Thess. iv. 7. Heb. iii. 1.
t Rom. iii. 20. & ix. 11. Tit. iii. 5.

Lord." This in the early ages would mean, "Be not ashamed of the Cross. Be not ashamed that thou preachest One that was crucified, but rather glory in it."

But the offence of the Cross never ceases. In one age men are offended at one thing, in another at another.

The age of our immediate forefathers seems to have stumbled at salvation by grace. In this age men stumble at the supernatural in Christianity, especially at the doctrine of the Sacraments as means not of instruction or of profession, but of grace. They stumble at such words of Christ as "As my Father sent me, so send I you," "Whosoever sin ye remit they are remitted unto them."

"Nor of me his prisoner." Very probably St. Paul, in writing this, had in his mind the defections of some like Demas, and he said, as an old man would say, "Behave not like these deserters," having no real fear that he would do as they had done.

"Be thou partaker of the afflictions of the Gospel." "All that will live godly in Christ Jesus must suffer persecution." "That no man should be moved by these afflictions, for yourselves know that we are appointed thereunto" (1 Thess. iii. 3).

"According to the power of God." The power which sustains us, and nerves us, and comforts us, and at last gives us the victory.

9. "Who hath saved us and called us with an holy calling," &c. "Saved us," that is, "by the death of his Son reconciling the world unto himself."

"Called us with an holy calling." A calling to holiness because a calling to be in the Church or Body of His Son.

"Not according to our works." Because salvation was entirely of grace, and this was seen in the characters of those who were called and obeyed the calling. Some were gross sinners (1 Corinth. vi. 11); some were persecutors even in spite of their

u Rom. viii. 28.
x Rom. xvi. 25. Ephes. i. 4. & iii. 11. Tit. i. 2. 1 Pet. i. 20.
y Rom. xvi. 26. Ephes. i. 9. Col. i. 26. Tit. i. 3. 1 Pet. i. 20.
z 1. Cor. xv. 51, 55. Heb. ii. 14.

[u] according to his own purpose and grace, which was given us in Christ Jesus [x] before the world began,

10 But [y] is now made manifest by the appearing of our Saviour Jesus Christ, [z] who hath abolished death, and hath brought life and immortality to light through the gospel:

---

9. "Before the world began." Literally, "before eternal ages."

growing conviction that those whom they persecuted were in the right (Acts ix. 5).

"According to his own purpose and grace, which was given us in Christ Jesus," &c. "That is, no one compelling, no one counselling Him, but of His own purpose, from the impulse of His own goodness, He saved us."

"Which was given us in Christ Jesus before the world began." That is, it was determined without beginning that these things should be done in Christ. This is no light consideration that from the first He willed it. It was not an after-thought.

10. "But is now made manifest by the appearing of our Saviour Jesus Christ." The appearing—the Epiphany. This means more than His appearance amongst His creatures on the day of His Birth. It denotes His whole redemptive work through His Incarnation, Death, and Resurrection, which men saw, though the meaning of it all as respects themselves was hidden from them till they were taught it by the Spirit of God.

"Who hath abolished death and hath brought life," &c. He abolished death by His Resurrection, because it was not the Resurrection of one single Person considered apart by Himself, but it was the Resurrection of an Adam, the last Adam, Who could have all his brethren in Himself when He died, and when He rose again.

"He hath abolished death." He hath changed its character, so that instead of being the end of a journey it is but a step in it.

The heathen, as a rule, even those who held the immortality of the soul, never fixed their minds upon anything beyond. They surmised, they hoped, at least they did not despair, but it was like looking into thick impenetrable darkness, whereas Christ has "brought life and immortality to light by the Gospel." He has

11 [a] Whereunto I am appointed a preacher, and an apostle, and a teacher of the Gentiles.

12 [b] For the which cause I also suffer these things: nevertheless I am not ashamed: [c] for I know whom I have || believed, and am persuaded

[a] Acts ix. 15. Eph. iii. 7, 8. 1 Tim. ii. 7. ch. iv. 17.
[b] Eph. iii. 1. ch. ii. 9.
[c] 1 Pet. iv. 19.
|| Or, *trusted.*

---

11. "Teacher of the Gentiles." So C., D., E., F., G., K., L., P., most Cursives, d, e, f, g, Vulg., Goth., Syriac; but ℵ, A., 17, omit "of the Gentiles."

illumined the darkness beyond by such words as "Because I live, ye shall live also" (John xiv. 19); "Father, I will that they also, whom thou hast given me, be with me where I am" (John xvii. 24); "Where I am, there shall also my servant be" (John xii. 26). "It doth not yet appear what we shall be, but we know that when he shall appear we shall be like him, for we shall see him as he is," (1 John iii. 2).

11. "Whereunto I am appointed a preacher, and an Apostle, and a teacher," &c. The same assertion, repeated almost verbatim, as he makes in 1 Tim. ii. 7. (See also Ephesians iii. 7, 8.) He constantly, in one form or other, asserts his commission. He knew nothing greater in itself or more humbling to himself than that he was "an ambassador for Christ, as though God did beseech men by him to be reconciled to God."

12. "For the which cause I also suffer these things: nevertheless I am not ashamed," &c. "For the which cause," *i.e.*, because of my commission to make known life and immortality. "I suffer these things," *i.e.*, bonds and imprisonment. It is natural to be ashamed of bonds, for robbers and murderers are those usually thrown into bonds and shut up in prisons, but my Master was crucified to save me and all the world, and the one thing in which I will glory is His Cross.

"I know whom I have believed, and am persuaded," &c. "In whom I have believed," rather, "have trusted." Does this "Whom" refer to God the Father or God the Son? Most commentators think to God the Father, but surely the Apostle at times commits himself or his work to the Lord Jesus, as in the 4th chapter of this Epistle. Nevertheless it is the same. St. Paul is the Apostle of God and also of Christ. "He is one of the sheep of Christ who are in His hand" (John x.), so that it seems extraordinary that Bishop Ellicott should say, "It need scarcely be said that ᾧ refers to God

d 1 Tim. vi. 20. e ver. 18. ch. iv. 8. f ch. iii. 14. Tit. i. 9. Heb. x. 23. Rev. ii. 25. g Rom. ii. 20. & vi. 17. h 1 Tim. i. 10. & vi. 3.

that he is able to [d] keep that which I have committed unto him [e] against that day.

13 [f] Hold fast [g] the form of [h] sound words,

---

the Father, 'I know whom I have believed,' seems to refer to Christ, the peculiar object of *Christian* faith."

"And am persuaded that he is able to keep that which I have committed unto him," &c. "That which I have committed unto him," or, as Revisers in margin, "that which He has committed unto me." There is very much grammatical discussion amongst commentators about which of these is the true application of *παραθηκὴ* (deposit), but surely there need be no discussion, for both must be true, not *may* be, but must be true. Whatever God commits to us (our own salvation, the salvation of others, the holding of the faith, the ministerial commission,) we must commit it to Him, because we have not strength to hold it of ourselves. We shall not be able to be faithful to it unless He gives us grace.

And so we can only commit to Him that which He has committed to us. We cannot commit to Him any sinful desire, any wrong course of action, any purely selfish project, for these are not from His inspiration; but any duty which He has laid upon us, any warfare in which He has enlisted us, any career of usefulness which He has opened out before us, these we can and must commit to Him.

"Against that day." Not the day of death, but the day of the Lord's appearing, and He is able to keep what we have committed to Him, for He is Almighty, He foresees all things, His providence orders all events.

13. "Hold fast the form of sound words, which thou hast heard of me," &c. This must be one of two things, either the oral Gospel, being the Life and Death and Resurrection of the Lord, which had not been committed to writing; or the chief articles of the Gospel, or of the faith collected into a short formula like a creed.

I scarcely think that it is the first, because the oral Gospel, which was undoubtedly the first form of it, was fast being superseded by the written form, particularly, as is most natural, in the case of St. Paul's churches, by the Gospel of St. Luke, so I think we must consider it to be the latter, *i.e.*, a short formula, or list of the chief articles of St. Paul's Gospel. That there was such a formula is

[l] which thou hast heard of me, [k] in faith and love which is in Christ Jesus. [l] ch. ii. 2. [k] 1 Tim. i. 14.

---

plain from many intimations in St. Paul's Epistles, as particularly in 1 Cor. xv. where a part of it is expressed as the Death, Burial, and Resurrection of the Lord, prefaced with "Moreover, brethren, I declare unto you, the Gospel which I preached unto you;" also in Romans i. 1, 2, where the Gospel is that "God's Son, Jesus Christ was made of the seed of David according to the flesh, and declared to be the Son of God with power," and again in Rom. ii. "Who shall judge the secrets of men by Jesus Christ according to my Gospel," and in this Epistle, "Remember that Jesus Christ, of the seed of David, was raised from the dead according to my Gospel" (ii. 8). There must have been, then, from the first, a form of words in which the Gospel or the faith was expressed. The necessities of the case demand it. In Ephes. iv. we read that there is "one faith" as there is "one Lord" and "one Baptism." Now this faith cannot be locked up in the breast of each one who believes it. It must take some objective form, or else it could not pass from one man to another, or be committed from one man to another. And this must have been the "form of sound words," not merely sound thoughts, but sound thoughts embodied in words.

We are told that "hold fast" is too strong a translation of ἔχε, which means simply, "have" or "hold," but surely we are not to be told that the Apostle would have us hold anything loosely, or "have" a thing which was of little importance, for it must have been something saving. Whatever "have" means, it must be "have" in the sense of possessing it as a thing of importance, and holding it firmly as such.

I do not mean by the above to say that the "form of sound words" is identical with the Apostle's Creed, but it must be some short form resembling it—a something that Timothy could carry about with him. It would be about Jesus Christ. It would be about the great facts of His Birth, Death, and Resurrection, rather than about His Circumcision or Baptism, or miracles, and so, from the intimations I have drawn attention to, it is.

"In faith and love which is in Christ Jesus." The holding fast is not to be intellectual merely, but in faith and love, with the heart, with the will, with submission of the whole spirit to God.

14 [l] That good thing which was committed unto thee
[l] 1 Tim. vi. 20. keep by the Holy Ghost [m] which dwelleth in us.
[m] Ro. viii. 11.
[n] Acts xix. 10. 15 This thou knowest, that [n] all they which are
[o] ch. iv. 10, 16. in Asia be [o] turned away from me; of whom are
Phygellus and Hermogenes.

---

15. "Phygellus." So A.; but ℵ, C., D., read, "Phygelus."
"Hermogenes;" most probably "Ermogenes," without breathing.

14. "That good thing which was committed unto thee keep by the Holy Ghost," &c. What was the good thing committed to Paul? It cannot have been the Holy Spirit, for he was to keep it by the Holy Spirit. Was it the form of sound words, or the mystery of godliness of 1 Tim. iii. 16, or something akin to it? Was it the grace of ordination or of the Apostolate conferred on him? If we are to distinguish it from the form of sound words it must be this. Chrysostom does not tell us explicitly what he thinks it to be, but rather insists on the danger of losing it, "For it is not in the power of a human soul, when instructed in things so great, to be sufficient for the keeping of them. And why? because there are many robbers, and thick darkness, and the devil still at hand to plot against us; and we know not what is the hour, what the occasion for him to set upon us."

"Through the Holy Ghost which dwelleth in us." We are thus to guard the deposit by giving all diligence to keep within us the Spirit of God. We are to give ourselves up to His leading, we are by all means of grace and prayer, and reading of Scripture, to invite His indwelling.

15. "This thou knowest, that all they which are in Asia be turned," &c. This cannot well mean that all in Asia, *i.e.*, all the Ephesian Christians, are turned from Christ and the Gospel. It must rather mean that very many are turned away from their allegiance to St. Paul. So many, that in the eyes of the depressed Apostle it seemed all.

Chrysostom supposes that it means all in Rome that were from Asia, *i.e.*, Proconsular Asia. They found it dangerous to themselves to seek him, and minister unto him, and so many of them behaved like Demas; but there was one great exception, for he goes on to say:

16, 17. "The Lord give mercy unto the house of Onesiphorus . . . .

16 The Lord [p] give mercy unto [q] the house of Onesipho-
rus; [r] for he oft refreshed me, and [s] was not
ashamed of [t] my chain:
17 But, when he was in Rome, he sought me
out very diligently, and found *me*.
18 The Lord grant unto him [u] that he may find
mercy of the Lord [x] in that day: and in how
many things he [y] ministered unto me at Ephesus,
thou knowest very well.

p Mat. v. 7.
q ch. iv. 19.
r Philem. 7.
s ver. viii.
t Acts xxviii. 20. Eph. vi. 20.
u Matt. xxv. 34-40.
x 2 Thess. i. 10. ver. 12.
y Hebr. vi. 10.

---

18. "Unto him" omitted by almost all authorities.

and found me." This means that Onesiphorus sought out the Apostle, and ministered to his wants when he was in Rome. This imprisonment, as Bishop Pearson remarks, must have been much closer than the first one, for it to be said that he sought him out diligently. This could not have been said respecting the Apostle's first detention when he was "dwelling in his own hired house, and receiving all who came in unto him" (Acts xxviii. 30, 31).

18. "The Lord grant unto him that he may find mercy of the Lord in that day . . . . thou knowest very well." Why should St. Paul pray that the Lord may have mercy upon him in particular "at that day," having invoked mercy from God upon his household, as in a measure apart from him; and why in the last chapter (verse 19), should he send a salutation to the household of Onesiphorus only?

The only fair explanation is that Onesiphorus was dead. This is in no way a prayer that God may alter his state, because he evidently died in a state of grace, but we have no reason whatever to believe that the moment a soul dies it is perfected. In every Christian Liturgy that has come down to us there are prayers for the departed; thus in that of St. Mark, "Give rest, O Lord our God, to the souls of our fathers and brethren who are departed in the faith of Christ," &c.

It is a primitive custom. It involves no change of state from condemnation to life no purgatory. No matter how fixed in the favour of God the state of the faithful departed is, they may be refreshed, and this is what the Prayers of the Ancient Liturgies ask of God.

CHAP. II.

[a] 1 Tim. i. 2. ch. i. 2.
[b] Eph. vi. 10.
[c] ch. i. 13. & iii. 10. 14.
|| Or, *by*.
[d] 1 Tim. i. 18.
[e] 1 Tim. iii. 2. Tit. i. 9.

THOU therefore,[a] my son, [b] be strong in the grace that is in Christ Jesus.

2 [c] And the things that thou hast heard of me || among many witnesses, [d] the same commit thou to faithful men, who shall be [e] able to teach others also.

---

1. "Thou therefore, my son, be strong in the grace that is in Christ Jesus." This assumes that it was in his power to be strong, because he had the means of grace, the Sacraments, the Scriptures, the examples of such men as Onesiphorus.

2. "And the things that thou hast heard of me, among many witnesses," &c. Were these "things" the Christian deposit? From the former verse and the succeeding one ("endure hardness") some have supposed that it was an account of the Apostle's own hardships; but some believe it to refer to the good deposit, particularly as what is in it is to be committed to others who, in their turn, are to teach others. I am inclined to think that it is the sum and substance of the Apostle's teaching, which would be the expansion of the short creed or deposit, and its practical application.

It would seem that we are taught by this verse that there was, even at this later period, a considerable amount of oral teaching upon all subjects of faith and doctrine, and even ritual, which was solemnly, in the assembled Church, committed by the Apostle to those who were to succeed him. Such is most likely to have been the case, and, indeed, the more we think about it the more difficult it is to believe that it could have been otherwise. (See my notes on 1 Cor. xi., and the excursus on apostolical traditions at the end of volume on Epistles to Corinthians).

3. "Thou therefore endure hardness, as a good soldier," &c. Rather (according to oldest MSS.) "Endure hardness with me," omitting "thou therefore" (*συγκακοπάθησον* instead of *σὺ οὖν κακοπάθησον*).

3 [f]Thou therefore endure hardness, [g]as a good soldier of
Jesus Christ.
4 [h]No man that warreth entangleth himself
with the affairs of *this* life; that he may please
him who hath chosen him to be a soldier.
5 And [i]if a man also strive for masteries, *yet*
is he not crowned, except he strive lawfully.

[f] ch. i. 8. & iv. 5.
[g] 1 Tim. i. 18.
[h] 1 Cor. ix. 25.
[i] 1 Cor. ix. 25. 26.

---

3. "Thou therefore endure hardness" (σὺ οὖν κακοπάθησον). So K., L., most Cursives, &c.; but א, A., C., D., E., F., G., P., 17, 31, 71, 80, Copt., Arm., Æth., read, "endure hardness with us" (συγκακοπάθησον).

"Soldier." Some MSS. read, "fellow soldier."

4. "Warreth." F., G., Vulg., add "for God."

"As a good soldier of Jesus Christ." It is as much the part of a soldier to endure evil as it is for him to be armed, or to be disciplined, or to be under a general.

"As a good soldier of Jesus Christ." Christ is the captain of our salvation, and He won the victory by enduring hardness, and was even made perfect through suffering (Heb. ii. 10).

4. "No man that warreth entangleth himself with the affairs of this life," &c. This does not allude so much to any soldier as to the soldier going on an expedition. If a soldier on the eve of a war so entangle himself, he would have to ask leave that he might attend to what he represented as urgent business, or if he were permitted so to do, to throw up his engagement. Now these words are addressed not to every Christian who is by his profession a soldier, but to the Christian minister whose ministry is ruined unless he is disengaged as far as can be from secular affairs. It is not so much the time spent on such matters as the engrossment of the mind by them. If a man is to be a successful minister he must give himself wholly to it, he must be "in" the things of his ministry (1 Tim. v. 16 note). Still this is not to be taken as excluding the minister under all circumstances from any other means of livelihood. St. Paul, whilst exercising the most active of ministries, spent some of his time working as a tent-maker,

5. "And if a man also strive for masteries, yet is he not crowned," &c. Striving for masteries alludes to the discipline or training of the athletes in the public games. Their training was not left to themselves, they were obliged to obey the directions of a public

k 1 Cor. ix. 10.
|| Or, *The husbandman, labouring first, must be partaker of the fruits.*

6 k || The husbandman that laboureth must be first partaker of the fruits.

7 Consider what I say; and the Lord give thee understanding in all things.

---

7. "The Lord give thee." So K., L., P., most Cursives; but ℵ, A., C., D., E., F., G., d, e, f, g, Vulg., Copt., Arm., read, "will give thee."

trainer, and if they disobeyed they were liable to be excluded altogether from the race. And so it is in the Christian race. Unless each soldier, and more particularly, each minister, submits to discipline, he may be altogether debarred from receiving the crown.

"Crowned." Of course not as a king, but as a victor. The difference is to be noted; men may receive a kingly crown out of favour or by descent, they cannot receive a victor's crown unless they have actually won the victory.

6. "The husbandman that laboureth must be first partaker of the fruits." There is a great difference amongst commentators respecting the application of this passage to Timothy as a labourer in the Gospel vineyard. The two former passages (verses 4 and 5) which illustrate from the soldier not encumbering himself, and the athlete observing the laws of the games, are said apparently by way of warning; but can this illustration of the husbandman be similarly taken? Only in the way that "that husbandman only who has endured the toil has a right (here the first right) to share the fruits."

I do not think that the Apostle can mean that hard labour in the Lord's vineyard carries its own reward along with it, and so urges Timothy to such hard labour. Blunt takes it as alluding to the honour of taking up the cross with his Master. "Here the same idea of suffering is carried out, the Apostle regarding it as the necessary result of ministerial labour in an age of persecution, and regarding it as a privilege that the ministerial labourer should be the first who should be called to bear the cross of his Master." The first meaning, though not without its difficulties, seems the best.

7. "Consider what I say: and the Lord give thee understanding," &c. I have given thee three plain illustrations from the daily life of the world, consider them, lay them to heart, and the Lord

8 Remember that Jesus Christ [1] of the seed of

[1] Acts ii. 30. & xiii. 23. Rom. i. 3. 4.

---

will give thee understanding in all things. The Lord Himself constantly used illustrations taken from the common natural intercourse of men with one another, so that He will honour thy attention to such instructions, and give thee the wisdom thou seekest after.

8. "Remember that Jesus Christ, of the seed of David was raised," &c. The connection seems to be this. In the previous verses he had been speaking of suffering, of enduring hardness, of warring, of striving for the victor's crown. Now he bids him ever remember his great Exemplar—His sufferings, and His victory after suffering. Thus it is applied by the Church to the sick and suffering. "There should be no greater comfort to Christian persons than to be made like unto Christ by suffering patiently adversities, trouble and sicknesses. For He Himself went not up to joy but first He suffered pain, He entered not into His glory before He was crucified."

So it may signify, "Nerve yourself for your contest with the powers of darkness by the remembrance of your Lord and Master, the captain of your salvation, how He was of the seed of David according to the flesh, and on this account the promised Messiah, and on this account also a Messiah Who partook of our nature, so that He experienced all its sinless infirmities. And how after enduring the extremity of suffering, He was raised from the dead in token that He had won the crown for which He contended."

The order of the original is "Remember that Jesus Christ was raised from the dead of the seed of David."

But this injunction to remember the Lord's Resurrection is capable of the widest application. The Resurrection is the seal of the truth of Christianity. For the Resurrection is the seal of the truth of the Lord's mission as the Christ the Son of God. It is the seal and assurance of the truth of all that the Lord had said of Himself, and of all that He had undertaken to do. It was the assurance from God Who raised Him from the dead, that He was God's own Son; that His Death was an all-sufficient sacrifice; that He would in due time raise us from the dead, and judge us; that we should be partakers of His Life; that because He lives we shall live also; that His Flesh shall be our meat indeed, and

m 1 Cor. xv. 1, 4, 20.
n Rom. ii. 16.
o Acts ix. 16. ch. i. 12.
p Ephes. iii. 1. Phil. i. 7. Col. iv. 3, 18.
q Acts xxviii. 31. Ephes. vi. 19, 20. Phil. i. 13, 14.
r Ephes. iii. 13. Col. i. 24.
s 2 Cor. i. 6.

David [m] was raised from the dead [n] according to my gospel:

9 [o] Wherein I suffer trouble, as an evildoer, [p] *even* unto bonds; [q] but the word of God is not bound.

10 Therefore [r] I endure all things for the elect's sakes, [s] that they may also obtain the salvation which is in Christ Jesus with eternal glory.

His Blood our drink indeed; and if there be any other promise of life uttered by Him, or contained in Him, of its truth His Resurrection is to be our assurance.

"According to my gospel." The Gospel of St. Paul was emphatically the doctrine of the Lord's Resurrection. Thus Rom. i. 1-3, "The gospel of God concerning his Son Jesus Christ our Lord, Who was made of the seed of David, according to the flesh, and declared to be the Son of God, with power according to the Spirit of holiness by the resurrection from the dead." Thus also in 1 Cor. xv. 1-10, he categorically declares the Gospel which he preached unto them, and this was that "Christ died for our sins, was buried, and rose again."

9. "Wherein I suffer trouble as an evildoer, even unto bonds," &c. At St. Paul's former detention he was an appellant, having appealed to Cæsar; now he was treated as a malefactor (κακοῦργος) as his Master had been.

"But the word of God is not bound." "It does not depend upon me whether the Word of God is preached or not. I am in bonds and unable to preach as I once did, but the Gospel is spreading everywhere."

10. "Therefore I endure all things for the elect's sakes, that they may," &c. A passage parallel to this, and illustrative of it, is to be found in Col. i. 24, "I, Paul . . . fill up that which is behind of the afflictions of Christ in my flesh for his body's sake, which is the church." (See note on it.) If he suffered for Christ, he suffered for those on whose behalf Christ suffered. Christ now needed no suffering on His own account, but His people did, and so the Apostle in suffering for His cause suffered for them.

"That they may also obtain the salvation which is in Christ

11 [t] *It is* a faithful saying: For [u] if we be dead with *him*, we shall also live with *him*:

t 1 Tim. i. 15.
u Rom. vi. 5, 8. 2 Cor. iv. 10.

---

11. "If we be dead." "If we died."

Jesus," &c. Though elected the call has to come to them, and to be accepted by them, and they have to continue in it and make it suro.

This entailed constant preaching to the heathen, constant efforts to keep the Church pure, and this implied danger of life and fierce opposition, "journeyings oft," "perils in the wilderness," "perils among false brethren."

11. "It is a faithful saying: For if we be dead with him, we shall also," &c. This is another and the last of the faithful sayings enunciated by the Apostle. It consists of four clauses or axioms, "If we be dead, we shall also live: if we suffer, we shall also reign: if we deny him, he also will deny us: if we believe not," &c. It has been supposed to be part of a Christian hymn, or, as Alford supposes, words uttered by some well-known Christian under the influence of the spirit of prophecy. Some, however, have supposed the words, "This is a faithful saying," to refer to the last verse, "I endure all things for the elects' sakes;" but this seems to me impossible, for the Apostle writes the last verse as an expression of his private feeling, using the first person singular. Such a saying could not be a proverbial one exalted into an universal axiom of the truth, which the faithful sayings all seem to be.

"It is a faithful saying, For if we be dead with him, we shall also," &c. It is difficult to explain the "for;" it may be a part of the original passage, which the Apostle reproduces, or it may be introduced by the Apostle himself to make a connection.

"If we be dead with him, we shall also live with him." It seems impossible to help referring back to Rom. vi. 8, "Now if we be dead with Christ, we believe that we shall also live with him." This, in the Epistle to the Romans, refers to our Death and Resurrection with Christ in Baptism. And why should it not in this place? It is sufficiently important if in Baptism we are made partakers of the Death and Resurrection of Christ (always, of course, presupposing that we continue thus in union with Him, and order our lives accordingly); it is indeed a faithful saying, and one which we should constantly bear in mind. It is really parallel to,

[x] Rom. viii. 17. 1 Pet. iv. 13.
[y] Matt. x. 33. Mark viii. 38. Luke xii. 9.
[z] Rom. iii. 3. & ix. 6.
[a] Numb. xxiii. 19.

12 [x] If we suffer, we shall also reign with *him*:
[y] if we deny *him*, he also will deny us:
13 [z] If we believe not, *yet* he abideth faithful:
[a] he cannot deny himself.

---

12. "*If we deny him.*" So D., E., K., L., P., most Cursives, d, e; but ℵ, A., C., read, "if we shall deny."

13. "He cannot deny himself." So K. and most Cursives, Vulg., Goth., Arm.; but ℵ, A., C., D., E., F., G., L., P., a few Cursives, read, "for"—"for he cannot," &c.

"If we have been planted together in the likeness of his death, we shall be also of his Resurrection" (Rom. vi. 5). This follows upon, "Remember that Jesus Christ, of the seed of David, was raised from the dead." Chrysostom considers that it refers to both deaths, that in baptism and that in suffering. "How are we dead with Him? This death, he means both of that in the laver, and that in suffering. For he says, 'Bearing about in the body the dying of the Lord Jesus.'"

12. "If we suffer, we shall also reign with him." This is a reproduction, almost verbatim, of Rom. viii. 17: "If so be that we suffer with him, that we may be also glorified together;" and also 1 Peter iv. 13: "But rejoice, inasmuch as ye are partakers of Christ's sufferings, that when his glory shall be revealed, ye may be glad also with exceeding joy." It seems as if both these places were slight expansions of this faithful saying.

"If we deny him, he also will deny us." Here is a stern faithful saying in contrast with the two first. But it is needful that we should be reminded of it: for this faithful saying is in the words of the Lord Himself, "Whosoever shall deny me before men, him will I also deny before my Father which is in heaven;" "O Lord, give us grace in all companies and on all occasions to confess thee."

13. "If we believe not, yet he abideth faithful: (for) he cannot deny himself." Various applications have been made of this verse. One is that in this he ratifies or clenches, as it were, the truth of the foregoing clauses. "If we be dead with him, we shall also live with him." This is true in itself, and quite independent of our belief. It is certain whether we believe it or not. "If we suffer with Him, we shall also reign with Him." This is as certain as the truth and unchangeableness of His own character. Having all

14 Of these things put *them* in remembrance, [b] charging *them* before the Lord [c] that they strive not about words to no profit, *but* to the subverting of the hearers.

15 Study to shew thyself approved unto God, a

b 1 Tim. v. 21. & vi. 13. ch. iv. 1.
c 1 Tim. i. 4. & vi. 4. Tit. iii. 9, 11.

---

power in His hands, He will never allow those who have suffered with Him to lose their reward. And if we deny Him, He also will deny us. We may not believe this now, but we shall find it fearfully true at the last.

"He cannot deny himself." He is the truth, and whatever He has uttered is true, and He has all power by which to carry out what He has promised or threatened, and all eternity in which to bring about that on which He has resolved.

If He were to be untrue to His word, He would be untrue to Himself. But He abideth faithful, for He is "the same yesterday, to-day, and for ever."

14. "Of these things put them in remembrance, charging them before the Lord," &c. "Of these things," that is, of what he had just been saying, of the soldier, the athlete, the husbandman, of constantly calling to mind the Lord's Resurrection, of the threefold or fourfold faithful saying.

"Charging them before the Lord." Reminding them of the Lord's Presence, and calling Him solemnly to hear the words as the words of the Holy Ghost and not of mere man.

"Words to no profit, but to the subverting of the hearers." These may be any words of error or heresy. They are scarcely words which describe the worst form of Gnosticism. They are equally applicable to words which attribute justification to the law, or to words which deny or explain away the Resurrection, to Jewish fables, and to distinction of meats and such things. All words of error have a tendency to subvert. Reverence for God would make us adhere to the exact teaching of His words, as we know not what a letting out of waters the entertainment of the least error may be.

15. "Study to show thyself approved unto God, a workman that needeth not," &c. This is the first duty of the minister—whether he preaches, teaches, reproves, exhorts, celebrates the Eucharist,

workman that needeth not to be ashamed, rightly dividing the word of truth.

[d] 1 Tim. iv. 7. & vi. 20. Tit. i. 14.

|| Or, *gangrene.*

[e] 1 Tim. i. 20.

16 But [d] shun profane *and* vain babblings: for they will increase unto more ungodliness.

17 And their word will eat as doth a || canker: of whom is [e] Hymenæus and Philetus:

---

or whatever he does, it is to be done in such a way as to meet the approval of God.

"A workman that needeth not to be ashamed," when his work and its results are to be examined at the last.

"Rightly dividing the word of truth." The word ὀρθοτομοῦντα signifies properly "cutting straight," and is applied to cutting a road, ploughing a furrow, and such things. The best translation of it is "rightly handling," or "rightly administering." How does he do this? when he handles not the Word of God deceitfully, when he does not put one truth forward to the disparagement or concealment of another; when he brings those truths into prominence on which all the rest depend, as the Incarnation of the Eternal Son, His atoning Sacrifice, His Resurrection as the pledge of the truth of all, His being Head over all things to the Church, which is His Body; on our acceptance by God wholly through His grace and merits; on His coming again and judging us all according to our works. If St. Paul rightly handles the truth of God in his Epistles, then no teacher can rightly handle it who does not put our belonging to a mystical Body in a most prominent place.

16. "But shun profane and vain babblings," &c. Chrysostom here reads "novelties of speech," καινοφωνίας, instead of κενοφωνίας; and says, "For they will not stop there. For when anything new has been introduced, it is ever producing innovations, and the error of him who has once left the safe harbour is infinite, and never stops."

17. "And their word will eat as doth a canker." Not a canker in the modern sense, but a tumour between inflammation and entire mortification—a gangrene will eat, literally, will have pasture, eating away all the contiguous flesh.

"Of whom is Hymenæus and Philetus."

18. "Who concerning the truth have erred, saying that the resurrection is passed already." This heresy is one of the oldest.

18 Who [f] concerning the truth have erred, [g] saying that the resurrection is past already; and overthrow the faith of some.

f 1 Tim. vi. 21.
g 1 Cor. xv. 12.

18. "The resurrection is passed." So A., C., D., E., K., L., P.; but ℵ, F., G., omit article before "resurrection."

Paul combats it in his first Epistle to the Corinthians, one of the earliest of his Epistles. The Resurrection appears to have been a doctrine particularly distasteful to the Greek mind, for when he enunciated it in his address on the Areopagus, we read, "When they heard of the Resurrection, some mocked, and others said, We will hear thee again of this matter" (Acts xvii. 32). Nothing demands more faith than a belief in the Resurrection of the flesh in one who has set before himself the power displayed in it.

"That the Resurrection is passed already," or that Resurrection is passed already. They, in all probability, asserted that the real Resurrection—the only one worthy of the attention of a spiritual man—was a resurrection of the soul or spirit. Tertullian describes their opinion thus: "Wherefore that also must be held to be the Resurrection, when a man is reanimated by access to the truth, and having dispersed the death of ignorance, and being endowed with new life by God, has burst forth from the sepulchre of the Old Man."

All this is very specious, and seemingly very spiritual, but it is very unbelieving. It makes one truth of God nullify another. God has told us that we must rise from sin to righteousness in our souls; but His Son has also told us that by His power and at His word we must rise to life and immortality in our bodies. If we reject this latter we must do so because we do not believe in the power and doubt the promises of God, or because we profanely set ourselves above the words of God, and choose among them which we will accept and which not.

"And overthrow the faith of some." The doctrine of the resurrection of the body is a sharp test of faith. St. Paul shows, in 1 Cor. xv. that they who disbelieve in their own resurrection cannot believe that Christ was raised, and if He was not raised "our faith is vain."

19. "Nevertheless the foundation of God standeth sure, having

h Matt. xxiv. 24. Rom. viii. 35. I John ii. 19.
‖ Or, *steady*.
i Nahum i. 7. John x. 14, 27. See Numb. xvi. 5.

19 Nevertheless[h] the foundation of God standeth ‖ sure, having this seal, The Lord [i] knoweth them that are his. And, Let every one that nameth the name of Christ depart from iniquity.

---

19. "The name of Christ." All authorities (ℵ, A., C., D., E., F., G., K., L., P., &c.) read, "the name of the Lord."

this seal, The Lord," &c. In order to understand this place we must first ask, why does the Apostle cite the words of Numbers xvi. 5, "The Lord will show who are his,"[1] but somewhat alters them in quoting them into, "The Lord knoweth them that are his"? Evidently because of the defection from the faith of Hymenæus and Philetus, and of those whose faith was overthrown by them. It is as if he said, "These men and their followers seem to be believers, but they are not really so." The Lord knoweth them that are His, *and no one else knows them.* It is strange, very strange, that men who seem so very spiritual as to deny the resurrection of the body on the highest evangelical grounds, should not belong to the Lord, but they do not. There is a Church which standeth—the firm foundation of God standeth—and on the foundation (Rev. xxi. 14), of this Church there are two seals engraved, each with a separate inscription. One of these is, "The Lord knoweth them that are his." Many may be in this Church by profession, but the Lord only knoweth whether they are truly His and will endure to the end: and *we* are not to build upon what is known only to God—we are not to say to ourselves, "I am known of God, and all else is of no consequence." No. Do I name the name of Christ? Am I a professing Christian? If so it is the Lord's will that I do not busy myself with speculations about my election, but taking His plain declaration respecting all who even so much as name His Name, I must depart from iniquity. Bishop Wordsworth has an excellent note:—"The solid foundation of God's Spiritual House, the Church, has these two mottos described upon it, 'The Lord knoweth them that are his' (Numb. xvi. 5; Nah. i. 7; John x. 14, 27). 'He seeth, loveth, and will preserve them from all peril.'

---

1 The words of the Septuagint are, "The Lord hath visited and known them that are his, and who are holy, and has brought them to himself;" but St. Paul here evidently did not intend to cite the words of the Septuagint, though they very accurately describe the doctrine usually imputed to him.

20 [k] But in a great house there are not only vessels of
gold and of silver, but also of wood and of earth; [k] 1 Tim. iii. 15.
[l] and some to honour, and some to dishonour. [l] Rom. ix. 21.
21 [m] If a man therefore purge himself from [m] See Isai. lii. 11.
these, he shall be a vessel unto honour, sanctified,

Here is a comfortable assurance of His favour towards us. And (a second seal or motto), 'Let all who name the name of Christ depart from iniquity' (Numb. xvi. 26; Isaiah lii. 3). Let all who profess to know the Lord and to worship Him, and who bear His Name into which they have been baptized, 'eschew all things contrary to their profession, and follow all such things as are agreeable to the same.' (Examples of a σφραγὶς, or gravure on a stone, may be seen in Zechariah iii. 9, and Rev. xxi. 14.)"

20. "But in a great house there are not only vessels of gold and of silver, but also," &c. The question arises, and a very important one it is, what are the vessels made to dishonour? He mentions some of wood and some of earth, but these are as useful and as necessary in their places as the vessels of gold and silver. Now this teaches us how very different his views of God's election are from what Predestinarians assume that they are. According to such, in the great house there are vessels not made for an humbler use, but to be broken and perish utterly—in fact, not only to perish, but to be tormented for ever, because the great Artificer has made them of wood rather than of gold or silver.

But this is by no means all. A vessel once made by the artificer cannot change itself. It cannot become of any other material than of that of which it was originally made. But here St. Paul represents vessels as changing themselves. This is absolutely incompatible with the idea that God has made a certain number of souls to be saved and a certain number to be destroyed. It is, on the contrary, the most surprising assertion of the freedom of the human will in Scripture: for a man is not only supposed to be able, but is responsible for changing himself from that which is typified by an earthen vessel into that which is typified by a golden one. Hymenæus and Philetus had fallen from being golden vessels (for they had faith, and some faith, or at least some spiritual discernment, is necessary for men to profess a spiritual resurrection), into earthen ones, but if they repented they might become gold or silver ones, that is, if

and meet for the master's use, *and* [n] prepared unto every good work.

22 Flee also youthful lusts: but [o] follow righteousness, faith, charity, peace, with them that [p] call on the Lord [q] out of a pure heart.

n ch. iii. 17. Tit. iii. 1.
o 1 Tim. vi. 11.
p Acts ix. 14. 1 Cor. i. 2.
q 1 Tim. i. 5 & iv. 12.

---

22. "That call on the Lord." A. only of all authorities reads, "with them that love the Lord."

they purged themselves from the error in question, and abstained from associating with those who held it. By the fact that a man has once fallen into this pernicious error, he is not condemned for ever, but by cleansing himself may recover himself, and become a vessel unto honour, sanctified, *i.e.*, by the Holy Spirit, and meet for the Master's use, Who has said, "I will be sanctified of them that come nigh me."

"And prepared unto every good work." Even though he do it not, he is fit for it and has a capacity for it. (Chrysostom.)

22. "Flee also youthful lusts: but follow righteousness, faith," &c. Timothy was now of middle age (between thirty-five and forty in all probability), but the inclinations of youth continue beyond that. Chrysostom speaks of all lusts being youthful: "If one be given to insolence, or a lover of power, or riches, or bodily pleasure, it is a youthful lust, and foolish. These things must proceed from a heart not yet established, from a mind not deeply grounded, but in a wavering state." But it is to be remembered that such words as these are not addressed to Timothy only, but are general precepts, or maxims, suited for all ministers at all times. And besides this, ministers, bishops, priests, deacons, require the most general precepts, as well as the particular ones suited to their order or grade in the ministry. If St. Paul had spoken to Timothy as a saint of God of very advanced holiness, which, from many indications in these Epistles he must have been, then these Epistles would not have been, as they are, a directory, or manual for all ministers of Christ in every age.

"But follow righteousness, faith, charity, peace, with them that call." "Follow," *i.e.*, pursue these good dispositions of mind, pursue them by prayer, by holy meditations, by exercising yourself in the practice of them, by diligently avoiding all that is contrary to them.

23 But [r] foolish and unlearned questions avoid, knowing that they do gender strifes.

24 And [s] the servant of the Lord must not strive; but be gentle unto all *men*, [t] apt to teach, || patient,

[r] 1 Tim. i. 4. & iv. 7. & vi. 4. ver. 16. Tit. iii. 9.
[s] Tit. iii. 2.
[t] 1 Tim. iii. 2, 3. Tit. i. ix.
|| Or, *forbearing*.

The reader will mark what I have asked him to notice several times before, that in giving us lists of graces or virtues to be attained to, St. Paul seldom puts them in the modern Evangelical order; he, on two other occasions, does not put faith at the beginning of the list, and this not because he would exalt anything above faith, but because he was not a slave to a system, as some of those who profess to follow him are.

The "peace" of this verse is undoubtedly primarily peace in the society or Church, as we learn from the two next verses.

23, 24. "But foolish and unlearned questions avoid, knowing," &c. These "foolish" and "unlearned" (or ignorant, or unrestrained) questions may be about any of the points which were debated in the first age. They may have been questions about meats and drinks, and divers washings; they may have been raised about some of the articles of the faith, as the Resurrection, but one thing is quite certain, they were not the questions of the more advanced Gnosticism; for St. Paul would never have told Timothy to avoid these speculations. He would have told him to put persons who entertained these blasphemies summarily out of the Church until they repented. "Foolish and unlearned questions" was not the name for heresies which deprived God of His Creatorship and Fatherhood, and Christ of His Sonship and unique Mediatorship, and made the universe to be intrinsically evil.

24. "And the servant of the Lord must not strive, but be gentle," &c. Is not the servant of the Lord to strive for the faith of the Gospel? (Phil. i. 27.) Yes, but not in the spirit of worldly strife: he must strive for the truth by putting it before men in the spirit of gentleness, as he proceeds to say, "be gentle unto all men." "How is it then," Chrysostom asks, "that he says, 'Rebuke with all authority,' and again, 'Let no man despise thy youth,' and again, 'Rebuke them sharply.' Because this is consistent with meekness. For a strong rebuke, if it be given with gentleness, is most likely to wound deeply; for it is possible, indeed it is, to

u Gal. vi. 1. 1 Tim. vi. 11. 1 Pet. iii. 15.
x Acts viii. 22.
y 1 Tim. ii. 4. ch. iii. 7. Tit. i. 1.
† Gr. *awake*.
z 1 Tim. iii. 7.

25 [u] In meekness instructing those that oppose
themselves; [x] if God peradventure will give them
repentance [y] to the acknowledging of the truth;
26 And *that* they may † recover themselves [z] out

---

touch more effectually by gentleness than to overcome by boldness."

"Apt to teach, patient." These two must go together. There must be aptitude for teaching, or the would-be teacher, if he has it not, must lay himself out for some other department of the ministry, as reading, visiting, consoling; but no matter what the aptitude for teaching, there must be patience, the patient inculcation, the patient watching the opportunity, the patient bearing with dulness, with ignorance, and with want of heart.

"Misbelievers are not to be met half-way by strife, but to have the truth set before them by those who are apt to teach, who can be patient with persons differing from themselves, and who will do their work in meekness, placing the result altogether in God's hands." (Blunt.)

25. "In meekness instructing those that oppose themselves; if God peradventure," &c. Observe, those that oppose themselves require not only teaching, but repentance. When men refuse the first principles of divine knowledge, it is not the head, but the heart, which is in fault, and the man requires a change of heart, viz., repentance. But can we say that all who now, in this age of the Church, oppose or withdraw themselves from Church teachers require repentance? No, we cannot; for teachers now are not Apostles, as he was who gave Timothy these instructions, and yet they who oppose the plain meaning of Scripture, or try to evade it, should be plainly warned that it is not our word, but God's. We must take heed that we faithfully reproduce the truth of God, and they who oppose must take equal heed that, in opposing us, they oppose not the Spirit of God.

26. "And that they may recover themselves out of the snare of the devil," &c. The word translated "recover themselves," is an unusual one. It seems to mean that they may "wake up to soberness out of," &c. The snare of the devil is a state of somnolence or stupefaction from which they must rouse themselves up.

of the snare of the devil, who are † taken captive by him at his will.

† Gr. *taken alive.*

Extraordinary differences of opinion have been exhibited by translators and commentators respecting the last clause "having been taken alive by him at his will," for the pronouns "by him," and "at his will" (or at the will of him) are different, and should properly refer to different persons. Bishop Ellicott renders it, "though holden captive by him to do God's will." Similarly Alford, "Having been taken by him in pursuance of God's will." Dr. Fairbairn translates or paraphrases it, "In meekness correcting those who oppose themselves, if peradventure God may give them repentance so that they may come unto the full knowledge of the truth, and that they may return to soberness (and so escape) out of the snare of the devil (by whom they had been taken captive) according to the will of Him (God) Who for this end seconds the efforts of His servant by giving the spirit of repentance." I cannot help thinking, however, that the grammatical difficulty is not great, for many instances are adduced in which two different pronouns coming close to one another refer to the same person. It seems a most unusual figure to describe the converting grace of God as "being taken alive by God at His will," especially when the Apostle had been speaking of men being snared by Satan. Bishop Jackson, in the Speaker's Commentary, seems to give the meaning that they may wake up and escape out of the snare of the devil who were taken captive by him according to the will of that evil one. The latter part seems to describe exactly the spiritual condition of many who at once, at the smallest solicitation of the devil, yield themselves to him.

CHAP. III.

[a] 1 Tim. iv. 1. ch. iv. 3. 2 Pet. iii. 3. 1 John ii. 18. Jude 18.
[b] Phil. ii. 21.

THIS know also, that [a] in the last days perilous times shall come.

2 For men shall [b] be lovers of their own selves,

---

1. "This know also, that in the last days perilous times shall come." "The last days." Are these the times of Christianity, that is, the whole period between the two Advents, or are they the times immediately preceding the Second Advent? The last is by no means impossible, for it was a first axiom with St. Paul and his brother Apostles to regard the Lord as "at hand," and to live in the constant expectation of His appearing.

"This know also," should rather be translated "but know this," as if he said, "I have been telling you how you are in meekness to instruct those that oppose themselves, and that God may give them repentance; but you must be forewarned that no exercise of meekness and patient instruction on your part will enable you (humanly speaking) to stem the torrent of ungodliness in the last days."

"Perilous times shall come." Properly, hard, difficult times. Some translate it "grievous."

In 1 Tim. iv., he had similarly forewarned Timothy. "Now the Spirit speaketh expressly that in the latter times some shall depart from the faith." It is to be remarked that in the present list of evil things, apostasy from the faith is not specifically mentioned. The key to its application seems set forth in the last words, "having a form of godliness, but denying the power thereof." All these evils are consistent (as we have daily evidence), with some outward profession of the faith, even with some degree of faith. In the former passage (1 Tim. iv.) he seems to set forth the fruits of apostasy from the fold, here the fruits of sinful living within it.

2. "For men shall be lovers of their own selves." Note how this is placed by the Apostle in the forefront of this evil array; and there is nothing more contrary to the truth of the mystical Body.

[c] covetous, [d] boasters, [e] proud, [f] blasphemers, [g] disobedient to parents, unthankful, unholy,

c 2 Pet. ii. 3.
d Jude 16.
e 1 Tim. vi. 4.
f 1 Tim. i. 20. 2 Pet. ii. 12. Jude 10.
g Rom. i. 30.

"If we are members one of another, the welfare of our neighbour is not his concern only, but that of the whole body, and the injury of our neighbour is not confined to him, but distracts with pain all else as well. If we are a building, whatever part is weakened it affects the whole, while that which is solid gives strength and support to the rest. So also in the Church, if thou but slightest thy neighbour, thou hast injured thyself. How? In that one of thy members has suffered no small hurt." (Chrysostom.)

"Covetous," *i.e.*, lovers of money. This naturally follows, for money is that which more than all else ministers to self.

"Boasters." This also naturally follows, for those who are selfish will arrogate to themselves all the credit of every thing.

"Proud." This also follows on selfishness, because the proud are the worshippers or admirers of self.

"Blasphemers." Translated by revisers "railers," by others "evil speakers."

"Disobedient to parents." Here seems a new departure. The Apostle had very strongly inculcated subjection and love in the family (Ephes. v. 22-33; vi. 1-4). He had characterized the opposite as one of the evil things into which God had permitted the heathen to fall (Rom. i. 30), and now he includes it among the sins of Christians in the last days. It is a very bad form of evil, in that it is beginning life badly. It is impiety in its first and earliest stage, because God has put our parents between us and Himself, and bids us reverence them till we can properly learn that He is the first and Universal Parent, worthy of all childlike reverence and confidence.

"Unthankful." If we are not thankful to those who are our first benefactors, who care for us when we are helpless, how shall we in after life show thankfulness to either God or man?

"Unholy." The first school of holiness is the family. Holiness is primarily separation, the separation in the family, and so the family typifies and prepares for the separation to God and the Church. Evil is naturally kept out of the family; purity is, one may say, naturally cherished in it for its own sake.

[h] Rom. i. 31.
[i] Rom. i. 31.
‖ Or, *make-bates*. Tit. ii. 3.
[k] 2 Pet. iii. 3.
[l] 2 Pet. ii. 10.
[m] Phil. 3. 19. 2 Pet. ii. 13, &c. Jude 4, 19.

3 [h] Without natural affection, [i] trucebreakers, ‖ false accusers, [k] incontinent, fierce, despisers of those that are good,

4 [l] Traitors, heady, highminded, [m] lovers of pleasures more than lovers of God;

---

3. "Without natural affection." This seems terrible in those naming the Name of Christ, that they should lose their natural, one might say their animal virtue—for the brute creatures at times display it intensely—but if men despise the teaching of Christ, what wonder if God permits them to despise the teaching of nature?

"Trucebreakers." Most translations agree in rendering this "implacable." If men have given up natural affection, how can they exercise social self-restraint, forbearance, and generosity?

"False accusers." Slanderers.

"Incontinent." Unable to restrain any passion—so that they are slaves to that which is lowest and most allied to the appetites of unreasoning creatures.

"Fierce." In this resembling savages and brute creatures, the denial of the power of godliness ending in their having no power over their own angry passions.

"Despisers of those that are good." Very probably "no lovers of good;" "haters of good" seems too strong. We should rather attach the idea of indifference to good, if we can. The Vulgate renders "sine benignitate."

4. Traitors (or betrayers), heady, high-minded," &c.

"Heady." Reaching forward without consideration, almost always in some evil course.

"High-minded." The same word as in 1 Tim. iii. 6 is rendered "lifted up with pride."

"Lovers of pleasures more than lovers of God." This means those who, whenever the service of God and the enjoyment of pleasure interfere with one another, invariably make some excuse for choosing the latter. How often does the poor pleasure of sloth keep from attendance at early Communion, and even from the later matins? How often does money spent in amusement prevent many from assisting missions and supporting works of piety

5 Having a form of godliness, but [n] denying the power thereof: [o] from such turn away.

6 For [p] of this sort are they which creep into houses, and lead captive silly women laden with sins, led away with divers lusts.

n 1 Tim. v. 8. Tit. i. 16.
o 2 Thess. iii. 6. 1 Tim. vi. 5.
p Matt. xxiii. 14. Tit. i. 11.

---

and mercy! How often does self-indulgence so enervate both body and mind, that there is no worship of God worth speaking of?

5. "Having a form of godliness, but denying the power thereof: from," &c. Attending church, singing hymns, repeating the responses, praising, or criticising the sermon, perhaps even at times receiving the Eucharist, but having no truly Christian life as the outcome of it all.

"From such turn away." Instruction is thrown away upon them. They must first put away that form of evil mind or practice, which prevents the truth from affecting them for good.

6. "For of this sort are they which creep into houses, and lead captive," &c. The Apostle here denounces, not, of course, the instruction of women, but the way in which these heretics set about the spread of their false doctrine. They did it clandestinely, endeavouring to make converts of those who, being yet under the dominion of sin, and having no sincere wish to be free from such dominion, used the excitement of the false teaching of these men as a set-off against the stern claims of righteousness and holiness. The thing exists now in this nineteenth century just as much as apparently it did in the first. Women being the softer and more impressible sex, as they are the first to receive the impressions of true religion, are also the more ready to receive the counterfeit. Constantly have we of the Church to put our people, especially the females, on their guard against the insidious practices of Plymouth brethren on the one side, and Romanists on the other.

Baur and other rationalists have asserted that this "creeping into houses," and "leading captive the silly ladies," was a characteristic of the later Gnosticism, and so is a proof of the late origin of the Epistle; but this seems to me a convincing proof that he and those like him have made up their minds that these Epistles must be rejected at all hazards. For what is more patent in the history of all religious opinion than this, that as women are the first to

7 Ever learning, and never able [q] to come to the knowledge of the truth.

8 [r] Now as Jannes and Jambres withstood Moses, so do these also resist the truth: [s] men of corrupt minds, [t] || reprobate concerning the faith.

q 1 Tim. ii. 4.
r Ex. vii. 11.
s 1 Tim. vi. 5.
t Rom. i. 28. 2 Cor. xiii. 5. Tit. i. 16.
|| Or, *of no judgment.*

---

receive impressions of what is true, so, on the other hand, are they easily led by what is wrong? In the very first preaching of the Gospel we read that the Jews of Antioch in Pisidia stirred up the devout honourable women against the Gospel. Thus St. John, or the Lord through him, has to warn two of the Churches of Asia to be on their guard against the influence of women in seducing to what is false (Rev. ii. 14, 20).

"Laden with sins."

7. "Ever learning, and never able to come to the knowledge of the truth." They could not come to the full knowledge of the truth, because they loved, and would not put away, their sins. Cherished sin prevents the faculties of the soul or spirit from embracing the full truth.

Some explain this "ever learning" as ever learning some new things, and yet never able to grasp the real truth.

8. "Now as Jannes and Jambres withstood Moses, so do these also resist," &c. It is difficult to account for St. Paul's mention of the names of these two magicians, except on this ground, that he is alluding to persons who opposed the spread of the truth of God by false miracles, just as these two magicians opposed the message of Moses by their enchantments. We have reason to believe from two or three passages that the Jews traded in magical deceptions, and employed them as a set-off to the true miracles of the Gospel—thus Elymas, a Jew in Cyprus (Acts xiii. 6), and the seven sons of Sceva, Jews in Ephesus (Acts xix. 14). It is clear also, as all history assures us, that Simon Magus did not sincerely repent, and so would go on using magical arts to hinder the spread of the Gospel. In only this way, that I can see, could the false teachers oppose the truth after the manner of the magicians in Pharaoh's time.[1]

---

1 The name of Jannes occurs as a noted magician in Pliny's "Natural History," xxx.

9 But they shall proceed no further: for their folly shall
be manifest unto all *men*, [u] as their's also was.
10 [x] But ‖ thou hast fully known my doctrine,
manner of life, purpose, faith, long-suffering,
charity, patience,
11 Persecutions, afflictions, which came unto
me [y] at Antioch, [z] at Iconium, [a] at Lystra; what
persecutions I endured: but [b] out of *them* all the
Lord delivered me.

u Ex. vii. 12. & viii. 18. & ix. 11.
x Phil. ii. 22. 1 Tim. iv. 6.
‖ Or, *thou hast been a diligent follower of.*
y Acts xiii. 45, 50.
z Acts xiv. 2, 5.
a Acts xiv. 19, &c.
b Ps. xxxiv. 19. 2 Cor. i. 10. ch. iv. 17.

---

10. "Hast fully known." So D., E., K., L., P., most Cursives; but ℵ, A., C., F., G., read, "didst fully know."

9. "But they shall proceed no further: for their folly shall be manifest," &c. This seems to allude to some exposure of the pretensions of these false teachers (which probably they incurred in Ephesus itself) which has not come down to us. As the Egyptian magicians could only imitate a few of the plagues, so the greater part of the miracles wrought by the servants of Christ were utterly out of the reach of the power of these impostors.

10. "But thou hast fully known my doctrine, manner of life, purpose," &c. "Doctrine"—what I taught; "Manner of life"—how I lived to what I taught. "Purpose," to establish the equality of the Gentiles as true members of Christ—for that was the leading purpose of his ministerial life. "Faith"—both what he held and what he realized.

11. "Persecutions, afflictions, which came unto me at Antioch," &c. These are particularly mentioned because they were the first with which Timothy was personally acquainted. Timothy knew all about the persecutions endured by the Apostles before he joined himself to him, so that this knowledge might well be mentioned here as showing his sincerity at the very first in embracing a persecuted Gospel.

Bishop Wordsworth remarks a sign of genuineness in this epistle, in that Antioch is mentioned without distinguishing which Antioch

---

2, and in "Apuleius Apol. II.," and they were mentioned, according to Eusebius ("Præp. Evang.," ix. 8), by Numenius of Apameia. (From Bishop Jackson, in "Speaker's Commentary.")

c Ps. xxxiv. 19. Matt. xvi. 24. John xvii. 14. Acts xiv. 22. 1 Cor. xv. 19. 1 Thess. iii. 3.
d 2 Thes. ii. 11. 1 Tim. iv. 1. ch. ii. 16.

12 Yea, and [c] all that will live godly in Christ
Jesus shall suffer persecution.
13 [d] But evil men and seducers shall wax worse
and worse, deceiving, and being deceived.

---

13. "Seducers." "Magicians," "jugglers."

it was. A forger of forty or fifty years later would have designated it as Antioch in Pisidia, whereas the Apostle uses no such mark of distinction, knowing that Timothy knew well which Antioch it was.

12. "Yea, and all that will live godly in Christ Jesus shall suffer persecution." This seems an axiom of universal application. Two of the beatitudes have reference to persecution. Our Lord also denounces woe on those who are without any persecution. "Woe unto you, Woe unto you, when all men speak well of you, for so did their fathers to the false prophets." It arises from the nature of things. The Christian religion allows not the smallest alliance or compromise with any form of evil whatsoever. It demands the whole heart and the whole life for Christ. The old form of evil, idolatry, which set the world against Christ, has in these parts passed away; but the spirit of the world remains in the Christian world. It is a spirit of laxity, whereas the Christian spirit is one of strictness—of love, it is true, but still of strictness. The holy life of the true Christian is a standing reproof of that of his neighbours, and they are at times not able to bear the contrast; and so they worry, they ridicule, they cut, they do all sorts of mean things; they draw disparaging contrasts between the deficiences in the lives of the truest saints and the high standard of the Gospel. And so they insinuate hypocrisy. But true Christians must remember that, though they assert the liberty and yet the strictness of the law of Christ, they must do what they can to avoid giving needless offence by the uncalled-for profession of spirituality or godliness, for the spirit of persecution is sin, and they must take heed lest they needlessly excite it.

13. "But evil men and seducers shall wax worse and worse," &c. "Seducers"—literally, magicians or jugglers. This confirms what I have said on verse 8. They were men who not only opposed the true doctrine of Christ by false doctrine, but the true miracles of

14 But [e] continue thou in the things which thou hast
learned and hast been assured of, knowing of whom thou hast learned *them*;
15 And that from a child thou hast known
[f] the holy scriptures, which are able to make thee

e ch. i. 13. & ii. 2.

f John v. 39.

---

15. "The holy scriptures." So A., C., E., K., L., P., most Cursives, &c.; but ℵ, D., F., G., omit article.

Christ (that is, wrought by His power by the hands of the Apostles,) by false miracles. Respecting the great prevalence of this form of evil in Ephesus, see Acts xix. 19.

14. "But continue thou in the things which thou hast learned, and," &c. So 1 Tim. iv. 16, "Continue in them." It requires great Christian effort to "continue" in what we have learned at the first; for to continue in these things is meant (by the Apostle, at least,) that we continue in the practice and realization of them.

"Knowing of whom thou hast learned them." If we adopt the reading of the received text, "of whom" in the singular (παρὰ τίνος), then this refers to St. Paul. It is equivalent to his saying, "Knowing that thou hast received them from an Apostle of Christ —one especially sent by Christ, and inspired by Him to make known all the counsel of God." If we, on the other hand, adopt the reading preferred by some (and having considerable authority), "of whom" in the plural, then it refers to Lois and Eunice, and it is as if he said, "Thou knowest well the piety and love of the truth of those who instructed thee in the Scriptures in thy childhood. God would direct such true children of His aright, so confidently adhere to what they have taught thee."

15. "And that from a child thou hast known the holy scriptures." By these St. Paul, of course, means the Scriptures of the Old Testament, as in the time of the childhood of Timothy no book of the New Testament was in existence.

We read in the first chapter of this Epistle of the unfeigned faith which was in his grandmother Lois and his mother Eunice; and here is an example of the working of this faith—they taught him from his childhood to revere and learn the Holy Scriptures.

"Which are able to make thee wise unto salvation through faith," &c. So the Lord had said, "Search the scriptures—they are they which testify of me" (John v. 39). Our Lord, in re-

wise unto salvation through faith which is in Christ Jesus.

[g] 2 Pet. i. 20, 21.

16 [g] All scripture *is* given by inspiration of

---

16. "All scripture is given by inspiration of God, and is profitable;" or, "every scripture God inspired is also profitable," &c.

proving the Sadducees, said, "Ye do err, not knowing the scriptures, nor the power of God" (Matt. xxii. 29). The Scriptures, then, coming from the God of Salvation, must be able to make men wise unto Salvation. But how?

"Through faith which is in Christ Jesus." Christ is the fulfilment of the Old Testament. His Faith is the key to all its mysteries; His Sacrifice give the import of all its sacrifices. Take the most precious of all prophecies—that of Isaiah liii. If we have no faith in Christ we can only ask when we read this prophecy, "Of whom doth the prophet speak this—of himself or of some other man?" but if we believe in Christ, then it is, as it were, the Gospel of Gospels, for of all Scripture it applies to our souls most directly the Sufferings and Death recorded in the Four Gospels.

16. "All scripture is given by inspiration of God, and is profitable," &c. There has been much controversy about the exact translation of this passage, but all are ultimately at one respecting its meaning, which is, that the Holy Scriptures are the gift of God to enable men to know what God desires that they should believe and do.

The two principal renderings are given in the Authorized Translation, and in the Revised of 1881. The first, "All Scripture is given by Inspiration of God and is profitable," asserts two things, "the Inspiration of Scripture," and its "profitableness." The second is, "Every Scripture inspired by God is also profitable." This seems, on the face of it, to make a distinction between some Scriptures and others—some as inspired and others not—the former being profitable and the latter not. Now we cannot think that St. Paul attempted here to emphasize any such distinction. He took "Scripture" in the sense in which the Jews usually understood it, as the canonical books of the Old Testament, and he declared that, being all God-inspired, they were profitable for doctrine, &c. With respect to the Canon of Scripture, he would believe that God had overruled by His providence the selection of the Books, so that

God, [h] and *is* profitable for doctrine, for reproof, for correction, for instruction in righteousness: [h] Rom. xv. 4.

---

none were admitted into the roll of Scripture except such as were God-inspired. Now the converse of this cannot be asserted, viz., that all the God-inspired books were included in Scripture; because we read of many writings of prophets, such as Iddo and others, which have not been preserved to us, and which are referred to in the Old Testament as if they contained, so far as Jewish history is concerned, the truth of God. So that if prophets were inspired men in what they wrote, as well as what they said, then God made a selection from many inspired writings, choosing some to be enshrined in the Canon and some not. Now this is very important, and emphasizes exceedingly the value of the old Testament Scriptures as being *select* books, selected by God, through the Jewish church, to be the guide of His people, and the preparation for the coming of His Son.

We cannot here enter upon the subject of inspiration. It is not verbal, *i.e.*, inspiration of the exact words, for in thousands of instances we do not know the exact words, nor if we knew them could we give the exact translation.

And it has not been sufficiently considered that the Books of Scripture are very different from one another, and require different sorts of inspiration. Thus in the New Testament the writers of the Gospels require a different inspiration to those who wrote the Epistles. The Gospels require the inspiration of memory, "He shall bring all things to your remembrance, whatsoever I have said unto you." And the Epistles require a knowledge of the internal state of the members of the Christian churches, and of the particular doctrine which they require; as, for instance, that the Corinthians required the truth of the holiness of the human body to be presented to them, and the Galatians required the inability of the law to justify, seeing that it was mere command—having no life, and so no strength, to enable men to obey the command.

Again, with respect to the Old Testament. The law of ritual in Leviticus, or of social and national righteousness in Numbers and Deuteronomy, required a different sort of inspiration to the historical books in which, from the vast number of incidents composing Jewish history, those are selected which unfold the Divine

i 1 Tim. vi. 11.
‖ Or, perfected.
k ch. iii. 21.

17 [i] That the man of God may be perfect, ‖ [k] throughly furnished unto all good works.

---

guidance of the nation; and the Psalms, being hymns for the use of the Church, required the inspiration of the poet, as well as of the ethical writer; and the prophets have their inspiration as special messengers of God, to reprove the sins or encourage the hopes of special times.

"And is profitable for doctrine, for reproof, for correction," &c. "For doctrine:" not so much for doctrine in our more restricted sense of the word, but for teaching, whether of faith or morals.

"For reproof:" conviction of sin, or of error.

"For correction:" "for setting right" literally—restoration of the weak or erring to the right way.

"For instruction in righteousness:" literally, for the discipline or training which is in righteousness.

On these four uses of Scripture Chrysostom remarks: "From thence we shall know whether we ought to learn, or to be ignorant of any thing. Thence we may disprove what is false, thence we may be corrected and brought to a right mind, may be comforted and consoled, and if anything is deficient we may have it added to us."

17. "That the man of God may be perfect, throughly furnished," &c. The man of God might be either the minister of Christ, who having to teach and expound the Scriptures must realize their inspirations and intent, or the private Christian who feeds on them, meditates on them day and night, and so is well able to fulfil his place in the Mystical Body.

"Throughly furnished unto all good works." Not merely taking part in them, but "throughly furnished," so that whatever part he takes he may do it well.

CHAP. IV.

I [a]CHARGE *thee* therefore before God, and the Lord Jesus Christ, [b]who shall judge the quick and the dead at his appearing and his kingdom;

2 Preach the word; be instant in season, out of season; reprove, [c]rebuke, [d]exhort with all longsuffering and doctrine.

a 1 Tim. v. 21. & vi. 13. ch. ii. 14.
b Acts x. 42.
c 1 Tim. v. 20, Tit. i. 13. & ii. 15.
d 1 Tim. iv. 13.

---

1. "Therefore." Omitted by ℵ, A., C., D., E., F., G., P., nine or ten Cursives, d, e, f, g, Vulg., Goth., Copt., Syriac; but retained by K. L., and most Cursives.

1. "At his appearing." "By his appearing." So ℵ, A., C., D., F., G., d, e, f, g, Vulg. (Amiat.), &c. See below.

1. "I charge thee therefore before God, and the Lord Jesus Christ," &c. I conjure or adjure thee, rather than I "charge" thee.

"Before God and the Lord Jesus Christ."

"At his appearing and his kingdom." The two words "His Epiphany" and "His Kingdom" are properly parts of the adjuration itself. "I adjure thee before God and Jesus Christ, and His Epiphany, and His Kingdom." Thus Moses calls heaven and earth to witness against the Israelites, that if they disobeyed God they should surely perish. (Deut. iv. 26.)

Notice God is the Judge of all—of all the earth, and yet He has committed all judgment to the Son.

2. "Preach the word," *i.e.*, the word of the Gospel. It does not mean preach the word of the Scriptures, but preach the Christ Who is witnessed to all through the Scriptures.

"Be instant in season, out of season." Properly, be urgent, press on. "Mr. ——," said a bishop of the last century to a preacher who by no means confined himself to his own parish, "I hear that you preach at all sorts of irregular times?" "My lord," was the rejoinder, "I preach at only two times, 'in season' and 'out of season.'"

"Reprove," *i.e.*, convince.

3 [e]For the time will come when they will not endure [f]sound doctrine; [g]but after their own lusts shall they heap to themselves teachers, having itching ears;

4 And they shall turn away *their* ears from the truth, and [h]shall be turned unto fables.

5 But watch thou in all things, [i]endure afflic-

[e] ch. iii. 1.
[f] 1 Tim. i. 10.
[g] ch. iii. 6.
[h] 1 Tim. i. 4. & iv. 7. Tit. i. 14.
[i] ch. i. 8. & ii. 3.

---

5. "Endure afflictions." A. only adds, "as a good soldier of Jesus Christ."

"Rebuke," *i.e.*, having convicted them of sin, expose it to them as sinful, as dishonourable to God and disgraceful to themselves.

"Exhort." Urge upon them to flee from the wrath to come, to repent and be converted.

"With all longsuffering and doctrine:" *i.e.*, be unwearied in bringing to bear upon them all the truth of Christ.

3. "For the time will come when they will not endure sound doctrine." "Sound doctrine," rather *the* sound doctrine such as St. Paul and his companions taught, which opposed itself to every form of sin and evil.

"After their own lusts shall they heap to themselves teachers." It need not be assumed that the Apostle here alludes to Gnostical teachers, rather I should think he alludes to the passion for novelty or human eloquence, which characterizes all ages of the Church, and to those teachers who pandered to it. This is one of the evils which naturally arise from teachers or pastors being chosen entirely by the congregation and dependent upon them for their means of subsistence, so that when tired of hearing the same wholesome truths they dismiss them.

4. "And they shall turn away their ears from the truth, and shall be turned unto fables." This is the Nemesis. They do not desire the truth of God, and so God gives them up to delusions that they should believe lies.

5. "But watch thou in all things," &c. Literally, be sober, but such must not be the rendering, because it gives to the English mind a very different idea from that which the Apostle means. Fairbairn's observations are good. It denotes a vigilant, wakeful, considerate frame of mind, which takes good heed to what is pro-

tions, do the work of [k] an evangelist, || make full proof of thy ministry.

6 For [l] I am now ready to be offered, and the time of [m] my departure is at hand.

7 [n] I have fought a good fight, I have finished *my* course, I have kept the faith:

k Acts xxi. 8. Eph. iv. 11.
|| Or, *fulfil*, Rom. xv. 19. Col. i. 25. & iv. 17.
l Phil. ii. 17.
m Phil. i. 23. See 2 Pet. i. 14.
n 1 Cor. ix. 24, 25. Phil. iii. 14. 1 Tim. vi. 12. Heb. xii. 1.

---

7. "A good fight." "The good fight."

ceeding around, and with calm and steady aim pursues its course. The Vulgate rendering is "Vigila."

"Do the work of an evangelist." The work of an Evangelist was the preaching or proclaiming the Gospel message, after which came the work of the Pastor or Teacher. Timothy, though he had the whole care and government of the church of Ephesus laid upon him, was not to remit this; just as St. Paul, who had on him the care of all the churches, was to the last a "preacher" as well as Apostle and teacher of the Gentiles. (1 Tim. ii. 7.)

"Make full proof of thy ministry." Fulfil thy ministry, neglect no part of it. Do thy utmost to render it effectual on all points.

6. "For I am now ready to be offered, and the time of my departure," &c. Literally, I am already being offered as a drink-offering (compare note on Phil. ii. 17). Observe how, in these last words of the Apostle, he applies sacrificial language to his approaching martyrdom. He would not have done this if he had thought, or had been inspired by the Spirit to think, that it was wrong in the sight of God to apply sacrificial terms to any thing except the Sacrifice of Christ upon the Cross.

"The time of my departure." Analysis—my dissolution, the separation of my soul from my body, and my body into its component parts. Some, however, refer it to a meaning of the verb ἀναλύω, which betokens departing from a banquet, others the loosing of a vessel to go on its voyage.

7. "I have fought the good fight." Not *a* good fight, as characterizing his own fight as good, but *the* good fight, *i.e.* the good fight of faith which he had exhorted Timothy to fight (1 Tim. vi. 2), and in which all the followers of Christ, by the fact of their being called soldiers, are engaged.

"I have finished my course." Rather "race," the race which all

o 1 Cor. ix. 25. Jam. i. 12. 1 Pet. v. 4. Rev. ii. 10.

8 Henceforth there is laid up for me o a crown of righteousness, which the Lord, the righteous

---

Christians have to run for the prize. To this course or race he had alluded some six or seven years before, in his charge to the elders of Ephesus, at Miletus, "Neither count I my life dear unto myself, so that I might finish my course with joy, and the ministry which I have received of the Lord Jesus." (Acts xx. 24.)

"I have kept the faith." How extraordinary that the Apostle should make this dying declaration. Was it not perfectly easy to him to keep so simple a thing as the truth of Christ incarnate, crucified, risen and ascended? Whether anything approaching to a temptation to deny any part of it had ever crossed his mind we know not. Only these words seem to imply that it was only by God's grace and by his own effort that he had done so. However, this place reads us, in these last days, a lesson. For the time may be close at hand respecting which our Lord asks, "When the Son of man cometh shall he find the faith on the earth?" (Luke xviii. 8.)

8. "Henceforth there is laid up for me a crown of righteousness, which," &c. The crown of righteousness, not the kingly crown, but the victor's crown; the crown assigned by God to him who had maintained his righteousness, wrought righteousness, battled for righteousness. "Be thou faithful unto death, and I will give thee a crown of life." This crown, whatever it was, was "of life," and "for righteousness." It has been noticed that St. Paul never in all his letters speaks as confidently as he does here, and this was on the very eve of his martyrdom. In Phil. iii. 12, 13, he writes, "not as though I had already attained, either were already perfect—I count not myself to have apprehended." In 1 Cor. ix. 27, "I keep under my body . . . . lest by any means when I have preached to others, I myself should be a castaway." How miserably, then, are they mistaken who encourage the merest neophytes, those who have only just begun to be religious, to apply these words to themselves; seeing they have only just begun to put on their armour or to start on their race, whilst the Apostle, having gained the victory, was putting off his armour and was finishing his race.

"Which the Lord, the righteous judge, shall give me at that day:" *i.e.*, not at the day of death, but the day of His appearing.

judge, shall give me [p] at that day: and not to me only, but
unto all them also that love his appearing. [p] ch. i. 12.

9 Do thy diligence to come shortly unto me:

10 For [q] Demas hath forsaken me, [r] having [q] Col. iv. 14. Philem. 24. [r] 1 John ii. 15.

All hope is concentrated on that day of His appearing. Thus Titus ii. 13, "Looking for that blessed hope and the glorious Epiphany of the great God and Saviour of us, Jesus Christ." Again, in St. John, "When he shall appear we shall be like him, for we shall see him as he is." (1 John iii. 2.)

Chrysostom remarks well: "He who loves His appearing will do every thing to ensure, before His general coming, a particular coming to himself. And how, you will say, is this possible? Hear from Christ, Who says, 'If a man love me, he will keep my words, and my Father and I will come to him, and make our abode with him.' And think how great a privilege it is that He Who will appear to all generally should promise to come to us in particular, for He says, 'We will come and make our abode with him.' If any man love His appearing he will do everything to invite Him to himself, and to hold Him that the light may shine upon him."

"And not to me only, but unto all them also that love his appearing." Notice how the Apostle is careful to assert that this crown will not be given to him only and to other great saints, but will be a gift bestowed upon all who look for the coming of the Lord in glory.

9, 10. "Do thy diligence to come shortly unto me: For Demas hath forsaken," &c. The Apostle was utterly alone and yearned for the comfort of the presence of such a fellow-helper and son in the faith.

"For Demas hath forsaken me, having loved," &c. Was this apostasy on the part of Demas? If so he would scarcely have gone back to Thessalonica, where Christ had so many followers, and St. Paul had so many friends. May we not ascribe it to unworthy cowardice? though, of course, it might lead to apostasy.

We should be very careful how we, in this age of security and freedom in professing the Gospel, condemn Demas. Have any of us lived in such an age as that of Nero? Have we ever seen any of our friends and fellow Christians dying deaths of inexpressible

loved this present world, and is departed unto Thessalonica; Crescens to Galatia, Titus unto Dalmatia.

s See ch. i. 15.
t Col. iv. 14. Philem. 24.
u Acts xii. 25. & xv. 37. Col. iv. 10.

11 [s] Only [t] Luke is with me. Take [u] Mark, and bring him with thee: for he is profitable to me for the ministry.

---

10. "Crescens to Galatia." So A., D., E., F., G., K., L., P., most Cursives; but א, C., a few Cursives, and Cod. Amiat. read, "Gallia."

agony, and being in doubt whether our turn might not come next? We trust that God will accept the disgrace that has attached to the name of this man for eighteen centuries as the punishment for his sin in abandoning His Apostle in his hour of loneliness.

"Crescens to Galatia." This Galatia is not improbably Gaul. So Eusebius iii. 4: "But of the rest that accompanied Paul, Crescens is mentioned by him as sent to Gaul." Theodoret also says that it means Gaul. The churches of Vienne and Mayence, we are told, claim Crescens as their founder.

"Titus unto Dalmatia." A district on the east coast of the Adriatic.

It has been asked whether these companions of St. Paul shared in any degree in the blame attached to Demas? We think it cannot possibly be so, for St. Paul attaches the stigma of worldliness to Demas, and in all fairness he would have blamed the other two if in the least degree they were companions of Demas in his desertion.

11. "Only Luke is with me. Take Mark, and bring him with thee," &c. St. Luke had been one of his most constant companions; he had been with him in his perilous voyage to Rome (Acts xxvii): and had been his companion at Rome, and now he alone is by the Apostle's side. But why was Mark also "profitable to him for the ministry?" May I suggest this—he had been at Rome as the companion or amanuensis of St. Peter, and had published from his lips that Gospel which contains such a graphic delineation of the incidents of our Lord's life. Such a man, with such knowledge of the earthly life of Christ, would be profitable even to St. Paul in the work of the ministry.

It is interesting to remember that when Paul and Barnabas set out on the first missionary journey to the heathen they had John Mark for their minister.

12 And [x] Tychicus have I sent to Ephesus.

13 The cloke that I left at Troas with Carpus, when thou comest, bring *with thee*, and the books, *but* especially the parchments.

x Acts xx. 4. Eph. vi. 21. Col. iv. 7. Tit. iii. 12.

---

12. "And Tychicus have I sent to Ephesus." No doubt to take the superintendence of the Church in the temporary absence of Timothy. In Coloss. iv. 7, St. Paul calls him "a beloved brother and a faithful minister and fellow servant in the Lord."

13. "The cloke that I left at Troas with Carpus, when thou comest," &c. There has been much difference of opinion respecting this "cloke." It is translated in the Vulgate by *pœnula*, a thick garment for winter's use. It has been supposed by Chrysostom to be a small case or bag for holding books. Some have even supposed it to be an Eucharistic vestment; but why should it not be the *pœnula*, to which meaning the word in Greek directs us?

In conversing upon the Inspiration of Scripture I have been more than once asked whether this direction of St. Paul to bring back his cloke was inspired? I answer, it does not require inspiration to direct that a cloke should be brought to him, but it requires the special providence of God that such a direction should be included in such an Epistle as this; and it seems to me to teach us much. It shows us that an Apostle might without sin be careful about property which might be useful to him, to his body as well as to his mind, as the books would be. And taken into consideration with the words which immediately precede respecting his martyrdom, it is very instructive: for, as Bishop Wordsworth says, "the mention of these minor details—the cloke, the books, and the parchments here specified—soon after these glowing aspirations for martyrdom, and these fervent aspirations for glory in the verses immediately preceding, is very affecting, interesting, and instructive, as showing that these aspirations and anticipations were not the outcome of fanatical enthusiasm." They are "touches of nature," showing that such organs of the Spirit of God as the Apostles were not ascetics, far above vulgar earthly wants, but men of like feelings with ourselves in all things.

Chrysostom has a quaint remark: "The cloke he requires, that he might not be obliged to receive one from another. For we see him making a great point of avoiding this."

14 [y] Alexander the coppersmith did me much evil: [z] the Lord reward him according to his works:

15 Of whom be thou ware also; for he hath greatly withstood || our words.

16 At my first answer no man stood with me, [a] but all *men* forsook me: [b] *I pray God* that it may not be laid to their charge.

17 [c] Notwithstanding the Lord stood with me,

y Acts xix. 33. 1 Tim. i. 20.
z 2 Sam. iii. 39. Ps. xxviii. 4. Rev. xviii. 6.
|| Or, *our preachings.*
a ch. i. 15.
b Acts vii. 60.
c Mat. x. 19. Acts xxiii. 11. & xxvii. 23.

---

14. "The Lord reward him." So E**., K., L., most Cursives, d, e, Vulg. (Amiat.); but ℵ, A., C., D*., E*., F., G., fourteen Cursives, f, g, Goth., Syriac, read, "shall reward."

"The books, but especially the parchments." The "books," probably *papyri;* the "especially" shows that the parchments were much more valuable. What were written in these books or parchments it is the idlest folly to conjecture; but being anxiously sent for at such a time by such a man, they must have contained what was very valuable.

14. "Alexander the coppersmith did me much evil: the Lord reward him."

15. "Of whom be thou ware also," &c. The overwhelming majority of the best authorities is in favour of the future tense—"the Lord will reward him." If, however, it be the optative, we are to remember that this curse upon this evil doer was from the Spirit which inspired St. Paul. He seems to have been an inveterate persecutor and opponent of the truth.

16. "At my first answer no man stood with me," &c. This was, in all probability, some trial which he had undergone during his second imprisonment, in which he was an accused person, charged with belonging to a *religio illicita,* the adherents of which the emperor had accused of setting fire to the city of Rome. "If the words may be taken technically, the 'first defence' might be on the first hearing, or '*actio prima,*' after which, if the judge was not satisfied, came an adjournment, '*ampliatio.*' The accused were usually assisted at their trial by an advocate who gave advice, and an orator or *patronus* who made the speech for his client . . . none such stood with St. Paul" (Bishop Jackson).

17. "Notwithstanding the Lord stood with me, and strengthened me; that," &c. This brings to our remembrance, "I am not alone,

and strengthened me; [d]that by me the preaching might be
fully known, and *that* all the Gentiles might hear:
and I was delivered [e]out of the mouth of the lion.
18 [f]And the Lord shall deliver me from every
evil work, and will preserve *me* unto his heavenly
kingdom: to whom *be* glory for ever and ever.
Amen.
19 Salute [h]Prisca and Aquila, and [i]the household of Onesiphorus.

d Acts ix. 15. & xxvi. 17, 18. Eph. iii. 8.
e Ps. xxii. 21. 2 Pet. ii. 9.
f Ps. cxxi. 7.
g Rom. xi. 36. Gal. i. 5. Heb. xiii. 21.
h Acts xviii. 2. Rom. xvi. 3.
i ch. i. 16.

---

18. "And the Lord." So E., F., G., K., L., P., most Cursives, Syriac, Æth.; but א, A., C., D., d, e, f, g, Vulg., Copt., Arm., omit "and."

because the Father is with Me." Similarly the Lord strengthened him at Corinth with the words, "Be not afraid; I am with thee" (Acts xviii. 9).

"That by me the preaching might be fully known, and that all the Gentiles might hear." This trial of the Apostle seems from this to have presented an opportunity which he never had had before of preaching the Gospel before the highest ones of the earth. It has even been supposed that Nero was present in person, and that the "lion" from whose mouth St. Paul was delivered was the emperor. It seems to have been somewhat of a proverbial saying to express deliverance from some tyrant or oppressor. Mr. Blunt gives two instances from the Apocrypha.

18. "And the Lord shall deliver me from every evil work, and will," &c. This is accounted by almost all commentators to be a reminiscence of the Lord's Prayer: "But deliver us from evil. For thine is the kingdom." Some notice that if this be the fact (and it seems very likely), the doxology was in the earliest times appended to the Lord's Prayer.

There was in the Apostle's belief but a very short time intervening between this utterance and his death by the sword: so that this deliverance cannot be one from martyrdom, but must be God's upholding him in the crisis he had to undergo. It seems parallel to that in our burial service: "Suffer us not at our last hour for any pains of death to fall from thee."

19. "Salute Prisca and Aquila, and the household of Onesiphorus." For Prisca (Priscilla) and Aquila, see notes on Acts

20 [k] Erastus abode at Corinth: but [l] Trophimus have I left at Miletum sick.

21 [m] Do thy diligence to come before winter.

k Acts xix. 22. Rom. xvi. 23.
l Acts xx. 4. & xxi. 29.
m ver. 9.

20. "Miletum;" rather, "Miletus."

xviii. 2. St. Paul from his first acquaintance with them kept up kindly and Christian communication with them all through his life. When he wrote his First Epistle to the Corinthians they were with him, and sent greetings to the Church of Corinth (1 Cor. xvi. 19). In Romans xvi. 3, 4, he greets them from Corinth, and here, at the close of his life, he desires to be remembered to them.

"The household of Onesiphorus." See notes on i. 16 of this Epistle.

20. "Erastus abode at Corinth: but Trophimus have I left at Miletum sick." If Erastus is the same as the chamberlain or treasurer of Corinth (Rom. xvi. 23), then Corinth was his home. He stayed then at Corinth after (as Bishop Wordsworth conjectures) St. Paul had paid some visit to that city, and evidently at the desire of the Apostle. It is conjectured, and with some probability, that as St. Paul had mentioned with deserved blame the defection of Demas, he made particular mention of these two companions for the purpose of exonerating them from any possible imputation of unfaithfulness. Trophimus could only have been left at Miletus in some interval between the first and second imprisonments. That he was left there in a state of sickness shows that the Apostle's gift of healing was not permitted by God to be employed for private needs, even for the purpose of securing to him the services of his closest friends, but was only to be used when there was some clear intimation of the Spirit that it was fitting.

21. "Do thy diligence to come before winter. Eubulus greeteth thee, and Pudens." This is the only mention of Eubulus. Nothing is known of him. His name does not appear in the Calendar.

"Pudens, and Linus, and Claudia." Pudens was an officer of the Roman army, who married Claudia, the daughter of the British king, Tiberius Claudius Cogidubnus. He with his wife and Linus are mentioned frequently by the poet Martial; and probably Pudens' name occurs in an inscription discovered in 1723 in

Eubulus greeteth thee, and Pudens, and Linus, and Claudia, and all the brethren.

Chichester. I give in a note the substance of the article in Smith's "Dictionary of the Bible."[1] A far more exhaustive account the reader will find in a note in Lewin's "Life of St. Paul," vol. ii., p. 392.

"And Linus." This man was no doubt the first Bishop of Rome. Irenæus thus speaks of him: "After that the blessed Apostles had founded the Church at Rome they committed the Bishoprick of that city to Linus. This Linus is mentioned by St. Paul in his Epistles to Timothy." Eusebius also mentions him as first Bishop of Rome: "After the martyrdom of Paul and Peter, Linus was the first that received the Episcopate at Rome" (bk. iii., ch. 11). In the Canon of the Mass his name is commemorated immediately

---

1 About the end of the sixteenth century it was observed that Martial, the Spanish poet, who went to Rome, A.D. 66, or earlier, in his twenty-third year, and dwelt there for nearly forty years, mentions two contemporaries, Pudens and Claudia, as husband and wife (Epig., iv. 13); that he mentions Pudens or Aulus Pudens in i. 32, iv. 29, v. 48, vi. 58, vii. 11, 97, Claudia or Claudia Rufina in viii. 60, xi. 53, and, it might be added, Linus in i. 76, ii. 54, iv. 66, xi. 25, xii. 49. That Timothy and Martial should have each three friends bearing the same names at the same time and place is at least a very singular coincidence. The Pudens of the poet was his intimate acquaintance, an admiring critic of his Epigrams, an immoral man if judged by the Christian rule. He was an Umbrian and a soldier; first he appears as a Centurion aspiring to become a Primipilus; afterwards he is on military duty in the remote north, and the poet hopes that on his return thence he may be raised to Equestrian rank. His wife Claudia is described as of British birth, of remarkable beauty and wit, and the mother of a flourishing family. A Latin inscription found, in 1723, at Chichester, connects a [Pud]ens with Britain and with the Claudian name. It commemorates the erection of a temple by a guild of carpenters, with the sanction of King Tiberius Claudius Cogidubnus, the site being the gift of [Pud]ens, the son of Pudentinus. Cogidubnus was a native king appointed and supported by Rome (Tacitus, Agricola, 14). He reigned, with delegated power, probably from A.D. 52 to A.D. 76. If he had a daughter she would inherit the name Claudia, and might, perhaps, as an hostage, be educated at Rome.

Another link seems to connect the Romanizing Britons of that day with Claudia and with Christianity. The wife of Aulus Plautius, who commanded in Britain from A.D. 43 to A.D. 52, was Pomponia Græcina, and the Rufi were a branch of her house. She was accused at Rome, A.D. 57, on a capital charge of "foreign superstition," was acquitted, and lived for nearly forty years in a state of austere and mysterious melancholy (Tacitus, Ann., xiii. 32). We know, from the Epistle to the Romans, xvi. 13, that the Rufi were well represented among the Roman Christians in A.D. 58.

On the whole it is difficult to believe that these facts add nothing to our knowledge of the friend of St. Paul and Timothy. They are treated at great length in a pamphlet entitled "Claudia and Pudens," by Archdeacon Williams, Llandovery, 1848; and more briefly by Dean Alford, "Greek Testament," iii. 104, ed. 1856.

n Gal. vi. 18. Philem. 25.

22 [n] The Lord Jesus Christ *be* with thy spirit. Grace *be* with you. Amen.

¶ The second *epistle* unto Timotheus, ordained the first bishop of the church of the Ephesians, was written from Rome, when Paul was brought before † Nero the second time.

† Gr. *Cæsar Nero*, or, *the emperor*.

---

22. "The Lord Jesus Christ." So C., D., E., K., L., P., most Cursives, d, e, f, g, Vulg., Syriac. A. reads, "the Lord Jesus." ℵ, F., G., reads, "the Lord," without addition.

after that of the Apostles: "As also of the blessed Apostles and martyrs, Peter and Paul . . . Simon and Thaddeus, Linus, Cletus, Clement," &c.

"And all the brethren." This shows that the names just mentioned were "of note among the brethren."

22. "The Lord Jesus Christ be with thy spirit. Grace be with you." These are the last words written by the Apostle in the New Testament. They echo his first words to the Thessalonian Church, to which he wrote, "Grace be unto you, and peace."

Bishop Jackson remarks: "The salutation is two-fold. To Timothy, and to his flock: 'The Lord Jesus be with THY spirit' (μετὰ τοῦ πνεύματός σοῦ); and to the flock, 'Grace be with *you*' (ἡ χάρις μεθ' ὑμῶν)."

EXCURSUS ON THE CHRISTIAN MINISTRY.

PART I.

The first act of the Lord after His Baptism was the designation of certain men to be His ministers (John i. 35-40). He inaugurated the ministry of the Church long before He founded the Church itself. A great principle is involved in this: it is that the Church is in no sense its own creation, neither is the ministerial office the creation of the Church. Now it is quite clear that if it had been His Will matters might have been ordered very differently. The Church might have been left to itself to choose its own ministry. Instead of appointing the ministry Himself, the Lord might have gathered together all His followers, and bid them select from themselves those whom they esteemed the most highly. On the Ascension of the Lord it might have been in a state like the Society of Friends, or, as I understand it, that of the Plymouth Brethren, having no settled ministry, but each assembly of the Christians in the upper rooms of particular houses (and several thousand persons must have required very many places of assembly), might have been left to assert its own independence, and to frame its doctrine and worship according to its own ideas of what is right and fitting. Such would have been the assertion of the absolute freedom of the Gospel, as some understand it, from its very outset. But the very contrary to this took place. The Lord appointed twelve, to whom He spoke very extraordinary words, "As my Father sent me, so send I you," "Whoso receiveth you receiveth me," &c. These twelve founded the Church. They preached the salutary words, the Holy Ghost pricked the hearts of the elect to receive those words, and then the Church commenced. Its beginning is described in the words, "Then they that (gladly) received his word were baptized, and the same day there were added unto them about three thousand souls. And they continued stedfastly in the Apostles' doctrine, and in (their) fellowship, and in the breaking of bread, and in the prayers . . . . and the Lord added to the Church daily such as were being saved" (Acts ii. 41, &c.).

And as it began, so it continued. The ministry of the New Testament from beginning to end is exercised either by these Apostles or under them. Till the conversion of St. Paul, or rather till the time of their dispersion to preach the Gospel, they appear to have acted in concert as one man, and their spokesman and leader seems to have been St. Peter. It is probable that many of them took the persecution after Stephen's speech as a warning for them to disperse, for after that we never read of the twelve, only of "the Apostles which were at Jerusalem."

During the years which intervened between the Day of Pentecost and the conversion of St. Paul, two other orders of the ministry seem to have been appointed or developed. Of that which is called the Diaconate we have a full account in Acts vi.: not so of the Presbyterate; there is not one word respecting its inauguration, and yet it must have been appointed very soon after Pentecost. For the circumstances of the case demanded it, which were something of this sort. Shortly after Pentecost there were above five thousand Christians in Jerusalem, and their number was daily increasing. These, no doubt, religiously attended the services in the vast temple, but where did they assemble for the special worship of the Church, the breaking of bread, or for instruction in the peculiar doctrines of Christianity? No doubt in the upper rooms of private houses; but, if so, there must have been a very large number of such rooms, for it would be a very large house which had a room in which one hundred and fifty or two hundred persons could assemble, and the Christians were not a wealthy community. These assemblies were no doubt presided over by the elders, who later on were called by St. Paul overseers, or episcopi, because of their so presiding. All these were, after the dispersion of the Apostles from Jerusalem, under one elder or episcopus, St. James. Whether he was an Apostle or not is uncertain. But one thing is certain, that all the congregations of the Church at Jerusalem were under him. It is impossible to suppose that the elders, if they wished, could displace him, or that they could assemble together and act without his authority, or that any of the separate congregations could assert an independence which they might suppose was inherent in them as congregations, according to the supposed principles of Christian liberty.[1] The presidency or episcopate of St. James, then, was the link with which they were connected with the Apostolic fellowship. Every notice of St. James in the New Testament shows that he was the bishop of Jerusalem in the present sense of the term bishop. The following deserve attention.

When St. Peter was delivered from prison he directed that tidings of his release should be conveyed to "James and to the brethren" (Acts xii. 17). This of itself, of course, would prove little or nothing, but taken in connection with other notices, it comes in like an undesigned coincidence between two parallel narratives, confirming the truth of both.

The next notice of St. James is the account of his presiding at the council held in Jerusalem respecting the circumcision of the Gentiles, and delivering his sentence *ex cathedrâ*, as it were: "My sentence is that we trouble not them which from among the Gentiles are turned unto God; but that we write unto them that they abstain," &c. (Acts xv. 19). That he should have so delivered the sentence in the presence of the Apostles is only to be accounted for by the fact that the perpetual oversight of the Church of Jerusalem had been committed to him.

The third notice is when St. Paul, on his arrival after his third journey, is reported to have "Gone in unto James, and all the elders were present" (Acts xxi. 18). The mention of his name here, as distinguished from the elders who were present, agrees with the other notices of his governing position.

He is mentioned in Gal. ii. 9 as the first of the three which "seemed to be pillars," and a little further on those Jewish Christians, on account of whose presence even Peter and Barnabas laid themselves open to reproof, are significantly said to have "come from James" (Gal. ii. 12).

The first of all the churches, then, was as strictly under episcopal regimen as any Church of any succeeding age, and its whole organization must have come direct from the Spirit of God, through the human instrumentality of the Apostles themselves.

Almost the whole of the remainder of the New Testament, Acts

---

1 This is by no means an unlikely supposition. The Assembly of the Council recorded in Acts xv. betrayed an agitated and uneasy state of feeling which, unless overruled by the calm decision of St. James, might have led to a fatal disruption, the basis of which would be the assertion of freedom in different congregations to act according to their respective views of the sort of Christianity to be imposed on the Gentiles.

and Epistles, is occupied with the Apostolic ministry of St. Paul. His Apostolic commission came, as he expressly states, not "of men, neither by man," *i.e.*, not by popular election, nor by designation of the other Apostles, but directly from Christ. His solemn setting apart to his office was by the express word of the Holy Ghost: "The Holy Ghost said, Separate me Barnabas and Saul for the work whereunto I have called them" (Acts xiii. 2). Yet even in his case the laying on of hands was not dispensed with. Though he had seen the Lord, and had been caught up into Paradise, he had yet to submit to the Divinely appointed rite. His life, as recorded in the New Testament, was spent in preaching the Gospel, founding churches, superintending them, revisiting them, writing letters to establish them in the truth which he at the first had preached to them, and to warn them against false teaching.

Now in what way, after what fashion, did he exercise his authority? I say it with the utmost reverence, he exercised his authority autocratically. He never allowed anyone (as, for instance, the older Apostles) to share his authority, and he never allowed it to be disputed. He based its exercise upon his Apostolical commission, which he asserted in very express terms at the beginning of most of his Epistles.

The following are instances: "Paul, a servant of Jesus Christ, called to be an Apostle . . . by whom (*i.e.*, by Christ Jesus) we have received grace and Apostleship" (Rom. i. 1-5). See also 1 Cor. i. 1; 2 Cor. i. 1; Gal. i. 1; Ephes. i. 1.

When he associates others with himself, as sending the opening salutation, he never joins these persons with himself as Apostles. It is Paul an Apostle, and Sosthenes our *brother*, Timothy our *brother* (1 Cor. i. 1; 2 Cor. i. 1; 1 Coloss. i. 1).

In the Epistle to the Galatians he intimates that he is equal in authority with Peter and John (Gal. ii. 9).

In the two Epistles to the Corinthians we find several direct assertions of his apostolical authority. "I think that God hath set forth *us* the Apostles last." "Am I not an Apostle?" "Have we not power to lead about . . . as the other Apostles," &c. "I am the least of the Apostles" (1 Cor. iv. 9; ix. 1, 5; xv. 9). Again, "I suppose I was not a whit behind the very chiefest apostles," and "In nothing am I behind the very chiefest apostles" (2 Cor. xi. 5; xii. 11).

Now he exercised this authority with all the love and tenderness of a parent. He never exercised it for selfish ends. He called himself, and he acted as, the least of all, and the servant of all. He abased himself; he worked with his own hands rather than be chargeable; he intreated his converts; he implored them; he was with them in meekness, and in fear, and in much trembling (1 Cor. ii. 3); he even made their prayers a condition of his own salvation (Phil. i. 19); but with all this he never let the reins of power out of his own hands, he never permitted his authority to be called in question, and he allowed no opposition.

The following instances will show that I have not overstated this: "I will come to you shortly, and will know, not the speech of them which are puffed up, but the power." "What will ye? Shall I come unto you with a rod, or in love, and in the spirit of meekness?" (1 Cor. iv. 19, 21).

The next case is exceedingly remarkable. The Church of Corinth, through its local presbytery or overseers, had passed over a case of the grossest immorality conceivable. This had come to the ears of St. Paul, and instead of mildly requesting them to assemble, and themselves adjudicate upon the matter, he sent to direct them what verdict they should pronounce, and what judgment they should inflict. "I verily, as absent in body, but present in spirit, have judged already, as though I were present, concerning him that hath so done this deed. In the name of our Lord Jesus Christ, when ye are gathered together, and my spirit, with the power of our Lord Jesus Christ, to deliver such an one unto Satan," &c. (1 Cor. v. 3).

The reader will perceive that the Apostle leaves nothing to the discretion of the Corinthian Church—to its congregations, its presbyters or overseers—but simply commands them to act according to his directions. If it be said that this was acting harshly, we reply that a worse case of laxity on the part of persons assuming to be a Church court could hardly be conceived. If he unceremoniously superseded them they richly deserved it.

Again, "I command, yet not I, but the Lord . . . so ordain I in all Churches." "I praise you, brethren, that ye remember me in all things, and keep the ordinances as I delivered them unto you." "The rest [of the regulations respecting the Eucharist] will I set in order when I come." "Concerning the collection for the saints, as I have given order to the Churches of Galatia, even so do ye" (1 Cor. vii. 10, 17; xi. 2, 34; xvi. 1, 10).

"If I forgave anything, to whom I forgave it, for your sakes forgave I it in the person of Christ." "Titus . . . remembereth the obedience of you all, how with fear and trembling ye received him." "Being absent, now I write to them which heretofore have sinned, and to all other, that if I come again I will not spare" (2 Cor. ii. 10; vii. 15, 16; xiii. 2). "I desire to be present with you now, and to change my voice, for I stand in doubt of you" (Gal. iv. 20).

"We have confidence in the Lord touching you, that ye both do and will do the things which we command you." "If any man obey not our word by this epistle, note that man." (2 Thess. iii. 4, 14.)

Upon the above I would remark that there is not one word in any Epistle of any organization in any Church which would remove that Church, for any purpose, from under his supervision. We have no word of any bishop, or local presbytery, or synod, or periodical conference, or union of congregations, or chapter, possessing any independent authority. Whatever ecclesiastical organization there was in these Churches the Apostle never recognizes it as a power or estate which had authority to sit in judgment on his letters.

Now in many of these Churches, particularly in the Corinthian, there must have been many persons endowed with special gifts of the Spirit. We should have thought that the abundant possession of such gifts would have made any Church comparatively independent of Apostolic control. But it was not so. The Spirit so ordered His influences that they never clashed with that Apostolic authority by which He Himself primarily worked.

On the contrary the Apostle demands that such persons, in token of their being inspired by the Spirit, should recognize his superior inspiration. "If any man think himself to be a prophet or spiritual, let him acknowledge that the things that I write unto you are the commandment of the Lord" (1 Cor. xiv. 37).

At the end of the eleventh chapter of his First Epistle to the Corinthian Church St. Paul tells the Church that when he comes he will set in order certain matters pertaining to the celebration of the Eucharist. How was it, seeing that there were in the Church many persons endowed with spiritual gifts, that they could not among themselves settle matters of detail of this sort? Simply because it was the will of God that all matters of any importance (and nothing connected with the due celebration of the Eucharist could be of small importance) should come to the Church through the Apostles.

We have now to consider by what means the Apostle was able to exercise control over Churches in all parts of the world. He must have had some special instrumentality for doing this, for he speaks of there coming daily upon him "the care of all the Churches" (2 Cor. xi. 28).

We have no difficulty in ascertaining this, for the Apostle had at least twenty persons attached to him, who were not merely his companions, but his ministers under his orders, like the staff of a commanding officer (Acts xix. 22; xx. 4).

The most prominent of these were Silas, Timothy, Titus, Epaphras, Erastus, Trophimus, Aristarchus, and Tychicus. The names of the rest which are mentioned in Scripture are Sosthenes, Luke, Mark, Apollos, Demas (before his defection), Epaphroditus, Crescens, Artemas, Eubulus, Sopater, Gaius (perhaps), Secundus, Jesus called Justus, Zenas. From the notices we have of these men we see that they did not follow him about for the sake of companionship, but to carry his messages to the Churches, and to bring back reports of their state to him.

First, Timothy. In the first notice of him (Acts xvi. 1-4) we read that the Apostle would have him go forth with him; then he left him with Silas at Berea (Acts xvii. 14). Then he sent for him again "to come to him with all speed" (xvii. 15). Then when at Athens, being troubled with doubts respecting the spiritual warfare of the Thessalonian Church, he sent him to Thessalonica (1 Thess. iii. 1, 2). Then he was comforted with the good news brought by Timothy, and wrote to them his First Epistle.

Then, on another occasion, he sent unto Macedonia two of them that ministered unto him, Timotheus and Erastus (Acts xix. 22). Again, "I have sent unto you Timotheus, who shall bring you into remembrance of my ways which be in Christ, as I teach everywhere in every Church." Again 1 Cor. xvi. 10. Again he was sent to the Philippians, that he might report their state to the Apostle (ii. 19), and this too almost immediately after St. Paul had sent Epaphroditus, whom he styles his brother and companion and fellow-soldier.

Respecting Titus, we learn from the 2nd Epistle to the Corinthians that between the sending of the first and second Epistle,

Titus had brought a report of their state to the Apostle who had sent him to them as his representative, for only in that capacity would such a church have received a subordinate like Titus "with fear and trembling" (2 Cor. vii. 15).

And he sends Titus again to them, and desires them to consider him as his (St. Paul's) "partner and fellow-helper" (2 Cor. viii. 23.)

Tychicus was another whom St. Paul actively employed in the same oversight. He dispatched him to Ephesus and to Colosse, evidently to see to the state of these Churches. To the Ephesians he writes: "That ye also may know my affairs, and how I do, Tychicus, a beloved brother and faithful minister in the Lord, shall make known unto you all things," &c. (vi. 21). To the Colossians: "All my state shall Tychicus declare unto you . . . . whom I have sent unto you . . . . that he might know your estate" (iv. 7, 8).

When in prison at Rome the Apostle sent him to Ephesus (2 Tim. iv. 12), and he also intimates to Titus that he might send Tychicus or Artemas to him, to bring him to the Apostle at Nicopolis (Titus iii. 12).

Such was the episcopate or oversight exercised by St. Paul over all the Churches which he had planted or founded—all closely watched or controlled in his absence by means of a large staff of subordinates who were his companions and disciples, and who consequently knew how he would act under any circumstances which might arise.

Not a single word respecting any independent action to be exercised by boards of presbyters or single congregations, so that they should be free to oppose him or his delegates in any matter in which the Church was concerned.

One point yet remains. What provision did he make for the government of these Churches after his death? We have full information on this point in his three last Epistles, one written shortly before his martyrdom (2 Timothy). These letters are written to two of his most active helpers; and from what they contain and from what they omit we can entertain no doubt as to how the Apostle would have the government of the Churches carried on after his decease.

They contain a solemn transmission of his Apostolical authority (so far as its governing element was concerned) to these two men, through whom, as his ministers, he had so long acted; and they totally omit to give any intimation that this authority was to cease and to be superseded by some oligarchical or (so called) democratic form. They provide for its continued exercise through individuals. They make no provision for its future exercise in synods of presbyters all officially equal, and deciding their differences by a majority of votes.

First they assume the continuance of the Apostolic authority in the persons of Timothy and Titus.

Proofs are "I besought thee to abide still at Ephesus . . . that thou mightest charge some that they teach no other doctrine" (1 Tim. i. 3). Here is authority given to Timothy over teachers and preachers. In the third chapter the qualifications needful in candidates for two orders of ministers, bishops and deacons, are set forth as if Timothy had both the sole choice of these persons and the sole power of ordaining them, the Apostle distinctly implying (verses 14 and 15) that in the choice or ordination of these men Timothy was to act for him.

In the fifth chapter the Apostle gives directions to Timothy respecting elders (or older persons), and widows, as if nothing was left to the discretion of the local authorities. The words in chapter vi. 3, "If any man teach otherwise," &c., taken in connection with other intimations which we have before noticed, evidently imply that St. Paul conveyed to Timothy his own authority over all teachers in the Ephesian Church. In 2 Tim. ii. 2, we have a very plain authority given to Timothy to look out and ordain teachers, and in verses 14 and 15, and in chap. iv. 2-4, directions to Timothy respecting his treatment of false teachers.

Similarly Titus was left in Crete that he might "set in order the things that are wanting, and ordain elders in every city" (Tit. i. 5). The qualifications of these bishops, or elders, are afterwards enumerated, as if Titus alone was responsible for their appointment and ordination. St. Paul also enjoins him to "rebuke sharply" (Tit. i. 13), "to rebuke with all authority" (ii. 15), and to "reject an heretic after the first or second admonition" (iii. 10).

Now these three Epistles are the only ones in which there are any directions whatsoever respecting the government of the churches. In no other Epistle is there one word respecting the choice, qualifications, or ordination of ministers, and those three Epistles are not written to Churches, but to Apostolic men to whom the Apostle was committing his authority.

Now if it had been the will of God that His Church should be ruled on some Presbyterian model, or that each separate congregation should rule itself independently of all other Churches, all such matters as ordinations of ministers would most certainly have been left to the Churches themselves. If God had intended that the lay people should be the source or depository of Church power, or that authority should in future reside in boards of presbyters, would not Epistles bearing on Church rule have been most certainly sent to them? Would they not have been plainly told that all ecclesiastical power had been entrusted to them—that is, to the laity—that they must in the interests of Christian liberty religiously guard the deposit from encroachment, and beware lest in the infancy of the Church an evil precedent should be established if they allowed even the companion and fellow-helper of an Apostle to usurp the authority inherent in the presbyters of the Church, or in each particular congregation itself? But no such words are written to them; they are never bidden to watch their rights with jealousy, they are admonished rather to obey and submit themselves.

Throughout the Pastoral Epistles we have no intimation that the authority committed to Timothy and Titus was transitory and abnormal, for, if so, seeing the uncertainty of human life, we should have had directions to these men to establish a permanent system—indeed such must have been on this hypothesis the main purpose of such Pastoral Epistles. But there is no hint in any part of these Epistles about forming Presbyteries or Apostolic directions as to their action, if already formed—no word to associate others with themselves (Timothy and Titus) as judges of either doctrines or persons. Timothy is directed to receive no accusation against an elder except before two or three witnesses, as if he alone were the judge (1 Tim. v. 19), and Titus is enjoined to reject a heretic after the first and second admonition (Tit. iii. 10).

If the office of such men as Timothy and Titus was temporary, I can only say that on all Presbyterian or Congregational principles it was established just at the wrong time; for the ecclesiastical powers committed to these men in the Pastoral Epistles must have seriously interfered with, or rather rendered impossible, the due action of any Presbyterian or Congregational system which might have been established by Divine authority. Just at the very time when the Churches were learning to walk alone, and with firm step, in their newly acquired Congregational or Presbyterian liberty, we have the Apostle himself binding on them the authority of individual rulers, and giving to these rulers not one word respecting the temporary nature of the authority he had committed to them, but actually implying that it should last till the Second Advent itself. (1 Tim. vi. 14; 2 Tim. iii. 1; iv. 1.)

From what has been adduced from Scripture in the foregoing pages, we gather that the government of the Churches founded by St. Paul was Apostolic, merging after the Apostle's death into Episcopal. By Episcopal government I mean government centred in one man; not, of course, so that one man should govern with the absolute autocracy of the inspired Apostle, but that in each place or neighbourhood there should be one centre, not many centres, of rule.

It is abundantly clear, then, from the Apostolical Epistles, that the power of ordaining and overseeing was not derived from the people through the presbyters to a president, or exercised by the people through deacons, or in popular assemblies, but authority was transmitted by the Apostles to the Apostolic delegates or vicars, and by them to individual overseers.

In the Epistles of the other Apostles there are no directions whatsoever respecting the government of the Church.

The messages of the Lord to the Angels of the Churches through St. John, are in all probability addressed to the Bishops of the respective Churches.

So far as to the principles on which the Apostolic Churches were governed. It must be abundantly clear to the reader that such principles could not develop into the organizations of the Presbyterian or Congregational bodies, and would necessarily develop into the Episcopacy, which early ecclesiastical history presents to us as flourishing in full vigour all over the world.

All Ecclesiastical history presents to us the phenomenon of the huge cities of the Roman Empire, Rome itself, Alexandria, Antioch, Jerusalem, Ephesus, having each but one ecclesiastical head, not elected annually, and not removable by the popular will.

Now seeing that, even on heathen testimony, there was an immense multitude of Christians in some of these cities, and seeing that the Churches were all this time under persecution, and so could not erect buildings of any size, it is clear that there must have been in these cities a great number of comparatively small congregations, each consisting of as many persons as a large room or court of a house would hold, and yet we read of but one supreme ecclesiastical governor or bishop in each of these cities, with whom all the separate congregations were in unison, as the centre or heart of the ecclesiastical κοινωνία.

Such is the natural outcome of the Apostolic precedent as it existed in the first of all Churches—that of Jerusalem—and as it was exercised by the Apostle St. Paul in all the Churches which he planted.

The earliest ecclesiastical writers exhibit the Church as governed on the paternal or monarchical principle.

Ignatius, who in his early years was a contemporary of the generation which knew the Apostles Peter and Paul, and lived long before the death of St. John, writes letters to several Churches in which the Episcopal regimen of the Churches is taken for granted. He speaks of Church government by bishops, presbyters, and deacons, as existing and recognized. He never for a moment supposes that the presidency of the first, the bishops, required to be pressed upon an unwilling Church, or a Church to which such a thing was new. The following is taken from the Epistle to Polycarp (Syrian Recension), "I will be instead of the souls of those who are subject to the bishop and the presbyters, and the deacons, with them may I have a portion in the presence of God."

From a multitude of other passages we select the following: "So that ye obey the bishop and the presbyters with an undivided mind, breaking one and the same bread" (To the Ephesians, ch. xx). "But be ye united with your bishop, and those who preside over you." "Neither do ye any thing without the bishop and presbyters" (To the Magnesians, vi. vii). In all the places in Ignatius which refer to Episcopal government there is not one which speaks of it as a new thing that the presbyters, deacons and people should be subject to a bishop elevated from among the presbyters. On the contrary it seems taken for granted in every place that it is the normal constitution of the Church, and normal in the sense of being established by God, and existing in all parts of the world.

The latest date assigned to the martyrdom of Ignatius is A.D. 116, that is, less than fifty years after the martyrdom of St. Paul. The teaching of his Epistles exactly accords with the Apostolic regimen which St. Paul worked through his large band of subordinates in every Church which he planted.

At the end of the second century, that is within seventy or eighty years after the martyrdom of Ignatius, we have the testimony of three fathers of the Church to the Ecclesiastical government of their times—and their times, that is, the times to which their memory of ecclesiastical masters reached back, must have extended to the former part of the century, and the elderly men whom they knew in their youth must have lived in the times of St. John.

One of these, Irenæus (A.D. 180), writes: "We are in a position to reckon up those who were by the Apostles instituted bishops in the churches, and (to demonstrate) the succession of these men to our own times, those who neither taught nor knew of anything like what these (heretics) rave about. For if the Apostles had known hidden mysteries, which they were in the habit of imparting to the perfect apart and privily from the rest, they would have delivered them especially to those to whom they were also committing the churches themselves. For they were desirous that these men should be very perfect and blameless in all things, whom also they were leaving behind as their successors, delivering up their own place of government to these men."

I would here interrupt the quotation, and remark that this exactly describes the conduct of St. Paul to the men whom he gathered around him, and through whom, as I have shown, he communicated with the various churches and ruled them. What can show the anxiety of St. Paul that those who were to succeed him should be "very perfect and blameless in all things," more than the Epistles to Timothy? Again, "The blessed Apostles, then, having founded and built up the Church (of Rome), committed unto the hands of Linus the office of the episcopate. Of this Linus, Paul makes mention in the Epistles to Timothy. To him succeeded Anencletus, and after him, in the third place after the Apostles, Clement was allotted the bishoprick." Again, "But Polycarp also was not only instructed by Apostles and conferred with many who had seen Christ, but was also by Apostles in Asia appointed bishop of the Church in Smyrna, whom I also saw in my early youth, for he tarried a very long time, and when a very old man gloriously and most nobly suffering martyrdom," &c. ("Against Heresies," book iii. ch. 3.)

Clement of Alexandria (A.D. 180-200) mentions the three orders in the words, "The promotions of bishops, of presbyters, and of deacons are imitations, as I conceive, of the angelic glory."

Clement could not have written such a sentence if he knew that the elevation of the episcopate proper above the other two orders was not from the first, but had taken place in his earlier years, or a little before; and he was a man of great power of mind and learning, and so could hardly have been in error upon a point like this.

And, in the third place, Tertullian, flourishing before the end of the century, writes: "But if there be any heresies which venture to plant themselves in the midst of the age of the Apostles, that they may therefore be thought to have been handed down from the Apostles, because they existed under the Apostles, we may say, 'Let them then make known the originals of their churches, let them unfold the rolls of their bishops, so coming down in succession from the beginning, that their first bishop had for his ordainer and predecessor some one of the Apostles, or of Apostolic men, so he were one that continued steadfast with the Apostles.' For in this manner do the Apostolic Churches reckon their origin, as the Church of Smyrna recounteth that Polycarp was placed there by John; as that of Rome doth that Clement was in like manner ordained by Peter. Just so can the rest also show those whom, being appointed by the Apostles to the episcopate, they have as transmitters of the Apostolic seed" (De Præscrip. Hær. xxxii.).

These testimonies, too, may be said to be from the whole Christian world of that time, for Irenæus was in Gaul, Clement in Alexandria, and Tertullian in Carthage.

Now these passages do not so much prove the early existence all over the world of episcopacy, as of episcopacy founded upon Apostolical succession. If episcopacy had been a late introduction into the Church, and established, as some suppose, by St. John, it could not have been cited as it is by Irenæus and Tertullian as handing down Apostolic doctrine; because if St. John went about the parts within easy reach of Ephesus for the sake of elevating worthy presbyters into bishops, who was it who did this good office for the rest of the world? If St. Paul, for instance, had established Presbyterian polity or anything like it in the Churches he had founded, is it in the least degree probable that such Churches would have universally exchanged their apostolically founded polity for the polity of another Apostle to whom they did not owe their conversion to Christ? Would they not have resisted to the uttermost any such an infringement of their liberties, particularly since St. Paul had in some shape or other constantly claimed the authority of Christ and of the Holy Ghost for what he said and did, and had asserted very strongly the equality of his commission with that of the other Apostles, including St. John? (Rom. i. 1-5; xv. 15-19; 1 Cor. ix. 1, 2; ii. Cor. xii. 12: Gal. i. 1; ii. 6-9).

For it is to be remembered that each of the three forms of rule which have been established amongst Christians—Episcopacy, Presbyterianism, and Congregationalism—embodies a principle: Episcopacy embodies the principle of Apostolic government continuing in paternal rule; Congregationalism, on the other hand, embodies the assertion of such absolute freedom, that any claims to outward unity by the whole mystical body are mischievous. Not only is every congregation absolutely free as against the claims of the Catholic Church, but each member of each particular Church, if he can get two or three to think with him, can establish a Church independent altogether of the Church from which they secede, and licence can scarcely be imagined to go further. In fact the worthy persons who hold this view may be congratulated upon having (humanly speaking) abolished a deadly sin, for on congregational principles no one can commit the sin of schism. Neither the universal Church, the national Church, the diocese, nor the congregation have any claims on strictly congregational principles upon the individual unit.

The mode of government carried on by St. Paul, as it appears in his Epistles, is as far as possible a continuation of the Apostolic. He seems to have had no idea that the Apostolate would cease, but that, as far as possible, it would be carried on in the persons of the Apostolic men whom he had attached to himself, as his disciples and fellow-workers. The existence of such men so trained and disciplined by him demands the continuance of Apostolic oversight or Episcopacy. Let the reader conceive the continuance of such persons in any city or neighbourhood, and he will realize how im-impossible it would be to maintain Presbyterian parity or congregational independence in their presence.

Now these Apostolic men are recognized in two of the writers whom I have cited—Irenæus and Tertullian—as the link between the Apostolic oversight and post-Apostolic episcopacy. Thus Irenæus: "They were very desirous that these men should be very perfect and blameless in all things, whom also they were leaving behind as their successors, delivering up their own place of government to these men." And Tertullian: "Let them unfold the roll of their bishops, so coming down in succession from the beginning that their first bishop had for his ordainer or predecessor, some one of the Apostles or of Apostolic men."

Again, the earliest ecclesiastical historian, Eusebius, takes notice of these "Apostolic men" thus: "That Paul preached to the Gentiles, and established Churches from Jerusalem and around as far as Illyrium, is evident both from his own expressions, and from the testimony of Luke in the book of Acts; and in what provinces Peter also proclaimed the doctrine of Christ—the doctrine of the New Covenant—appears from his own writings . . . throughout Pontus, Galatia, Cappadocia, Asia, and Bithynia. But how many, and which of these, actuated by a genuine zeal, were judged suitable to feed the Churches established by these Apostles, it is not easy to say, any further than may be gathered from the writings of Paul. For he, indeed, had innumerable fellow-labourers, or as he himself calls them, fellow-soldiers, in the Church. Of these the greater part are honoured with an indelible remembrance by him in his Epistles, where he gives a lasting testimony concerning them. Luke also in his Acts, speaking of his (St. Paul's) friends, mentions them by name. Timothy, indeed, is recorded as having first received the Episcopate at Ephesus, as Titus also was appointed over the Churches in Crete. . . . But of the rest that accompanied St. Paul, Crescens is mentioned by him as sent to Gaul. Linus, whom he has mentioned in his Second Epistle to Timothy as his companion at Rome, has been before shown as the first after Peter that obtained the Episcopate at Rome," &c.

"But the manner and times of the Apostolic succession shall be mentioned by us as we proceed in our course."

This corroborates the statements of Irenæus and Tertullian, to which we have drawn attention, of the origin of Episcopacy through Apostolic succession. So that, under God, the real institutor of Episcopacy was not St. John, but St. Paul.

On the hypothesis set forth by Irenæus, Tertullian, and Eusebius, there is no break in the Apostolical government. On the hypothesis of Bishop Lightfoot and others there is a break of such a sort that the earliest Episcopate proper cannot be called Apostolic as proceeding from the Apostles, but through the action of St. John may have Apostolic sanction.

But if we are to gather the will of God from the teaching of the whole New Testament, it was never His intention that the Apostolate should cease. It was to be carried on through the successors of the Apostles after their departure, as it had been to a great extent before.

Has the reader duly considered this fact, that from the Day of Pentecost to the close of the New Testament history, there is no ministry exercised, except that of Apostles? With the exception of the address of St. Stephen, and two or three sentences spoken by Philip the Deacon to the Eunuch, and a sentence by Agabus, there is not one word recorded as spoken by anyone except an Apostle. For instance, we have not one word recorded as spoken by Silvanus, or Barnabas, or Timothy, or Titus, or Tychicus. Not one single independent act of Ordination, or Excommunication, or Confirmation by any follower of St. Paul. The whole canvas is, as it were, filled by the Apostle St. Paul.

Now if such a fact has any significance—and significance, it seems to me, it must have—it is that during all Christian times the Apostolate was not to cease; as, properly understood, it has not.

It may be asked, Have not the miracles of the Apostles ceased? We rejoin, we cannot tell whether God has decreed that there should be no more miracles, or whether the Church has grown cold in faith, so that she has not the faith required by the Lord in Matthew xvii. 20.

If it be asked, has not Apostolic inspiration ceased? we must answer that we think not. There are many books or parts of books written by bishops and priests since Apostolic times, which seem to have been written under Divine assistance; and we must remember that, of the original band of twelve Apostles, monuments of the inspiration of two only have been preserved to us, and that some of the Epistles of St. Paul have perished.

In all probability God has continued to the present holders of the Episcopate the unifying, and transmitting, and governing powers of the Apostolate; and this is, if duly considered, a very great thing indeed.

Note.—The part of the preceding Excursus between pages 312 and 322 I have taken nearly verbatim from my chapter on Church Government, in the seventh chapter of "Church Doctrine Bible Truth." What I have thus copied consists almost wholly of citations of passages in the Pauline Epistles, with short remarks on their application. This I composed with very great care when I wrote the volume in question; and I do not see that I am required to alter it in this new volume, in which it seems necessary to have some essay or excursus on the Christian Ministry, in elucidation of the Pastoral Epistles.

PART II.

The question presents itself, what is the conception of the Church of Christ which we find in Holy Writ, and is the idea of a ministry derived from Apostolic succession consonant with it or not?

We are at no loss for the scriptural, or should we not say, Divine conception of the Church. We have it in the tersest, and perhaps most condensed form in St. Paul's Epistle to the Colossians (ii. 19), "The Head, from which all the body by joints and bands having nourishment ministered, and knit together, increaseth with the increase of God." There are one or two precisely similar descriptions which I give in a note.[1]

The Divine Conception, then, of the Church is that of an organization, a human body, all the parts of which partake of life, because they are all united in one living frame, under One Head. It is clear, then, that in the Divine Conception or Idea, there must of necessity be means of communicating the life or sensation of the Head to the remotest parts of the Body. The various limbs or members do not hold, *so far as the conception of a body is concerned*, direct or personal communion with the head, but indirect, through the nerves, the joints, and bands. So that the whole

---

1 "He gave some (as) apostles, and some (as) prophets, and some (as) evangelists, and some (as) pastors and teachers; for the perfecting of the saints, for the work of the ministry, for the edifying (or building up) of the body of Christ. Till we all come in the unity of the faith, and of the knowledge of the Son of God, unto a perfect man, unto the measure of the stature of the fulness of Christ: . . . may grow up in all things into him which is the head, even Christ: from whom the whole body fitly joined together and compacted by that which every joint supplieth, according to the effectual working in the measure of every part, maketh increase of the body unto the edifying of itself in love." (Eph. iv. 11-16.) Again (1 Cor. xii.), "As the body is one, and hath many members . . . so also is Christ . . . ye are the body of Christ, and members in particular. And God hath set some in the church, first apostles, secondarily prophets, thirdly teachers, after that miracles, then gifts of healing . . . Are all apostles? are all prophets?" &c. So also Rom. xii. 4-9.

system of the human body is a system of interpositions—no member having direct communication with either head or heart; all the communication is indirect through certain means of conjunction. Now is there no *direct* communication between God or Christ, and each member? Certainly, most certainly, the spirit of each man must have intercourse with the Father of Spirits. He must come to God as if there was no other being in the universe except himself and God; but notwithstanding this, it is not the will of God that His kingdom should be looked upon as consisting of Himself and an innumerable number of separate units. His ultimate design is to "gather together in one all things in Christ" (Ephes. i. 10), and the Church is the preparation for this.

The whole Church, in its primary conception, is a system of means. God might teach each and every member by Himself, and yet He teaches each member of the Church by others. He might preach the Gospel Himself as He preached the law from the top of Sinai by Himself, but He preaches to us through the lips of others, reserving to Himself the power of impression only. The same with admission into the mystical body. He might admit each and every member by some invisible action of His own, but instead of this, His Spirit baptizes by the hands of man, He buries them with Christ, raises them again in Him, grafts them into His Body, and makes them His members by means of earthly human agents, who are His means or mediums for this purpose, and whom at His own will and pleasure He interposes between Himself and each person saved. The same with the mystical feeding in the Eucharist. He blesses the elements through tho lips of others. He distributes them by the hands of others, and that which is bestowed, if we are to measure it by the terms used in the first occasion by the Great Institutor, must be immeasurably great.

So that the first conception of the Church is that of a system of means—a system of means to take each Christian unit out of its natural isolation, and to make it one, not of a worldly society, but of a mystical body, of whose union under its Divine Head, the most transcendental things are spoken. In accordance with this, the Apostles were prepared by the Lord to be parts of a system of means. Such words as "He that receiveth you receiveth me," "Whatsoever ye shall bind on earth shall be bound in heaven," "As my Father sent me, so send I you," "Whosoever sins ye remit, they are remitted unto them," are only consonant with the fact that with respect to His Church, these Apostles were to be mediating ministers—interposed by God Himself, between Himself and those on whom He desired to confer certain benefits.

Furthermore, the Lord utters the parable of the Vine and the Branches to describe the Kingdom He was preparing them to administer. Now this parable asserts a system of mediation or interposition from beginning to end. The roots are interposed between the ground and the stem, the stem is interposed between the roots and branches—the larger branches into which the stem first divides itself are interposed between the stem and the smaller branches, and the smaller branches again are interposed between the branches which support them and the tendrils—no leaf or tendril having direct communication with the stem. This parable teaches us that the Apostolic connection between Christ and the smallest fruit-bearing branch is never intended to cease—the Apostles are to merge into Apostolic men, and these into ordinary ministers, and these into ordinary Christians. Such, if Christ be Divine, was the Divine idea or conception, and such it appeared in the Pentecostal Church, and the Churches planted among the Gentiles by the Apostles.

So that this idea of organization was in the Divine Conception, and ruled the outward form of the Church from the very first; it was anterior to the Church, and was, one may say, the mould into which it was cast. It existed anterior to any needs which might affect the Church from without, and oblige it to alter its form or constitution.

And now we must set before ourselves an opposite theory of the Church and its ministry, one set before us by one (till lately) of our chief and most honoured ecclesiastical rulers.

> "The kingdom of Christ, not being a kingdom of this world, is not limited by the restrictions which fetter other societies, political or religious. It is in the fullest sense free, comprehensive, universal. It displays this character not only in the acceptance of all comers who seek admission, irrespective of race, or caste, or sex, but also in the instruction and treatment of those who are already its members. It has no sacred days or seasons, no special sanctuaries, because every time and every place alike are holy. Above all, it has no sacerdotal system. It interposes no sacrificial tribe or class between God and man, by whose intervention alone God is reconciled and man forgiven. Each individual member holds personal communion with the Divine Head. To Him immediately he is responsible, and from Him directly he obtains pardon, and draws strength.
>
> "It is most important that we should keep this ideal definitely in view, and I have therefore stated it as broadly as possible. Yet the broad statement, if allowed to stand alone, would suggest a false impression, or at least would convey only a

half truth. It must be evident that no society of men could hold together without officers, without rules, without institutions of any kind; and the Church of Christ is not exempt from this universal law. The conception, in short, is strictly an *ideal*, which we must ever hold before our eyes, and which should inspire and interpret ecclesiastical polity, but which nevertheless cannot supersede the necessary wants of human society, and if crudely and hastily applied, will lead only to signal failure. As appointed days and set places are indispensable to her efficiency, so also the Church could not fulfil the purposes for which she exists without rulers and teachers, without a ministry of reconciliation, in short without an order of men who may in some sense be designated a priesthood. In this respect the ethics of Christianity present an analogy to the politics. Here also the ideal conception and the actual realization are incommensurate and in a manner contradictory. The Gospel is contrasted with the Law as the spirit with the letter. Its ethical principle is not a code of positive ordinances, but conformity to a perfect Exemplar—incorporation into a Divine Life—the distinction is most important, and eminently fertile in practical results. Yet no man would dare to live without laying down more or less definite rules for his own guidance, without yielding obedience to law in some sense; and those who attempt to discard all such aids are often farthest from Christian perfection.

"This qualification is introduced here to deprecate any misunderstanding to which the opening statement, if left without compensation, would fairly be exposed.

"This then is the Christian ideal, a holy season extending all the year round—a temple confined only by the limits of the habitable world—a priesthood co-extensive with the human race.

"Strict loyalty to this conception was not held incompatible with practical measures of organization. As the Church grew in numbers, as new and heterogeneous elements were added, as the early fervour of devotion cooled and strange forms of disorder sprang up, it became necessary to provide for the emergency by fixed rules and definite officers."

Now in reading this, we cannot help thinking that there must be some mistake, some radical error, for here we have what we must hold to be a Divine Conception or Ideal which never has been, and never can be realized. We are told, for instance, that above all "it has no sacerdotal system," for "each individual member holds personal communion with the Divine Head," and yet a few sentences further on, this is corrected by the words, "The Church could not fulfil the purposes for which she exists, without rulers and teachers, without a ministry of reconciliation, in short, without an order of men, who may in some sense be designated a priesthood." Here then is an ideal of Almighty God which in its working needs to be supplemented, or rather corrected, by the action of men. I cannot see that I am misrepresenting this. I have read over the whole passage many times, I have transcribed it carefully, and I cannot but gather from it that the opinion of the writer is, that the Divine Conception as far as possible excludes means, and yet that it cannot be worked except by a system of means. In idea, *i.e.*, in the Divine Idea, it has above all no priests, and yet in its working it must have them, or it cannot "fulfil the purposes for which it exists," that is, we must assume, the purposes for which God caused it to exist.

There must be some error in some part of the reasoning, and the error is, that an ideal or conception of the Church is imputed to God which is not His. The Church in His Mind is a system of means (at least so He has assured us by His Son and His Holy Apostles, John xv., 1 Cor. xii., Ephes. iv., Col. ii.), and the ideal which is imputed to Him is a system without means—I mean, of course, without means administered by men—without interposition or intervention, or anything of the kind.

Now the first thing which we have to correct in the above extract is the assumption that there is any inherent antagonism between each individual holding personal communion with God, and what is called Sacerdotalism, or a system of means administered by men. Has there ever been, in the history of the world, anything which can be properly called Sacerdotalism? Undoubtedly there has, and that is the Jewish sacrificial system. The most pious persons of the Israel of God, as far as we can gather from the Old Testament, came to God through this system; but did this in any way hinder, or even deteriorate from, their personal access to Him and feeling of dependence upon Him? Let the book of Psalms testify. The sacerdotal system enabled the Psalmist to say, "I will go into thine house with burnt offerings, and will pay thee my vows which I promised with my lips, and spake with my mouth when I was in trouble: I will offer unto thee fat burnt sacrifices with the incense of rams: I will offer bullocks and goats." Here is as hearty a recognition as is possible of the sacrificial or sacerdotal system, but how does the Psalmist proceed? "O come hither and hearken, all ye that fear God, and I will tell you what he hath done for my soul. I called unto him with my mouth, and gave him praises with my tongue. If I incline unto wickedness in my heart, the Lord will not hear me. But God hath heard me, and considered the voice of my prayer. Praised be God, who hath not cast out my prayer, nor turned his mercy from me." (Psalm lxvi. 12-18.)

Again, in a Psalm a little before this (lxiii.), "O God, thou art my God, early will I seek thee. My soul thirsteth for thee; my flesh also longeth after thee, in a barren and dry land, where no water is. Thus have I looked for thee in holiness, that I might behold thy power and glory. For thy loving kindness is better than the life itself. My lips shall praise thee." Again, the Psalm before this (lxii), "My soul truly waiteth still upon God, for of him cometh my salvation. He verily is my strength and my salvation, he is my defence, so that I shall not greatly fall. . . . Nevertheless, my soul, wait thou still upon God, for my hope is in him. In God is my health and my glory, the rock of my might, and in God is my trust. O put your trust in him alway, ye people; pour out your heart before him, for God is our hope."

Now can language, setting forth individual communion with God, be more direct and loving than this? and yet these are the utterances of men between whom and Himself God had interposed a sacrificial tribe, or class. How is it, then, that their intercourse with God should be so intimate and direct? For a very simple reason indeed: God had ordained not one, but two things. He had ordained (so, at least, we must assume), that each Israelite should come to Him directly in his own spirit; and He had also ordained that each Israelite should use sacrifice and burnt offering as a means of approach. If an Israelite was loyal to God, he would endeavour to realize both these means of access, and God would reward him with the sense of His presence and protection; but if he held up his head aloft, and said to himself, I have intercourse with God in my soul and spirit; what need I with these sacrifices? Then God would not come near to that man, He would "behold him afar off."

It is a great mistake to suppose that the Old Testament dispensation is a system of means, *i.e.*, of priestly interventions, in contrast with the New Testament, which is supposed to be, in its ideal, a system of direct intercourse. As far as we can ascertain from Scripture, the conception of the two in the Divine Mind is the contrary. There are two parables embodying the Divine conception of each respectively—that in Isaiah v. of the "Vineyard on the very fruitful hill,"—that in John xv. of the "Vine and the branches." In the first of these, which is supposed to represent the Israelites under the sacerdotal system, there is a vineyard of plants, each a separate organism, each receiving its share of rain and sunshine from heaven by itself. In the other (John xv.), there is but one Vine, One Stem, from which the farthest branch receives its nourishment; and as this vine is supposed to overspread the earth, there must be innumerable interventions, or interpositions, of branch between branch everywhere, at all times, no one single branch receiving its life alone, by itself, but each and every one through mediation or interposition.

And if we look to the Church of the Old Testament, the highest things are said of it. Israel is God's Son, His firstborn. It is His people, His inheritance, but it is never said to be His Body, and it is never said to be His Vine, but only His vineyard. Its quasi-sacraments are never said to be, or implied to be, channels of grace. Its ministry is a ministry of ceremonies, not of Sacraments—of law, not of Grace. Its unity is the unity of a nation, not of a Mystical Body. To its ministers are never said the words, "As my Father sent me, so send I you." They are never commissioned to feed men with the Body and Blood of one at the right hand of God.

So that the Christian Church is far more than the Jewish National Polity a system of "interpositions" and "interventions." The fact that the Christian system of intervention is for spiritual ends increases its importance, dignity, and essential necessity.

We shall now be able to see what truth there is in certain statements which we find in this celebrated excursus.

1. "The Christian idea, therefore," the Bishop writes, "was the restitution of this immediate and direct relation with God which was partly suspended, but not abolished, by the appointment of a sacerdotal tribe." Now let the reader remember that the Christian system was not the restitution of something wholly, or partially suspended, but the creation of an absolutely new thing, the joining together or inherence of believing men in one Body in Christ. We have shown that, so far as its spiritual results in men's souls were concerned, the Book of Psalms shows that direct intercourse with God was not even partially suspended under the Levitical system, and the Church of Christ, from the first, adopted the devotional Book of the Old Covenant as its own: but the New Testament commenced with, and to its close maintained, the most astonishing principle of exclusive mediation: "No man cometh unto the Father but by Me." Now, by saying this, does the Eternal Son mean to shut the door against any poor isolated soul who would approach to God, not having heard of Christ, and so not naming His Name? No, but He means that, wherever His Gospel is preached—the Gospel of His Incarnation, Death, Resurrection, and Ascension—there must be preached contemporaneously with it its unifying principle of

one life in Him: the Gospel, that is, of the true Vine, of the one Body, of the New Creation (κτίσις), the Gospel of the living and unifying Bread. (John vi.; 1 Cor. x.)

Now the first conception of this Gospel demands means, or interpositions, such as the similitude of the Vine and the human body demands; and, as a system of means, it began to be at the day of Pentecost; and, as a system of means, it was taught and administered by St. Paul, and, though with many distortions and many misapplications and exaggerations, such it has continued ever since. The system of means, as it appears in 1 Cor. xii., one of the first of the Epistles, written within twenty-five years after the Lord's Ascension, contains the whole conception.

The New Dispensation, then, is not a return to an old state of things, but it is an altogether new state of things, a new organization, a new system of new means, a new and living way, all things new.

2. The Bishop makes the institutions of Christianity to be, not the creation of the Divine Will at the first, but the creatures of circumstances. "As the Church grew in numbers, as new and heterogeneous elements were added, as the early fervour of devotion cooled, and strange forms of disorder sprang up, it became necessary to provide for the emergency by fixed rules and definite officers."

Now what does this mean? It means that the first principle of the Church, the principle which discountenanced interposition and intervention, could not last for twenty years, or, indeed, anything like it, for in Corinthians xii. we have a system of officers as complete as at any future time, and we have also the recognition of traditions respecting Divine worship (xi. 1), which must have had their beginning some, if not many, years before. Now, if we take into consideration what I have shown to be the fact, that the Lord prepared His Apostles to be the ministers of a system of mediations or interventions, and that He Himself describes it beforehand as such (John xv.); then the first principle of the Church has never been contravened. The conception in the Divine Mind was embodied from the first in the then first planted Church at Jerusalem, and in the churches planted by St. Paul. (Acts ii. 42, xi. 30, xiv. 23, &c.) The Church was never unofficered.

3. Again, the Bishop writes, "The Apostles never lost sight of the idea (that the perfection of the Church was to be without means) in their teaching. They proclaimed loudly that 'God

dwelleth not in temples made with hands,' they indignantly denounced those who 'observed days and months, and seasons, and years.' This language is not satisfied by supposing that they condemned only the temple worship in the one case—that they reprobated only Jewish Sabbaths and New Moons in the other. It was against the false principle that they waged war; the principle which exalted means into an end, and gave an absolute intrinsic value to subordinate aids and expedients."[1] Now I say it with all reverence to the memory of the departed Bishop, it would have been a new thing to St. Paul to have been told that in the Epistle to the Galatians he waged war against the false principle which "exalted the means into an end;" on the contrary, he was most certainly reprobating the use of certain means themselves, which were characteristic of an effete system which some of his Galatian converts, through a deep-seated unbelief in the Divine Greatness of Christ, were adopting. If St. Paul was waging war against this false principle alluded to, the first thing which he would have done would have been to forbid the celebration of the Eucharist on the first day of the week. He would have said, "I lay it solemnly upon you to have no fixed day of the week for the celebration of the Eucharist; especially do not have it on the first day of the week; by so doing you will introduce into the Church an evil principle, contrary to the first principle of its existence, which is, that in the Divine conception it has no sacred days or seasons."

Again, the Bishop proceeds, "These aids and expedients (of observances of days, &c.), for his own sake and for the good of the society to which he belonged, a Christian could not afford to hold lightly or to neglect. But they were no part of the essence of God's message to man in the Gospel; they must not be allowed to obscure the idea of Christian worship."

At first one might think that this might be dismissed with such a remark as, Whoever in his senses thought that they did form part of such essence? The great fact of St. Paul's Gospel is the

---

[1] Bishop Lightfoot explains the "days and seasons and months and years" of Gal. iv. 10, as Jewish ones. I have shown in my notes on this verse (along with others) that the observance of such days on the part of a converted Gentile would betray disloyalty to Christ, and a deep-seated unbelief in the all-sufficiency of His system, as compared with that of Moses.

Lord's Resurrection. How is it possible that the keeping of a weekly, or an annual commemoration of such an event could obscure the idea of Christian worship? Nevertheless, it may be instructive to dwell for a moment on the principle which underlies such a matter as the keeping of the day of the Resurrection. We have in England and Scotland two established churches. In one of these there is an annual as well as a weekly commemoration of the day of the Lord's Resurrection, as well as of other great events concerning Him, such as His Birth, Death and Ascension. In the other such annual commemorations are sternly forbidden. But when we come to look into the matter a little closer, we find a very marked difference between the conception of the Gospel put forth by the two Christian bodies respectively. The one puts in the foreground the historical form—the record of the Death, Burial, and Resurrection of the Eternal Son, including, of course, His Incarnation, Birth, and Human Life. The other (the Kirk) keeps these things in the background, and has as its real creed certain abstract doctrines as predestination, election, reprobation, and final perseverance. Now the Church, holding forth the historical Gospel, naturally, we may say, retains such annual commemorations as that of the Nativity and Ascension. She could not do otherwise, holding, as she does, such historical facts as the Incarnation of the Word, His appearance amongst us in human nature, the Divine character manifested in His human life, Crucifixion at the Passover, the Burial, the life-resuming, and life-imparting Resurrection on the third day, and Ascension on the fortieth day, to be the Gospel; and a Christian body which on principle puts certain abstract doctrines as her foremost exhibition of Divine truth, as naturally could not have a Christian year.

4. "But," the Bishop proceeds, "the careful student will also observe that this idea (of an universal priesthood—of the religious equality of all men,) has hitherto been imperfectly apprehended; that throughout the history of the Church it has been struggling for recognition, at most times discerned in some of its aspects, but at all times wholly ignored in others," &c. Now the principle alluded to by the bishop is not alone in this. Many are the truths—even the aspects of Christianity which have been struggling for recognition all through its history; but what does the bishop mean by "religious equality"?—he surely must confound it with "official equality" (*i.e.*, in the Christian Church). There never has been

from the earliest history of the Christian Church, "official equality" (Acts v. 13); St. Paul ignores it, and in his very first Epistle (1 Thess. v. 12) says what is directly contrary to it; but if by "religious equality" be meant the equality of a layman's personal religion with a clergyman's, then it appears to me that this, whenever and wherever it is known, has always been most fully recognized. I can only say for myself (and I may say also for all those with whom I have acted in my ministerial life) that I have always regarded personal religion in a layman with more respect than the same in a clergyman, because the layman's personal religion seems always more voluntary, and less required by the needs of his official position. But in saying this I am not fighting with a mere shadow, but with a misconception which is doing a vast amount of mischief, for those who now lay out their whole strength in order to rob the Church of England (of which the writer of the Essay is a high official), of its revenues, are doing it on the ground of asserting "religious equality," and the Bishop ought to have been careful not to lend his sanction to such ambiguity of expression.

But I have made this last quotation from the Bishop's Excursus for another purpose. I believe that it may be said with infinitely more truth respecting what I have shown to be the Divine Conception, or Ideal of the Church, viz., that it is an organization in and under Christ—that "the careful student will observe that *this* idea has hitherto been very imperfectly apprehended." If it had been at all adequately apprehended, it would have saved the Catholic Church from the Papacy on the one side, and from such disuniting principles as Congregationalism on the other. For the Papacy is, as it were, a new branch springing out of the Church after all the original branches had been divided from the stem, and so asserting itself as to demand that all the branches, large or small, of the whole universal Church, should be re-engrafted into it, and made to spring from it, and be in fellowship with it on peril of loosing their hold on Christ. And Congregationalism, on the other side, asserts that there must not be any intervening branches whatsoever between any twig or tendril, and Christ; the Church is an unnatural tree, having no branches, but the huge trunk covered with sprigs having no connection with either the branches or with one another.

The strength of the ministry is the realization of the Apostolical Succession. This is outwardly or ecclesiastically assured to us by the bishops, but each individual minister has to realize that he has not spiritually ascended from the people, but that he is spiritually descended from Christ through the Apostles. The constant falling back upon this, the continual making acts of faith in this, will more than ought else save him from being proud and overbearing in the exercise of his priestly functions. The proud, overbearing bishops, as is very well known, are just those who disclaim any connection by succession with the Apostles. The true realization of the Apostolic succession is, "looking to the rock whence we are hewn, and to the hole of the pit whence we are digged" (Isa. xli. 1)—looking to the self-sacrificing, humble, homeless, persecuted men whom God set forth as the first ministers of His Church (1 Cor. iv. 9-13).

And now we must, as it were, gather into a focus the teaching of the Bishop's Essay, or Excursus. It seems to be written with the view of establishing Episcopacy upon what the author assumes to be a lower basis than that of direct Apostolical Succession, and that is upon Apostolical Sanction, the Sanction being apparently that of St. John, as contrasted with that of St. Paul and the other Apostles. Now this seems strange. The action of St. Paul, as described in the New Testament, is eminently fitted to train men as successors of the Apostles (see above, pp. 318, &c.); and, respecting the action of St. John in this matter, we can gather nothing from the Sacred Volume.

Moreover, two of the most ancient ecclesiastical writers, and the chief ecclesiastical historian, as I have shown, consider the Apostles generally as the originators of episcopacy. Eusebius evidently does this with reference to St. Paul in words which, from their importance, I shall quote again: "But how many, and which of these, actuated by a genuine zeal, were judged suitable to feed the Churches established by these Apostles, it is not easy to say, any further than may be gathered from the writings of St. Paul. For he indeed had innumerable fellow-labourers, or, as he calls them, fellow-soldiers in the Church. Of these the greater part are honoured with an indelible remembrance by him in his Epistles, where he gives a lasting testimony concerning them." Then, having mentioned Timothy as appointed by him Bishop of Ephesus, and Titus of Crete, he goes on, "But of the rest that accompanied Paul, Crescens is mentioned by him as sent to Gaul. Linus, whom he has mentioned in his Second Epistle as his companion at Rome, has been before shown to have been the first after Peter that obtained the Episcopate at Rome. Clement also, who was appointed the third Bishop of this Church, is proved by him to have been a fellow-labourer and fellow-soldier with him."

And what St. Paul did we may be sure that the rest of the Apostles did also. It was only natural if they wished the Churches which they had planted to continue under something of Apostolic oversight.

Now the Bishop seemingly takes no notice of this, the most salient point in the history of Church government, but assumes that the Pauline churches were under some sort of Presbyterian or Congregational government, all memory of which had utterly perished in the course of less than half a century, and which, in twenty years, had grown so effete, that another Apostle, St. John, had to supersede it in about twenty or twenty-five years after St. Paul's death.

Now this action on the part of St. John seems to me attended with very great difficulty indeed, for, as I have said, it assumes that an almost universal presbyterate, established by the rest of the Apostles, was superseded by an episcopate ordained by one who was not their father in Christ.

Very weighty words on this subject were written by the late Dean Millman ("History of Christianity," vol. ii., book ii., ch. iv.), "The later the date which is assumed for the general establishment of the Episcopal Authority, the less likely it was to be general. It was only during the first period of undivided unity that such an usurpation, for so it must have been according to this theory (the earlier establishment of a presbyterian polity), could have been universally acquired. All presbyters, according to this view, allowed themselves to be deprived of their co-ordinate and co-equal dignity. The further we advance in Christian history, the more we discover the common motives of human nature to work. In this case alone are we to suppose them without influence. Yet we discover no struggle, no resistance, no controversy. The uninterrupted line of bishops is traced by the ecclesiastical historians up to the Apostles; but no murmur of remonstrance against this usurpation has transpired."

This appears to me incontrovertible, but Bishop Lightfoot seems not to have apprehended it in the least, and supposes the original presbyterian polity to have been so weak that an aged Apostle, living far from the centre of the world's or the Church's influence, was, by his mere breath, able to supersede it. But Presbyterianism seems to me to be by no means a weak polity. It is very strong and decisive against opinions which it holds to be heretical; it maintains, or has in times past maintained, a very effective discipline against what it conceives to be wrong-doing. The fault which is inherent in its very essence is that it appears to be disintegratory. There are now three powerful bodies of Presbyterians in Scotland, all of which hold precisely the same creed (and a very long one), and yet there is, I am told, not an approach to anything like a basis of union between them. The traditions of their elders keep them apart.

The Bishop of Durham acknowledges that Episcopacy is so inseparably interwoven with all the traditions and beliefs of men like Irenæus and Tertullian, that they betray no knowledge of a time when it was not. He has altered his opinion respecting the genuineness of the Greek Recension of the letters of St. Ignatius, so that he acknowledges that some of the strongest assertions of the Divine origin of the Episcopal office are written by him early in the second century. He acknowledges that the mother Church of Christendom, that of Jerusalem, was Episcopal long before the Apostles were removed from the scene. So also with Antioch. So with Asia Minor. So with Rome. So with the churches of Gaul. He considers them closely connected with, and probably descended from, the churches of Asia Minor. So with the churches of Africa, (224). He acknowledges that the Church of Alexandria had always one ruler, though he contends that there are doubts respecting his having boen Episcopally ordained.[1]

Crete and Thrace and Athens received Episcopacy certainly very early in the century. But there is a doubt about Corinth, which, considering the state of anarchy in the Church there, is probably not unlikely; and the Bishop of Philippi is not mentioned in Polycarp's Epistle.[2] These two last surmises seem the sole argument

[1] The reader will find a full examination of this matter in Mr. Gore's work on "The Ministry," note B, p. 357.

[2] May not the Valens, whose conduct is so severely blamed in ch. x. as having fallen into some temptation from avarice, have been the Bishop? The words seem to imply that he had been a Presbyter, but had been advanced to some higher post. The words (Hefele) are "Nimis contristatus sum pro Valente, qui Presbyter factus est aliquando apud vos, quod sic ignoret is locum qui datus est ei."

which the Bishop can adduce for the revolution effected by the influence of St. John. Now I would ask the reader to consider for what purpose the origin of Episcopacy is made to depend upon St. John's influence. It is for the purpose of making a break, or gap, between the Apostolic and the present Church—a gap, or break, which the Bishop says, "will not allow us to unchurch other Christian communities differently organized." This, no doubt, is at the bottom the reason why Episcopal government is dated as late as possible—I do not say by the Bishop, but by the German writers whose opinions he reproduces. It is that a previous Presbyterianism, or Congregationalism, being assumed, these "otherwise constituted Christian communities" may yet be acknowledged as parts, "visible parts," of the Catholic Church. Now I can assure the reader that this consideration weighs with me, I hope, quite as much as with the Bishop, but it is to be remembered that we do not think of unchristianizing them—on the contrary, we hold that many of them are better Christians than ourselves. But we believe that they repudiate the things by and for which the Catholic Church, as a visible community, maintains its succession from the Apostles.

For instance, the Catholic Church maintains that Episcopacy carries on that government in the hands of one man, which the Apostles undoubtedly exercised; this the "otherwise constituted communities" deny, and its denial is one of the first terms of their existence as bodies or communities separate from the Catholic Church.

Then the Catholic Church holds an historical Gospel, whereas the Christian bodies alluded to, without denying the facts of the Divine History of Redemption, put the facts in the background, and certain doctrines, principally abstract, in the foreground. Now, according to such very ancient witnesses as Irenæus and Tertullian, the Apostolic succession was the guard and guarantee of a certain body of truth, Catholic truth, as contained in the creeds handed down from the Apostles themselves. But the leading principle of the transmission of Christian truth amongst these bodies is, that each man, and certainly each community, derives its creed direct from the Bible, as if the Church had begun to exist with the sect, or even the individual, who first discovered the truth which is held to the fore. I am not exaggerating this. The whole past of the Church, as the transmitter of the truth, is either ignored or denied.

It is a fact that a very pious writer, some of whose hymns are sung by all of us, declared, in very express terms, that if any man had learnt some Christian truth by the teaching of others without having learnt it himself direct from the Bible, that man was a thief.

Then the Catholic Church holds its own Unity as an outward Visible Body, and holds that the continued Episcopate is a most essential factor in this Unity. Now this the "otherwise constituted bodies" absolutely disclaim. They contend that the Unity is only inward and invisible. So that it is absurd to claim on behalf of a number of souls united by religious sentiment only, the succession which is given for an exactly opposite purpose—that there should be an outward body having a corporate union over and above the bond of mere sentiment.

Then in the next place the "otherwise constituted bodies" absolutely repudiate Sacerdotalism in every form and shape. It is difficult to define this sacerdotalism. The Bishop of Durham never actually defines it. I should think from carefully considering the first pages of his essay, that in his eyes it would be a system of means, such as the Sacraments, Church government, &c., administered by agents more or less distinctly authorized.

As far as I know, there is not one of the "otherwise constituted bodies" which holds anything like absolution, as set forth in the formularies of the Church of England, and yet if there is any one thing in the Christian system which would seem to require a commission, it is this absolution; if penitent sinners, that is, are to have any faith in it, and to receive any comfort from it.

Another of the functions which would seem to require a commission, is the celebration of the Eucharist. If the Eucharist is the distribution of mere emblems—outward signs with no inward part, though they may have some edifying effect on a devout receiver—then it would seem that no commission is required in the ministrant; but if we are to accept the words in which St. Paul speaks of the Eucharist as a most mysterious means of Union in the One Body (1 Cor. x. 17), then it would seem that if any thing in the Church requires a commission, it would be this, seeing that the Apostle makes the Oneness of the Church to depend upon it.

The administration of the rite of Confirmation seems to require a commission, transmitted from those who in the first age laid hands on the disciples. That a Church minister should go about a diocese and say to God, "We make our humble supplications unto thee for these thy servants, upon whom (after the example of Thy Holy Apostles) we have now laid our hands to certify them, by this sign, of thy favour and gracious goodness towards them" —this I say certainly seems to require some authority from the Church, and that authority transmitted downwards from the first administrators of the rite.

And lastly, with reference to Ordination itself, which is the means of Church continuity, and of handing down from one generation to another all power to perform the functions which pertain to the Church as a visible and yet mystical body, these "otherwise constituted bodies" with which we have most to do, seem to have, of set purpose, held it as of little consequence, and so taken no pains respecting its continuity. I am told that this has been the case with the Presbyterians of Scotland in times past. It has certainly not been continuous in the most powerful sect in this country, the Wesleyan. The Congregationalists, as far as I can understand, look upon election by the members of their communities as constituting the minister's only valid title to exercise his functions, though they have certain services which are simply the recognition by neighbouring ministers of what the people have done.

We then do not unchurch any of these "otherwise constituted bodies." If there be an outward visible body with continuous life, they unchurch themselves. They deliberately reject all the things which the Church Catholic holds as constituting its Catholicity in all times and places. They repudiate all acts and functions which require authority transmitted from the past. We are not their judges. We only carry out their judgment on themselves in cutting themselves off from the past, not only in the matter of its superstitions or extravagances, but in the matter of its transmissive functions, of its testimony to the Apostolic doctrine of the Person of Christ in its creeds, and of its sacraments, as being veritable means of the highest conceivable grace and pledges of its unity as one Body.

Again, I repeat, we do not unchristianize them, for we hold that they may be, and numbers of them are, better Christians than we are; but their action, and indeed their existence in a state of separation destroys, as far as it is possible for man to destroy, the

Divine Conception of the Church as the Vine of which Christ is the Stem, and the Body of which He is the Head.

NOTE.—The above excursus was written a short time before the death of the great prelate whose essay on the ministry in his notes on the Epistle to the Philippians I have been forced to consider. I would gladly have declined the task, but this I felt to be impossible. If excursus, or short essays, on the teaching of books of Scripture are to be admitted at all, there must be one on the bearing of the Pastoral Epistles on the Christian ministry. Some complained that I had not published such an excursus at the end of my volume on the Acts. But the proper place for such an essay would be in connection with the Pastoral Epistles. If I undertook such a work at all reference must be made to the Bishop of Durham's excursus. Respect for the Bishop's position, and the influence of his celebrated essay demanded it. And as I have the misfortune to differ from him on so fundamental a principle as the Divine Conception of the Christian ministry, I must write what I conceive to be the truth on this matter, and I trust that I have done so with all respect and charity.

CHISWICK PRESS:—C. WHITTINGHAM AND CO., TOOKS COURT, CHANCERY LANE.

OPINIONS OF THE PRESS.

THE GOSPELS.

From THE CHURCH QUARTERLY, *October*, 1883.

"It is far the best practical Commentary that we know, being plain-spoken, fearless, and definite, and containing matter very unlike the milk and water which is often served up in [so-called] practical Commentaries. . . . For solid Church teaching it stands unrivalled. Nothing could be better than the notes on the Sermon on the Mount, and the practical lessons drawn with convincing clearness from our Lord's words on the subject of Almsgiving, Prayer, and Fasting. Throughout the whole book the writer is ever on the watch for general principles and teaching applicable to the wants of our own day, which may legitimately be deduced from the Gospel narrative."

From THE CHURCH TIMES, *February* 23*rd*, 1883.

"The question of the origin of the Four Gospels is well treated, and a more succinct account of the real standing of the Evangelists with respect to each other, or to a supposed original document from which all copied, could scarcely be found than that contained in these few pages. Some few pages introductory to the critical portion of the volume, and explaining the elements of textual criticism, bring us to the text of the Commentary itself. Throughout the whole of its pages the same evidence of scholarship and critical acumen, which distinguishes all the author's work, is apparent; while the faculty of conveying such knowledge to the minds of the least learned in a simple and forcible manner, is abundantly preserved, and will procure for this work the position of one of the best of popular commentaries. Many of the notes extend beyond the scope generally implied by the term, and become full explanations of doctrinal subjects such as will prove of immense value to the student as well as to the general reader. We may cite as an instance of this exhaustive process the lengthy note on St. Matt. xvi. 18, and those notes on the Parables, which, severally treated in their entirety, present a more intelligible meaning than when explained in short disjointed notes. Finally, it remains to mention the fact, which, however, goes without saying, that the tone of the Commentary is thoroughly Catholic, so that the reader will find here a firm defence of the supernatural and divine character of the Gospel story, which never condescends to the tone of much of modern criticism, but remains true to primitive Catholic teaching."

From CHURCH BELLS, *November* 18*th*, 1882.

"It is written in a clear and sensible style, with a healthy tone; and its practical portions are devout without being wearisome or 'goody.'"

From THE CHURCH REVIEW, *November*, 1883.

"A valuable and substantial contribution to the literature of the New Testament is made by Mr. Sadler in the volume now before us. . . . It might be said that every page of the work lights up the grand historical character of the Church as the one supreme authority for the authenticity and interpretation of the books of Scripture."

From The Church Times, *December 21st*, 1883.

"We have much pleasure in announcing the issue of 'The Gospel according to St. John, with Notes, Critical and Practical,' by the Rev. M. F. Sadler (George Bell and Sons), a companion volume to his gloss on St. Matthew, and a redemption of the pledge he gave therein to carry on his labours to the remaining Gospels. This is admirably done, being exactly what is wanted for that large and increasing class of readers who need the results of genuine scholarship and sound vigorous thought, but who are repelled by any surface display of erudition, and still more by dryness of treatment, ... The admirable lucidity, which is the distinctive quality of Mr. Sadler's style, comes out markedly in his annotations, whether they take the form of pithy clearings up of verbal difficulties or more elaborate dissertations on important points of doctrine; and he is a good judge in selecting the best matter supplied by his precursors, such as Olshausen, Stier, Godet, and, above all, St. Augustine, whose commentary on St. John is one of that Father's ablest works. This is much less of a mere grammatical inquiry than Professor Westcott's volume in the 'Speaker's Commentary,' but it is much more of a theological explanation, and that of a far sounder and deeper school."

From The Literary Churchman, *December 7th*, 1883.

". . . Apart from these longer and more continuous glosses, the reader constantly meets with single pithy notes, which by their clear common sense solve a difficulty at once, and satisfy the understanding promptly, so that this is quite the best popular commentary on S. John we know, without implying by that epithet that even advanced students of Biblical literature will not find ample profit in consulting it."

From The Church Times, *October 3rd*, 1884.

"We gladly chronicle the third instalment of Prebendary Sadler's clear and sensible Commentary on the Gospels, which exactly meets the needs of that large and increasing class, which, without pretending any interest in the more abstruse problems of scholarship in connection with the Greek Testament, is desirous of having in its hands a trustworthy guide to the actual meaning of the sacred writers, and some plain statement of the results accepted by that calmer type of scholars who understand the nature of evidence, and are not disposed to admit the validity of unsupported conjecture, however original and brilliant, as proof. . . . . The notes, as always with Mr. Sadler, are singularly lucid, pithy, and to the point."

From Church Bells, *November 22nd*, 1884.

"This is a work of a veteran scholar and divine to whom the Church owes much. Prebendary Sadler's writing is characterized by great clearness of style, and he has a remarkably persuasive way of putting things. His sermons, as well as his 'Church Doctrine Bible Truth,' &c., have done much towards furnishing the parochial clergy with materials for feeding their flocks. In this commentary he aims at a yet more important object, the instruction of the educated classes. He has carefully compared the original Scriptures with the authorized and revised versions, and has set himself to meet objections of scientific sceptics, and he has achieved great success. . . . . The volume is full of thoughts and suggestions for preachers as well as for general readers."

From The Saturday Review, *February 21st*, 1885.

"We can recommend his book to devout and cultivated Churchmen who want to read the Gospels for instruction as well as for edification."

From The Church Quarterly, *January*, 1885.

"In reading the notes upon the text, the feature which strikes us most is their intensely practical character. Mr. Sadler has a remarkable faculty of bringing the teaching of the incidents of our Lord's life on earth to bear upon the circumstances of our own time. Even where the points brought out are well worn and familiar, there is a freshness in his manner of treating them which adds greatly to the charm and value of the Commentary."

From The Church Times, *July 3rd*, 1886.

"Indeed, one great merit in this commentary and its companion volumes is the frequency with which notes are found, which are capable of being each expanded into useful sermons. They are like very strong essences or tinctures, which will bear considerable dilution before being employed medically, though for convenience they are usually kept in the more portable form."

From The Church Quarterly, *July*, 1886.

"We must begin our notice of this volume by offering Prebendary Sadler our hearty congratulations on the completion of his work on the four Gospels. The previous volumes were all reviewed in our columns as they appeared, and we have no hesitation in extending the welcome which we gave to them to their present companion. It is no slight distinction for a writer, after having made his reputation by what is confessedly the best popular work on Church doctrine, to have produced what we hold to be the best popular commentary on the Gospel narrative. There is no other occupying quite the same ground, and we cordially recommend these four volumes, in the now familiar blue binding, as for practical purposes the most useful to the general reader."

From Church Bells, *July 2nd*, 1886.

"Mr. Sadler's excellent qualities as a theological writer and expositor are so well known that we need only introduce the reader to this, his last Commentary on the Gospels, completing the series, by saying that it presents the same features as its predecessors. It is somewhat longer than any of the other three, a circumstance quite intelligible to those who consider how a commentator's view of his responsibility must enlarge as he proceeds with his work. To begin at the beginning, the Introduction is excellent, clear, concise, and full. In short, it says all that need be said on the authorship of the Gospel, and says it well."

From The Irish Ecclesiastical Gazette, *Nov. 6th*, 1886.

"Originality of treatment, depth of insight, and thorough grasp of the practical side of Divine truth characterize these commentaries of Mr. Sadler on the four Gospels."

THE ACTS OF THE HOLY APOSTLES.

From THE GUARDIAN, *July*, 1887.

"We find, however, in the notes on St. Luke and the Acts the same freshness in thought and style, the same direct and independent consideration of the themes brought up on the sacred pages, the same knowledge of what has been said by others, the same masterly use, alike without subservience and without neglect, of the great and varied stores which our predecessors have left to us of these days who study the New Testament. The result is that Mr. Sadler's Commentary is decidedly one of the most unhackneyed and original of any we have. It will often be found to give help where others quite fail to do so, and its special value will be to the preacher or teacher who has to give oral and practical instruction; Mr. Sadler's strong point being decidedly in pointing the application to contemporary thought and to life, its trials and its duties, of the divine words with which he has to deal."

From CHURCH BELLS, *July 8th*, 1887.

"We can hardly imagine a commentary better adapted than Mr. Sadler's for giving to the reader an antidote to that unsettling influence which is now going about in the world, making people have a different set of religious opinions every month or so."

From THE CHURCH QUARTERLY REVIEW.

"There is vigour and freshness about his writings which makes it a pleasure to read them, while there is certain to be much that is instructive, and their tone and tendency are equally certain to be sound and edifying. This short commentary on the Acts of the Apostles is no exception to the rule, and it well supports the established reputation of its author."

From THE CHURCH TIMES, *August 26th*, 1887.

"Prebendary Sadler's useful commentary on the New Testament is advanced another important stage by the issue of this volume on the Acts of the Apostles, a part of Scripture whose interest and value seems to increase daily, as investigation into the beginnings of the Christian Church are pressed on with fresh vigour, alike by those who wish to prove Christianity a mere human evolution out of materials lying to hand in the Augustan era, and those who accept it as a divine revelation. Much of the work which has been done of late years in connexion with the Acts and other Pauline records has been devoted chiefly to the externals of history, geography, antiquities, and the like, rather than to the religious teaching which they contain; and this fact makes a gloss from a theologian like Mr. Sadler all the more welcome."

THE EPISTLES.

From Church Bells, *May* 18*th*, 1888.

"Mr. Sadler carries on his work with unabated vigour, and now we have some hope of his being able to give us a commentary on the whole of the New Testament. Undoubtedly such a work when completed will be of great value, as giving a well-thought-out exposition of the whole of the sources from which we derive the history of the founding, as well as the doctrines, of the Christian Church, and this, too, an exposition which supplies, not the mere personal opinions of its writer, although it is everywhere tinged by his individuality, but the historical meaning of the teaching of individual writers and of the Church at large. The 'introduction' to the present volume is excellent, giving all the requisite information without any unnecessary waste of words."

From The Church Times, *June*, 1888.

"There are three excursuses at the end of the volume, on Justification, on Election, and on the Christology of St. Paul, all carefully written, but with most pains bestowed upon the second. We do not know a better book than this Commentary to put into the hands of an intelligent Evangelical who is beginning to doubt the soundness of the system he has heretofore accepted, and is striving to find his way out and up into a higher and clearer atmosphere."

From The Church Quarterly Review.

"We hail with pleasure this addition to the Commentary on the New Testament. . . . . . We think this volume will certainly sustain the high position which Mr. Sadler has gained as a practical interpreter of Holy Scripture."

From The Irish Ecclesiastical Gazette, *April* 18*th*, 1890.

"Incomparably the best Commentary on the New Testament extant."

From The Banner, *May* 23*rd*, 1890.

"Ordinary readers could hardly have a better exposition of the sacred books."

From The Literary Churchman, *February* 6*th*, 1891.

"This volume will be found to present all the characteristic excellences of Mr. Sadler's method; and it would be hard, indeed, to find any points of objection to these terse, thoughtful, Church-like notes."

www.ingramcontent.com/pod-product-compliance
Lightning Source LLC
Chambersburg PA
CBHW020324240426
43673CB00039B/914
* 9 7 8 3 3 3 7 3 8 1 3 3 2 *